International Liability Regime for Biodiversity Damage

The Nagoya-Kuala Lumpur Supplementary Protocol on Liability and Redress to the Cartagena Protocol on Biosafety, adopted on 15 October 2010 in Nagoya, Japan, provides an international liability regime for biodiversity damage caused by living modified organisms (LMOs). Its adoption marks a significant development in the legal design for international environmental liability regimes, as it incorporates, for the first time in global treaties, an administrative approach to liability.

This book examines the Supplementary Protocol from both practitioner and academic perspectives. In its three parts the book explores the historical development, legal significances, and future implementation of the core provisions of the Supplementary Protocol, focusing specifically on its incorporation of an administrative approach to liability for biodiversity damage and its relation to civil liability. Contributors to the volume include Co-Chairs of the negotiating group and the negotiators and advisors from some of the key negotiating Parties, offering valuable insights into the difficult-to-read provisions of the Supplementary Protocol. The book demonstrates the significant changes in the political configuration of environmental treaty negotiations which have come about in the twenty-first century, and argues that the liability approach of the Supplementary Protocol has important implications for future development of international liability regimes under international environmental law.

Akiho Shibata is Professor of International Law at the Graduate School of International Cooperation Studies (GSICS), Kobe University, Japan. He was a member of the Japanese delegation to negotiate the Nagoya-Kuala Lumpur Supplementary Protocol from 2006–2010.

Routledge Research in International Environmental Law

Available titles in this series:

Forthcoming titles in this series:

International Liability Regime for Biodiversity Damage

The Nagoya-Kuala Lumpur Supplementary Protocol

Edited by
Akiho Shibata

Routledge
Taylor & Francis Group

LONDON AND NEW YORK

First published 2014
by Routledge

2 Park Square, Milton Park, Abingdon, Oxon OX14 4RN
711 Third Avenue, New York, NY 10017, USA

Routledge is an imprint of the Taylor & Francis Group, an informa business

First issued in paperback 2016

British Library Cataloguing in Publication Data
A catalogue record for this book is available from the British Library

Library of Congress Cataloging in Publication Data
International liability regime for biodiversity damage:
the Nagoya-Kuala Lumpur supplementary protocol/
edited by Akiho Shibata.
    pages cm. –
    (Routledge research in international environmental law)
    Includes bibliographical references and index.

    1. Liability for environmental damages.
    2. Convention on Biological Diversity (1992).
    Protocols, etc., 2010 Oct. 29.
    3. Biodiversity conservation – Law and legislation.
    4. Environmental law, International.
    I. Shibata, Akiho, 1965– editor of compilation.
    K955.I55 2014
    346.04′6 – dc23   2013042206

ISBN 978-1-138-66698-6 (pbk)
ISBN 978-0-415-72242-1 (hbk)
ISBN 978-1-315-84974-4 (ebk)

Typeset in Baskerville
by Florence Production Ltd, Stoodleigh, Devon, UK

Contents

Illustrations

Figures

Tables

Contributors

Reynaldo Ariel Alvarez-Morales is a Senior Researcher at the Center for Research and Advanced Studies in the Department of Genetic Engineering, Mexico. Until August 2013, he held the position of Executive Secretary of the Intersecretarial Commission of Biosafety and Genetically Modified Organisms, and, in such capacity, he was the head of a Mexican delegation to negotiate the Nagoya-Kuala Lumpur Supplementary Protocol (2004–2010).

John Barkett is a Partner in the Miami office of Shook, Hardy & Bacon, LLP, and an Adjunct Professor of Environmental Law at the University of Miami Law School, USA. He is also a Fellow of the American College of Environmental Lawyers and the Special Master overseeing the Consent Decree governing the restoration of the Florida Everglades in the USA.

Edward H. P. Brans is an Attorney at Law at Pels Rijcken & Droogleever Fortuijn in The Hague, Netherlands. He has participated in various studies sponsored by the European Commission on the EU's Environmental Liability Directive and its application, one of them being the REMEDE project (Resource Equivalency Methods for Assessing Environmental Damage in the EU). His major publications include *Liability for Damage to Public Natural Resources: Standing, Damage and Damage Assessment* (Kluwer Law International, 2001) and *Environmental Liability in the EU: The 2004 Directive Compared with US and Member State Law* (co-editor, Cameron May, 2006).

J. Thomas Carrato is Chief Executive of Creative Biotech Solutions, LLC. As Associate General Counsel for Monsanto Company, he led the industry delegation of the Global Industry Coalition in the negotiations of the Nagoya-Kuala Lumpur Supplementary Protocol on Liability and Redress, and is a primary author, Executive Director Emeritus, and member of the Executive Committee of 'The Compact, a Contractual Mechanism for Response in the Event of Damage to Biological Diversity Caused by the Release of a Living Modified Organism'. He holds his BS in Statistics from Stanford University, USA, and his JD *Juris* (*summa cum laude*, first in class) from Seattle University School of Law, USA. He is admitted to practice law in the states of California, Washington, Missouri and before the US Supreme Court.

Dorith H. Dongelmans is Senior Advisor on Legal Affairs at the Ministry of Security and Justice in The Netherlands. She has worked as an Attorney at Law at Pels Rijcken & Droogleever Fortuijn in The Hague, Netherlands, for more than five years. She graduated in 2007 from the University of Leiden (civil law and corporate law, *cum laude*), Netherlands.

Eriko Futami is a postgraduate student of environmental law at Waseda University School of Law, Japan. She holds an LLB and an LLM from Waseda University. Her publications include 'Liability for the Restoration of Biodiversity Damage: Comparison with EU Environmental Liability Directive, OPA, and CLC (1) (2)', *Waseda Law Journal*, Vol. 63, Nos. 1 and 2 (2013) (in Japanese).

Kathryn Garforth is Programme Officer (2012–present) for Access and Benefit Sharing, the Secretariat of the Convention on Biological Diversity, United Nations Environment Programme. She served as a Legal Officer (2007–2012) for the Cartagena Protocol on Biosafety in the same Secretariat. She holds an LLB from Osgoode Hall Law School, Canada, and a Master of Environmental Studies from York University, Canada. Her major publications include 'Biosafety, the Cartagena Protocol, and Sustainable Development' (co-author), *Legal Aspects of Implementing the Cartagena Protocol on Biosafety* (Cordonier Segger, Perron-Welch & Frison eds, Cambridge, 2013); 'Review of Issues, Instruments and Practices Relevant to Liability and Redress for Damage Resulting from Transboundary Movements of Living Modified Organisms' (co-author), *Biosafety Technical Series 3* (Secretariat of the Convention on Biological Diversity, 2012); and 'Life as Chemistry or Life as Biology? An Ethic of Patents on Genetically Modified Organisms', *Patenting Lives: Life Patents, Culture and Development* (Gibson ed., Ashgate, 2008).

Phil Goldberg is a Partner in the Public Policy Group in the Washington, DC, office of Shook, Hardy & Bacon, LLP, specialising in developing and communicating liability-related public policies, and is an aide to several Democratic Members of Congress in the USA.

Mahlet Teshome Kebede is a Biosafety Expert and Environmental Lawyer working for the African Union Commission (2006–present). She prepared briefing documents for the African group on the operational texts of the Nagoya-Kuala Lumpur Supplementary Protocol (2007–2010). She has also provided inputs on the draft national biosafety laws of Ethiopia (National Biosafety Proclamation of 2009), Nigeria (Biosafety Bill of 2007), Swaziland (Biosafety Bill of 2008), and Malawi (Revised Biosafety Act of 2010). She holds an LLB (2002) and an MA in Development Studies (2006) from Addis Ababa University, Ethiopia.

Alejandro Lago Candeira is Director of the UNESCO Chair for the Environment at the Rey Juan Carlos University in Madrid, Spain. He was a member of the EU delegation to negotiate the Nagoya-Kuala Lumpur Supplementary Protocol (2004–2010). He is also a Professor of Environmental Law at the School of Legal Praxis at the Complutense University, Spain, and Coordinator and Professor at the International University of Andalusia, Spain. His major publications include 'International Environmental Commitments', *Environmental Policy Observatory* (yearly since 2007) (co-author with Blanca Lozano); 'The Success of a Negotiation: The Nagoya Protocol on Access to Genetic Resources and Benefit Sharing', *Ambienta* (March 2011); and 'Access to Genetic Resources and Benefit Sharing', *Documentación Social: Revista de Estudios Sociales y de Sociología Aplicada*, no. 145 (April–June 2007).

René Lefeber is a Professor of International Environmental Law at the Faculty of Law, University of Amsterdam, and is Deputy Legal Advisor in the International Law Division of the Netherlands Ministry of Foreign Affairs. He served as a Co-Chair of the negotiation groups concerning liability and redress in the context of the Cartagena Protocol on Biosafety (2004–2010). His major publications include *Transboundary Environmental Interference and the Origin of State Liability* (Kluwer Law International, 1996).

Rodrigo C. A. Lima is a lawyer, currently employed at Agroicone & Plataformaagro (April 2013–present), a consulting company in Brazil. He is also a PhD candidate in international law at the Catholic University of São Paulo (PUC-SP). Previously, he was a researcher and the General Manager at the Institute for International Trade Negotiations (ICONE) in Brazil, where he focused on agriculture, trade and environmental international negotiations, and regulatory issues. He has experience on non-tariff barriers debate in negotiations and policy-making decisions relating to the World Trade Organization, the Convention on Biological Diversity, the Cartagena Protocol on Biosafety, and the United Nations Framework Convention on Climate Change and its Kyoto Protocol. He holds a Master in International Law from Universidade Federal de Santa Catarina. His major publications include *Sanitary and Phytosanitary Measures in the WTO: Neo-protectionism or Defense of Legitimate Objectives* (Aduaneiras, 2005) (in Portuguese).

Jimena Nieto Carrasco is Special Adviser in the International Affairs Office, the Ministry of the Environment and Sustainable Development, the Republic of Colombia. She served as a Co-Chair of the negotiation groups concerning liability and redress in the context of the Cartagena Protocol on Biosafety (2004–2010). She is currently serving as the Chair of the Compliance Committee under the Cartagena Protocol on Biosafety (2013–2015). She is a lawyer from the Colegio Mayor de Nuestra Señora del Rosario, Colombia, and teaches international environmental law at Universidad Externado de Colombia, Universidad de los Andes and the Colegio Mayor de Nuestra Señora del Rosario, Colombia. She holds an LLM in Public International Law from the London School of Economics and Political Science, UK.

Gurdial Singh Nijar is Director of the Centre of Excellence for Biodiversity Law (CEBLAW) and Professor of Law at the Faculty of Law, Universiti Malaya in Malaysia. He was a key negotiator representing Malaysia in the development of the Nagoya-Kuala Lumpur Supplementary Protocol (2004–2010). He is an advocate and solicitor of Malaysia and is admitted as a barrister of the Supreme Court of the Australian States of New South Wales and Victoria. He holds an LLB from Kings College London and a PhD from Universiti Malaya. His major publications include *Liability and Redress under the Cartagena Protocol on Biosafety: A Record of Negotiations for Developing International Rules* (co-author, CEBLAW/NRE, Universiti Malaya, 2008); 'Incorporating Traditional Knowledge in an International Regime on Access to Genetic Resources and Benefit Sharing: Problems and Prospects', *European Journal of International Law*, Vol. 21, No. 2 (2010); 'The Nagoya-Kuala Lumpur Supplementary Protocol on Liability and Redress to the Cartagena Protocol on Biosafety: An Analysis and Implementation Challenges', *International Environmental Agreements: Politics, Law and Economics (online first articles)* (1 August 2012); and *Nagoya-KL Supplementary Protocol: A Record of Negotiation, Vol. 2* (co-author, CEBLAW, Universiti Malaya, 2012).

Tadashi Otsuka is a Professor of Law at Waseda School of Law, Japan (2001–present). His major publications include *Environmental Law* (3rd edn., Yuhikaku, 2010) (in Japanese); *Environmental Risk and the Precautionary Principle* (co-editor, Yuhikaku, 2010) (in Japanese); *Emissions Trading Scheme in Japan and Measures Concerning Global Warming* (Iwanami Shoten, 2011) (in Japanese); *Earthquake, Nuclear Power Plant Accident and Environmental Law* (co-editor, Minjiho Kenkyukai, 2013) (in Japanese).

Akiho Shibata is a Professor of International Law at the Graduate School of International Cooperation Studies (GSICS), Kobe University, Japan. He was a member of the Japanese delegation to negotiate the Nagoya-Kuala Lumpur Supplementary Protocol (2006–2010). He received an LLB and an LLM from Kyoto University, Japan, and an LLM in International Legal Studies (1993) from New York University School of Law, USA. He was an invited professor at the Faculty of Law, University of Grenoble, France (2013). His major publications in English include *UN Peace-Keeping Operations: A Guide to Japanese Policies* (co-author, UNU, 1999); 'The Court's Decision *in Silentium* on the Sources of International Law: Its Enduring Significance', *The ICJ and the Evolution of International Law: The Enduring Impact of the Corfu Channel Case* (Bannelier, Christakis & Heathcote eds, Routledge, 2012); and 'International Environmental Lawmaking in the First Decade of the Twenty-First Century: The Form and Process', *Japanese Yearbook of International Law*, Vol. 54, Year 2011 (2012).

Elmo Enrico Thomas is Deputy Director of Research, Science and Technology at the Ministry of Education, Namibia (2007–present). He was a member of the Namibian delegation to negotiate Nagoya-Kuala Lumpur Supplementary Protocol (2006–2010) and the chief African negotiator (2009–2010). He holds a BSc in Genetics and Biochemistry (1995) from the University of Stellenbosch, South Africa, and a Master in Biotechnology (2006) from Flinders University of South Australia, Australia.

Dire Tladi is Principal State Law Advisor (international law), Office of the Chief State Law Advisor in the Republic of South Africa, a Member of the United Nations International Law Commission (2012–present), and a Professor of International Law at the University of Pretoria, South Africa. He was a member of the South African delegation to negotiate the Nagoya-Kuala Lumpur Supplementary Protocol (2004–2010). Previously, he was a Legal Counsellor at the Permanent Mission of South Africa to the United Nations and Extraordinary Professor at University of Stellenbosch, South Africa. His major publications relevant to environmental law include *Sustainable Development in International Law: Analysis of Key Enviro-Economic Instruments* (PULP, 2007); 'Liability Protocol to the Basel Convention on Transboundary Movement of Hazardous Wastes: An Overview', *South African Journal of Environmental Law and Policy*, Vol. 7 (2000); and 'Civil Liability in the Context of the Cartagena Protocol: To Be or Not to Be (Binding)', *International Environmental Agreements: Politics, Law and Economics*, Vol. 10 (2010).

Worku Damena Yifru is Senior Legal Officer (2013–present) and was Programme Officer of Biosafety Policy and Law at the Seretariat of the Convention on Biological Diversity, United Nations Environment Programme (2001–2013). He was the head of the Policy and Legislation Department at the Environmental Protection Authority of Ethiopia until 2001 and was a member and a legal advisor of the Ethiopian delegation to negotiate the Cartagena Protocol on Biosafety, and the International Treaty on Plant Genetic Resources for Food and Agriculture. He holds an LLB (1988) from the Faculty of Law, Addis Ababa University, and an LLM in Environmental Law (1995) from the London School of Economics and Political Science, UK. His major publications include 'Access to Genetic Resources in Ethiopia', *African Perspectives on Genetic Resources: A Handbook on Laws, Policies and Institutions* (Nnadozie *et al.* eds, Environmental Law Institute, 2003); 'Liability and Redress', in *The Cartagena Protocol on Biosafety: Reconciling Trade in Biotechnology with Environment and Development?* (Bail, Falkner and Marquard eds, Earthscan, 2002).

(All information is correct as of 31 August 2013)

Acknowledgements

It was on 15 March 2011, four days after the Great East Japan Earthquake, at Akasaka Grand Prince Hotel in Tokyo, when an idea of publishing a book on the Nagoya-Kuala Lumpur Supplementary Protocol on Liability and Redress was first informally discussed with some of the participants attending an international symposium organised by the Ministry of Foreign Affairs of Japan (MOFA). In stark contrast with the invitees to the Nagoya ABS Protocol component of the same symposium, most of whom cancelled the visit to Japan, our friends involved in the negotiation of the Supplementary Protocol demonstrated a strong solidarity by showing up in Tokyo, despite difficult conditions, and successfully completed all of the symposium agenda. My first thanks, therefore, go to those participants, many of whom are the contributors to this book, including Alejandro, Ariel, Elmo, Dire, Jimena, Tom, Worku, Professor Otsuka and Duncan Currie of Greenpeace International.

My thanks go also to Michiko Miyano, Nobu Kikuchi and Hiro Ichiba of MOFA's Global Environment Division, who showed great confidence in me in negotiating the Supplementary Protocol, often as the spokesperson of the Japanese delegation. Without such experience, I could not have had either such a close comradeship with the negotiators nor the strong personal attachment to the product of the negotiation.

The development of this book with its coherent theme was possible because its contributors and I, the editor, on several different occasions, had the chance to meet in person and discuss their respective contributions. I would like to thank the following friends and contributors for providing such occasions: Edward for organising a meeting in The Hague in September 2011; Tom and Sarah Lukie of Croplife International for letting me use the margin of Compact's advisory committee meetings in Tokyo in February 2012 and in Seattle in May 2013 to discuss the book project; Mr Saigo and his colleagues at the Japanese Ministry of Agriculture, Forestry and Fisheries for organising a workshop on the implementation of the Supplementary Protocol in Tokyo in February 2013; and, on a more personal level, René and Amy Hindman for inviting me to their home in The Hague in January 2012 to discuss the book project, the whaling case in the ICJ and instructing me on how to open a champagne bottle.

On many such occasions, I was accompanied by able students from the Graduate School of International Cooperation Studies (GSICS), Kobe University, as note takers. They include Mai Fujii, Yoko Onishi and Masakuni Ueta. Osamu Inagaki, another PhD student at GSICS, assisted me with checking the consistency of footnotes and formatting.

The financial assistance for the publication of this book from the Kobe University Rokkodai Koenkai is greatly appreciated. My contributions to this book are a partial result of a research project funded by a Grant-in-Aid for Scientific Research (C) (2012–2014), Japan Society for the Promotion of Science (JSPS).

Attending negotiation meetings in Montreal, Cartagena, Bonn, Mexico City, Putrajaya, Kuala Lumpur and Nagoya means the role of husband and daddy for two daughters must be compromised. My final thanks for understanding go to Yuri, Haruka and Makoto.

This book is dedicated to all those who made the adoption of the Nagoya-Kuala Lumpur Supplementary Protocol on Liability and Redress possible on 15 October 2010.

A. S.
15 October 2013

Abbreviations

ABS	Access and Benefit Sharing
Ad Hoc WG	Open-Ended *Ad Hoc* Working Group of Legal and Technical Experts on Liability and Redress in the Context under the Cartagena Protocol on Biosafety (2004–2008)
AIA	Advance Informed Agreement
Antarctic Liability Annex	Annex VI on Liability Arising From Environmental Emergencies to the Protocol on Environmental Protection to the Antarctic Treaty 2005
ATCM	Antarctic Treaty Consultative Meeting
Basel Liability Protocol	Basel Protocol on Liability and Compensation for Damage Resulting from Transboundary Movements of Hazardous Wastes and Their Disposal 1999
Bunker Oil Pollution Convention	International Convention on Civil Liability for Bunker Oil Pollution Damage 2001
Cartagena Protocol	Cartagena Protocol on Biosafety to the Convention on Biological Diversity 2000
CBD	Convention on Biological Diversity 1992
CLC	see Oil Pollution Liability Convention
COP	Conference of the Parties
COP-MOP	Conference of the Parties serving as the Meeting of the Parties
ECJ	European Court of Justice/Court of Justice of the European Union
EU	European Union
EU-ELD	European Union Environmental Liability Directive/ Directive 2004/35/CE of the European Parliament and of the Council of 21 April 2004 on environmental liability with regard to the prevention and remedying of environmental damage
FAO	Food and Agriculture Organization of the United Nations

GATT	General Agreement on Tariffs and Trade
GFCC	Group of the Friends of the Co-Chairs Concerning Liability and Redress in the Context of the Cartagena Protocol on Biosafety (2008–2010)
GIC	Global Industry Coalition
GM	genetically modified
GMO	genetically modified organism
GRULAC	Group of Latin American and Caribbean countries
HGT	Horizontal Gene Transfer
HNS Convention	International Convention on Liability and Compensation for Damage in Connection with the Carriage of Hazardous and Noxious Substances by Sea 1996
ICJ	International Court of Justice
ILC	International Law Commission
IMF	International Monetary Fund
IPPC	Integrated Pollution Prevention and Control
Kiev Protocol on Civil Liability	Protocol on Civil Liability and Compensation for Damage Caused by the Transboundary Effects of Industrial Accidents on Transboundary Waters to the 1992 Convention on the Protection and Use of Transboundary Watercourses and International Lakes and to the 1992 Convention on the Transboundary Effects of Industrial Accidents 2003
Kyoto Protocol	Kyoto Protocol to the United Nations Framework Convention on Climate Change 1997
LMO	living modified organism
Lugano Convention on Civil Liability	Convention on Civil Liability for Damage Resulting from Activities Dangerous to the Environment 1993
Oil Pollution Liability Convention	International Convention on Civil Liability for Oil Pollution Damage 1992
PCA	Permanent Court of Arbitration
SDR	Special Drawing Rights
SPS Agreement	Agreement on the Application of Sanitary and Phytosanitary Measures
Supplementary Protocol	Nagoya-Kuala Lumpur Supplementary Protocol on Liability and Redress to the Cartagena Protocol on Biosafety 2010
TBT Agreement	Agreement on Technical Barriers to Trade
TEG	Technical Expert Group on Liability and Redress
UN	United Nations
UNEP	United Nations Environment Programme
VCLT	Vienna Convention on the Law of Treaties
WTO	World Trade Organization

1 Introduction

The Nagoya-Kuala Lumpur Supplementary Protocol on Liability and Redress

Akiho Shibata

The adoption of the *Nagoya-Kuala Lumpur Supplementary Protocol on Liability and Redress to the Cartagena Protocol on Biosafety* (Supplementary Protocol) on 15 October 2010 in Nagoya, Japan,[1] was an epoch-making event both for the field of environmental diplomacy and for academia interested in the study of international environmental law generally, and environmental liability in particular. The Supplementary Protocol provides international rules and procedures in the field of liability and redress relating to living modified organisms (LMOs) in response to damage caused by those LMOs to the conservation and sustainable use of biological diversity, taking also into account risks to human health.

The adoption of the Supplementary Protocol came when the international community was still suffering from the Copenhagen disaster in December 2009, where climate change negotiations collapsed, and was losing confidence in multilateral environmental diplomacy. Indeed, the Supplementary Protocol was the first universal environmental treaty adopted since the Stockholm Convention on Persistent Organic Pollutants in 2001. The political configuration of environmental treaty negotiations had undergone a significant change in the first decade of the twenty-first century, and the international community was searching for new ways to effectively create international environmental law.[2] Similar to the climate change negotiations, the issue of LMOs in general and the legal design for liability arising from them in particular could no longer be seen as a simple north-south divide, as had previously been the case in 2000 when the Cartagena Protocol

---

1 Nagoya-Kuala Lumpur Supplementary Protocol on Liability and Redress to the Cartagena Protocol on Biosafety, adopted by Decision BS-V/11 in its Annex on 15 October 2010, UNEP/CBD/BS/COP-MOP/5/17 (29 November 2010), pp. 68–75. A certified true copy is available at http://treaties.un.org/pages/CTCs.aspx (section XXVII 8.c) (accessed 1 August 2013). See also Appendix 1 of this book.

2 Akiho Shibata, 'International Environmental Lawmaking in the First Decade of the Twenty-First Century: The Form and Process', *Japanese Yearbook of International Law*, Vol. 54, Year 2011 (2012), pp. 31–34.

on Biosafety (Cartagena Protocol),[3] with its controversial Article 27 on liability and redress, was adopted.[4]

How was the adoption by consensus of the Supplementary Protocol at Nagoya possible both substantively and procedurally? By inviting the Co-Chairs of the negotiating group and the negotiators and advisors from the key negotiating Parties, including the African Union, the European Union, Japan, Malaysia, Mexico, Namibia and South Africa to contribute, this book delves into the minds of those who were at the forefront of the extremely intricate negotiations.

On a more profound, theoretical level, the Supplementary Protocol was negotiated and adopted when, within the academia, the 'sensibility' of negotiating an international environmental liability regime was seriously questioned.[5] The Protocol on Liability and Compensation for Damage resulting from Trans-boundary Movement of Hazardous Wastes and Their Disposal under the Basel Convention (Basel Liability Protocol), adopted in 1999, has not attracted many ratifications from the Parties to the Basel Convention and still has not entered into force.[6] The same is true for liability regimes negotiated and adopted within the European context in previous decades.[7] The United Nations' International Law Commission (ILC) has been wandering over the concept of 'international liability' since 1978,[8] and in 2006, adopted instead the 'Principles on Allocation of Loss in the Case of Transboundary Harm Arising out of Hazardous Activities'.[9] The initial

---

3   Cartagena Protocol on Biosafety to the Convention on Biological Diversity, adopted on 29 January 2000, entered into force on 11 September 2003, *United Nations Treaty Series*, Vol. 2226, p. 208.

4   Kate Cook, 'Liability: "No Liability, No Protocol"', in Christoph Bail, Robert Falkner and Helen Marquard eds, *The Cartagena Protocol on Biosafety: Reconciling Trade in Biotechnology with Environment and Development?* (Earthscan, 2002), pp. 371–384.

5   Jutta Brunnée, 'Of Sense and Sensibility: Reflections on International Liability Regimes as Tools for Environmental Protection', *International and Comparative Law Quarterly*, Vol. 53, No. 2 (2004), pp. 351–368. See also, Anne Daniel, 'Civil Liability Regimes as a Complement to Multilateral Environmental Agreements: Sound International Policy or False Comfort?' *Review of European Community and International Environmental Law*, Vol. 12, No. 3 (2003), pp. 225–241; Malgosia Fitzmaurice, 'Chapter 14: International Responsibility and Liability', in Daniel Bodansky, Jutta Brunnée, and Ellen Hey eds, *The Oxford Handbook of International Environmental Law* (Oxford University Press, 2007), pp. 1010–1035.

6   As of 1 August 2013, 11 Parties deposited their instruments of ratifications, etc. out of 20 necessary to bring the Protocol into force. Available at www.basel.int/Countries/StatusofRatifications/TheProtocol/tabid/1345/Default.aspx (accessed 1 August 2013).

7   Convention on Civil Liability for Damage Resulting from Activities Dangerous to the Environment, adopted on 21 June 1993 (not in force), *European Treaty Series, No.150* [Lugano Convention on Civil Liability]; Protocol on Civil Liability and Compensation for Damage Caused by the Transboundary Effects of Industrial Accidents on Transboundary Waters to the 1992 Convention on the Protection and Use of Transboundary Watercourses and International Lakes and to the 1992 Convention on the Transboundary Effects of Industrial Accidents, adopted on 21 May 2003 (not in force), Doc. ECE/MP.WAT/11-ECE/CP.TEIA/9 [Kiev Protocol on Civil Liability].

8   Alan E. Boyle, 'Globalising Environmental Liability: The Interplay of National and International Law', *Journal of Environmental Law*, Vol. 17, No. 1 (2005), pp. 3–26.

9   Draft principles on the allocation of loss in the case of transboundary harm arising out of hazardous activities: Text of the draft principles and commentaries thereto, *ILC Report 2006*, UN Doc. A/61/10 (2006) [Allocation of Loss Principles].

enthusiasm for developing international civil liability regimes, forcibly urged in Principle 13 of the 1992 Rio Declaration on Environment and Development,[10] seemed to fade. As an attempt to find a way out of this liability occlusion, the Supplementary Protocol, while retaining the concept of liability and redress, has taken an innovative approach that is now widely called the 'administrative approach' to liability. The legal structure of this new liability regime that commanded consensus of the negotiating Parties at Nagoya needs detailed and critical examination; this is the primary aim of this book.

The Supplementary Protocol deals with damage caused by LMOs, a politically and socially sensitive issue.[11] An LMO is defined in the Cartagena Protocol as 'any living organism that possesses a novel combination of genetic material obtained through the use of modern biotechnology'. The term 'modern biotechnology' in turn is defined as the application of (a) in vitro nucleic acid techniques, including recombinant deoxyribonucleic acid (DNA) and direct injection of nucleic acid into cells or organelles; or (b) fusion of cells beyond the taxonomic family, which overcome natural physiological reproductive or recombination barriers and are not techniques used in traditional breeding and selection.[12]

The international community acknowledges both the benefits[13] and the risks[14] of biotechnology, which is still developing and progressing. By addressing LMOs, the new treaty intends to regulate certain consequences arising from the utilisation of biotechnology for both research and commercial purposes, particularly in the agricultural sector. Thus, the Supplementary Protocol is at the forefront of science and technology and their applications.[15] At the same time, genetically modified

---

10   Principle 13 of the Rio Declaration states: 'States shall develop national law regarding liability and compensation for the victims of pollution and other environmental damage. States shall also cooperate in an expeditious and more determined manner to develop further international law regarding liability and compensation for adverse effects of environmental damage caused by activities within their jurisdiction or control to areas beyond their jurisdiction.' See also Rüdiger Wolfrum, 'Liability for Environmental Damage: A Means to Enforce Environmental Standards?' in Karel Wellens ed., *International Law: Theory and Practice: Essays in Honour of Eric Suy* (Martinus Nijhoff, 1998), pp. 565–578.

11   See generally Mark A. Pollack and Gregory C. Shaffer, *When Cooperation Fails: The International Law and Politics of Genetically Modified Foods* (Oxford University Press, 2009).

12   Art. 3 (g), (h) and (i), Cartagena Protocol.

13   Agenda 21, Chapter 16, para. 16.1, adopted at Rio Conference on Environment and Development, 1992: The biotechnology 'promises to make a significant contribution in enabling the development of, for example, better health care, enhanced food security through sustainable agricultural practices, improved supplies of potable water, more efficient industrial development processes for transforming raw materials, support for sustainable methods of afforestation and reforestation, and detoxification of hazardous wastes.'

14   5th preambular paragraph of Cartagena Protocol: 'Aware of the rapid expansion of modern biotechnology and the growing public concern over its potential adverse effects on biological diversity, taking also into account risks to human health.'

15   For an overview of the development of biotechnology and its implications for international law, see Francesco Francioni and Tullio Scovazzi eds, *Biotechnology and International Law* (Hart, 2006). More particularly on the genetic engineering and its implications on trade law, see Daniel Wüger and Thomas Cottier eds, *Genetic Engineering and the World Trade System: World Trade Forum* (Cambridge University Press, 2008).

(GM) crops such as GM soybeans and GM canola have already been produced in large quantities and marketed globally. The area and the number of countries producing such GM crops and vegetables/fruits are steadily increasing across all five continents (see Figure 1.1 and Table 1.1). If one includes LMOs used in laboratory research, field trials for public health purposes[16] and industrial applications,[17] the use of LMOs can now be considered as ubiquitous in modern society.

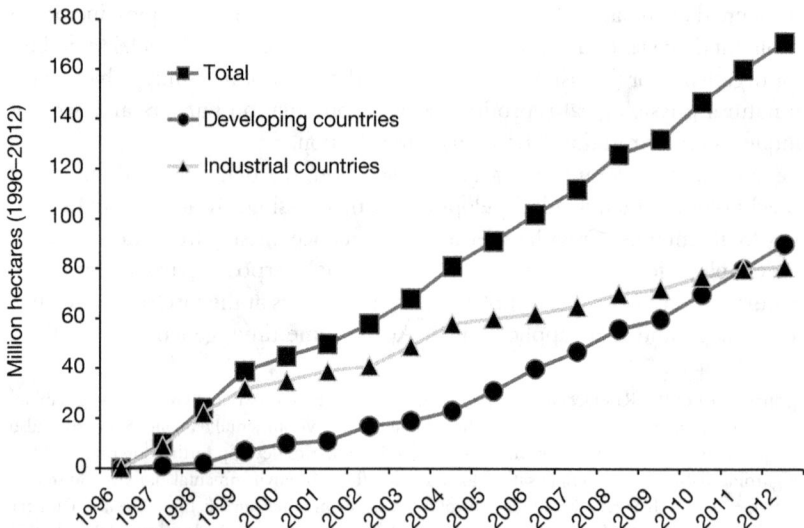

Figure 1.1 Global area of biotech crops in million hectares (1996–2012)

Source: International Service for Acquisition of Agri-Biotech Applications (IASSS), Brief 44: Global Status of Commercialized Biotech/GM Crops: 2012. www.isaaa.org/resources/publications/briefs/44/ (accessed 1 August 2013).

16   Cf. genetically modified mosquitoes developed and approved for field trial in Malaysia. Data available from Biosafety Clearing House of the CBD Secretariat: http://bch.cbd.int/about/ (accessed 1 August 2013).

17   For example, in Japan, from 2004 to 2009, 912 LMOs for scientific research purposes, 726 LMOs for mining and manufacturing purposes, 124 LMOs for medical and pharmaceutical purposes, and 98 LMOs for agricultural, forestry and fishery purposes have been approved for contained use. Chuo Kankyo Shingikai Yasei Seibutsu Bukai Idenshi Kumikae Seibutsu Sho-iinkai (Subcommittee on Genetically Modified Organisms, Central Environment Council of Japan), *Idenshi Kumikae Seibutsuto no Shiyotou no Kisei niyoru Seibutsu no Tayosei no Kakuho nikansuru Horitsu (Cartagena Ho) no Sekou Jokyo no Kentou nitusite (Report on the Examination of Implementation of the Cartagena Law)*, August 2009, p. 12. Available at www.env.go.jp/press/press.php?serial=11502 (accessed 1 August 2013).

Table 1.1 Global area of biotech crops by country 2012 (million hectares)

Country	Total	Crops	Country	Total	Crops
Africa					
South Africa	2.9	Mz, Sb, Ct	Burkina Faso	0.3	Ct
Sudan	<0.05	Ct	Egypt	<0.05	Mz
Asia and Pacific					
India	10.8	Ct	China	4.0	Ct, Pa, Pp, Tm, SP
Pakistan	2.8	Ct	Philippines	0.8	Mz
Australia*	0.7	Ct, Cn	Myanmar	0.3	Ct
Europe					
Spain	0.1	Mz	Portugal	<0.05	Mz
Czech Republic	<0.05	Mz	Romania	<0.05	Mz
Slovakia	<0.05	Mz			
North America					
USA*	69.5	Mz, Sb, Ct, Cn, St, Al, Pa, Sq	Canada*	11.6	Cn, Mz, Sb, St
Latin America					
Brazil	36.6	Sb, Mz, Ct	Argentina*	23.9	Sb, Mz, Ct
Paraguay	3.4	Sb, Mz, Ct	Uruguay	1.4	Sb, Mz
Bolivia	1.0	Sb	Mexico	0.2	Ct, Sb
Chile*	1.0	Mz, Sb, Ct	Colombia	<0.05	Ct
Honduras	<0.05	Mz	Cuba	<0.05	Mz
Costa Rica	<0.05	Ct, Mz			

* Country: Country not Party to the Cartagena Protocol (as of 31 August 2013)

Al: Alfalfa; Cn: Canola; Ct: Cotton; Mz: Maize; Pa: Papaya; Pp: Poplur; Sb: Soybean; SP: Sweet Potato; Sq: Squash; St: Sugar Beet; Tm: Tomato

Source: International Service for Acquisition of Agri-biotech Applications (IASSS), Brief 44: Global Status of Commercialized Biotech/GM Crops: 2012. www.isaaa.org/resources/publications/briefs/44/ (accessed 1 August 2013).

However, unlike oil spills polluting the ocean or nuclear power plant accidents spreading radioactive material, there has not yet been a scientifically confirmed case of environmental damage caused by LMOs. The treaty negotiators were tackling a hypothetical problem of environmental damage that may potentially be caused by LMOs without any actual experience of it. The state-of-the-art science and technology involved in LMOs, their already complex global supply chains and the lack of actual environmental damage caused by them to date have been identified as formidable challenges in designing a liability regime involving LMOs, for which existing liability regimes may not serve as a complete model.[18]

During the negotiation of the Supplementary Protocol, some participants (some with good and some with bad intentions) tried to revive the political, social and even emotional divide over LMOs that had been partially sealed off by the Cartagena Protocol. A lack of actual cases of environmental damage caused by LMOs allowed, on the one hand, idealistic and sometimes emotional claims of establishing an impenetrable liability regime responding to all hypothetically conceivable scenarios including catastrophic events. On the other hand, it also prompted conservative and sometimes hostile attitudes towards the practical necessity of such a regime. However, the adept Co-Chairs of the negotiating group steered the discussion towards a focus on the technicalities of the legal structure of an acceptable liability regime, taking full account of the realities of the 'GM world' as described above.

Unlike the negotiations over a climate change regime or the Nagoya Protocol on access and benefit-sharing (ABS) relating to genetic resources,[19] the substantive negotiation of the Supplementary Protocol rarely involved ministers or other political figures. It was conducted mostly by those officers responsible for administrative management of LMOs and their legal advisors who knew the substantive issues the best. Pragmatism prevailed in the negotiation. The non-politicisation of the negotiation achieved by focusing on the practical and legal issues of a liability regime for biodiversity damage was one important factor in the successful adoption of the Supplementary Protocol. The Supplementary Protocol keeps a fair distance from potentially divisive issues related to LMOs themselves, essentially by freezing the controversy and leaving them to the determination of each State. The result was the insertion in 18 places in the Supplementary Protocol of the famous phrase: 'in accordance with its domestic law'.

---

18   Cf. Kareen L. Holtby, William A. Kerr and Jill E. Hobbs, *International Environmental Liability and Barriers to Trade: Market Access and Biodiversity in the Biosafety Protocol* (Edward Elgar, 2007), pp. 87–88.

19   The Nagoya Protocol on Access to Genetic Resources and the Fair and Equitable Sharing of Benefits Arising from their Utilization to the Convention on Biological Diversity was adopted on 29 October 2010 in the same city of Nagoya, two weeks after the adoption of the Supplementary Protocol. For an account of its final 'political' endeavour to adopt the ABS Nagoya Protocol by consensus, written by the Minister of the Environment of Japan and the Chairperson of the 10th Conference of the Parties to CBD, see Ryu Matsumoto, *Kankyo Gaiko no Butaiura: Daijin ga kataru COP10 no Shinjitsu (The Behind the Scenes of the Environmental Negotiation: The Minister Talks the Truth at COP10)* (Nikkei BP Marketing, 2011).

Thus, the Supplementary Protocol was able to shelve many of the potential difficulties and complexities particular to biotechnology and LMOs.[20] Instead, its legal design is premised mainly on addressing biodiversity damage in an international liability regime. This aspect of the Supplementary Protocol may have profound precedential and theoretical implications that reach beyond LMOs and biotechnology.

The Supplementary Protocol addresses damage that is defined as 'an adverse effect on conservation and sustainable use of biological diversity, taking also into account risks to human health' (Article 2 (2) (b) and Article 2 (3)).[21] This is the first ever global treaty that defines 'biodiversity damage' and establishes the legal consequences arising from such damage. As international law continues to grapple with a generally acceptable concept of environmental damage,[22] the agreement on the concept of biodiversity damage and, more significantly, on its legal consequences was almost a miracle, especially in the context of the treaty negotiated under the United Nations auspices by 160 or so Parties to the Cartagena Protocol. This miracle, however, had been achieved by extensive political compromise and adept drafting technique, making the Supplementary Protocol difficult to comprehend for first-time readers. This book will shed light on some of the most controversial, and thus most difficult-to-read, provisions of the Supplemental Protocol.

This book does not intend to be a comprehensive commentary on all 21 articles and five preambular paragraphs of the Supplementary Protocol. Instead, this book examines in depth the highlights of the Supplementary Protocol from the perspective of both the negotiators and academia. The most significant feature of the Supplementary Protocol from the perspective of both diplomacy and academic study is its incorporation of an administrative approach to liability for biodiversity damage, rather than a fully fledged civil liability regime. Three chapters examine the prelude to, the negotiation over and the legal significance of this core feature of the Supplementary Protocol that underlies all other issues examined in this book.

20 For example, the issues of patent liability and socio-economic aspects of LMOs have been identified by Cullet in 2004 as such difficulties and complexities. Philippe Cullet, 'Liability and Redress for Modern Biotechnology', *Yearbook of International Environmental Law*, Vol. 15 (2004), pp. 165–177.

21 See Appendix 1 of this book. See also Juan-Francisco Escudero Espinosa, 'The Definition of Damage Resulting from Transboundary Movements of Living Modified Organisms in Light of the Cartagena Protocol on Biosafety', *Canadian Yearbook of International Law*, Vol. 47 (2009), pp. 319–341.

22 See Francesco Francioni ed., *International Responsibility for Environmental Harm* (Kluwer, 1991); Peter Wetterstein ed., *Harm to the Environment: The Right to Compensation and the Assessment of Damages* (Clarendon Press, 1997); Michael Bowman and Alan Boyle eds, *Environmental Damage in International and Comparative Law: Problems of Definition and Valuation* (Oxford University Press, 2002). On the jurisprudence of the United Nations Compensation Commission, see Cymie R. Payne and Peter H. Sand eds, *Gulf War Reparations and the UN Compensation Commission: Environmental Liability* (Oxford University Press, 2011). For a historical development on the concept of environmental damage under international law, see Yukari Takamura, 'Kankyo Songai ni taisuru Kokusaihojo no Sekinin Seido' (Liability Regimes for Environmental Damage under International Law: Developments and Problems), in Tadashi Otsuka *et al.* eds, *Shakai no Hatten to Kenri no Souzo (Social Development and Creation of Rights)* (Yuhikaku, 2012), pp. 711–736.

This book is composed of three parts. Part I addresses the international legal context and the negotiating history underlying the Supplementary Protocol. In Chapter 2 ('A new dimension in international environmental liability regimes: a prelude to the Supplementary Protocol'), Akiho Shibata, a professor of public international law at Kobe University, Japan, and a legal advisor to the Japanese delegation negotiating the Supplementary Protocol between 2006 and 2010, examines the legal structure of the Supplementary Protocol, and questions whether its conceptual underpinning that lays the foundation of administrative approach to liability has any preludes in general international law (as opposed to US, EU and other domestic practices). After an examination of the discussion in the United Nations International Law Commission (ILC) under the agenda item 'international liability', he concludes that the two-tiered structure of the ILC Allocation of Loss Principles adopted in 2006 was the true international law prelude to the administrative approach to liability for environmental damage. As such, he argues that the Supplementary Protocol is firmly grounded on a general theory of liability as accepted by the ILC that bestows it with legitimacy and the power to pull States towards its acceptance.

In Chapter 3 ('Negotiating the Supplementary Protocol: the Co-Chairs' perspective'), René Lefeber and Jimena Nieto Carrasco, the Co-Chairs of the *Ad Hoc* Working Group and the Group of Friends of Co-Chairs (GFCC) tasked with negotiating a liability regime under the Cartagena Protocol between 2004 and 2010, examine the history of the six-year negotiations leading to the adoption of the Supplementary Protocol. The Co-Chairs disclose that it was at their initiative that an administrative approach to liability was put on the table as one option among several approaches to liability. Further, they note that they had to resort to innovative initiatives and techniques such as 'Blueprint' and 'Core Elements Paper' to expedite the negotiations and the 'confessionals' to comprehend the bottom lines of the delegations' instructions. They also endeavoured to engage the civil society and business representatives in the negotiation, while effectively employing both behind-the-scenes bilateral talks with the recalcitrant parties and, occasionally, closed meetings of the GFCC. Now, they seek to reveal the purposes and intentions of those initiatives, and evaluate their effectiveness. Without the leadership that the Co-Chairs exemplified, and the pressures that they exerted at pivotal moments of the negotiation, the Supplementary Protocol might not have borne fruit.

In Part II, this book analyses both the significance and critiques of the Supplementary Protocol. In Chapter 4 ('The legal significance of the Supplementary Protocol: the result of a paradigm evolution'), René Lefeber, a professor of International Environmental Law at the University of Amsterdam and a legal counsel to the Dutch Ministry of Foreign Affairs at the time of the negotiation, argues that the Supplementary Protocol was a result of a paradigm evolution, rather than a paradigm change, as its administrative approach to liability, or in his terminology 'regulatory liability', for environmental damage was a gradual and incremental evolution from domestic and regional precedents. He posits the liability approach of the Supplementary Protocol in the historical development of States' obligations under international law to address transboundary harm caused by activities within their jurisdictions or under their control. He interprets the core obligation under Article 5 (1) of the Supplementary Protocol as providing for the obligation imposed on the States importing LMOs to ensure that response measures be taken in the event of biodiversity damage caused by a transboundary movement of LMOs. He also postulates the industries' self-regulation demonstrating their corporate social responsibility (the Compact) as an important development that fills a regulatory gap.

In Chapter 5 ('Administrative approach to liability: its origin, negotiation and outcome), Alejandro Lago Candeira, the UNESCO Chair at Juan Carlos University in Spain and a leading negotiator of the EU delegation, examines how the EU position during the negotiation influenced not only some specific provisions of the Supplementary Protocol, but also the overall legal framework of the liability instrument under the Cartagena Protocol. He explains how the adoption in 2004 of the EU Directive on Environmental Liability based on an administrative approach and occurring just after the initiation of the negotiation process in the context of Article 27 of the Cartagena Protocol, entirely conditioned the approach of the EU to this negotiation. After the rejection of the EU's 'two-stage approach' of first adopting non-legally binding guidelines in order to gain experience before considering a legally binding instrument and after the agreement at the 2008 Bonn meeting to 'work towards' a legally binding treaty, he argues, the degree of flexibility for the EU was strictly reduced to the limits of its internal legislation, namely the 2004 EU Directive. According to his evaluation, the final outcome is a mixed interaction of different situations and contexts during the negotiation and not a comprehensive 'exportation' of EU internal law to the international sphere. He even declares that the EU was afraid of doing so due to its lack of experience in implementation, but the EU position had clearly been driving the outcome.

In Chapter 6 ('A scientific perspective on the Supplementary Protocol'), Reynaldo Ariel Alvarez-Morales, the former Executive Secretary of the Mexican Inter-Secretarial Commission of Biosafety and Genetically Modified Organisms and head of the Mexican delegation to the Supplementary Protocol negotiations, examines two of the most controversial issues related to the Supplementary Protocol: the claim to include in addition to LMOs themselves the 'products thereof' in the scope of the Supplementary Protocol (Article 3) and the definition of 'operator' (Article 2 (2) (c)). These provisions on the scope of the Supplementary Protocol and the definition of 'operator' as a liable entity constitute the legal foundation of the international liability regime for biodiversity damage established by the Supplementary Protocol. Against the expectation that these issues were a lawyer's niche, the contribution by Alvarez-Morales is extremely informative in understanding the scientific justifications behind those provisions, justifications he himself advocated very effectively during the negotiation. He identifies special features of biodiversity damage that may be caused by LMOs and argues that the relevant provisions of the Supplementary Protocol are the proper reflection of a scientific understanding of the issue. He concludes by highlighting the continuing important role of science and scientist in the implementation process of the Supplementary Protocol.

As highlighted by Shibata and Lago Candeira, some leading negotiating Parties from developed countries were unwilling to establish a legally binding civil liability regime for biodiversity damage caused by LMOs that would involve a fundamental change to their domestic legal systems and, consequently, would leave little chance for them to ratify the outcome. However, Gurdial Singh Nijar from Malaysia, probably the most influential negotiator and the leader of the 'Like-Minded Friends' campaigning for a legally binding instrument, composed of 82 countries,[23] argues in Chapter 7 ('Civil liability in the Supplementary Protocol') that for many developing countries, the adoption of an international civil liability treaty was the whole purpose of negotiation under Article 27 of the Cartagena Protocol. The grudging compromise, on both sides, was an anomalous and self-standing provision in Article 12 entitled 'Implementation and Relation to Civil Liability'. Nijar tells his story of how this Article came about and interprets the first half of paragraph 1 of Article 12 by linking it with the second half; that is to say that it leaves it to Parties to implement their existing or new civil liability laws to take response measures. Although the civil liability provision in the Supplementary Protocol is 'spectacularly deficient', he sees the potential, with the review provision under Article 13 and with experience and in the ripeness of time, that the process established by the Supplementary Protocol could well lead to the establishment of a mature regime incorporating substantive international rules on liability and redress for damage caused by LMOs. Thus, in his view, eschewing any reference to civil liability when discussing the Supplementary Protocol is 'woefully inaccurate'.

Nijar's argument is corroborated by a brief explanation on the legal and administrative situations prevalent in Africa in Chapter 8 ('One legally binding provision on civil liability: why it was so important from the African negotiators' perspective') by Elmo Thomas and Mahlet Teshome Kebede. Thomas is from Namibia and was one of the negotiators of the African Group, and Kebede is an African Union lawyer who provided legal advice to the Group during the negotiations. They argue that for many African Parties that had just begun to establish their administrative apparatus to implement the Cartagena Protocol, the administrative approach to liability would place additional demands upon the still-fragile national authorities, and, therefore, African nations favoured a legally binding civil liability regime that would make use of their existing judicial systems. In their view, the rules on civil liability enter into the picture when administrative regulations have proved ineffective in preventing damage, and, as this is the case in national laws of most African and other developing countries, an adequate civil liability system recognised in the international arena in the form of a binding treaty would allow the claimant to obtain compensation through due process of law.

In the traditional international regimes of civil liability, a provision on financial security to cover the potential liabilities of operators with an established financial

23   Gurdial Singh Nijar, Sarah Lawson-Stopps and Gan Pei Fern, *Liability and Redress under the Cartagena Protocol on Biosafety: A Record of the Negotiations for Developing International Rules*, Vol. I (Centre of Excellence for Biodiversity Law, 2008), p. 387.

limit of the liabilities in order for them to be insurable had always become one of the most complex and controversial issues in negotiations.[24] Even after the adoption of the treaty, the provisions on financial security remained one of the thorniest issues for many States in their consideration of whether to ratify the regime. Under the Supplementary Protocol, although it does not directly oblige the liable operator to pay compensation for the damage but, instead, obliges it to take reasonable response measures, the operator may still be financially liable to reimburse the 'costs and expenses of, and incidental to, the evaluation of the damage and the implementation of any such appropriate response measures' taken by the competent authority if the competent authority has exercised its discretion to implement the required response measures (Article 3 (4), Article 3 (5) and Article 8). Accordingly, a possibility of requiring some kind of financial security of the operators to cover this indirect liability had also become a controversial issue under the Supplementary Protocol. Article 10 (1) of the Supplementary Protocol on financial security uniquely stipulates that the Parties 'retain the right to provide, in their domestic law, for financial security', instead of the usual provision under civil liability conventions obliging the operators to establish such financial security.[25]

In Chapter 9 ('Trade and the Supplementary Protocol: how to achieve mutual supportiveness'), Rodrigo C. A. Lima objectively and critically examines the legal implications of Article 10 of the Supplementary Protocol in light of the WTO rules, particularly the national treatment principle, the general exception provision under GATT Article XX (b), the rules under the Agreements on technical barriers to trade (TBT) and on the application of sanitary and phytosanitary measures (SPS). Lima is a lawyer from Brazil with a vast experience of non-tariff barriers debates in negotiations under multilateral environmental agreements including the Cartagena Protocol. As Article 10 (2) requires the Parties to the Supplementary Protocol to exercise the right referred to in Article 10 (1) above 'in a manner consistent with their rights and obligations under international law, taking into account the final three preambular paragraphs of the (Cartagena) Protocol', he sets forth clear requirements established by the WTO rules and its precedents, taking into account also the precautionary approach under the Cartagena Protocol. He also argues that if a Party to the Supplementary Protocol chooses to adopt a financial measure on imported LMOs generally, without scientific evidence to justify such measure to protect biodiversity, we may expect cases that can reach the Dispute Settlement Body of the WTO.

The analysis of the Supplementary Protocol in Chapter 10 ('The Supplementary Protocol: a treaty subject to domestic law?') by Worku Damena Yifru and Kathryn Garforth is overtly critical. Yifru and Garforth are from the CBD Secretariat, who provided valuable logistical and legal support to the negotiation. They argue that

---

24 Fitzmaurice, see note 4, p. 1031.
25 For example, Article 14 (1) of the Basel Liability Protocol provides in part: 'The persons liable under Article 4 shall establish and maintain during the period of the time limit of liability, insurance, bonds or other financial guarantees covering their liability under Article 4 of the Protocol for amounts not less than the minimum limits specified in paragraph 2 of Annex B.'

the Supplementary Protocol does not actually establish binding international obligations upon its Parties in its core provisions on the definition, the scope, the response measures and their implementation because the treaty is fundamentally subjected to the domestic law of each Party. They claim that this situation could perhaps be attributed to the nature of rules based on an administrative approach. They suggest that some negotiating Parties were more concerned with the retention of their existing domestic legal systems than establishing true international rules, and the core provisions of the Supplementary Protocol, when examined with a critical eye, actually reflect this leeway in the name of flexibility. In addition, as Article 16 (4) reflects the controversial trade and environment debate, the Supplementary Protocol seemed to be severed from the rest of international law – past, present and future, which according to Yifru and Garforth, is 'a logical impossibility'.

It is clear that the true legal value of the Supplementary Protocol can only be assessed by examining its (future) implementation at the domestic level. Part III of this book addresses this important issue of the implementation of the Supplementary Protocol at both the international and domestic level.

Dire Tladi, currently a member of the International Law Commission and formerly a member of the South African delegation to negotiate the Supplementary Protocol, foreshadows in Chapter 11 ('Challenges and opportunities in the implementation of the Supplementary Protocol: re-interpretation and re-imagination') a situation in which the hard-fought compromises in the Supplementary Protocol may be reopened in the form of its re-interpretation and re-imagination, potentially affecting its implementation. Defining re-interpretation and re-imagination as tools that States and other actors may use to mould their rights and obligations under a treaty in a manner that is more favourable for them, Tladi identifies the opportunities for such re-interpretation and re-imagination in the process of a State drafting its implementation laws, in the process of its review in the Conference of the Parties serving as the Meeting of the Parties to the Supplementary Protocol (COP-MOP) and in the dispute settlement process under the WTO. Both the discretion explicitly provided under the Supplementary Protocol and the ambiguity that allows national implementers the license of re-interpretation and re-imagination permit such moulding of rights and obligations under the Supplementary Protocol, and he identifies provisions on the definitions of damage and operator, on financial security and on civil liability as the primary targets of such re-interpretation and re-imagination. However, he cautions that the transboundary character of the Supplementary Protocol may pose an implementation challenge in that while a country of import (where the damage is most likely to occur) is free, within certain constraints, to apply the Supplementary Protocol as it has re-interpreted or re-imagined, enforcement in the country of export or third country may prove difficult if such re-interpretation or re-imagination is not acceptable to the latter.

On the issue of domestic implementation, this book invites 'outsiders' to the negotiation with expertise on domestic laws to gain an objective analysis of the Supplementary Protocol from the perspective of domestic lawyers.

In Chapter 12 ('The Supplementary Protocol and the EU Environmental Liability Directive: similarities and differences'), Edward H. P. Brans and Dorith H. Dongelmans, Dutch practicing lawyers with extensive research experience in EU environmental liability law, examine meticulously the details of the Supplementary Protocol and compare them with the relevant provisions of the EU Environmental Liability Directive (EU-ELD). They find a significant overlap between the Supplementary Protocol and the EU-ELD. Both regimes cover damage to natural resources, apply an administrative approach and are focused on the actual remediation of environmental damage in lieu of monetary compensation. The Supplementary Protocol's flexibility may signify that the regime will not be implemented in a uniform manner worldwide, but, conversely, it could be an advantage for European legislators to have opportunity to pick and choose those elements of the Supplementary Protocol that are similar to the EU-ELD. They also find important and more fundamental differences between the Supplementary Protocol and EU-ELD, namely in the scope of both regimes and their measures of damages. According to Brans and Dongelmans, these differences are such that they make a smooth implementation of the Supplementary Protocol into EU law less likely. They question whether Article 3 (6) of the Supplementary Protocol can overcome the difference in scope of both regimes and their measures of damages. This is an important indication that despite the negotiators' efforts to the contrary, an objective reading of the Supplementary Protocol may require some amendments to some Parties' existing legislation in order to effectively implement the Supplementary Protocol.

In Chapter 13 ('A Japanese approach to the domestic implementation of the Supplementary Protocol'), Eriko Futami, a postgraduate student, and Tadashi Otsuka, a professor of environmental law at Waseda University School of Law, Japan, who have written extensively in the field of environmental liability law, examine objectively the provisions of the Supplementary Protocol to see whether the current Japanese Cartagena Law adequately responds to the legal requirements of the Supplementary Protocol and to what extent, if any, it needs to be amended to effectively implement its provisions. As Futami and Otsuka state, the Japanese implementing legislation of the Supplementary Protocol will establish the first ever liability system in Japan for environmental damage *per se*, including the biodiversity damage. Futami and Otsuka introduce the main features of the current Japanese Cartagena Law, which implements the Cartagena Protocol, and identify both the merits and drawbacks in using this legislation to implement the Supplementary Protocol. As the Japanese Cartagena Law explicitly addresses the adverse effect of LMOs on the biological diversity, for Japan, the concept of biodiversity damage is much easier to swallow as long as it can be addressed through existing administrative legislation specifically dealing with the LMOs and their negative impact on biodiversity, and not by general tort law under its civil code. On the other hand, Futami and Otsuka identify a major gap in the Law's current scope of possible measures that could be ordered against 'users of LMOs', who will be equivalent to the 'operators' under the Supplementary Protocol. As the current Japanese Cartagena Law is premised on the prevention of adverse effects from

LMOs, it allows the competent authority either to 'suspend' the use of LMOs or 'remove' (or 'recall' in certain other situations) the LMOs. According to Futami and Otsuka, these measures would not include 'restoration measures' as required under the Supplementary Protocol. They also identify the difference between the threshold of 'adverse effects on biodiversity' under the current Cartagena Law and the 'biodiversity damage' under the Supplementary Protocol, suggesting incorporation of the concept of biodiversity damage into the Cartagena Law, with the changes necessary to allow precautionary measures in cases where the expected damage is not 'significant'.

Chapter 14 ('The industry's Compact and its implication for the Supplementary Protocol') by J. Thomas Carrato, John Barkett and Phil Goldberg does not relate directly to the implementation of the Supplementary Protocol but to an industry's instrument called 'The Compact: A Contractual Mechanism for Response in the Event of Damage to Biological Diversity Caused by the Release of a Living Modified Organism', which, according to the authors, can complement the Supplementary Protocol by more effectively protecting biodiversity from potential damage caused by LMOs. The Compact is a private sector mechanism that States can use to assure that a person or business responsible for releasing an LMO that causes damage to biological diversity remediates that damage. After recapping the biotech industry's engagement in the negotiation of the Supplementary Protocol and how this Compact came about, they explain how it works and how it can be used to complement the liability and redress remedies available to a State under the Supplementary Protocol. They argue that the Compact and Supplementary Protocol provide States with two viable options for assuring that a responsible party will remediate damage to biological diversity caused by its release of an LMO. The authors also suggest that the Compact, which is based on a similar platform and common concepts, can be a resource for States in completing their task of implementing the Supplementary Protocol, including the Compact's detailed definitions of key terms, such as damage to biological diversity, causation and determinations pursuant to science-based evidence.

In Chapter 15 ('Conclusion: beyond the Supplementary Protocol'), Akiho Shibata, summarising the 14 chapters, identifies the core issues that needed to be examined in order to appropriately comprehend the significance and *problématique* of the Supplementary Protocol, and discusses its future implications on the fundamental thinking on the legal design of environmental liability regimes under international law.

Part I

The context and negotiation

2 A new dimension in international environmental liability regimes

A prelude to the Supplementary Protocol

Akiho Shibata

I Introduction

The Nagoya-Kuala Lumpur Supplementary Protocol on Liability and Redress to the Cartagena Protocol on Biosafety (Supplementary Protocol) is an international liability regime for environmental damage. When it enters into force, it will be a legally binding treaty providing for the legal consequences of causing damage, defined as 'an adverse effect on the conservation and sustainable use of biological diversity' (Article 2 (2) (b)). Biodiversity being a part of natural environment, the Supplementary Protocol *is* an international environmental liability regime of global applicability. As of 31 January 2014, it attracted 51 signatories and 21 ratifications, approvals and accessions, including the European Union (EU).[1] The 40 ratifications the Supplementary Protocol requires to enter into force (Article 18 (1)) is a challenge, but it is within sight.

The news of the successful adoption of the Supplementary Protocol and its steady support from States in the form of signatures and ratifications must have come as a surprise to those who doubted the 'sensibility' of negotiating environmental liability regimes.[2] In 1992, Principle 13 of the Rio Declaration on Environment and Development urged the States 'in an expeditious and more determined

---

1 United Nations Treaty Collection, *Multilateral Treaties Deposited with the Secretary-General*, Chapter XXVII, 8.c: Nagoya-Kuala Lumpur Supplementary Protocol on Liability and Redress to the Cartagena Protocol on Biosafety, Status as of 31 January 2014. Available at http://treaties.un. org/pages/ParticipationStatus.aspx (accessed 31 January 2014). Most recently Cambodia acceded to it on 30 August, Guinea-Bissau accepted it on 24 September, Burkina Faso acceded to it on 4 October, Romania ratified it on 4 October, Hungary ratified it on 9 December, and the Netherlands accepted it on 30 December 2013.

2 Jutta Brunnée, 'Of Sense and Sensibility: Reflections on International Liability Regimes as Tools for Environmental Protection', *International and Comparative Law Quarterly*, Vol. 53, No. 2 (2004), pp. 351–368.

manner to develop further international law regarding liability and compensation for adverse effects of environmental damage'.[3] The international community succeeded in creating such regimes on voluminous papers with extensive negotiation costs and time, only to find out later that except for a few maritime oil pollution liability regimes,[4] no regime has attracted enough ratification from States to make it enforceable.[5] Thus, there were indeed reasons for scepticism. Against all these odds, the Supplementary Protocol revived the environmental liability regime under international law with its important conceptual evolution, an evolution that has been extensively discussed, and, finally, accepted in the United Nations. This chapter will shed some light on the international legal context in which this conceptual evolution has occurred.

It is, however, necessary first to establish the legal framework under which the negotiation and adoption of the Supplementary Protocol had occurred, as it could have been the case that such a framework had already tightly restricted the outcome, leaving little to no room to incorporate such an evolution occurring in the context of general international law. The examination of such legal framework focuses not only on the interpretation of Article 27 of the Cartagena Protocol on Biosafety (Cartagena Protocol),[6] but also on the legal regime established by the Convention on Biological Diversity (CBD)[7] as a whole. As this chapter will illustrate, there was indeed a very small window of opportunity for the negotiators to adapt to new trends and ideas in the field of environmental liability, and to learn from past mistakes.

3 Rio Declaration on Environment and Development, adopted on 16 June 1992, UN Doc. A/CONF.151/26/Rev.1, Vol. I (1992).

4 International Convention on Civil Liability for Oil Pollution Damage, adopted on 29 November 1969 as amended (in force), *United Nations Treaty Series*, Vol. 973, p. 3, and the Protocol to amend the Convention, adopted on 27 November 1992, entered into force on 30 May 1996, *United Nations Treaty Series*, Vol. 1956, p. 255 [Oil Pollution Liability Convention]; International Convention on Civil Liability for Bunker Oil Pollution, adopted on 23 March 2001, entered into force on 21 November 2008, IMO/LEG/CONF.12/19 (27 March 2001).

5 Convention on Civil Liability for Damage Resulting from Activities Dangerous to the Environment, adopted on 21 June 1993 (not in force), *European Treaty Series, No. 150* [Lugano Convention on Civil Liability]; Basel Protocol on Liability and Compensation for Damage Resulting from Transboundary Movements of Hazardous Wastes and Their Disposal, adopted by Decision V/29 on 10 December 1999 (not in force), UNEP/CHW.5/29 (1999), p. 88, Annex III [Basel Liability Protocol]; Protocol on Civil Liability and Compensation for Damage Caused by the Transboundary Effects of Industrial Accidents on Transboundary Waters to the 1992 Convention on the Protection and Use of Transboundary Watercourses and International Lakes and to the 1992 Convention on the Transboundary Effects of Industrial Accidents, adopted on 21 May 2003 (not in force), ECE/MP.WAT/11-ECE/CP.TEIA/9 [Kiev Protocol on Civil Liability].

6 Cartagena Protocol on Biosafety to the Convention on Biological Diversity, adopted on 29 January 2000, entered into force on 11 September 2003, *United Nations Treaty Series*, Vol. 2226, p. 208.

7 Convention on Biological Diversity, adopted on 5 June 1992, entered into force on 29 December 1993, *United Nations Treaty Series*, Vol. 1760, p. 79.

II The legal framework for designing a liability treaty under the CBD regime

1 Article 27 as an open-ended framework

The origin of the Supplementary Protocol is in Article 27 of the Cartagena Protocol,[8] a controversial and ambiguous provision. Putting aside the controversy as to whether Article 27 could be considered as a mandate or even a duty to commence the negotiation to elaborate international rules and procedures, it was intentionally silent as to the nature of liability and the scope of damage, leaving the negotiating Parties to determine these fundamental elements of liability regimes.

On the other hand, Article 27 as originally drafted was fairly clear as to the scope of activities that may cause such damage by providing that these rules and procedures would deal with 'damage resulting from transboundary movements of LMOs'. This strongly indicated that the new instrument would address damage occurring *during* the transboundary movements of LMOs. This restrictive view on the scope of activities is similar to that under the Basel Liability Protocol,[9] and was invoked by certain negotiating States during the early years of negotiation on the Supplementary Protocol. However, the negotiating Parties decided to broaden the scope of the Supplementary Protocol to cover at least those activities explicitly mentioned in Article 4 of the Cartagena Protocol.[10] Finally, Article 3 (1) of the Supplementary Protocol provides that the Supplementary Protocol 'applies to damage resulting from LMOs which find their origin in a transboundary movement'. In theory, the application of the Supplementary Protocol may be triggered decades after the importation of a LMO, when its availability and use would have been totally domesticated.[11]

---

8   Article 27, Cartagena Protocol: 'The Conference of the Parties serving as the meeting of the Parties to this Protocol shall, at its first meeting, adopt a process with respect to the appropriate elaboration of international rules and procedures in the field of liability and redress for damage resulting from transbounday movements of living modified organisms, analysing and taking due account of the ongoing processes in international law on these matters, and shall endeavour to complete this process within four years.'

9   Article 3 (1) and (2) of the Basel Liability Protocol states that the 'Protocol shall apply to damage due to an incident occurring during a transboundary movement of hazardous wastes . . . from the point where the wastes are loaded on the means of transport in an area under the national jurisdiction of a State of export', and 'until the time . . . completion of disposal has occurred.'

10   An important turn in the negotiations of this matter occurred when, at the fifth meeting of the Open-Ended Working Group in March 2008, the Co-Chairs introduced their 'Core Elements Paper', which suggested an option of a legally binding instrument based on an administrative approach with a wide scope of activities to be covered (broad functional scope), and with narrow scope of damage limited only to damage to biological diversity. Core Elements Paper, submitted by the Co-Chairs, UNEP/CBD/BS/WG-L&R/5/CRP.1 (15 March 2008), reproduced in Appendix 4 of this book.

11   The only condition under the Supplementary Protocol (Article 3 (4)) is that it 'applies to damage resulting from a transboundary movement of living modified organism that started after the entry into force of this Supplementary Protocol for the Party into whose jurisdiction the transboundary movement was made.'

Thus, Article 27 of the Cartagena Protocol was not so much a golden rule to be strictly complied with, but rather a flexible general framework to direct the negotiators. It is thus important to note the latter part of Article 27, where it directed the negotiators to 'tak(e) due account of the ongoing processes in international law on these matters'. Within the flexible framework provided in Article 27, the information regarding liability discussions undertaken in other international and regional forums could have been legitimately referred to during the negotiations and, as this chapter will shortly demonstrate, did indeed set an important context in which the Supplementary Protocol came to take its final legal design and was accepted by the negotiating Parties.

At the beginning of the new century, States negotiating Article 27 of the Cartagena Protocol, and, later, the Supplementary Protocol must have had, at the least, the following processes in their minds: (a) the experience from the Basel Liability Protocol adopted in 1999; (b) the discussion on international liability within the United Nations International Law Commission (ILC), which culminated in the adoption on its second reading of the draft texts on the Prevention of Transboundary Harm in 2001, as well as on the Allocation of Loss in 2006; (c) the environmental liability discussion within the European Union (EU), which led to the adoption in 2004 of the Environmental Liability Directive (EU-ELD); (d) the adoption in 2005 of a new treaty on liability arising from Environmental Emergencies in Antarctica; and (e) the UNEP's work on guidelines for the development of national legislation on liability and compensation for damage caused by activities dangerous to the environment.[12]

2 CBD-Cartagena framework

This being said, the Supplementary Protocol is only 'supplementary' to the Cartagena Protocol, and it is negotiated and successfully adopted as a new treaty based on and within the framework of the legal regime established by the Cartagena Protocol. The Cartagena Protocol, for its part, was negotiated and adopted based on and within the framework of the legal regime established by the CBD. This legal relationship between the Supplementary Protocol, on one hand, and the Cartagena Protocol and CBD, on the other, is articulated in paragraphs 1 and 2

---

12 During the negotiations on the Supplementary Protocol, the Secretariat produced information papers on 'recent developments in international law relating to liability and redress'. UNEP/CBD/BS/WG-L&R/1/INF/4 (15 April 2005); UNEP/CBD/BS/WG-L&R/2/INF/5 (27 January 2006); UNEP/CBD/BS/WG-L&R/3/INF/2 (10 January 2007); UNEP/CBD/BS/WG-L&R/4/INF/2 (4 October 2007); UNEP/CBD/BS/WG-L&R/5/INF/1 (3 February 2008); UNEP/CBD/BS/GF-L&R/1/INF/1 (27 January 2009).

It was not so much these documents that influenced the negotiations, but rather the personal experience and knowledge of some delegates who actually made proposals and interventions based upon such experience or knowledge that made a real difference in the process of negotiation on the Supplementary Protocol. Many of the contributors to this book were such influential negotiators with vast experience and knowledge, and the present author was much privileged and honoured to have had an opportunity to work with them.

of Article 16, originally proposed by Japan and modelled after Article 4 of the Protocol on Environmental Protection to the Antarctic Treaty:[13]

Article 16 Relationship with the Convention and the Protocol

1   This Supplementary Protocol shall supplement the Protocol and shall neither modify nor amend the Protocol.

2   This Supplementary Protocol shall not affect the rights and obligations of the Parties to this Supplementary Protocol under the Convention and the Protocol.[14]

The Cartagena Protocol was negotiated and adopted on the basis of Article 19 (3) of the CBD,[15] and, in its final form, it does not conceive LMOs as generally and inherently hazardous or dangerous to the environment. Consequently, the advance informed agreement (AIA) procedure and its scheme of operation under the Cartagena Protocol is different in its legal nature from the prior informed consent (PIC) procedure provided for hazardous wastes and pesticides under the Basel Convention on hazardous wastes and by the Rotterdam Convention on hazardous chemicals and pesticides.[16] Under the AIA procedure, it is the impor-ting country, based on its risk assessment carried out in a scientifically sound manner, that determines whether a certain LMO could be considered as risky to its environment and thus become subject to special regulations, including import bans. Thus, as one authority says, '(t)he fact that the Protocol does not seek to establish an internationally binding assessment of the risks that may derive from LMOs means that risk assessment and decision-making rest on the authority of each individual party to the Protocol'.[17]

Although the Cartagena Protocol does not conceive LMOs as inherently hazardous, it does allow Parties to make distinction between LMOs (cf. GM soybeans) and non-LMOs (cf. non-GM soybeans) and to impose distinct regulations only on LMOs as specifically provided in the Cartagena Protocol. This distinction

13 Protocol on Environmental Protection to the Antarctic Treaty, adopted on 4 October 1991 at the 11th Special Consultative Meeting of the Antarctic Treaty, entered into force on 14 January 1998, *Handbook of the Antarctic Treaty System*, 9th edn (US Department of State, 2002), p. 18.

14 Paragraphs 3 and 4 of Article 16 underwent revisions, as these paragraphs came to reflect the controversial 'trade and environment' issue.

15 Article 19 (3), CBD: 'The Parties shall consider the need for and modalities of a protocol setting out appropriate procedures, including, in particular, advance informed agreement, in the field of the safe transfer, handling and use of any living modified organism resulting from biotechnology that may have adverse effect on the conservation and sustainable use of biological diversity.'

16 Catherine Redgwell, 'Biotechnology, Biodiversity and Sustainable Development: Conflict or Congruence?', in Francesco Francioni and Tullio Scovazzi eds, *Biotechnology and International Law* (Hart, 2006), p. 69.

17 Laurence Boisson de Chazournes and Makane Moise Mbengue, 'Trade, Environment and Biotechnology: on Coexistence and Coherence', in Daniel Wüger and Thomas Cottier eds, *Genetic Engineering and the World Trade System: World Trade Forum* (Cambridge University Press, 2008), p. 210.

is one of the reasons as to why some large GM crop-producing countries, such as the United States, Canada and Argentina, elected to stay outside of the Cartagena regime. However, the Parties to the Protocol themselves had been entrusted to negotiate an international liability regime under the Cartagena Protocol with the very fine and delicate mandate of designing a legal regime to address damage arising from LMOs without assuming them as inherently hazardous to the environment. For example, during the early stages of the negotiation, a proposal to oblige Parties to apply strict liability for damage as if activities involving LMOs are all ultra-hazardous was considered. This proposal, however, was considered as prejudicing the delicate compromise reached in 2000.

The Cartagena Protocol as the basis of the Supplementary Protocol also established important parameters on the scope of damage and the definition of LMOs that cause such damage under the new liability regime. Although Article 27 of the Cartagena Protocol did not specify what kind of damage could be treated in the elaboration of international rules in the field of liability, both the CBD and the Cartagena Protocol referred to 'adverse effect on the conservation and sustainable use of biological diversity, taking also into account the risks to human health'.[18] The language of the latter part of this phrase, referring to human health, was deliberately left open for the Parties to interpret. For example, Japan posits that 'since the CBD does not provide as its objective the protection of human health and the human beings cannot be considered a part of living organisms protected under the CBD, the Cartagena Protocol under the CBD should be interpreted as providing for the protection of human health only as an incidental element when taking measures to ensure the protection of biological diversity'.[19] Although there was an attempt to renegotiate this delicate compromise, the Supplementary Protocol as finally adopted faithfully follows the legal framework established by its predecessors, and defines damage as 'an adverse effect on the conservation and sustainable use of biological diversity, taking also into account risks to human health' (Article 2 (2) (b)).

The same solution was achieved as to the definition of LMOs that may cause damage to the biological diversity. The make-or-break issue at the final hours of negotiation on the Supplementary Protocol was whether to refer to LMOs as 'living modified organisms and products thereof'. The proponents of expanding the

---

18 See Article 8 (g), CBD. However, the enabling provision in Article 19 (3) does not contain the latter part referring to the human health, see note 15. The Cartagena Protocol is consistent in using this exact phrase throughout the Protocol. See, for example, fifth preambular paragraph, Articles 1 (objective), 4 (scope), 15 (risk assessment), and 18 (handling, transport, packaging and identification), Cartagena Protocol; and paragraph 1 of its Annex III on Risk Assessment. See generally Juan-Francisco Escudero Espinosa, 'The Definition of Damage Resulting from Trans-boundary Movements of Living Modified Organisms in Light of the Cartagena Protocol on Biosafety', *Canadian Yearbook of International Law*, Vol. 47 (2009), pp. 319–341.

19 Kankyosho (The Ministry of the Environment), Idenshi Kumikae Seibutsu to no Shiyo to no Kisei niyoru Seibutsu no Tayosei no Kakuho ni Kansuru Houritsu no Kaisetsu (Commentary on the Law Ensuring Biological Diversity through the Regulation on the Use of Living Modified Organisms) (modified on 1 April 2007), p. 1. Available at www.bch.biodic.go.jp/bch_2.html (accessed 1 August 2013).

definition of LMOs to include also the products of LMOs (for example, tofu and soy sauce made from GM soybeans) argued that as long as the modified genes can be traceable and are proven to be the cause of damage, such products should also be within the scope of the new liability regime. These same proponents also pointed to Article 20 (3) (c) of the Cartagena Protocol and paragraph 5 of its Annex III on Risk Assessment, both of which refer to the concept of 'products thereof, namely, processed materials that are of living modified organism origin, containing detectable novel combinations of replicable genetic material obtained through the use of modern biotechnology'. Based on these provisions, they argued that the products of LMOs, as well as LMOs themselves, have already been within the scope of the mother treaty. The majority of Parties, however, considered such arguments unconvincing.[20] First, the reference to the 'products thereof' in the Cartagena Protocol was limited strictly to the risk assessment and within the context of discretionary technical or informational procedures. Second, the phrase 'products thereof' cannot be detached from its context as provided in paragraph 5 of the Annex III, as risks associated with the 'products thereof' should be considered in the context of the risks posed by the recipients or parental organisms, that is the living organisms. In other words, in no way were the 'dead' materials that are of LMO origin intended to be within the scope of the Cartagena Protocol. Finally, the opponents reminded the negotiators that the issue of 'products thereof' had already been extensively discussed during the negotiation of the Cartagena Protocol,[21] and it was finally agreed not to include the 'products thereof' within the scope of the Protocol, but instead refer to them only within the context of risk assessment and its discretionary informational procedures.[22]

In its final draft, retaining the legal framework provided by the Cartagena Protocol, the Supplementary Protocol deleted all references to the 'products thereof' or any other similar formulas from its text. Nonetheless, during the informal contact group discussion, it became evident that the domestic regulations of some Parties implementing the Cartagena Protocol, including those Parties opposing the inclusion of the phrase, have been made applicable to cases of potential adverse effects caused by processed materials that are of LMO origin. The members of the contact group considered that the existence of such domestic regulations, based most probably on an interpretation of Article 27 of the Cartagena Protocol, cannot be ignored or rejected. Hence, in the Report of the Meeting, this fact was recognised: the 'Parties to the (Cartagena) Protocol hold different understandings of the application of Article 27 of the Protocol to processed materials that are of living modified organism-origin. One such understanding is that Parties may apply the Supplementary Protocol to damage caused by such

---

20   See Chapter 6 of this book, by Reynaldo Ariel Alvarez-Morales for a scientific justification for excluding 'products thereof'.

21   Report of the Fifth Meeting of the Open-Ended *Ad Hoc* Working Group on Biosafety, UNEP/CBD/BSWG/5/3 (3 September 1998), para. 36.

22   Report of the Sixth Meeting of the Open-Ended *Ad Hoc* Working Group on Biosafety, UNEP/CBD/ExCOP/1/2 (15 February 1999), para. 51 (statement by China) and Appendix I: Draft Protocol on Biosafety.

processed materials, provided that a causal link is established between the damage and the LMO in question'.[23] It was clearly understood by the negotiators that even in these rare cases of domestic regulations, the applicability of the Supplementary Protocol is conditioned on the fact that the original LMO (cf. GM soybeans), and not the processed materials (cf. tofu), must have been subject to the transboundary movement.

Thus, the legal framework for designing a liability treaty under the CBD regime was both open-ended and confined. It was open-ended as to the innovative ideas and developments relating to liability discussions in the ongoing processes in international law, especially as to the approaches to the concept of liability. At the same time, it was confined to the fundamental tenets of the CBD regime, the Supplementary Protocol being its integral part. Repelling the attempts to renegotiate the agreement reached in 2000, the definition of damage addressed by the Supplementary Protocol and the scope of LMOs that will be the cause of such damage were streamlined with its mother treaties. Only the scope of activities that fall under the Supplementary Protocol seemed to go beyond the original textual intention as reflected in Article 27 of the Cartagena Protocol, but this was all with the ultimate goal of designing a liability regime that will respond to the real needs of the Parties. No Party will be content to have a liability regime applicable for biodiversity damage caused only *during* the transboundary movement of LMOs.

III The administrative approach to liability in the Supplementary Protocol at a glance

As examined above, Article 27 was open as to the nature of liability to be established under the Cartagena Protocol, and the same article specifically mandated the negotiators to take due account of the ongoing processes in international law in this regard. The experience of the 1999 Basel Liability Protocol was a cause of scepticism, both in academic and diplomatic circles,

---

23 Report of the Fifth Meeting of the Conference of the Parties to the Convention on Biological Diversity serving as the Meeting of the Parties to the Cartagena Protocol on Biosafety, UNEP/CBD/BS/COP-MOP/5/17 (29 November 2010), para. 133. See also Appendix 3 of this book.

　　This paragraph cannot be considered as reflecting an 'agreement relating the treaty which was made between all the parties in connection with the conclusion of the treaty', which, for the purpose of the interpretation of a treaty, may comprise the context of the treaty, as provided in Article 31 (2) (a) of the Vienna Convention on the Law of Treaties (VCLT). First, and regarding the substance, the paragraph reflects the 'different understandings' of the treaty; only one such understanding has been cited here. Second, and regarding the form, it is still an open question as to whether a statement of understanding or agreement reflected in the final report of a conference of the parties (COP), adopted usually by consensus, but sometimes by majority decision-making, can be considered as an agreement relating to the treaty 'between all the parties'. See Mark Villiger, *Commentary on the 1969 Vienna Convention on the Law of Treaties* (2009), pp. 429–431; Anthony Aust, *Modern Treaty Law and Practice* (2nd edn, 2007), pp. 235–238.

for negotiating and adopting a full-fledged international civil liability regime for environmental damage.[24] The process leading up to the adoption in 2004 of the EU Environmental Liability Directive (EU-ELD),[25] although not yet widely known at the time other than in Europe and by experts specialising in the EU environmental law, was convincing evidence that the international endeavour to harmonise domestic civil law on environmental liability would be a formidable, if not impossible, mission to accomplish.[26] It is therefore understandable that the Co-Chairs proposed at the end of the first meeting of the Open-Ended *Ad Hoc* Working Group of Legal and Technical Experts on Liability and Redress in the Context of the Cartagena Protocol on Biosafety (*Ad Hoc* WG) in 2005, on their own initiative, an option of 'administrative approaches based on allocation of costs of response measures and restoration measures'[27] as one of the possible approaches to liability under the Cartagena Protocol. One of the Co-Chairs was from the EU, with vast experience in the diplomatic negotiations on international environmental liability regimes, including the Basel Liability Protocol, and being also well informed of the academic trends in the field. The EU was quick to support such an option as viable, and promptly submitted textual proposals before the third meeting of the *Ad Hoc* WG held in February 2007;[28] meanwhile, other delegations were still struggling to grapple with the concept.

24 From the academia: Brunnée, see note 2. From practitioners involved in the negotiations: Anne Daniel, 'Civil Liability Regimes as a Complement to Multilateral Environmental Agreements: Sound International Policy or False Comfort?' *Review of European Community and International Environmental Law*, Vol. 12, No. 3 (2003), pp. 225–241.

25 Directive 2004/35/CE of the European Parliament and of the Council of 21 April 2004 on environmental liability with regard to the prevention and remedying of environmental damage, *Official Journal of the European Union 2004*, L 143/56.

26 For an account of the process leading up to the EU-ELD, including the 2000 White Paper based on private law approach to ensure access to justice, and the Working Document in 2001, which proposed for the first time an administrative approach to environmental liability, see Mai Fujii, 'EU Kankyo Liability Shirei ni okeru "Gyousei teki approach": Sono Kokusaiho eno Shisa' (The Administrative Approach in the EU Environmental Liability Directive), *Kokusai Kyoryoku Ronshu (Journal of International Cooperation Studies)*, Vol. 17, No. 2 (2009), pp. 143–145.

27 Report of the Open-Ended *Ad Hoc* Working Group of Legal and Technical Experts on Liability and Redress under the Cartagena Protocol on Biosafety, UNEP/CBD/BS/COP-MOP/2/11 (27 May 2005), p. 12. See the Co-Chairs' account of this proposal in Chapter 3 of this book. See also the Co-Chairs' 'encouragement' to discuss the administrative approach: Report of the Open-Ended *Ad Hoc* Working Group of Legal and Technical Experts on Liability and Redress in the Context of the Cartagena Protocol on Biosafety on the work of its third meeting, UNEP/CBD/BS/WG-L&R/3/3 (15 March 2007), p. 7, para. 45; Report of the Open-Ended *Ad Hoc* Working Group of Legal and Technical Experts on Liability and Redress in the Context of the Cartagena Protocol on Biosafety on the work of its fourth meeting, UNEP/CBD/BS/WG-L&R/4/3 (13 November 2007), p. 5, paras 23–25.

28 EU submission of 6 October 2006, Compilation of submissions of further views and proposed operational texts with respect to approaches, options and issues identified as regards matter covered by Article 27 of the Cartagena Protocol on Biosafety, UNEP/CBD/BS/WG-L&R/3/INF/1 (7 December 2006), p. 13.

This very brief account of the origin of the administrative approach to liability in the negotiation of the Supplementary Protocol[29] strongly suggests that it was an initiative of the people who knew of the EU-ELD and its process. Without challenging this suggestion, it is the author's argument in this chapter that while initiated by the EU, the final acceptance by all the negotiating Parties of this new approach to liability in an international treaty must have been based on its global legitimacy – its pedigree and coherence, to use Professor Thomas Franck's legitimacy criteria[30] – beyond its acceptance in the European context. Indeed, the core normative features of the administrative approach to liability exemplified by the Supplementary Protocol have been carefully examined within the context of the ILC by international law experts of the highest reputation under the agenda item of 'International liability for injurious consequences of acts not prohibited by international law'. The examination by the ILC culminated in the adoption in 2006 of the *Principles on the allocation of loss in the case of transboundary harm arising out of hazardous activities* (Allocation of Loss Principles), with the commentaries thereto,[31] and the United Nations General Assembly had taken note of these Principles the same year.[32] The discussion on international liability in the ILC had occurred in parallel with, but not necessarily linked to, the negotiations on the Supplementary Protocol, but, as will be examined in this chapter, it served as an important legal background that facilitated the global acceptance of the Supplementary Protocol based on the administrative approach to liability. The international community was ready in 2010 to adopt a new approach to liability in international law with, as its latent basis, the ILC's background work of almost 30 years on international liability.

It is thus necessary to analyse the core normative features of the administrative approach to liability incorporated in the Supplementary Protocol at the outset. In essence, the Supplementary Protocol obliges its Parties to establish a domestic legal system that effectively addresses biodiversity damage caused by LMOs by requiring the operator who has the control of the LMOs at issue to take response measures to prevent, minimise, contain and mitigate such damage, and restore the damaged biological diversity (Articles 12 (1) and 5 (1)). In this process, the Supplementary Protocol mandates the competent authority of the Parties to identify the operator, evaluate the damage and determine which response measures should be taken by the operator. Further, it allows the authority to implement appropriate response measures if the circumstances so require, and to obtain reimbursement of the costs from the liable operator (paragraphs 2, 4 and 5 of Article 5).

---

29 See Chapter 5 of this book, by Alejandro Lago Candeira for a discussion on the role of the EU in the negotiations of the Supplementary Protocol, with a particularised emphasis on its administrative approach to liability.

30 Thomas M. Franck, *The Power of Legitimacy among Nations* (Oxford University Press, 1990).

31 Draft principles on the allocation of loss in the case of transboundary harm arising out of hazardous activities: Text of the draft principles and commentaries thereto, *ILC Report 2006*, UN Doc. A/61/10 (2006) [hereinafter *2006 Text and Commentary*], p. 101.

32 UN Doc. A/RES/61/36 (2006): Allocation of loss in the case of transboundary harm arising out of hazardous activities, adopted on 4 December 2006.

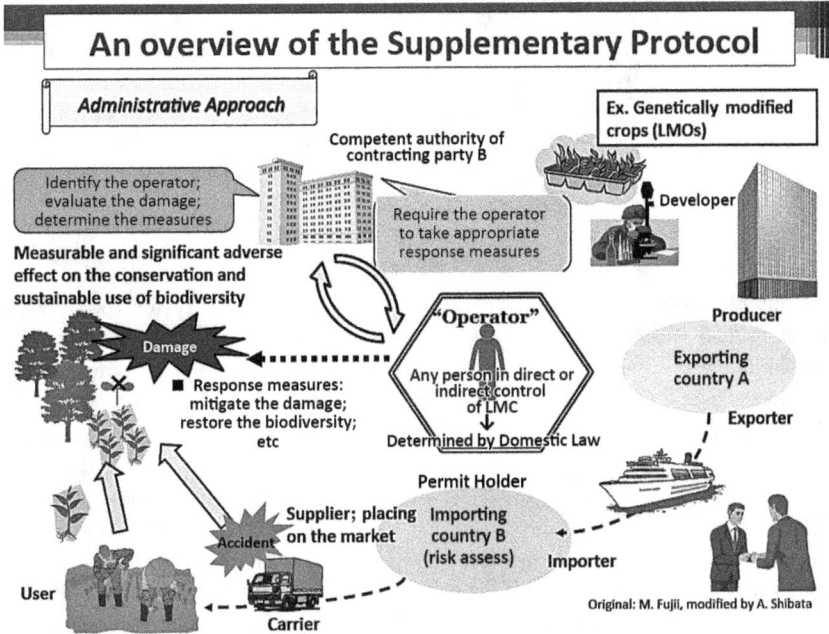

Figure 2.1 An overview of the Supplementary Protocol (administrative approach)

Thus, the legal regime of the Supplementary Protocol is premised on the following four normative features:

(a) It addresses damage to biodiversity, and not traditional damage to persons, property or economic interests.

(b) The content of liability, namely the legal consequences of causing such damage, shall be for the operator to take response measures to contain and mitigate such damage, and to restore the damaged biological diversity to its original condition or to its nearest equivalent, in lieu of monetary compensation. Monetary obligations arise only when it is the competent authority that takes response measures and requests reimbursement for such measures from the operator. In fact, nowhere in the Supplementary Protocol does the word 'compensation' actually appear.

(c) The liability of the operator is incurred in relation to the administrative organ of the government, rather than in relation to the victim of such damage. As such, the obligation of the operator will be pursued largely utilising the administrative apparatus and procedures, rather than in the courts.

(d) The liability is imposed on the operators, usually private actors involved in the development, export, import, marketing or use of LMOs, instead of territorial States where such activities take place. Thus, administrative approach to liability *is not* administrative liability in the sense of State liability, where the legal consequences of damage are channelled to a State.

These features represent the core normative structure of an administrative approach to liability. Having all these features, the Supplementary Protocol is the first international treaty of global applicability that adopts an administrative approach to liability for biodiversity damage. These features will be examined in more detail below, in relation to specific provisions under the Supplementary Protocol.

1 Liability for biodiversity damage

To reiterate, the Supplementary Protocol establishes liability for biodiversity damage, and it defines damage as 'an adverse effect on the conservation and sustainable use of biological diversity, taking also into account risks to human health' (Article 2 (2) (b)). The CBD provides for both the concept of damage to biological diversity (Article 14 (2)), and that of adverse effect on (or damage to) the conservation and sustainable use of biological diversity (Article 19 (3)), the latter being consistently used within the context of LMOs. The discussion in the CBD regime as to the distinction or the similarity between these two concepts has not been determinative thus far.[33] The practice of States, on the other hand, suggests that the Parties to the CBD and the Cartagena Protocol consider these two concepts interchangeable. For example, the Japanese law implementing the Cartagena Protocol uses the term 'adverse effect on biological diversity', and the Ministry of the Environment seems to understand the term to be synonymous to 'adverse effect on conservation and sustainable use of biological diversity'.[34] As such, at least for the purpose of this chapter, these two concepts can be used interchangeably.

The Supplementary Protocol addresses damage to biodiversity, and, in light of the standard formula of recoverable 'damage' under international legal instruments (here, using the Basel Liability Protocol as an example), it excludes the traditional damage to persons ('loss of life or personal injury') and to property ('loss of or damage to property'), and, arguably, pure economic loss ('loss of income directly deriving from an economic interest in any use of the environment'). This interpretation is confirmed by, first, the text of Article 12, which refers to 'material

---

33 See the latest discussion on 'damage to biological diversity' under Article 14 (2) of CBD, Note by the Executive Secretary: Synthesis report on technical information relating to damage to biological diversity, UNEP/CBD/COP9/20/Add.1 (20 March 2008). In 2010, the 10th Conference of the Parties to the CBD decided to resume discussion on 'liability and redress' under Article 14 (2) of the CBD at the twelfth Conference of the Parties planned to be held in 2014. Paragraph (b) (vii), Decision X/9 (2010): The multi-year programme of work for the Conference of the Parties for the period 2011–2020 and periodicity of meetings, Report of the tenth meeting of the Conference of the Parties to the Convention on Biological Diversity, UNEP/CBD/COP/10/27 (20 January 2011), p. 144.

34 See Idenshi Kumikae Seibutsu to no Shiyo to no Kisei niyoru Seibutsu Tayousei no Kakuho ni kansuru Houritsu (Law Ensuring Biological Diversity through the Regulation of Use of Living Modified Organisms), Law No. 97 of 5 June 2003, as amended [Cartagena Law]. For more details on the Japanese Cartagena Law, see Chapter 13 of this book, by Eriko Futami and Tadashi Otsuka.

or personal damage' as distinct from 'damage' as defined above, and, second, the *travaux préparatoires* of the Supplementary Protocol.

Article 12 was a hard-fought provision arising out of grudging compromise between, on one hand, those Parties who wanted to have an international civil liability treaty for damage caused by LMOs, and, on the other hand, those who rejected such an endeavour as unrealistic and unwise.[35] The obligations in paragraphs 1 and 2 of Article 12 are clearly distinguished in relation to the different type of damage each paragraph addresses. Paragraph 1 addresses damage as defined in Article 2 (2) (b) of the Supplementary Protocol, that is biodiversity damage, whereas paragraph 2 addresses traditional damage referred to as 'material or personal damage', with a condition that it applies when such traditional damage is 'associated with' the biodiversity damage. The reasons for this distinction are obvious. First, the obligation to implement the administrative approach to liability as reflected in the Supplementary Protocol as regards to biodiversity damage is clearly established by the first sentence, as well as by the first half of the second sentence of paragraph 1. Second, on the other hand, as per the latter part of the second sentence starting from the phrase 'and may, as appropriate' in paragraph 1, there is no such obligation on the Parties to address biodiversity damage by civil liability law. Third, as regarding the traditional damage under paragraph 2, the Parties are obliged to apply their civil liability law, but only 'with the aim' of providing adequate domestic law on civil liability to address such traditional damage associated with biodiversity damage.[36] The complex structure of Article 12 can be illustrated as follows:

35 See Chapter 7 of this book, by Gurdial Singh Nijar on the negotiation on Article 12.

36 It should be noted, however, that the Supplementary Protocol does foresee a domestic legal system in which response measures may be ordered by the court by applying civil liability law. This is explicit in the second sentence of paragraph 7 of Article 5: 'Parties may, as appropriate, assess whether response measures are already addressed by their domestic law on civil liability.' This provision was inserted by the insistence of Brazil, as, according to its explanation, under its domestic legal system, such response measures in response to damage would usually be ordered by the court in applying civil liability law. On the contrary, in the Japanese legal system, the monetary compensation is the principal remedy under its civil liability law (tort law), and, unless there is a specific legislation to the contrary, the action for restoration would not be claimed as part of redress for damage. Tadashi Otsuka, *Kankyoho* (*Environmental Law*) (3rd edn, Yuhikaku, 2010), p. 679.

If the Supplementary Protocol can be interpreted as allowing the application of civil liability law to require the operator to take response measures without introducing an administrative approach, the second sentence of Article 12 (1) could be interpreted as not obliging its Parties to introduce in its domestic law an administrative approach to liability, but, rather to implement only 'response measures' that could be ordered through the application of civil liability law and by the court 'as appropriate'. However, the text of Article 5 (7) and Article 12 (1) does not explicitly allow for such an interpretation. Moreover, such an interpretation militates against the specific obligations provided in Article 5 (1) to (6) to establish an administrative scheme to respond to biodiversity damage, and, therefore, against the object and purpose of the Supplementary Protocol. On this issue, see different views expressed explicitly or implicitly by Gurdial Singh Nijar in Chapter 7, and by Worku Damena Yifru and Kathryn Garforth in Chapter 10 of this book.

Table 2.1 Structure of Article 12 implementation and relation to civil liability

	By administrative approach (response measures)	*By civil liability law (compensation)*
Biodiversity damage as defined in the Supplementary Protocol	Obligation to implement	Discretion to implement
Material or personal damage associated with biodiversity damage	(no provision)	With the aim to provide

Until the fifth meeting of the *Ad Hoc* WG in Cartagena in March 2008, the negotiating document did indeed contain the entire range of possible damage within the scope of damage to be addressed by the new instrument. It was the Core Elements Paper submitted on the initiative of the Co-Chairs at that meeting that clearly set the options for combining those core elements for the future liability regime under the Cartagena Protocol. In the Core Elements Paper, the Co-Chairs distinguished the scope of damage to be addressed by two different instruments (Piece A and Piece B).[37] In Piece A, the administrative approach to liability would be a legally binding instrument, and would address '(d)amage to the conservation and the sustainable use of biological diversity' only. On the other hand, in Piece B, civil liability would be non-legally binding guidelines for implementation in domestic law, and would address '(a)ny type of damage resulting from the transboundary movement of LMOs to legally protected interests, including damage to the conservation and sustainable use of biological diversity not redressed through administrative approach (no double recovery)'. The concept of damage to 'legally protected interests' is creative as it includes not only the traditional interests protected by most of the legal systems of the world – namely damage to persons and property – but also pure economic loss through the impairment of the environment, and, possibly, damage to public goods if these are already protected by the domestic law of the Parties. By setting these items of damage aside to be addressed by civil liability guidelines, the administrative approach to liability, as was submitted by the Co-Chairs, addressed squarely the non-traditional damage to environment *per se*, namely damage to biodiversity.[38] Although the Core Elements Paper as such was not accepted by the Parties as the basis of further negotiation, the agreement at the Bonn meeting in May 2008 to 'work towards a legally binding instrument on an administrative approach with one article on civil liability' was premised on the basic normative structure proposed by the Co-Chairs in the Core Elements Paper. The administrative approach to liability will address biodiversity damage, whereas civil liability applies to traditional damage, and, as long as the domestic law permits, pure economic loss and damage to public goods.

37 Core Elements Paper, see note 10.
38 See also the explanation on the Core Elements Paper by the Co-Chairs in Chapter 3 of this book.

Thus, the Supplementary Protocol as based on an administrative approach to liability addresses damage to biodiversity, intentionally distinguishing it from the traditional damage to persons and property, pure economic loss and other damage that is capable of being addressed by domestic civil liability laws of some countries. Damage to biodiversity is a kind of damage to environment *per se*, or 'orphan damage',[39] and it has perplexed both the practitioners and theorists as to the proper response in legal terms. An administrative approach to liability, as exemplified in the Supplementary Protocol, can be one answer to that question at the level of international law. The specific definition of biodiversity damage in the Supplementary Protocol and its significance, as well as potential problems associated wherewith, will be discussed below in subsection 3.

2 Liability as response measures

Under international law, the term 'liability' has been used by scholars and stipulated in documents in a variety of contexts to mean many different things. The 1972 Stockholm Declaration on Human Environment referred, in Principle 22, to 'liability and compensation' for environmental damage, and it was contrasted with the term 'responsibility' in Principle 21, namely in reference to the responsibility of territorial States to ensure that transboundary environmental damage would not occur.[40] Some non-English speaking scholars use the term 'liability' to generally convey the obligation to pay monetary compensation, including reparation for wrongful acts.[41] This may well be because the English term 'liability' had not been translated into an appropriate corresponding term in other languages. The Institut de Droit International (IDI) takes the position that the terms 'liability' and 'responsibility' should be distinguished in relation to the subject that is either liable or responsible, with 'liability' applicable to operators (including States *qua* operators), and 'responsibility' to States.[42] The treaty practice has been fairly consistent up until recently in using the term 'liability' to convey monetary compensation for damage. In this treaty practice, the term 'liability' refers to either: (a) the liability for damage of an operator incurred under the domestic law of the Parties to a treaty that intends to harmonise their domestic civil liability laws (civil liability for damage: e.g. 1969 Oil Pollution Liability Convention, 1999 Basel Liability Protocol); or (b) the liability for damage of a State incurred under international law irrespective of an existence of wrongful act by that State (State liability for damage: the only example being the 1972 Space Object Liability

39   On 'orphan damage', see Chapter 5 of this book, by Alejandro Lago Candeira.

40   Principles 21 and 22, Stockholm Declaration on Human Environment, adopted on 16 June 1972, UN Doc. A/CONF.48/14/Rev.1 (1972). See also Louis B. Sohn, 'The Stockholm Declaration on the Human Environment', *Harvard International Law Journal*, Vol. 14 (1973), pp. 485–502.

41   Pierre-Marie Dupuy, 'International Liability for Transfrontier Pollution,' in Michael Bothe ed., *Trends in Environmental Policy and Law* (Erich Schmidt Verlag, 1980), p. 364.

42   Responsibility and Liability under International Law for Environmental Damage, Resolution adopted at Strasbourg Session, *Annuaire de l'Institut de droit international* (1997), Vol. 67, Tome II, pp. 486–513.

Convention).[43] Thus, according to this fairly established treaty practice, the term 'liability' signifies the obligation to pay monetary compensation as a direct legal consequence of causing damage, irrespective of whether the act causing such damage was wrongful or not.

The Supplementary Protocol, however, does not explicitly provide the substantive content of liability, although, in its title and in Article 1, it declares that the treaty is on 'liability and redress'. It does not contain a typical liability provision, such as, for example, 'the person who notifies in accordance with Article 6 of the (Basel) Convention, shall be liable for damage . . .' (Article 4, Basel Liability Protocol). Instead, Article 5 (1) of the Supplementary Protocol provides that 'Parties shall require the appropriate operator or operators, in the event of damage, . . . to (c) Take appropriate response measures'. A superficial reading of this provision may seem to negate the establishment in the Supplementary Protocol of liability as a direct legal consequence of causing damage. However, if one examines its legal structure as a whole, with the support of its *travaux préparatoires*, the Supplementary Protocol indeed establishes the liability for biodiversity damage, requiring operators to take response measures.

By interpreting Article 5 (1) in conjunction with the first half of Article 12 (1), the operators will be required, pursuant to domestic law of the Parties, to take appropriate response measures. This obligation of the operator under the domestic law will be a consequence of such operator being in control of the LMO (Article 2 (2) (c)) that caused damage (Article 4 on causation). Thus, the operators at the domestic law level are obliged to take response measures for damage that was caused by an LMO under their control. At the international law level, however, the Parties are obliged to provide domestic laws that address damage to biodiversity in a way that the operators are required to take response measures in the event of such damage. This reading of Article 5 (1) can be confirmed by Article 5 (3), which provides straightforwardly that 'the operators shall be required to take appropriate response measures so as to avoid such damage' in a situation where there is a sufficient likelihood that damage will result. Paragraph 1 on the normal instances of damage, and paragraph 3 on the situation where such damage is likely to occur, have been separated in compromise to accommodate those Parties rejecting the phrase 'imminent threat of damage'.[44] However, the paragraphs are on the same rationale as to the legal consequence for the operators in control of LMOs to be obliged to take appropriate response measures for biodiversity damage caused by those LMOs.

The above interpretation of Article 5 (1) can also be supported by its *travaux préparatoires*. At the beginning of the first meeting of the Group of Friends of Co-Chairs (GFCC) in February 2009, there were two types of provisions stipulating the core of an administrative approach: one directed the Parties to require

---

43 Convention on International Liability for Damage Caused by Space Objects, adopted on 29 March 1972 (in force), *United Nations Treaty Series*, Vol. 961, p. 187.

44 On the issue of 'imminent threat of damage', see Chapters 3 and 6 of this book, by René Lefeber and Jimena Nieto Carrasco, and Reynaldo Ariel Alvarez-Morales, respectively.

the operators to take response measures, and another directly addressing the operator to take the response measures.[45] The negotiations focused on whether to use 'shall' or 'should', rather than the two differing stipulations, as they were thought by the negotiators to be similar in their substance. Two texts that remained towards the end of the meeting were: (a) 'The Parties shall require the operator to immediately inform the competent authority of damage or the imminent threat of damage . . .'; and (b) 'In the event of damage, . . . an operator shall . . . evaluate the damage . . . and take appropriate response measures'.[46] In order to streamline the provision without changing the substantive content of these two texts, it was agreed by the negotiators to stipulate them into a single provision as follows:

> Article 7 (2): Parties shall require the operator, in the event of damage [or imminent threat of damage], subject to any requirements of the competent authority, to: (a) immediately inform the competent authority; (b) evaluate the damage [or imminent threat of damage]; and (c) take appropriate response measures.[47]

Thus, from this negotiating history of Article 5 (formerly 7), it is clear that its specific stipulation does not intend to militate against the establishment of liability of the operator to take response measures as a direct legal consequence of causing damage by an LMO under its control.

Uniquely in comparison with the previous treaty practice as examined above, the Supplementary Protocol provides as liability for damage an obligation to take response measures, rather than to pay monetary compensation. Moreover, the extent of the liability, that is the extent of the response measures that the operator is obliged to take as a legal consequence of causing damage to biodiversity by an LMO under its control, is far-reaching. The operators are required to take 'reasonable actions' to:

(i) Prevent, minimise, contain, mitigate, or otherwise avoid damage as appropriate;

(ii) Restore biological diversity through actions to be undertaken in the following order of preference:

(a) Restoration of biological diversity to the condition that existed before the damage occurred, or its nearest equivalent; and where the competent authority determines this is not possible;

---

45 See Annex to Decision BS-IV/12: Liability and redress under the Cartagena Protocol on Biosafety, UNEP/CBD/BS/GF-L&R/1/2 (2 December 2008), Section IV on Primary compensation scheme: A. Elements of administrative approach based on allocation of cost of response measures and restoration measures, Operational texts 9, 10, 10 alt, 11, and 11 alt.

46 Proposed operational texts on liability and redress in the context of Article 27 of the Biosafety Protocol, as of 26 February 2009 (on file with the author), Operational texts 10 and 11.

47 Report of the Group of the Friends of the Co-Chairs on liability and redress in the context of the Cartagena Protocol on Biosafety on the work of its first meeting, UNEP/CBD/BS/GF-L&R/1/4 (27 February 2009), p. 12.

(b)   Restoration by, *inter alia*, replacing the loss of biological diversity with other components of biological diversity for the same, or for another type of use either at the same or, as appropriate, at an alternative location.

(Article 2 (2) (d))

Perhaps with the exception of EU Member States already required by the EU-ELD to impose similar measures, the implementation of this far-reaching obligation imposed on the operators to take response measures as a liability for causing damage to biodiversity was thought to be a huge challenge, even for a country such as Japan with its developed legal system and administrative apparatus. Initially, Japan thought it necessary to insert a flexibility clause into the definition of response measures, such as 'to the extent it is technically and economically feasible' or 'as appropriate'.[48] When it became clear that the other negotiating Parties would not agree to such a clause, Japan sought, instead, at the very least, certain flexibility in the manner in which a Party implements these response measures through its domestic law (Article 5 (8)).[49] With the criteria of 'reasonableness' built into the definition of response measures, in addition to possible formal exemptions that may be provided by domestic law (Article 6), this flexibility as provided in the Supplementary Protocol will definitely promote the ratification process for many countries that would need a trial-and-error period for its implementation, without in any way compromising the objective of the Supplementary Protocol to establish the liability of operators to take appropriate response measures, including the far-reaching restoration measures provided in Article 2 (2) (d).

What, then, will one make of the reference to Principle 13 of the Rio Declaration in the second preambular paragraph of the Supplementary Protocol? Was not the Supplementary Protocol based on an administrative approach to liability in order to overcome the mistakes of previous civil liability regimes negotiated, but never enforced, under the mandate of Principle 13? This clause was proposed by a Co-Chair very late in the negotiations during the final two days of the extended fourth and last meeting of GFCC.[50] In response, Japan initially opposed the proposal, arguing that there were substantive differences between Principle 13 and the draft Supplementary Protocol. Japan indicated that the former refers to 'liability and compensation for adverse effects of environmental damage',[51] whereas the

48   Report of the First GFCC, ibid., p. 10 (Article 2 (f)).

49   Report of the Group of the Friends of the Co-Chairs on liability and redress in the context of the Cartagena Protocol on Biosafety on the work of its second meeting, UNEP/CBD/BS/GF-L&R/2/3 (14 February 2010), p.11 (Article 7 (1)); Report of the Group of the Friends of the Co-Chairs on liability and redress in the context of the Cartagena Protocol on Biosafety on the work of its third meeting, UNEP/CBD/BS/GF-L&R/3/4 (19 June 2010), p. 12 (Article 5 (8)).

50   The negotiating text at the beginning of the fourth meeting of GFCC did not include a preambular paragraph referring to Principle 13 of the Rio Declaration. See Draft texts for further negotiations (appendices I and II to the report of the third meeting of the Group of the Friends of the Co-Chairs), UNEP/CBD/BS/GF-L&R/4/2 (25 August 2010), p. 5.

51   Principle 13, Rio Declaration on Environment and Development, see note 3.

Supplementary Protocol intentionally avoided using the term 'compensation'. However, as the negotiations were nearing the final stage of creating a package deal, Japan, being the host of the meeting, did not pursue such a theoretical opposition. Japan was content to have a much clearer preambular paragraph in the Supplementary Protocol, indicating its true significance that was already agreed by the negotiating Parities: '*Recognizing* the need to provide for appropriate response measures where there is damage or sufficient likelihood of damage, consistent with the Protocol' (fourth preambular paragraph).[52]

3 Liability pursued by administrative organ of State

Under the Supplementary Protocol, in principle, the liability of the operator will not be pursued in a court based on a claim by a victim of damage. Instead, the liability will be pursued by an administrative organ of the State Party to the Supplementary Protocol. The legal authority of such a State organ to pursue the operator's liability would most likely be provided in administrative (or public) law, rather than in civil (or private) law. Thus, the administrative approach to liability is sometimes referred to as an administrative law (or public law) approach.[53]

The pivotal role of the administrative organ in the administrative approach to liability is reflected in paragraphs 2–6 of Article 5 of the Supplementary Protocol. After providing in paragraph 1 the liability of the operator for causing biodiversity damage through an LMO under its control (see above), paragraph 2 of Article 5 provides that '(t)he competent authority shall: (a) Identify the operator which has caused the damage; (b) Evaluate the damage; and (c) Determine which response measures should be taken by the operator. The sequence of paragraphs 1 and 2 is important. It is in the process of *implementing* (and not *establishing*) the liability of the operator already incurred by the fact of its causing damage (paragraph 1) that the functions of the competent authority would be exercised (paragraph 2). Even in such an implementing process, the role of the competent authority to pursue and execute the operator's liability to take response measures is central to the effective functioning of the Supplementary Protocol. Most likely, under its domestic law, although not legally required to do so under the Supplementary Protocol, the competent authority of a Party, after identifying the operator that has caused the damage, and after evaluating the damage, would issue an administrative order based on its legal authority provided under public law to take response measures either in generic ('appropriate measures') or more specific ('measures to contain the damage', for example) terms. Under paragraphs 4 and 5 of Article 5, the competent authority itself may implement the appropriate response measures when, in particular, the operator has failed to do so. In such a situation, the

---

52   Draft texts for further negotiations, UNEP/CBD/BS/GF-L&R/4/2, see note 50, p. 5.
53   Ludwig Krämer, 'Directive 2004/35/EC on Environmental Liability', in Gerrit Betlem and Edward Brans eds, *Environmental Liability in the EU: The 2004 Directive Compared with US and Member State Law* (Cameron May, 2006), p. 34.

competent authority 'has the right to recover from the operator the costs and expenses of, and incidental to, the evaluation of the damage and the implementation of any such appropriate response measures'.

It is true that the effective functioning of the Supplementary Protocol is premised on the existence of a robust administrative apparatus and dedicated personnel with the capacity to quickly cope with the situation of biodiversity damage, including the capacities to assess the nature and extent of damage, to analyse its cause (which LMO has caused damage) and to determine the causal connection to identify a liable operator or operators. This was one of the reasons that some developing countries participating in the negotiation process showed, at best, a leery support for the idea of an administrative approach to liability under the Supplementary Protocol.[54] It is also true, however, that among the salient possible approaches to liability regime, including a full-fledged civil liability regime and a State liability regime, the negotiating Parties could agree, as a legally binding liability regime for biodiversity damage caused by LMOs, only to the one based on an administrative approach. Strangely, the developing countries did not show much interest in the capacity-building component of the package as proposed initially in the Core Elements Paper in 2008[55] and in the final drafting of Decision BS-V/11 (2010).[56] A strong capacity-building regime, theoretically, could have overcome, or, at least, alleviated their hesitancy towards an administrative approach to liability.

In the administrative approach to liability, the concept of damage takes on a substantially different function from that under the regular civil liability systems. Under the civil liability systems, the concept of damage determines the parameters for monetary compensation, and, consequently, the evaluation of damage into monetary value becomes its critical exercise. On the contrary, under the administrative approach, the concept of damage functions primarily as a trigger for the operator and the administrative organ to take action in relation to damage. Under the administrative approach, as is most often the case, the determination as to whether 'damage' had occurred will be made by the competent authority (Article 5 (2)), and based on such determination, the competent authority will require the operator to take response measures to prevent, contain and mitigate the damage, and, if necessary, to restore the damaged biodiversity. This trigger is for the good cause of conservation and sustainable use of biodiversity. As such, a good faith determination of the competent authority would most likely be considered as authoritative as long as the situation at hand is within the general contours of the definition of 'damage'. Indeed, this was why the definition of

---

54 See Chapter 8 of this book, by Elmo Thomas and Mahlet Techome Kebede.
55 Piece D: Complementary Capacity-Building Measures, Core Elements Paper (2008), see note 10.
56 Section C: Complementary Capacity-Building Measures, Decision BS-V/11 (2010): International rules and procedures in the field of liability and redress for damage resulting from transboundary movements of living modified organisms, UNEP/CBD/BS/COP-MOP/5/17 (29 November 2010), p. 63; see also Appendix 2 of this book. During the fourth meeting of GFCC, the discussion on Section C of the draft decision took only one hour.

'damage' under the Supplementary Protocol became a less controversial issue, and a provision on 'evaluation of damage' became unnecessary.[57]

The Supplementary Protocol defines damage to biodiversity in relation to its measurability and its significance (paragraphs 2 (b) and 3 of Article 2). In other words, it defines damage in relation to its quality and quantity, but it does not provide in itself the substantive criteria as to what constitutes biodiversity, a measurable and significant adverse effect to which will amount to damage as defined in the Supplementary Protocol. The CBD defines 'biological diversity' as the 'variability among living organisms from all sources including, *inter alia*, terrestrial, marine and other aquatic ecosystems and the ecological complexes of which they are part; this includes diversity within species, between species and of ecosystem'.[58] This definition is far from setting the precise outlines of object 'biological diversity', damage to which shall incur legal liabilities. The discussion within the CBD regime refers to 'loss of biological diversity',[59] but its relationship to damage to biological diversity is still not clear. In its *Pulp Mills* judgment in 2010, while positively incorporating the concept of biodiversity into the term 'aquatic environment', and examining substantively the parties' arguments on 'effects on biodiversity',[60] the International Court of Justice (ICJ) seemed to assimilate the harmful effect on biodiversity as that on fauna and flora of the river.[61]

Thus, the Supplementary Protocol leaves significant discretion to its Parties to set substantive criteria as to what constitutes biological diversity, and what constitute damage to so-defined biological diversity. The EU wanted to ensure that this discretion is explicitly spelled out in the Supplementary Protocol. At its insistence, Article 3 (6) was inserted: 'Parties may use criteria set out in their domestic law to address damage that occurs within the limits of their national jurisdiction'. This provision also helped countries such as Japan that have unique criteria of gauging adverse effects to biological diversity. For example, under the Japanese Cartagena Law, which will also provide the basic legal framework for

---

57 Indeed, it was at the first meeting of GFCC in 2009, after the negotiating Parties agreed to work towards a legally binding instrument on administrative approach, that they decided to delete a section on 'evaluation of damage', and to integrate its texts into the definition of response measures. Note by the Executive Secretary: Decision BS-IV/12: liability and redress under the Cartagena Protocol on Biosafety, UNEP/CBD/BS/BF-L&R/1/2 (2 December 2008), p. 6; Report of the first GFCC, UNEP/CBD/BS/GF-L&R/1/4, see note 47, p. 10.

58 Article 2, CBD. 'Ecosystem' is defined as 'a dynamic complex of plant, animal and micro-organism communities and their non-living environment interacting as a functional unit'.

59 According to Decision VII/30, 'biodiversity loss' is defined as 'the long-term or permanent qualitative or quantitative reduction in components of biodiversity and their potential to provide goods or services, to be measured at global, regional and national levels'. Paragraph 2 of Decision VII/30 (2004): Strategic plan, future evaluation of progress, UNEP/CBD/COP/DEC/VII/30 (13 April 2004). This definition of biodiversity loss should be taken into account when considering the concept of damage to biological diversity, but the former is not necessarily the same as the latter. Note by the Executive Secretary, UNEP/CBD/COP/9/20/Add.1 (2008), see note 33, paras 4, 12–15.

60 Case concerning Pulp Mills on the River Uruguay (Argentina v. Uruguay), Judgment on 20 April 2010, *ICJ Reports 2010*, paras 202, 260–261.

61 Ibid., para. 262.

implementing the Supplementary Protocol, only the native and wild species of animals and plants are considered for the object of possible adverse effects caused by LMOs, excluding, for example, cultivated crops and non-native species.[62]

Not denying the possibility of some variations as to the scope of protected 'biodiversity' among the Parties implementing the Supplementary Protocol,[63] a lack of a precise and binding definition of biodiversity damage in the Supplementary Protocol itself, and allowing the Parties to use their domestic law criteria to address such damage would not, however, cause significant difficulty in operationalising the administrative approach to liability. Again, under the Supplementary Protocol, the definition of damage at the international level primarily functions as a trigger for the action that will prevent, contain and mitigate damage, and, if necessary, restore the damaged biodiversity. For this triggering function, certain discretion on the part of competent authorities is desired, provided that a corresponding domestic law provides for more precise criteria that would curtail abusive exercise of power by the competent authority vis-à-vis the operator. Article 5 (6) of the Supplementary Protocol actually foresees such a judicial (or administrative) review of the decision made by the competent authority.

4 Liability imposed on operators

As examined above, the Supplementary Protocol places the liability on the operator who is defined as 'any person in direct or indirect control of the LMO which could, as appropriate and as determined by domestic law, include, *inter alia*, the permit holder, person who placed the LMO on the market, developer, producer, notifier, exporter, importer, carrier or supplier' (Article 2 (2) (c)). The term 'notifier' refers to those entities that notify of the intentional transboundary movement of an LMO as required under Article 8 of the Cartagena Protocol, and, thus, could include a State Party of export. However, since the operator can only be a person (including a legal person) who is in the chain of business involving that LMO and in control of that LMO, the State that has notified of such movement in accordance with its legal mandate will not be identified as an operator, unless the State functions as a State enterprise engaged in LMO exports by itself. Thus, under the Supplementary Protocol, there is no liability attached to States based on their functions in the AIA procedure under the Cartagena Protocol. Neither the Party of export that needs to ensure the accuracy of information provided to the importing Party (Article 8 (1) of the Cartagena Protocol), nor the Party of import that conducts the risk assessment, and, based on such assessment, consents to the import of a LMO (Article 10 of the Cartagena Protocol), would be held liable under the Supplementary Protocol based only on the fact that they assume these duties under the Cartagena Protocol. Further, the territorial State where the LMO that caused damage was developed, produced, and from which the LMO was exported

---

62 See Chapter 13 of this book, by Eriko Futami and Tadashi Otsuka.
63 See Chapters 10 and 12 of this book, by Worku Damena Yifru and Kathryn Garforth, and Edward H. P. Brans and Dorith H. Dongelmans, respectively.

(most probably with its permission), nor the territorial State where the damage occurred by an LMO that was imported and used in that State (most probably with its permission), would be held liable under the Supplementary Protocol based solely on the basis of its territorial jurisdiction over those activities by private actors involving the LMO at issue.

Thus, the Supplementary Protocol rejects State liability when understood as a liability for damage imposed on States solely on the basis of their jurisdiction or control over an activity that caused damage. Even the option of residual State liability did not attract much attention in negotiations, and was ultimately dropped without any substantive discussion.[64] The Supplementary Protocol is without prejudice to the possibility of States incurring international responsibility for wrongful acts (Article 11).

Beyond the clear rejection of State liability, and, consequently, the clear choice of operator's liability based on the so-called polluter-pays principle,[65] the definition of operator under Article 2 (2) (c) of the Supplementary Protocol is extremely open-ended. First, the core criterion of 'control' has been expanded to include 'indirect control'. Second, the listing of possible actors is only illustrative. Finally, the identification of the operator will ultimately be subject to the domestic law of each Party. It is, therefore, clear from this textual reading that the Supplementary Protocol at the international law level did not channel the liability to any particular actor in the chain of activities involving LMOs. More importantly, the peculiarity of this definition resides in the fact that the concept of 'control' is linked not to the activity involving an LMO, but to the LMO itself. This peculiarity had further legal consequences on the provision on causation (Article 4), as, under the Supplementary Protocol, it is the causal link between the damage and the LMO (and not the activity) that must be proved in order to establish liability. Thus, the logic of the Supplementary Protocol is as follows: first, damage to biodiversity is caused by an LMO; second, that LMO is under 'direct or indirect control' of an operator; third, it is, therefore, (presumed) that the operator has caused the damage (Article 5 (2) (a)); and, finally, as a consequence, that operator is liable to take appropriate response measures.

There were several factual, legal and policy reasons behind this unwieldy text on the definition of operator. First, the Supplementary Protocol covers several different types of damage scenarios, each of them directing us to a different operator as the appropriate person to take response measures. In case of illegal

64 A section on 'residual State responsibility' remained in the document only as a reminder until the fourth and final meeting of GFCC. Draft texts for further negotiation, UNEP/CBD/BS/GF-L&R/4/2 (2010), see note 50, p. 19. The document had two operational texts both in brackets: 'Where a claim for damages has not been satisfied by an operator, the unsatisfied portion of that claim shall be fulfilled by the State where the operator is domiciled or resident'; and 'For damage resulting from transboundary movement of living modified organisms, primary liability shall be that of the operator with residual State liability [to the State of the operator].'

65 No provision in the Supplementary Protocol refers explicitly to the concept or principle of polluter-pays. However, during the negotiations, some Parties expressly referred to the principle when opposing the residual State liability and, thus, supporting the operator's liability.

use or accidental spill of LMOs, one might assume that an actor who has the operational control of the activity that is illegal, or having caused the accident, would be held liable. However, in discussing unexpected and unforeseen biodiversity damage caused by an authorised use of a GM crop by a farmer, some Parties argued that it is unfair to impose liability on the 'innocent poor farmer' who has no knowledge of LMOs, nor the capacity to respond to or pay for the biodiversity damage. In such cases, they argued, the operator should be identified at the upper stream of the LMO business chain, e.g. permit holder, exporter, producer or developer. Second, some Parties already have a domestic legal framework in place, ready to implement the future Supplementary Protocol with their own definition of operators, and these Parties wanted to make sure that the definition of operator under the Supplementary Protocol would not exclude the ones already provided in their domestic law. Third, some scientists in the negotiations argued convincingly that the process of biodiversity damage by LMOs will invariably be long-term, latent and cumulative, so that a legal regime premised on the need to establish an activity that caused the damage through the LMO would never function effectively. According to these scientists, illegal use or accidental spills of LMOs do not in themselves cause damage to biodiversity. A person having the operational control of such activity at the time of an incident may be required to take necessary measures to avoid adverse effects on biodiversity under the Cartagena Protocol (Article 18 of the Cartagena Protocol), but the same person may not necessarily be the appropriate operator to take the response measures under the Supplementary Protocol when the eventual biodiversity damage actually occurs.

Thus, departing from the previous treaty practice on liability regimes, the Supplementary Protocol, under the name of 'liability' treaty, imposes an obligation on the operator to take response measures, including far-reaching restoration measures, as a legal consequence of causing damage to biodiversity. The liability of the operator is effectuated by administrative organs of States through their regulations, rather than in their domestic courts initiated by victims claiming for monetary damages. Under the Supplementary Protocol, the concept of damage functions as a trigger for the operator and the competent authority, prompting them to act, and certain discretion on the part of the administrative organ in determining the precise scope of such damage is warranted. The Supplementary Protocol, at the same time, leaves the channelling of liability open-ended, leaving it to the determination by the domestic law. This characteristic may be considered as particular to a liability regime for diversity damage caused by LMOs, as the Supplementary Protocol covers very different potential damage scenarios, and the nature of such damage is usually long-term, latent and cumulative, making the determination of one particular 'activity' as the cause of damage extremely difficult.

IV ILC's work on international liability as a context

The international environmental liability regime established under the Supplementary Protocol is thus an evolution from the previous conventional liability regimes. Its acceptance by over 160 Parties to the Cartagena Protocol as reflected in its consensus adoption was, of course, a result of political compromise of the Parties within the specific context of the negotiations under the Cartagena Protocol. At the same time, the liability regime in the Supplementary Protocol, it is argued, was one coherent case in the general trend towards re-conceptualisation of liability under international law. Its precedential value, therefore, would emanate from it being firmly grounded on a theoretical underpinning accepted by the international community. After 30 years of work on international liability with the aim to progressively develop or to codify international law, the ILC has come to recognise a distinct need to address the case of damage to the environment *per se* and a new idea of addressing such damage by effective response measures in addition to monetary compensation.[66] This recognition by the ILC came after several turn-arounds in the approaches to the concept of international liability and was based on a conceptual redirection of liability into a regime of 'allocation of loss'. This movement was led since 2002 by an Indian special rapporteur, Pemmaraju S. Rao. Based on his reports, the ILC, with its 34 international law experts from around the world, after thorough examination of recent State practice and theories, adopted in 2006 the Allocation of Loss Principles with its conceptual redirection of liability. The process leading up to the adoption of these principles sets an important context in which the Supplementary Protocol was negotiated from 2004 and finally adopted in 2010.

The main issues relating to the concept of liability discussed in the ILC, and their culmination in the Principles, correspond quite neatly to the core elements of the administrative approach to liability in the Supplementary Protocol as examined above. This correspondence between the two instruments relates to the basic approach to the concept of liability, rather than to the scope, and, consequently, the specific legal structure of their respective instruments. The scope of the two instruments differs. First, the ILC Principles apply to hazardous activities that have 'a high probability of causing significant transboundary harm or a low probability of causing disastrous transboundary harm';[67] whereas the Supplementary Protocol, as discussed above, is neutral as to the hazardous nature of activities involving LMOs. Second, the ILC Principles apply to transboundary harm through the physical consequences of activities themselves, excluding those consequences caused by State policies such as trade;[68] whereas the Supplementary Protocol applies to those LMOs that find their origin in a transboundary movement, including by trade (Articles 3 (1) and (2)). Perhaps, except for an unintentional transboundary movement of LMOs, such as GM pollen crossing the boundary by wind (Article 3 (3) referring to Article 17 of the Cartagena Protocol),

---

66 This section is based on the author's previous work: Akiho Shibata, 'Kiken Katsudo kara shojiru Ekkyo Higai no sai no Sonshitsu Haibun ni kansuru Shogensoku' (Principles on the allocation of loss in the case of transboundary harm arising out of hazardous activities), in Shinya Murase and Koji Tsuruoka eds, *Henkakuki no Kokusaihou Iinkai (International Law Commission at a Crossroads)* (Shinzansha, 2011), pp. 273–296.

67 Paragraph 2 of commentary to Principle 1, *2006 Text and Commentary*, p. 117.

68 Paragraph 12 of commentary to Principle 1, ibid., p. 121.

the bulk of the cases of biodiversity damage addressed by the Supplementary Protocol would not fall under the definition of 'transboundary damage' in the ILC Principles.

1 The 'two-fold purpose'

The legal regime of allocation of loss adopted by ILC consists of two sub-regimes of victim compensation scheme, on one hand, and of environmental liability scheme, on the other. These two schemes are interrelated, but grounded on the different legal bases. This 'two-fold purpose'[69] is reflected in Principle 3 of the ILC Allocation of Loss Principles:

> Principle 3: Purposes
>
> The purposes of the present draft principles are:
>
> (a) to ensure prompt and adequate compensation to victims of transboundary damage; and
> (b) to preserve and protect the environment in the event of transboundary damage, especially with respect to mitigation of damage to the environment and its restoration or reinstatement.

The separation of these two purposes was reintroduced, and finally adopted, only at the last session in 2006, because the ILC wanted to 'emphasize the more recent concern of the international community to recognize protection of the environment *per se* as a value by itself without having to be seen only in the context of damage to persons and property'.[70] This was an important change from its 2004 draft, in which the objective of the principles had been integrated into one sentence emphasising the provision of compensation to the victim of damage, including damage to the environment.[71] The 2004 draft considered that 'damage to environment *per se* is actionable requiring prompt and adequate compensation', which includes not only monetary compensation to the claimant, but also 'the reimbursement of reasonable measures of restoration and response'.[72]

The final 2006 draft does not deny the possibility of States being the victim of environmental damage.[73] In such cases, the monetary compensation for environmental damage would be composed of 'loss or damage by impairment of the environment', 'the costs of reasonable measures of reinstatement of the . . .

---

69 Paragraph 1 of commentary to Principle 3, ibid., p. 140.

70 Paragraph 6 of commentary to Principle 3, ibid., p. 142.

71 2004 Draft Principle 3: Objective: 'The present draft principles aim at ensuring prompt and adequate compensation to natural or legal persons, including States, that are victims of transboundary damage, including damage to the environment'. *Report of International Law Commission 2004*, UN Doc. A/59/10 (2004) [hereinafter *2004 Draft Text and Commentary*], p. 155.

72 Paragraph 14 of commentary to Principle 3, *2004 Draft Text and Commentary*, p. 192.

73 See the definition of 'victim' in paragraph (f) of Principle 2: 'victim means any natural or legal person or State that suffers damage'. *2006 Text and Commentary*, p. 108.

environment, including natural resources' and 'the costs of reasonable response measures'.[74] The monetary compensation for environmental damage will be realised through the scheme of victim compensation, mainly as provided in Principle 4 on prompt and adequate compensation and Principle 6 on international and domestic remedies. It should be noted, however, that in Principle 4, the core provision requiring the State to take 'all necessary measures to ensure that prompt and adequate compensation is available for victims' (paragraph 1) is stipulated in a hortatory language using 'should'. Paragraph 2 also uses the hortatory language, stating, '(t)hese measures should include the imposition of liability on the operator or, where appropriate, other person or entity'.

Clearly, in separating the purpose of preserving and protecting the environment from that of victim compensation, the emphasis of the 2006 Principles was placed on Principle 5, focused on response measures. The link between the two is recognised, as the ILC 'gives a prominent place to the protection and preservation of the environment', which is provided in Principle 3 (b), and to 'the associated obligations to mitigate the damage and to restore or reinstate the same to its original condition to the extent possible',[75] which is provided in Principle 5. Principle 5 (b) provides that upon the occurrence of an incident that results in damage:

> (T)he State of origin, with the appropriate involvement of the operator, shall ensure that appropriate response measures are taken and should, for this purpose, rely upon the best available scientific data and technology.
>
> (Principle 5 (b))

Although the ILC's Allocation of Loss Principles does not provide a definition of response measures, it is stated in its commentary that such measures should include 'clean-up and restoration measures' and the measures to 'contain geographical range of the damage'.[76] It is clear that Principle 5 addresses mainly environmental damage, without denying the possibility that such response measures may also mitigate and restore damage to persons and property.

Thus, the ILC Allocation of Loss Principles came to recognise the different rationale applicable in the scheme of environmental liability from that of victim compensation. The scheme of victim compensation (Principle 3 (a)) mainly relates to traditional damage to persons and property (Principle 2 (a) (i) and (ii)) (except where one can recognise the State as a victim of the environmental damage), and the liability is pursued through prompt and adequate monetary compensation to the victim (Principle 4) supported by a judicial and administrative system of

---

74 See the definition of 'damage' in paragraph (a) of Principle 2: 'damage means significant damage caused to persons, property or the environment; and includes: (i) loss of life or personal injury; (ii) loss of, or damage to, property, including property which forms part of the cultural heritage; (iii) loss or damage by impairment of the environment; (iv) the costs of reasonable measures of reinstatement of the property, or environment, including natural resources; (v) the costs of reasonable response measures'. Ibid., p. 107.

75 Paragraph 6 of commentary to Principle 3, ibid., p. 142.

76 Paragraph 1 of commentary to Principle 5, ibid., p. 167.

international and domestic remedies (Principle 6). On the other hand, the scheme of environmental liability (Principle 3 (b)) relates to damage to the environment *per se* (Principle 2 (a) (iii), (iv) and (v)),[77] and the liability is pursued through effective response measures (Principle 5). This subtle change of emphasis occurred only in the last two years of ILC discussion. The ICJ in its judgment on *Gabcikovo-Nagymaros Project* case recognised the 'limitations inherent in the very mechanism of reparation of this type of damage (to the environment)'.[78] The Court, in its judgment in 1997, emphasised the importance of prevention; the ILC, in addition, emphasised in its 2006 Allocation of Loss Principles the importance of response measures once environmental damage occurred, despite any preventative measures.

2 Allocation of loss

In 2003, Special Rapporteur Rao explained the reasons for providing a legal regime for allocation of loss in lieu of an international liability regime as follows:

> The focus on allocation of loss instead of the development of an international liability regime is well in tune with the emerging thinking on the subject which is focused on facilitating a more equitable and expeditious scheme of compensation to the victims of transboundary harm. Given the difficulties and constraints of traditional tort law or civil liability regimes, the 1996 Working Group of the Commission had already set in motion a more flexible approach, divorced from private law remedies or from strict or absolute liability as a basis for the compensation scheme proposed.[79]

Rao also stated that the term 'allocation of loss' would be clearly distinguishable from the term 'reparation' in the context of State responsibility for international wrongful acts, and would be used to avoid the term 'compensation' so as not to link the topic too closely to the topic of civil liability.[80]

The substantiation of the concept of liability differed significantly among the three special rapporteurs who addressed this topic. The first special rapporteur, Quentin-Baxter of New Zealand, tried to stipulate a procedural scheme based on an equitable balance of interests among the relevant States to avoid, minimise

---

77 According to the ILC commentary, sub-item (iii) on loss or damage by impairment of the environment may include, in addition to pure economic loss, the loss of non-use value of the environment. Paragraphs 11–13, 15, 17–18 of commentary to Principle 2, ibid., pp. 127–132. See also Alan Boyle, 'Chapter 10: Liability for Injurious Consequences of Acts not Prohibited by International Law', in James Crawford, Alain Pellet, and Simon Olleson eds, *The Law of International Responsibility* (Oxford University Press, 2010), p. 103.

78 Case concerning the Gabcikovo-Nagymaros Project (Hungary/Slovakia), Judgment of 25 September 1997, ICJ Reports 1997, p. 78, para. 140.

79 Pemmaraju S. Rao, Special Rapporteur, First report on the legal regime for allocation of loss in case of transboundary harm arising out of hazardous activities, UN Doc. A/CN.4/531 (21 March 2003), p. 17, para. 38.

80 *Yearbook of International Law Commission [Yearbook of ILC] 2003*, Vol. I, p. 102, para. 64.

and make reparations for transboundary environmental damage. From 1985, the second special rapporteur, Barboza of Argentina, instead tried to focus on the strict liability of the territorial State that authorised or permitted a hazardous activity within its territory that caused transboundary damage.[81] However, by the time he submitted his last report in 1996, the liability was shifted from the State of origin to the operator, and, as a consequence, his draft moved away from the scheme of State liability and came closer to that of civil liability.[82] The African proposal on liability regime during the negotiations of the Cartagena Protocol was based on Barboza's concept of liability,[83] which unfortunately had not had the support of the ILC so that even after 10 years of work, not even a single text was sent to the drafting committee for adoption.[84]

On the contrary, the concept of 'allocation of loss' put forward by Rao was based on a flexible approach where the liability would not be channelled invariably to a specific entity under specific circumstances. According to Rao, the State should be able to design an appropriate regime combining international and domestic liability schemes to achieve an equitable allocation of loss among the relevant actors, including operators, insurance companies, industry funds and governments, taking into account the specific circumstances of each incident.[85] Under the Allocation of Loss Principles, 'it is not considered necessary to predetermine the share for the different actors or to precisely identify the role to be assigned to the State', and '(t)he freedom of States to choose one option or the other in accordance with its particular circumstances and conditions is the central theme of the (P)rinciples'.[86]

---

81 See Alan Boyle, 'State Responsibility and International Liability for Injurious Consequences of Acts Not Prohibited by International Law: A Necessary Distinction?', *International and Comparative Law Quarterly*, Vol. 39 (1990), p. 6.

82 Julio Barboza, Special Rapporteur, Twelfth report on international liability for injurious consequences arising out of acts not prohibited by international law, UN Doc. A/CN.4/475 (13 May 1996).

83 Worku Damena, representing the Ethiopian government during the final stages of the negotiations on Cartagena Protocol and the 'author' of the African draft text on liability and redress, confessed that his texts 'were much influenced by the International Law Commission Draft Articles of 1991 on Liability for Injurious Consequences of Acts Not Prohibited by International Law, which basically envisage that a state of origin will be strictly liable for harm to the environment'. Worku Damena, 'Liability and Redress', in Christoph Bail, Robert Falkner and Helen Marquard eds, *The Cartagena Protocol on Biosafety: Reconciling Trade in Biotechnology with Environment and Development?* (Earthscan, 2002), p. 367. See also Kate Cook, 'Liability: "No Liability, No Protocol"', ibid., pp. 371–384.

84 Instead of basing their discussion on Barboza's report, a working group was established in 1996 and produced a separate report (Report of the Working Group, International liability for injurious consequences arising out of acts not prohibited by international law, UN Doc. A/CN.4/L.533, reproduced in *Yearbook of ILC 1996*, Vol. II, Part 2, Annex I, p. 100), which became the basis of an important decision in 1997 to separate the aspects of prevention and liability. *Yearbook of ILC 1997*, Vol. II, Part 2, p. 59.

85 Statement of Rao, Special Rapporteur, at 2805th meeting of ILC, *Yearbook of ILC 2004*, Vol. I, p. 101, para. 46; Report of the Working Group, *ILC Report 2002*, UN Doc. A/57/10 (2002), p. 226, paras 452–455.

86 Paragraph 9 of general commentary and Paragraph 39 of commentary to Principle 4, *2006 Text and Commentary*, p. 112, p. 166.

Thus, the concept of allocation of loss was deliberately chosen to delink its discussion from the previous treaty practice of liability regimes for damage, imposing the obligation to pay monetary compensation on either the operator or the territorial State, and to convey the flexibility as to both the entities to be liable, together with the associated content of liability. The emancipation by the ILC of the concept of liability from the previous treaty practice of civil liability and State liability was an important international law context within which the Parties negotiating the Supplementary Protocol were able to consider, and able to finally accept, a unique scheme of an administrative approach to liability for biodiversity damage.

3 Response measures

In the Commission discussion, some expressed doubts about incorporating the obligations to take response measures within the concept of liability.[87] However, the Commission justified itself by stating that in theory and in practice, the response measures are associated with the costs of damage, and, in particular, with damage to the environment.[88] It is true that in some civil liability treaties, in case an incident that causes damage or creates a grave and imminent threat of causing damage occurs, the costs of preventative measures in response to such an incident to prevent, minimise or mitigate loss or damage, or to effect environmental clean-up, are included in the compensable damage.[89] In addition, under those treaties, the costs of measures of reinstatement that aim to assess, reinstate or restore damaged or destroyed components of the environment are also included in the compensable damage.[90] However, none of these practices makes the taking of preventative or reinstatement measures obligatory under the treaty.[91]

It is in very recent, and still rare cases, such as the 2003 Kiev Protocol on Civil Liability, in which the treaties paraphrased the measures to prevent, minimise or mitigate possible damage, or to arrange for environmental clean-up, as 'response measures'. Under the legal framework of liability, these treaties provided for a distinct obligation of the operator to take such response measures as separate from its obligation to pay monetary compensation.[92] The 2005 Annex VI on Liability

---

87 Statement of Mr. Matheson, at the 2807th meeting of ILC, *Yearbook of ILC 2004*, Vol. I, p. 116, para. 10.

88 Statement of Rodriquez Cedeno, Chairman of the Drafting Committee, at the 2822nd meeting of ILC, *Yearbook of ILC 2004*, Vol. I, p. 201, para. 15.

89 See Article 2 (2) (c) (v), (e), and (h), Basel Liability Protocol, see note 5; Article 1 (6) (b), (7), and (8), Oil Pollution Liability Convention, see note 4.

90 Article 2 (2) (c) (iv) and (d), Basel Liability Protocol, see note 5; Article 2 (6) (a), Oil Pollution Liability Convention, see note 4.

91 Article 6 of the Basel Liability Protocol, see note 5, is discreet in providing for the obligation of a person in operational control of hazardous wastes at the time of an incident to take measures only to mitigate damage, and not to take preventative or reinstatement measures as defined in the Protocol.

92 Article 6, Kiev Protocol on Civil Liability, see note 5.

arising from Environmental Emergencies to the Protocol on Environmental Protection to the Antarctic Treaty (Antarctic Liability Annex)[93] is another example of providing for an obligation of its Parties to require their operators to take prompt and effective 'response action' to environmental emergencies (Article 5). The 'response action' is defined as 'reasonable measures taken after an environmental emergency has occurred to avoid, minimise or contain the impact of that environmental emergency, which to that end may include clean-up' (Article 2 (f)). It is interesting to note that under the 2005 Antarctic Liability Annex, these response actions are distinct from the preventative measures 'that are designed to reduce the risk of environmental emergencies and their potential adverse impact' (Article 3). However, it must be emphasised that neither of these precedents provides for the obligation to take response measures as a legal consequence of causing damage. Under the Kiev Protocol, the obligation to take response measures arises when an industrial accident involving a hazardous activity occurs, and the liability of the operator for damage relates only to the costs of such response measures presumably taken by others. Similarly, under the 2005 Antarctic Liability Annex, the obligation to require its operators to take response action arises when an activity of that operator causes an environmental emergency defined as an 'accidental event that . . . results in, or imminently threatens to result in, any significant and harmful impact on the Antarctic environment' (Article 2 (b)). In fact, nowhere in the Annex does the term 'damage' appear, and the liability of the operator is to 'pay the costs of response action taken by Parties' (Article 6 (1)).[94]

Thus, Principle 5 of the ILC Allocation of Loss Principles, providing for an obligation to ensure that appropriate response measures are taken when an incident that results in damage occurs, is grounded on a few recent treaty practices, but with a subtle expansion on two fronts. First, the concept of 'response measures' under the ILC Principles would include restoration measures,[95] although a demarcation line between those and the 'measures of reinstatement'[96] was not clear-cut. Second, the obligation to take response measures arises when an incident that 'results in damage' occurs. Thus, the ILC has already recognised in 2006 the need

---

93 Annex VI to the Protocol on Environmental Protection to the Antarctic Treaty: Liability Arising From Environmental Emergencies, Attachment to Measure 1 (2005) [Antarctic Liability Annex], adopted at the 28th Antarctic Treaty Consultative Meeting on 17 June 2005 (not in force), *Final Report of the 28th Antarctic Treaty Consultative Meeting (2005)*, p. 63.

94 'Under the Liability Annex, the liability arises not from the fact that the damage was caused by one's activity, but from the fact that the operator, having caused an environmental emergency that may have significant and harmful impact on the Antarctic environment, did not take the required response action to avoid or minimize such impact.' Akiho Shibata, 'How to Design an International Liability Regime for Public Spaces: The Case of the Antarctic Environment', in Teruo Komori and Karel Wellens eds, *Public Interest Rules of International Law: Towards Effective Implementation* (Ashgate, 2009), p. 352.

95 Paragraph 1 of commentary to Principle 5, *2006 Text and Commentary*, p. 167.

96 According to ILC, the 'measures of reinstatement' would include those measures 'to assess, reinstate, or restore damaged or destroyed components of the environment or where this is not possible, to introduce, where appropriate, the equivalent of these components into the environment'. Paragraph 15 of commentary to Principle 2, ibid., pp. 130–131.

to provide, under a flexible concept of allocation of loss, for an obligation to take response measures including restoration measures as a legal consequence of causing an incident that results in damage to the environment. This recognition sets an international law context in which the Supplementary Protocol attempted to provide for an obligation of the operator to take such measures as a direct legal consequence of causing damage to biodiversity through an LMO under its control. The ILC's background work on international liability can be considered as a final stepping stone for the Supplementary Protocol to establish an administrative approach to liability for damage to the environment at the global level.

4 Operator's liability and the role of States

Principle 5 does not place the obligation to take response measures squarely on the operators, defined as 'any person in command or control of the activity at the time the incident causing transboundary damage occurs' (Article 2 (g)). Paragraph (a) obliges the State of origin where the hazardous activity is carried out to 'promptly notify all States affected or likely to be affected of the incident and possible effects of the transboundary damage'. Then, in paragraph (b), as examined above, 'the State of origin, with the appropriate involvement of the operator, shall ensure that appropriate response measures are taken'. Further, in paragraph (d), it is the States affected, or likely to be affected, by the transboundary damage that are obliged 'to take all feasible measures to mitigate and if possible to eliminate the effects of such damage'. According to the commentary, the measures that must be taken by the affected States include necessary response measures.[97]

The original proposal by Special Rapporteur Rao on Principle 5 (b) was premised on the understanding that the operator will take the response measures. However, the 2004 ILC drafting committee restructured it to impose the obligation on the State of origin instead, explaining that 'the role of the operator (should not be put) in any secondary or residuary', and should be 'equal' to that of States.[98] Then, the final 2006 version of the commentary explains that the operator has 'a primary' role in operationalising any such measures as soon as an incident occurs.[99] Although in the final 2006 version the role of the operator in taking the response measures has been strengthened, it is clear from its text and commentaries that the obligation under Principle 5 to take response measures is not exclusively placed on the operator, and that Principle 5 foresees an allocation of such obligations placed also on the State of origin or even the affected States.

When Special Rapporteur Rao proposed to re-conceptualise liability into allocation of loss with its inherent flexibility as to both the entities to be liable, together with the associated content of liability, there was some criticism from the Commission members that his new concept deviated from the principle of

---

97   Paragraph 10 of commentary to Principle 5, ibid., pp. 170–171.
98   Paragraph 6 of commentary to Principle 5, *2004 Draft Text and Commentary*, p. 209.
99   Paragraph 8 of commentary to Principle 5, *2006 Text and Commentary*, p. 169.

polluter-pays.[100] Rao, in response, stated that 'if the Commission focused solely on "polluter pays" principle, it would end up with operator liability and nothing more', but he posited that this was not the intention of the Commission.[101] The ILC considered that the 'polluter-pays principle is an essential component in underpinning the present draft principles',[102] but was very discreet in not recognising its binding status under general international law.[103] With regard to Principle 5 specifically, there was also support for 'the role of the State of origin, which might need to take action if the operator lacked adequate means or simply failed to take the required action'.[104] Thus, 'the real underlying principle is not that "operators" are always liable, but that the party with the most effective control of the risk at the time of the accident or has the ability to provide compensation is made primarily liable'.[105] Reflecting this real underlying principle, the ILC's Principle 4, within the context of prompt and adequate compensation, provides that 'imposition of liability (should be) on the operator or, where appropriate, other person or entity'.

Thus, it was a deliberate choice of the ILC, at least at the level of international law, to allow some flexibility in channelling the liability to relevant actors, with the recognition that a primary role in taking response measures should be placed on the operators. At the same time, the ILC recognised the important role of States, including the affected States, in the process of responding to the incident that results in damage. It is true that the ILC's Allocation of Loss Principles did not expressly endorse an administrative approach to liability. However, its underlying concept directs States to design a liability regime for damage to the environment with an appropriate role of relevant States in the process of taking response measures, while placing a primary role on the operator. This concept, accepted by the ILC in 2006, is extremely receptive to a liability regime in which, while channelling the primary obligation to take response measures to the operators, the administrative organ of the State where the damage has occurred plays an essential role in realising the process of taking such response measures. The ILC's Principle 5 (d) explicitly provided for the obligation of the affected States to take feasible measures to mitigate, and to eliminate, the effects of damage. In the context of damage caused by LMOs subject to transboundary movement, the importing State is expected to play a comparable role to the affected States.

---

100 Statement of Ms Escarameia, at 2805th meeting of ILC, *Yearbook of ILC 2004*, Vol. I, p. 98, para. 21. Topical summary of the discussion in the Sixth Committee of the General Assembly during its fifty-ninth session, UN Doc. A/CN.4/549/Add.1 (7 May 2005), p. 20, para. 84.

101 Statement of Mr. Rao, Special Rapporteur, at 2805th meeting of ILC, *Yearbook of ILC 2004*, Vol. I, p. 101, para. 46.

102 Paragraph 2 of commentary to the Preamble, *2006 Text and Commentary*, p. 115.

103 Paragraphs 11–15 on commentary to Principle 4, ibid., pp. 144–117. See also Pemmaraju S. Rao, Special Rapporteur, Third report on the legal regime for the allocation of loss in case of transboundary harm arising out of hazardous activities, UN Doc. A/CN.4/566 (7 May 2006), p. 19, para. 27.

104 Statement of Mr. Gaja, at 2807th meeting of ILC, *Yearbook of ILC 2004*, Vol. I, pp. 120–121, para. 59.

105 Paragraph 10 of commentary to Principle 4, *2006 Text and Commentary*, pp. 154–155.

The administrative approach to liability as exemplified in the Supplementary Protocol, with its open-ended definition of 'operator', and the essential role played by the importing State to pursue the liability of the operator, can be considered as a faithful model of specific implementation of the ILC's Allocation of Loss Principles. As such, the Supplementary Protocol is firmly grounded on a theory of liability as accepted by the ILC, which was taken note by the United Nations General Assembly.

V Conclusion

This chapter sought to demonstrate that the Nagoya-Kuala Lumpur Supplementary Protocol on Liability and Redress to the Cartagena Protocol on Biosafety, based on an administrative approach to liability, emerged out of an inevitable evolution that takes into account the past experience of civil liability regimes, as well as the long and arduous theoretical examination within the United Nations International Law Commission on the concept of international liability. For sure, the Supplementary Protocol was not a mutant. Neither, however, was it just a transposition of a regional model to the global level. It did have a prelude, a global pedigree that bestows it the legitimacy and the power to pull States towards its acceptance.

The Supplementary Protocol established, for the first time in the history of international law, an international environmental liability regime of global applicability based on an administrative approach to liability. The administrative approach to liability as exemplified in the Supplementary Protocol involves a conceptual evolution from the previous treaty practice on liability. With an explicit mandate provided in Article 27 of the Cartagena Protocol, the negotiating Parties were able to take into account the experience and discussion in other forums, particularly on the basic concept and approach to liability for damage to the environment. In this context, the difficulties encountered by civil liability treaties such as the 1999 Basel Liability Protocol in garnering support in the form of ratifications from States, and the academic warnings against the 'sensibility' of negotiating such treaties, were noted. During the negotiations on the Supplementary Protocol, the initiative was taken by a Co-Chair and the delegation of the EU to introduce into the discussion an administrative approach to liability modelled after their 2004 Environmental Liability Directive.

In addition, the global acceptance of the new approach to liability requires global pedigree. The ILC's work on international liability, with its fundamental conceptual redirection of the issue into a flexible regime of 'allocation of loss' proposed by an Indian special rapporteur in 2002, sets an important context in which the Supplementary Protocol was negotiated, and finally adopted by consensus. The emancipation by the ILC of the concept of liability from the previous treaty practice of civil liability and State liability was a latent background that facilitated creative thought among the negotiators, culminating in them accepting an administrative approach to liability. The Supplementary Protocol needed only a small step beyond the ILC's recognition of providing an obligation to take response measures, including restoration measures, when an incident that results in damage to the environment *per se* occurs. The ILC also recognises an important role of the States, including the affected States, in effectuating the primary role of operators in taking such response measures. This paved the way to accepting an administrative approach to liability in the Supplementary Protocol, which, while placing the liability on the operator and denying liability imposed on States based on their jurisdiction or control over the relevant activities, provides for a central role of the competent authority of the importing Party in the effective functioning of the regime.

The precedential value of the Supplementary Protocol for international environmental liability regimes lies in the fact that it is firmly grounded on a general theory of liability as accepted by the ILC that was taken note by the United Nations General Assembly.

3 Negotiating the Supplementary Protocol

The Co-Chairs' perspective

René Lefeber and Jimena Nieto Carrasco

I Introduction

> Some delegations reiterated longstanding positions, with some calling for no liability provisions and others characterizing 'zero' liability as unacceptable.[1]

On 15 October 2010, the Nagoya-Kuala Lumpur Supplementary Protocol on Liability and Redress to the Cartagena Protocol on Biosafety (Supplementary Protocol) was adopted in Nagoya, Japan.[2] This was the culmination of a process that started with the adoption of the Cartagena Protocol on Biosafety to the Convention on Biological Diversity (Cartagena Protocol) on 29 January 2000 in Montreal, Canada. Pursuant to the Cartagena Protocol, '[t]he Conference of the Parties serving as the meeting of the Parties to this Protocol shall, at its first meeting, adopt a process with respect to the appropriate elaboration of international rules and procedures in the field of liability and redress for damage resulting from transboundary movements of living modified organisms, analysing and taking due account of the ongoing processes in international law on these matters, and shall endeavour to complete this process within four years' (Article 27). This provision was a hard-fought compromise between States that pursued substantive provisions on liability and redress in the Cartagena Protocol and States that did not want to include any such provisions in the Protocol.[3]

The regulation of human-induced genetic mutations and the regulation of liability for damage resulting from such mutations are both contentious issues and, combined, are capable of concocting a politically toxic potion. Doubts were

1 Highlights from the Sixth Session of the Open-Ended *Ad Hoc* Working Group on Biosafety (BSWG-6), Monday, 15 February 1999, *Earth Negotiations Bulletin*, Vol. 9, No. 111, Tuesday, 16 February 1999.

2 The authors would like to thank Mai Fujii, PhD Student at Kobe University, for the reconstruction of the negotiations in a factual paper which was of great assistance in the development of this Chapter.

3 On the negotiations of Article 27 of the Cartagena Protocol, see Kate Cook, 'Liability: "No Liability, No Protocol"', in Christoph Bail, Robert Falkner and Helen Marquard eds, *The Cartagena Protocol on Biosafety: Reconciling Trade in Biotechnology with Environment and Development?* (Earthscan, 2002), pp. 371–384.

expressed as to whether it would be possible to elaborate international rules and procedures in the field of liability and redress for damage resulting from transboundary movements of living modified organisms (LMOs), at least not in the form of a legally binding instrument. Reference was made to the 'graveyard' of civil liability conventions in the context of multilateral environmental agreements. Several such conventions had been adopted in the years preceding the commencement of the work under the Cartagena Protocol, but these instruments were not likely to ever enter into force. In particular, the negotiations on the Basel Protocol on Liability and Compensation to the Basel Convention on the Control of Transboundary Movements of Hazardous Wastes and their Disposal (Basel Liability Protocol) had been long, difficult and cumbersome, and seasoned negotiators were dreading the prospect of another cycle of even longer, more difficult and more cumbersome negotiations. On the one side, some argued that the harmonisation of rules and procedures on civil liability had not been a successful enterprise, in particular pointing out that it had not been possible even in the European Union to harmonise domestic civil liability regimes. On the other side, it was argued that the incorporation of substantive provisions on liability and redress in the Cartagena Protocol had only been foregone on the understanding that a legally binding instrument would eventually be adopted and that such an instrument would contain rules and procedures on civil liability. According to this view, there were ample and successful examples of civil liability conventions, in particular in the field of nuclear damage and oil pollution damage.

The Cartagena Protocol entered into force on 11 September 2003 and the first Conference of the Parties Serving as the Meeting of the Parties (COP-MOP) to the Cartagena Protocol was convened from 23 to 27 February 2004 in Kuala Lumpur, Malaysia. By that time, the preparatory work for the negotiations had already commenced. In the preceding years, the Intergovernmental Committee for the Cartagena Protocol on Biosafety had met three times to prepare for the entry into force of the Cartagena Protocol, including work on liability and redress. Among other recommendations, it had extended an invitation to Parties to convene a workshop on liability and redress.[4] Such a workshop was eventually convened from 2 to 4 December 2002 in Rome, Italy. At this workshop, René Lefeber and Jimena Nieto Carrasco were elected as Co-Chairs. Their election had been arranged by Xueman Wang, the officer in charge of the Secretariat of the Convention on Biological Diversity (CBD). She approached René, with whom she had worked during the Netherlands' Presidency of the Sixth Conference of the Parties of the United Nations Framework Convention on Climate Change. Together, they decided to approach Jimena, with whom René had worked during the final stages of the negotiations of the Basel Liability Protocol and the Cartagena Protocol, to complete the team.

---

4   Paragraph 5 of Recommendation 3/1 (2002), Liability and redress, Report of the Intergovernmental Committee for the Cartagena Protocol on Biosafety on the work of its third meeting, UNEP/CBD/ICCP/10 (28 May 2002). p. 31.

Although both René and Jimena were elected as Co-Chairs for the workshop in Rome, Jimena chose not to sit on the podium in order to enable her to actively participate in the discussions from the floor during the day so that she could better present the perspective of the developing countries that were not growing genetically modified crops at that time. However, she worked with René and the Secretariat through the nights to prepare the report on the workshop. Preparing the report proved to be one of the most difficult tasks in the process as the workshop initiated the discussion from scratch and thus the discussions had to be captured in the form of a narrative that would reflect all of the positions and issues raised. In addition, the Co-Chairs were pressed to develop scenarios on the basis of those discussions as some participants challenged the need for rules and procedures on liability and redress. These participants could not imagine any scenarios in which international rules and procedure might be needed in the field of liability and redress for damage resulting from transboundary movements of LMOs.[5]

The workshop on liability and redress foreshadowed a long and winding process that started in earnest with the adoption of the mandate calling for such process at the first meeting of the Parties to the Cartagena Protocol.[6] Pursuant to the mandate, one expert meeting would be convened to prepare the foundation for the negotiations, which themselves would be conducted in an open-ended working group. Five meetings of the working group were planned prior to the deadline provided in Article 27 of the Cartagena Protocol, which was within four years of the adoption of the mandate. Although the meeting of the Parties was only required to 'endeavour' to meet the deadline, the Protocol encouraged that all efforts be oriented towards completion of the process by 27 February 2008, including the acquisition of such funds that would not be covered by the core administrative budget of the Cartagena Protocol, but were necessary for the organisation of meetings, as well as the participation of developing country representatives.

II Outline

> [D]elegates attentively followed presentations on the scientific, technical and legal issues of liability and redress, with several expressing satisfaction with their content and quality.[7]

At the meeting of the Group of Legal and Technical Experts on Liability and Redress, which took place from 18 to 20 October 2004 in Montreal, Canada, the

---

5   Report of the Workshop on Liability and Redress in the Context of the Cartagena Protocol on Biosafety, UNEP/CBD/BS/COP MOP/1/INF/8 (2003), Annex.

6   Decision BS-I/8 (2004), Establishment of an Open-Ended *Ad Hoc* Working Group of legal and technical experts on liability and redress in the context of the Protocol, UNEP/CBD/BS/COP-MOP/1/15 (2004), p. 102.

7   Highlights of the *Ad Hoc* Group on Liability and Redress: Wednesday, 25 May 2005, *Earth Negotiations Bulletin*, Vol. 9, No. 313, Thursday, 26 May 2005.

Table 3.1 Meetings on liability and redress (2002–2010)

Meetings (relevant outcome)	Place and dates	Meetings (relevant outcome)	Place and dates
Workshop on Liability and Redress	Rome, 2–4 December 2002	*Ad Hoc* Working Group 5	Cartagena, 12–19 March 2008
COP-MOP1 (Decision BS-I/8)	Kuala Lumpur, 23–27 February 2004	Group of Friends of Co-Chairs under *Ad Hoc* WG*	Bonn, 7–10 May 2008
Technical Group of Experts	Montreal, 18–20 October 2004	COP-MOP (Decision BS-IV/12)	Bonn, 12–16 May 2008
Ad Hoc Working Group 1	Montreal, 25–27 May 2005	Group of Friends of Co-Chairs 1	Mexico City, 23–27 February 2009
COP-MOP2 (Decision BS-II/11)	Montreal, 30 May–3 June 2005	Group of Friends of Co-Chairs 2	Putrajaya, 8–12 February 2010
Ad Hoc Working Group 2	Montreal, 20–24 February 2006	Group of Friends of Co-Chairs 3	Kuala Lumpur, 15–19 June 2010
COP-MOP3 (Decision BS-III/12)	Curitiba, 13–17 March 2006	Group of Friends of Co-Chairs 4	Nagoya, 6–11 October 2010
Ad Hoc Working Group 3	Montreal, 19–23 February 2007	COP-MOP5 (Decision BS-V/11)	Nagoya, 11–15 October 2010
Ad Hoc Working Group 4	Montreal, 22–26 October 2007		

* During the fifth meeting of the *Ad Hoc* WG, a group of Friends of Co-Chairs was established under the WG. The *Ad Hoc* WG requested the Co-Chairs to convene a meeting of Friends of Co-Chairs prior to the COP-MOP4.

authors of this chapter were again elected as Co-Chairs. Again, at this meeting, Jimena chose not to sit on the podium in order to be able to actively participate in the discussions. It would be the last opportunity for her to do so as developing countries informally expressed concerns that 'their' Co-Chair should be seen to assume responsibility for the process.

The Co-Chairs started the process by emphasising that rules and procedures on liability and redress might contribute to the prevention of damage in addition to performing compensatory and corrective functions. However, in view of the regulations contained in the Cartagena Protocol, such rules and procedures on liability and redress should facilitate rather than prohibit transboundary movements of LMOs. Appropriate rules and procedures could therefore only be developed after an in-depth exchange of views on the complex legal and technical issues involved.

Through such an in-depth exchange of views, the Co-Chairs sought to deflect political interest in the matter, to create a common knowledge base and to find common ground for the ensuing negotiations. At the same time, the Co-Chairs were aware that many participants would come to the negotiations without in-depth knowledge of either the legal or technical issues. It was therefore important to reserve ample time for technical presentations and discussions, and to avoid rushing into negotiations. The Co-Chairs wished to start from scratch and take it slow.

The first step in this process was to identify issues and options available in order to address such in further discussion. The Co-Chairs invited the experts to raise issues they considered relevant for the development of rules and procedures in the field of liability and redress for damage resulting from transboundary movements of LMOs. They pursued and obtained agreement that all issues and options would be listed in an outline irrespective of whether one or another expert considered the issue relevant, pertinent or legally sound. An example of such an issue was the matter of choice of instrument. The Cartagena Protocol called for a process with respect to 'the appropriate elaboration of international rules and procedures' (Article 27). The view was expressed that the group, through its process, might come to the conclusion that it would not be appropriate to elaborate any rules or procedures (the zero option). This view was challenged as an interpretation of Article 27 that was not in good faith. Under the agreed rules of engagement, however, the zero option would also be an option and had to be included in the outline.[8]

At the same time, it was understood that the agreed rules of engagement would militate against the incorporation of issues and options that were not listed at this initial stage of the process. It was therefore important to the Co-Chairs that administrative approaches based on allocation of the costs of response measures and of restoration measures would be included in the outline. This innovative approach to liability had only recently surfaced at the international level. States had not entrenched themselves in rigid positions with respect to this approach. Hence, this option might be within the zone of possible agreement once properly introduced, discussed and understood. At the time, this administrative approach to liability, or regulatory liability, had been considered in the framework of the European Union and the Antarctic Treaty Consultative Meeting (ATCM). However, the negotiations in the ATCM had not yet been finalised, and although the European Union had adopted a directive on environmental liability based on this approach, it did not have any experience with its application and refrained from introducing it as an option. The Co-Chairs drew the attention of meeting participants to these developments and suggested inclusion of administrative approaches to liability as an option in the outline.[9]

---

8   Report of the Open-Ended *Ad Hoc* Working Group of Legal and Technical Experts on Liability and Redress under the Cartagena Protocol on Biosafety, UNEP/CBD/BS/COP-MOP/2/11 (2005), p. 17 (Option 6: No instrument).

9   Report of the Open-Ended *Ad Hoc* Working Group of Legal and Technical Experts on Liability and Redress under the Cartagena Protocol on Biosafety, UNEP/CBD/BS/COP-MOP/2/11 (2005), p. 12, Section IV.A (d).

The outline prepared by the expert group would be submitted to the first meeting of the Open-Ended *Ad Hoc* Working Group of Legal and Technical Experts on Liability and Redress in the Context under the Cartagena Protocol on Biosafety (*Ad Hoc* WG). At the first meeting, René and Jimena were elected as permanent Co-Chairs and would henceforth both sit on the podium. At the meeting, the agreement of the Parties was procured as to the outline, as revised by the working group, which would constitute the basis for the future work and, hence, the negotiations. In addition, to advance the work forward, Parties and observers were invited to develop and submit further options for the issues outlined and suggestions for the elaboration of the options into rules and procedures on liability and redress. The Co-Chairs were requested to synthesise these submissions.

III Operational text

The result was a highly technical, legal and conceptual discussion. Although one observer noted that this process did little to clarify the issues in any significant way, several others viewed this approach, along with the strong leadership from the Co-Chairs, as very useful, since it resulted in the formulation and collation of operational texts.[10]

What followed the adoption of the outline was an uneventful, but important phase in the process. The *Ad Hoc* WG worked diligently for several years and produced proposals for rules and procedures on liability and redress (operational text proposals) in between and during its meetings up to and including its fourth meeting. The Co-Chairs allowed ample time for regional and other groups to meet during the working group meetings, as these meetings were the only opportunity to coordinate positions for many participants. By that time, the negotiations no longer attracted much political attention.

The time had come for the Co-Chairs to provide their perspective on the potential outcome of the negotiation process. At the third meeting of the working group, at the informal request of several participants, they presented a 'Blueprint' for a decision by the meeting of the Parties to the Cartagena Protocol.[11] This Blueprint contains a matrix of the possible approaches to liability (State responsibility, State liability, civil liability, administrative approach) together with the issues identified in the outline (scope, damage, primary compensation scheme, supplementary compensation scheme, settlement of claims). The Blueprint did not prejudge the discussion on the choice of instrument, but it provided the first indication that the rules and procedures could take the form of a mixture of binding

---

10 Summary of the Second Meeting of the Open-Ended *Ad Hoc* Working Group on Liability and Redress in the Context of Cartagena Protocol on Biosafety, 20–24 February 2006, *Earth Negotiations Bulletin*, Vol. 9, No. 345, Monday, 27 February 2006.

11 Report of the Open-Ended *Ad Hoc* Working Group of Legal and Technical Experts on Liability and Redress in the Context of the Cartagena Protocol on Biosafety on the Work of its Third Meeting, UNEP/CBD/BS/WG-L&R/3/3 (2007), Annex I.

and non-binding elements. At the fourth meeting of the *Ad Hoc* WG, the Co-Chairs convened an informal brainstorming session to discuss the choice of instrument under the Chatham House Rule; accordingly, participants were free to use the information received, but neither the identity nor the affiliation of the speaker(s) or of any other participant was to be revealed. This enabled participants and Co-Chairs to speak freely and permitted the Co-Chairs to invite the working group to reflect on options for a hybrid instrument, that is an instrument with binding and non-binding elements.[12]

During and between working group meetings, Parties and observers were invited to develop and submit proposals for operational text to address the issues in the outline. The effective participation in the negotiations by observers, businesses and civil society alike was facilitated through the granting of an opportunity to submit proposals and the reflection of all proposals, from Parties and observers alike, without attribution in the working document. The Co-Chairs were tasked with synthesising the operational text proposals into a single working document for the next meeting. At the request of some Parties, the working document would not contain any attributions of the operational text proposals. These Parties wished to contribute to the process, but indicated that they did not have a mandate to present proposals and would have to refrain from contributing if contributions were not anonymous. The anonymous presentation of proposals in the working documents prepared by the Co-Chairs had a positive impact on the consideration of proposals. Proposals were reviewed on their merits rather than their origin. This approach also enabled participants not to entrench themselves in their positions. The Co-Chairs, who still had a document with attributions in front of them, observed some smooth changes of positions.

At the second meeting of the working group, industry representatives from CropLife International invited all participants to a reception. CropLife International had organised the reception to announce that the agro-biotechnology industry would not repeat the mistake it had made during the negotiations of the Biosafety Protocol. At that time, industry representatives opposed the development of an international instrument to regulate transboundary movements of LMOs, including in particular any liability and redress provisions. The active participation of the agro-biotechnology industry in the negotiations on liability and redress enabled informal dialogue to explore alternative solutions, including the option of self-regulation. In the field of liability and redress, examples of self-regulation existed with respect to oil pollution damage.[13] The Co-Chairs encouraged the private sector to consider such forms of self-regulation as they hoped that the

---

12   Report of the Open-Ended *Ad Hoc* Working Group of Legal and Technical Experts on Liability and Redress in the Context of the Cartagena Protocol on Biosafety on the Work of its Fourth Meeting, UNEP/CBD/BS/WG-L&R/4/3 (2007), para. 33.

13   The Tanker Owners Voluntary Agreement concerning Liability for Oil Pollution (TOVALOP) and CRISTAL Contract Regarding a Supplement to Tanker Liability of Oil Pollution (CRISTAL) became operational in 1968 and were ended in 1997; and 1974 Offshore Oil Pollution Agreement (OPOL) is operational since 1974.

establishment of an industry-wide fund could help advance the negotiations on a supplementary compensation scheme that would apply in the event that damage is not, or not fully, redressed. Such a scheme could, for example, be applicable in the event that the source of damage cannot be identified, that the liable person can avail him or herself of a defence based on an exonerating or mitigating circumstance, that liability is limited in amount or in time, or that the available financial security is insufficient to cover the damage. If, as LMO developers maintained, the release of biotechnology products on the market following a risk assessment is safe, there would be no reason to be afraid of liability. The Co-Chairs indicated that a confidence-building measure, such as the establishment of an industry-wide fund, might facilitate transboundary movements of LMOs into those countries that were not favourably disposed towards the use of modern biotechnology. If, however, a biotechnology product would cause damage to biological diversity in spite of the assessed risks, it would only be appropriate to be held accountable for the damage. CropLife International accepted the challenge and initiated discussions among its members to explore the design of such a confidence-building measure.

IV Negotiating text

Many [delegates] said they had arrived in Cartagena with clear instructions based on the revised working draft, setting out which cards they may, or may not trade. Those cards had been held tightly throughout the week and many were surprised to have some of those cards taken off the table, by virtue of the framework of the core elements paper. Others commented the paper served as 'shock therapy' and at least facilitated a showing of cards.[14]

By the fourth meeting of the *Ad Hoc* WG, the compilation of operational text proposals covered 78 pages.[15] The time had come to weed out the proposals that did not make sense or were no longer supported by Parties. By the end of the fourth meeting, the working document had been reduced to 51 pages.[16] It was pointed out that there was only one meeting of the working group left and that negotiations had not even started in earnest. The Co-Chairs were running out of time. They knew it, but could not say it.

At the very start of the fifth meeting of the working group in Cartagena, Colombia, which ran from 12 to 19 March 2008, the Parties would have to be

---

14 Working Group Highlights: Monday, 17 March 2008, *Earth Negotiations Bulletin*, Vol. 9, No. 433, Tuesday, 18 March 2008.

15 Synthesis of Proposed Operational Texts on Approaches and Options Identified Pertaining to Liability and Redress in the Context of Article 27 of the Biosafety Protocol, UNEP/CBD/BS/WG-L&R/4/2 (2007).

16 Report of the Open-Ended *Ad Hoc* Working Group of Legal and Technical Experts on Liability and Redress in the Context of the Cartagena Protocol on Biosafety on the Work of its Fourth Meeting, UNEP/CBD/BS/WG-L&R/4/3 (2007), Annex II.

induced to commence the negotiations in earnest. The Co-Chairs had carefully planned the sequence of the meeting, starting on a Wednesday and running to the next Wednesday. At this meeting, they would introduce a 'Core Elements Paper' that they had developed between sessions. The introduction of the Core Elements Paper would be a matter of timing. At the start of the meeting, the Co-Chairs allowed negotiations to take place in two contact groups, which met in parallel. It appeared, as expected, that not much progress could be made in the contact groups. The Co-Chairs made use of this time to invite Parties and observers to 'confessionals'. These one-on-one meetings between the Co-Chairs and delegations sounded out red lines to assess whether the Core Elements Paper represented a zone of possible agreement. This legitimised the introduction of the Core Elements Paper as adjusted on the basis of the negotiations and confessionals. It was introduced on Saturday to allow delegations time to reflect on it and contact their capitals. The Co-Chairs indicated that delegations could accept the Core Elements Paper (in which case the negotiations would still be on track), reject it (in which case the negotiations would collapse), or negotiate its contents further (in which case there would still be a long way to go).

The Core Elements Paper struck a balance between the different positions that had been advanced in the working group.[17] It had become clear to the Co-Chairs over the years and from the confessionals that a legally binding instrument providing for civil liability was not within the zone of possible agreement. Hence, the only prospect for a legally binding instrument would be one providing for an administrative approach to liability. The proposed approach envisaged that a person involved in the chain of an LMO (from development through export and import to use) would be required to respond to damage caused by that LMO (primary compensation scheme). Such an approach to liability is viable and appropriate for damage to public goods, such as biological diversity, but not for traditional damage, such as personal injury, property damage and economic loss. A civil liability regime is required to provide redress for these types of damage. To address traditional damage, the Core Elements Paper envisaged the establishment of guidance for Parties to develop their respective domestic law in this area.

It was also not within the zone of possible agreement to require the establishment and maintenance of financial security for unlimited liability, as such a requirement would erect a trade barrier and insurance coverage would not be available on the insurance market. This meant that there would be a risk that damage would lie where it had fallen, unless such risk could be minimised through the creation of multiple layers of liability. Since several Parties had rejected the establishment of a fund financed by the private sector, Parties would have to finance a supplementary compensation scheme that would apply in the event damage was not, or not fully, redressed by the primary compensation scheme. For this reason, the Core Elements Paper envisaged a supplementary compensation scheme that would have to be financed by the Parties to the Cartagena Protocol and would only be triggered in the event of damage not covered by the primary compensation scheme.

17   For the Core Elements Paper, see Appendix 4 of this book.

In the run up to the fifth meeting of the *Ad Hoc* WG, the discussions among the members of CropLife International had come to fruition. It was important to the Co-Chairs that CropLife International announce the private sector initiative before the introduction of the Core Elements Paper. The Co-Chairs hoped that the private sector initiative might make the Core Elements Paper more palatable; in particular, they hoped that Parties would agree to finance a supplementary compensation scheme if damage was not, or not fully, covered by the primary compensation scheme and/or the private sector initiative. CropLife International announced the private sector initiative on Friday afternoon. Although the private sector initiative did not provide for a supplementary compensation scheme, it did overcome a serious disadvantage of the administrative approach to liability. The exercise of jurisdiction necessary to implement the administrative approach can only be based on the principle of territoriality. Hence, it would only enable the channelling of liability to a person within the territorial jurisdiction of the State of import, and not to a foreign developer or an exporter of an LMO. The private sector initiative overcomes this by channelling liability to the developer irrespective of whether the developer has its primary or a subsidiary presence in the State of import. Pursuant to the initiative, each participating developer accepts liability for its products in a contractual mechanism that would be concluded between developers of agro-biotechnology products. A State would be a third-party beneficiary in the event of damage to biological diversity caused by such a product to an area within the limits of its national jurisdiction.

On Monday, several Parties indicated that they could accept the Core Elements Paper as the basis for the removal of operational text proposals. Other Parties neither accepted nor rejected the Core Elements Paper in full, but wished to negotiate its contents before using it as a basis to remove operational text proposals. It was, however, not realistic to expect progress on substance if the process would not be adjusted to the new phase in the work of the working group. It would no longer be practicable to allow all Parties and observers to participate on an equal footing in the negotiations if progress was to be made. Pressed for time and pressured by the need to make progress, the *Ad Hoc* WG decided to establish a Group of Friends of the Co-Chairs (GFCC) that would represent the different negotiating positions. The agreed rules of engagement allowed for representatives of one group to rotate at the negotiation table to participate in the discussion of a particular issue, provided that at any time no more than the maximum number of representatives of that group would participate. This restricted setting, in which the final text was eventually agreed upon, reflects one of the challenges of contemporary international environmental lawmaking, which has been described by Akiho Shibata as 'how to balance the legitimacy claim of global participation and the effectiveness claim of actually creating necessary and effective norms in timely manner'.[18]

18 Akiho Shibata, 'International Environmental Lawmaking in the First decade of the Twenty-First Century: The Form and Process', *Japanese Yearbook of International Law*, Vol. 54, Year 2011 (2012), p. 34.

Up to the fifth meeting of the *Ad Hoc* WG, the G77 and China met to coordinate the positions of developing countries. Although the members of the G77 and China held fundamentally different views on genetic modification, which had become apparent during the negotiations of the Cartagena Protocol, liability and redress involved a financial component that might enable the group to identify and pursue common objectives along a North-South divide. However, the meeting of the G77 and China at which the Core Elements Paper was discussed would prove to be their last in this process. The G77 and China could not agree on a common position as its members held fundamentally different views on many elements of the Core Elements Paper. As a result, the Core Elements Paper drove the group definitely apart. This had a profound impact on the negotiation process. The predictable bipolar divide that had hitherto facilitated environmental negotiations at the global level turned into a cluttered multipolar pool from which different coalitions emerged at different stages of the process adding a new dimension to an already complicated negotiation process.

The negotiations on the Core Elements Paper commenced on Tuesday morning and would continue until the early hours of the next morning. Representatives from various observers also stayed up all night, 'guarding' the entrance of the room and adding to the sense of urgency among the negotiators in the room.[19] By the next morning, the Core Elements Paper had served its purpose. Agreement on an element was immediately implemented in the working document by the removal of operational text proposals that were not in accordance with such an element. This resulted in the further reduction of the working document to 27 pages.[20] At last, the working group had produced a basis for the negotiations, but the negotiations on the remaining operational text proposals had yet to start and the deadline for the completion of the negotiations was approaching. In fact, the deadline of 27 February 2008 had already lapsed by the time of the fifth meeting of the *Ad Hoc* WG, which was convened from 12 to 19 March 2008. Since the next meeting of the COP-MOP to the Cartagena Protocol had been scheduled over 12 to 16 May 2008, there was some extra time. However, at the fifth meeting of the working group, whether the outcome of the negotiations would consist of a legally binding instrument could not be resolved, nor could the issue of whether this instrument would contain international rules and procedures on civil liability for traditional damage. In other words, some fundamental decisions on the legal nature and scope of the rules and procedures had yet to be taken.

At the fifth meeting of the working group, a group of Like-Minded Friends of civil liability was established. This was a sizeable group involving eventually

---

19   A civil society perspective can be found in Third World Network, Liability and Redress for Damage Resulting from GMOs: The Negotiations under the Cartagena Protocol on Biosafety (2012).

20   Report of the Open-Ended *Ad Hoc* Working Group of Legal and Technical Experts on Liability and Redress in the Context of the Cartagena Protocol on Biosafety on the Work of Its Fifth Meeting, UNEP/CBD/BS/WG-L&R/5/3 (2008), Annex II.

82 Parties.[21] The group consisted of developing country Parties as well as some developed country Parties, but several developing country Parties from Asia and Latin America were not part of it. This group insisted on addressing civil liability in a legally binding instrument. Although the group recognised that a comprehensive civil liability regime was not likely to emerge from the negotiations, it indicated that nothing would emerge from the negotiations if a legally binding instrument providing for the administrative approach to liability would not include one provision on civil liability. However, at that time, the adoption of a legally binding instrument had not yet been agreed either.

At the fourth COP-MOP (COP-MOP4) to the Cartagena Protocol held in Bonn, Germany, from 12 to 16 May 2008, a contact group was established with a composition that was almost identical to the Group of the Friends of the Co-Chairs established at the fifth meeting of the *Ad Hoc* WG. In this contact group, the questions that Parties had dodged for so long finally had to be answered. For this purpose, the Co-Chairs formulated two interlocking questions that were to be answered sequentially: (a) 'Is there an objection to work towards a legally binding instrument on an administrative approach?'; and (b) 'Is there an objection to work towards including in such a legally binding instrument one article on civil liability?' A negative response to either of these two questions would result in the breakdown of the negotiations. Yet, two Parties provided a negative response to the first question, namely Paraguay and Peru. Since many Parties indicated, in response to a third question posed by the Co-Chairs, that they would not agree to work exclusively towards a non-legally binding instrument, the Co-Chairs suspended the meeting of the contact group and invited Paraguay and Peru to bilateral meetings with the Co-Chairs to assess whether their concerns could be accommodated. It appeared that these countries had been led to believe that an affirmative answer to the first question meant that they would be bound by the instrument without the need for them to express their consent to be bound in accordance with the law of treaties. After it had been clarified that the instrument would include provisions on the expression of consent to be bound, the contact group was resumed, the same question was presented, and there were no more negative responses.

The Co-Chairs proceeded to the second question, which resulted in one negative response, namely from Japan. Japan indicated that there would not be much point in meeting with the Co-Chairs; it wished to directly engage with the Like-Minded Friends of civil liability in a bilateral meeting facilitated by the Co-Chairs. Japan indicated at this meeting that it was willing to work towards a legally binding instrument on an administrative approach with an article on civil liability, provided that such an article left it at the discretion of Parties to develop a domestic civil liability regime. Although this could not be agreed upon, it was agreed that such

---

21 Gurdial Singh Nijar, Sarah Lawson-Stopps and Gan Pei Fern, *Liability and Redress under the Cartagena Protocol on Biosafety, A Record of Negotiations for Developing International Rules*, Vol. I (Centre of Excellence for Biodiversity Law, 2008), Annex I, p. 399.

a discretionary approach would be reflected in the negotiation text alongside a mandatory approach proposed by the Like-Minded Friends of civil liability. When this agreement was introduced in the contact group, two delegations asked for a timeout to consult their capitals, and these Parties, apparently, should not have remained silent when the second question was posed. At this late juncture, if these Parties would not go along with the consensus, the negotiations would collapse and the blame would fall on them. Under this pressure, the delegations concerned obtained consent from their capitals. The negotiations could move forward, but time had run out to complete them in Bonn. Since the question of the choice of instrument had been resolved, Parties agreed to continue the negotiations with the aim of completing them at the next meeting of the COP-MOP in 2010 in Nagoya, Japan. For this purpose, the Group of the Friends of the Co-Chairs Concerning Liability and Redress in the Context of the Cartagena Protocol on Biosafety (GFCC) was officially established.[22] Up to this point, the Co-Chairs had been scrambling for money to convene meetings, but now that the process was finally heading towards a successful outcome, the Parties were scrambling for the honour of hosting a meeting!

Table 3.2 Composition of the Group of Friends of Co-Chairs (GFCC)*

African Group Parties: Six (6)	Rotation (often represented by Burkina Faso, Cameroon, Egypt, Ethiopia, Liberia, Namibia, South Africa)
Asian and Pacific Group Parties: Six (6)	Bangladesh (later Iran), China, India, Malaysia, Palau (later Republic of Korea), the Philippines
European Union: Two (2)	Represented by Spain (EU Presidency) and the European Commission
Central and Eastern European Parties: Two (2)	Rotation (often represented by Czech Republic, Slovenia, Republic of Moldova)
Group of Latin American and Caribbean Parties: Six (6)	Rotation (often represented by Bolivia, Brazil, Colombia, Ecuador, Mexico, Panama, Paraguay, Peru)
Other Interested Parties: Four (4)	Japan, New Zealand, Norway, Switzerland
Co-Chairs: Two (2)	René Lefeber (Netherlands), Jimena Nieto Carrasco (Colombia)

* This is the official GFCC established by Decision BS-IV/12 (2008) at COP-MOP4. At the fifth meeting of the *Ad Hoc* WG in Cartagena in March 2008, an informal group of Friends of Co-Chairs was established under the WG, and this group met again prior to the COP-MOP4 in Bonn. The composition of this informal group was slightly different from the official GFCC established by Decision BS-IV/12. For the composition of the informal group under the *Ad Hoc* WG, see UNEP/CBD/BS/WG-L&R/5/3 (25 March 2008), paragraph 88 (c).

22 Decision BS-IV/12 (2008), Liability and redress under the Cartagena Protocol on Biosafety, para. 1, UNEP/CBD/BS/COP-MOP/4/18 (2008), p. 84.

V Outcome

> [O]ne delegate said the last few days had resembled a poker game, with parties gambling on other players declaring their hands before them. . . . [M]any are wondering who holds the cards, and whether any single party is willing to go for broke.[23]

Although it had been agreed in Bonn to include a provision on civil liability in a legally binding instrument providing for an administrative approach to liability, the contents of that provision had yet to be agreed. The European Union had agreed to such a provision in Bonn on its understanding that it could be formulated in a non-binding manner. The Like-Minded Friends of civil liability were, however, not going to be satisfied with such a Pyrrhic victory. The ensuing confrontation between the Like-Minded Friends and the European Union at the second meeting of the GFCC in Putrajaya, Malaysia, held from 8 to 12 February 2010, was gruesome and brought the negotiations to the brink of collapse. The Co-Chairs had to resort to convening long meetings in closed sessions to overcome the crisis. The resulting provision was formulated in a binding manner, yet had a procedural nature (Article 12 (2) of the Supplementary Protocol). Accordingly, Parties must provide for adequate rules and procedures in their domestic law on civil liability for specified types of traditional damage associated with damage to biological diversity. The content of the domestic law was thus completely left at the discretion of the Parties, provided that the resulting rules and procedures were 'adequate'. The need to assess the effectiveness of this provision was explicitly mentioned in the provision on the assessment and review of the Supplementary Protocol (Article 13). Resigning to this outcome, the Like-Minded Friends forewent the development of guidance for rules and procedures in domestic law on civil liability and, hence, what would be 'adequate'.

At the third meeting of GFCC from 15 to 19 June 2010 in Kuala Lumpur, Malaysia, the major controversy concerned the application of the Supplementary Protocol to imminent threats of damage. Several developing country Parties opposed such an application. These Parties were concerned that any discretion to decide whether there is a threat and whether that threat is imminent might be abused. Considerable economic losses might be incurred following the unwarranted closure of borders for transboundary movements of LMOs, notably perishable agricultural crops. In particular, the resulting delays might impact on land-locked States as such crops are predominantly shipped in bulk by rail, road or inland navigation vessels. In the end, it was agreed to limit the number of references to 'sufficient likelihood of damage' in the text of the Supplementary Protocol to only one operative provision (Article 5 (3)) and one recital in the preamble (fourth recital). Furthermore, a Party applying response measures on the basis of a

---

23   COP/MOP 4 Highlights: Thursday, 15 May 2008, *Earth Negotiations Bulletin*, Vol. 9, No. 440, Friday, 16 May 2008.

sufficient likelihood of damage will have to demonstrate that such application is science-based.

The end game of the negotiations in October 2010 in Nagoya, Japan, involved two South-South confrontations. These confrontations related to the establishment of financial security and the application of the Supplementary Protocol to products of LMO. As for the establishment of financial security, the discussion was no longer about the introduction of an obligation to require financial security in the Supplementary Protocol, but the attribution of a right of Parties to require financial security at the point of import of an LMO. It was argued that the introduction of such a requirement by a Party in domestic law might conflict with the obligations of that Party under international trade law. Such a conflict might arise if the import of an LMO did not involve a risk that could justify such a trade-related environmental measure. However, if such a measure can be justified in particular circumstances, the absence of a provision related to financial security in the Supplementary Protocol might be interpreted as an agreement not to attribute a right of Parties to require financial security. The Parties concerned took the matter into their own hands and resolved it in a bilateral meeting without any assistance of the Co-Chairs, and presented their solution to the Group of the Friends of the Co-Chairs. Accordingly, Parties would 'retain' the right to provide, in their domestic law, for financial security (Article 10 of the Supplementary Protocol). This provision could neither be interpreted as the attribution of a new right to a Party nor as removing existing rights from a Party under international law.

As for the final outstanding issue, the application of the Supplementary Protocol to products of LMOs, the civilised disagreement on the matter turned vicious when some participants started to doubt and question whether mutual respect was expressed. Several participants were neither on speaking terms in the meeting any longer nor in the margins of the meeting. The Co-Chairs invited these participants to a meeting to clear the air in order to move, gradually, towards resolving the substantive matter. The Cartagena Protocol applies to transboundary movements of LMOs, but not to transboundary movements of products of LMOs. However, the annex to the Cartagena Protocol on risk assessment refers to 'risks associated with living modified organisms or products thereof'.[24] The controversy turned on the question of whether damage caused by products of LMOs was 'damage resulting from transboundary movements of living modified organisms' (Article 27 of the Cartagena Protocol). The Co-Chairs were called on to provide an interpretation of the text of the Supplementary Protocol if the references to products of LMOs were removed. They advised that Parties would not be prevented from applying the Supplementary Protocol to damage caused by products of LMOs, provided that a causal link is established between the damage and the LMO in question. This interpretation enabled the removal of the references to products of LMOs from the text of the Supplementary Protocol on the

---

24   For the full text, see Annex III, para.5, the Cartagena Protocol.

understanding that such interpretation would be reflected in the report of the meeting of the Parties.[25] Although not all Parties wished to subscribe to the Co-Chairs' interpretation, none of them wished to challenge it either. Eventually, it was agreed to disagree on the matter and thus leave it at the discretion of Parties to apply the Supplementary Protocol to damage caused by products of LMOs.

Following the resolution of these two outstanding issues, the meeting of the Parties to the Cartagena Protocol adopted, on 15 October 2010, the decision on liability and redress that includes the Supplementary Protocol. Although it is common practice to name a treaty after the place where it is adopted, as a tribute to the host State, exceptions have been made to this practice. For example, the Cartagena Protocol on Biosafety, which was adopted in Montreal, was named after Cartagena to honour the host of the penultimate meeting and to recognise the role played by the Minister of the Environment of Colombia, Juan Mayr Maldonado. The negotiations could not be completed at that meeting, but it had been a critical step towards the adoption of the Cartagena Protocol. An exception was acceptable in this case, because Montreal is the seat of the Secretariat of the CBD and the default meeting venue. Since the Supplementary Protocol would be adopted in Nagoya, which had offered to host the fifth meeting of the COP-MOP to the Cartagena Protocol, the Co-Chairs wished to pay tribute to the host city Nagoya by giving the Supplementary Protocol its name. However, the Co-Chairs also wished to acknowledge the role of Malaysia in the process. Malaysia had hosted the meeting where the mandate of the process was adopted (in 2004), as well as two meetings of the GFCC in 2010. The result is unusual, yet not unprecedented.

Following its announcement at the fifth meeting of the *Ad Hoc* WG in March 2008, the private sector initiative had met with fierce criticism from civil society, some Parties as well as other sectors of industry (in particular the grain traders, small and medium enterprises), and the public research sector. The Co-Chairs had not anticipated the extent and intensity of this criticism. The proposed contractual mechanism would not be more than a complementary instrument to the international rules and procedures on liability and redress for damage resulting from transboundary movements of LMOs. However, it appeared from the criticism that the complex contractual mechanism was not initially fully understood. In particular, concerns were expressed that it might become an alternative to those rules and procedures. This criticism eventually became an incentive for CropLife International to engage civil society, Parties and other sectors of industry in the further development of the initiative. CropLife International organised regional dialogues for which invitations were extended to Parties, members of civil society and other sectors of industry. The dialogues provided a platform to raise questions and provide advice to CropLife International. The Co-Chairs were invited to

25 Report of the Fifth Meeting of the Conference of the Parties to the Convention on Biological Diversity Serving as the Meeting of the Parties to the Cartagena Protocol on Biosafety, UNEP/CBD/BS/COP-MOP/5/17 (2010), para. 133, reproduced in Appendix 3 of this book.

facilitate the dialogues.[26] The dialogues resulted in numerous amendments of the proposed contractual mechanism. These amendments would not accommodate all criticism, as there were red lines for industry that could not be crossed, including the provisions related to exemptions, financial limits and time limits. The contractual mechanism for response in the event of damage to biological diversity caused by the release of a living modified organism, called the Compact, became operational in 2010 before the Supplementary Protocol was adopted.[27] The decision on liability and redress, adopted by the COP-MOP5 of the Cartagena Protocol, refers to it in the preamble. It notes, 'initiatives by the private sector concerning recourse in the event of damage to biological diversity caused by living modified organisms'.[28]

VI Toolbox

> One smiling delegate attributed the general lack and lag of response to jetlag, sleep deprivation and/or celebratory *sake*. Was finishing Liability a liability?[29]

The adoption of the Supplementary Protocol was the culmination of a multi-year international negotiation process that involved many stakeholders. Multiple factors contributed to the successful outcome of the process. At different stages of the process, different factors were at work and all factors were interdependent. The following factors were decisive:

(a) *Election of leaders of the process.* When a chair informs participants of a meeting that he or she is in their hands, the participants should beware an imminent change in the way the meeting is conducted. The chair is responsible for conducting the meeting and the orderly conduct of the meeting is a pre-requisite for progress on substance. A meeting benefits from electing a seasoned negotiator as a chair, but progress on substance will be more expeditious if the chair knows the subject matter. To share the responsibility and to represent different interest groups in the negotiations, there is merit in electing co-chairs, preferably one from a developed and one from a developing country, even though two chairs cannot represent all interests. Although it could be agreed

---

26   Dialogues were held in Asia (Singapore in January 2009 and the Philippines in January 2010), America (Costa Rica in June 2009), Europe (Belgium in November 2009), and Africa (Kenya in August 2010).

27   For the text of the Compact, as amended on 18 September 2012, see www.biodiversitycompact. org (accessed 1 August 2013).

28   Preamble, Decision BS-V/11 (2010): International rules and procedures in the field of liability and redress for damage resulting from transboundary movements of living modified organisms, UNEP/CBD/BS/COP-MOP/5/17 (2010), p. 62. See also Appendix 2 of this book.

29   'COP/MOP 5 Highlights, Monday, 11 October 2010', *Earth Negotiations Bulletin*, Vol. 9 No. 529, Tuesday, 12 October 2010.

to elect (new) co-chairs at every meeting, continuity, in particular between meetings, militates in favour of the election of co-chairs on a permanent basis. Yet, more often than not, you will have spent your co-chairs by the end of the process as a result of the unpopular decisions they have to take to move the process forward.

(b) *Deflection of (too much) political interest in the process.* The negotiations on liability and redress in the context of the Biosafety Protocol were susceptible to attracting political attention. A high political profile of negotiations is not likely to contribute to the creation of an atmosphere that is conducive to the discussion of technical and legal aspects, let alone to the development and evolution of instructions that provide sufficient flexibility for participants to explore alternative solutions. Given the level of political interest at the time of the adoption of the Cartagena Protocol, it was imperative to deflect political interest in the process. At the end of the process, the Co-Chairs were wondering whether they had been too successful, as there did not seem to be much political interest in the outcome of the negotiations.

(c) *Creation of a common knowledge base.* In the initial stages of negotiations, there should be ample opportunity to present and exchange information. This will not only strengthen the knowledge of participants, but also contribute to the mutual understanding of different perspectives and the creation of internal jargon of the microcosmos that are individual negotiation communities. Provided that Parties continue to be represented by the same people, at least a critical mass of them, unnecessary confusion and irritation in subsequent stages of the negotiations can be avoided.

(d) *Allowing for effective participation of observers.* International agreements are adopted by States. Yet, it may well be the observers, including non-State actors, who will have to work with the outcomes. They usually have thorough knowledge of technical aspects and often a realistic perspective on the implementation of the outcomes. Negotiations will therefore benefit from the effective participation of observers, and this may also prevent agitated participants from lamenting that diplomats do not know what they are talking about. All participants need to understand the evolution of the negotiations and the negotiating text; the best way to achieve this is to allow them to observe the negotiations and, where possible, to participate.

(e) *Managing time.* A deadline for the completion of negotiations provides focus, but it makes time a scarce commodity. Negotiators on tight schedules from all over the world convene to meet for a limited number of days – the era of international conferences lasting for months is long gone. Meetings are expensive and it is important to make the most of them; as a result, international labour standards on working time are violated and healthy eating and sleeping habits ignored. Yet, the process must allow for presenting and exchanging information, regional coordination, effective participation of observers, explaining and testing positions, and finding solutions. In this pressure cooker, it is the responsibility of the chair to manage time, process and people. It is up to the chair to transmit a sense of direction and urgency to negotiators, without which chaos can erupt at any time. However, lack of patience will only move the negotiations backward.

(f)   *Investing in social capital.* Throughout the negotiation process, it is important to accumulate social capital, that is to establish and maintain networks within the negotiating community, build trust between participants (it is a lot about people), and develop and enforce norms governing the negotiations (rules of engagement). Besides the formal rules of procedure, numerous additional rules of engagement, appropriate for each stage of the process, must be deployed to move the process forward. Such informal rules, more often than not proposed by the chair, are agreed to by all, but have to be enforced by the chair. The respect for such rules depends on the trust in the chair.

(g)   *Building consensus.* Pursuant to its rules of procedure, the Meeting of the Parties to the Cartagena Protocol was required to adopt most of its decisions by consensus. The process of achieving consensus takes time, as it involves the demonstration that certain proposals will eventually meet with a formal objection. It must first be understood what the reasons are for such a position and then such position will need to be tested, in particular when it becomes clear that such a position is not or is no longer supported by other Parties. There is often more than one road that leads to Rome (or, in this case, from Rome). Taking time to explore alternative routes may lead to solutions that accommodate national interests or, at least, not impair such interests. Furthermore, when one Party is showing flexibility, other Parties will be more inclined and more pressured to show some flexibility as well. Slowly but surely, Parties will assume ownership of the evolving negotiated text. Such ownership is even more important than achieving consensus, as only true ownership will enhance the probability that the instrument will enter into force and attract broad participation. As of January 2014, 20 States and the European Union have expressed their consent to be bound to the Supplementary Protocol. Although there are still 20 States to go, there is, in the minds of the Co-Chairs, no doubt that the Supplementary Protocol will enter into force.

Part II

The significance and critiques

4 The legal significance of the Supplementary Protocol

The result of a paradigm evolution

René Lefeber[1]

I Introduction

Since its identification in the Hong Kong Special Administrative Region in 1997, the Avian Influenza Virus A/H5N1 has spread to other parts of the world, infecting domesticated and wild birds. The airborne virus is transmissible between birds and occasionally from birds to people, but it has not yet been found to transmit between people. Among infected humans, the respiratory illness caused by the virus proved to have a high fatality rate (approximately 60 per cent). The American National Institute of Health directed pathogenic research to monitor natural mutations and prepare emergency measures in case of an outbreak. In early 2012, it was revealed that the genetic modifications of the virus had produced a variety that transmits between mammals without the loss of its pathogenic characteristics. The virus may – or may not – evolve naturally into a genetically mutated variety with such features. The news caused widespread concern. The publication of the research details was considered a security risk as such details might be used to develop a biological weapon. At the same time, the presence of the genetically modified virus was a safety risk, as its release into the environment would pose a public health threat. The research was criticised and its potential benefits challenged, casting doubts on the proper balancing of the benefits and risks involved. Irrespective of the propriety of having the research conducted, this example demonstrates that the development of living modified organisms (LMOs) may be hazardous.

The technology used to modify the genetic properties of living organisms was developed in the early 1970s and commercialised in the early 1980s. Ever since, the benefits and risks of this new technology have been the subject of debate. Notwithstanding the ongoing debate, this technology has spread, and genetically modified organisms have been developed and released into the environment of many countries, notably through genetically modified crops such as soybeans, canola and corn. Such releases only took place following the identification and

1 The views expressed in this paper are the author's and do not necessarily reflect those of the Minister of Foreign Affairs or the Government of the Kingdom of the Netherlands. The author thanks Amy Hindman for her comments on this paper.

assessment of any risks to the environment and human health. Risk assessments enable authorities to balance socioeconomic benefits and the risks of adverse effects to the environment and human health of an intentional release. Only when risks are considered to be manageable and acceptable are releases likely to be permitted. This example demonstrates that genetically modified crops do not belong to the same risk category as genetically modified viruses.

Since adverse effects may occur in spite of risk management measures or as a result of the failure to identify the risk of adverse effects, the allocation of the costs of such effects should be anticipated and regulated. This became a contentious issue during the negotiations in the late 1990s on an international agreement that would regulate and facilitate transboundary movement of LMOs in a safe manner. It was argued by many developing countries that transboundary movements should only be permitted if the allocation of the costs of any adverse effects was regulated. Proposals were introduced that would address such adverse effects through the introduction of civil liability provisions.[2] According to other negotiating States, in particular developed countries, the issue was too complex and controversial to be resolved in the time available for the negotiations. The controversy became a major obstacle in the negotiation process, as was effectively communicated through the slogan 'No Liability, No Protocol'. Eventually, the Cartagena Protocol on Biosafety (Cartagena Protocol) was adopted on 29 January 2000 without substantive liability provisions as a result of a procedural solution to the controversy. It provides for a further process to address liability and redress for damage resulting from transboundary movements of LMOs (Article 27 of the Cartagena Protocol). These negotiations commenced on 25 May 2005 after several technical expert meetings and an agreement on the organisation of the process.[3] A long, winding and complex negotiation process ensued, a process that has, for now, ended with the adoption of the Nagoya-Kuala Lumpur Supplementary Protocol on Liability and Redress to the Cartagena Protocol on Biosafety (Supplementary Protocol) on 15 October 2010.

The adoption of the Supplementary Protocol merits an assessment of whether this liability instrument reflects multilateral treaty practice in addressing liability for damage to the environment or contains elements that contribute to the progressive development of international law in this field. To that end, this chapter will first revisit the responsibilities that flow from the principle that the polluter must pay for the damage caused (Section II). It will subsequently address the responsibility of States for internationally wrongful acts (Section III), the responsibility of States for the injurious consequences of activities under their jurisdiction or

---

2   Text proposals are contained in Revised Consolidated Text of the Draft Articles, UNEP/CBD/BSWG/5/Inf.1 (23 February 1998). On the negotiations related to liability, see Kate Cook, 'Liability: "No Liability, No Protocol"', in Christoph Bail, Robert Falkner and Helen Marquard eds, *The Cartagena Protocol on Biosafety: Reconciling Trade in Biotechnology with Environment and Development?* (Earthscan, 2002), pp. 371–384.

3   On the negotiations, see further Chapter 3 of this book, by Jimena Nieto Carrasco and myself.

control (Section IV) and the responsibility of the private sector for the injurious consequences of their activities (Section V).

II The polluter-pays principle

The development of LMOs through biotechnology, as well as their use, will normally be a commercial activity. Such use may be contained in laboratories or controlled in field trials, or involve the release of the organisms into the environment for application in agricultural or industrial production processes or products. Governments may, however, be involved in the development and use of LMOs. Such involvement may not only originate in commercial interests (State enterprises), but also in their sovereign interests, including military,[4] food security and public health interests.

The risks associated with LMOs have prompted governments to regulate their development and use for governmental and non-governmental purposes. In view of the expected socioeconomic benefits of the technology, some governments allow and encourage the application of the technology, in particular through public research institutes. Other governments, however, have assessed that the risks for the environment and human health, in particular by the release of LMOs into the environment, outweigh any socio-economic benefits. The balancing of risks and benefits results in domestic policy choices to allow or prohibit the development and/or use of LMOs. When making such choices, a government will have to take into account its international obligations, including those under international trade law.

The conduct of any activity may cause damage or create a risk of causing damage to the interests of others. The level of damage and risk depends on the nature of the activity. The introduction of a new technology to conduct an activity tends to carry a higher risk because the long-term effects cannot be assessed before gaining experience with the technology. The development and use of LMOs is considered to carry a potentially significant risk and has, therefore, been subjected to national and international procedures to assess the risks associated with the genetic modification of a living organism. When such a risk materialises, damage may be caused to the interests of others. Such damage may manifest itself as traditional damage to private goods (i.e. personal injury, property damage, economic loss). Damage incurred by an organic farmer as a result of the contamination of his organic crops by the genetic material of a neighbouring farmer's modified crops provides an example. Claims for such traditional damages resulting from LMOs have been brought in several jurisdictions, in particular the United States and Canada.[5] The harm may also take the form of damage to public goods, notably

---

4   E.g. Convention on the Prohibition of the Development, Production and Stockpiling of Bacteriological (Biological) and Toxin Weapons and on their Destruction, adopted 10 April 1972, *United Nations Treaty Series*, Vol. 1015, p. 163.

5   See Stuart J. Smyth and Drew L. Kershen, 'Agricultural Biotechnology: Legal Liability Regimes from Comparative and International Perspectives', *Global Jurist Advances*, Vol. 6, Issue 2 (2006), pp. 1–78.

the environment and human health. An example is the loss of wild species relatives by the spread of genetically modified crops and, notably, the cost of actions to prevent further loss or to restore the loss; another example is the infection of people with an unintentionally released genetically modified virus and, notably, the costs of medical screening and/or inoculation following such release.

A potential legal basis for holding States liable for such damage is the principle that the polluter must pay for the pollution caused by him or her. This principle has an economic origin. Accordingly, operators must internalise the costs of pollution caused by their activities. The economic objectives of the principle are an optimal allocation of the means of production and maximisation of production value. It is, however, not clear whether the principle only applies to the person in control of the polluting activity or also to the State under whose control the activity is conducted. It could be argued that the application of the principle should be extended to that State because it can permit or prohibit the activity and, if it permits the activity, may benefit from the activity through the contribution of that activity to its gross national product.[6] According to such an extended application of the principle, a State must require operators within its jurisdiction or control to internalise the transboundary costs of their activities. In this form, the principle could be applied as a principle of international law to be invoked by States if the external costs of activities within their jurisdiction or control, such as damage to third parties, are not internalised. However, the application of the principle at the international level is not supported by existing international instruments and case law.[7]

III The responsibility of States for internationally wrongful acts

International law imposes general and, as the case may be, specific rules on States regarding activities within their jurisdiction or control, including commercial activities. With respect to LMOs, specific rules are contained in the Cartagena Protocol for intentional and unintentional transboundary movements of LMOs. The rules of this Protocol are predominantly procedural in nature. The Cartagena Protocol does not impose substantive obligations on exporting States with respect to intentional transboundary movements, nor does international law contain any general rules on the export of technology and products to third States with the aim of preventing the occurrence of damage therein.

---

6   René Lefeber, *Transboundary Environmental Interference and the Origin of State Liability* (Kluwer Law International, 1996), pp. 2–3; Advocate-General Juliane Kokott in European Court of Justice Case C-188/07, Commune de Mesquer v. Total France SA and Total International Ltd, Conclusion of 13 March 2008, paras 142–143.

7   Arbitral Tribunal, Case Concerning the Auditing of Accounts Between the Kingdom of the Netherlands and the French Republic Pursuant to the Additional Protocol of 25 September 1991 to the Convention on the Protection of the Rhine Against Pollution by Chlorides of 3 December 1976, Award of 12 March 2004, *Reports of International Arbitral Awards*, Vol. 25, p. 312, para. 103.

With respect to unintentional transboundary movements, the Cartagena Protocol requires States to take appropriate measures to prevent such movements (Article 16 (3)). This provision reflects a general rule of international law that requires States to take appropriate measures to prevent activities within their jurisdiction or control from causing transboundary damage. This obligation binds all States by virtue of customary international law.[8] Although the corresponding provision in the Cartagena Protocol does not explicitly refer to a threshold of damage, it appears from its context that it is subject to such a threshold. Response measures are only required if the release of an LMO leads or may lead to an unintentional transboundary movement that is likely to have 'significant adverse effects of the LMO on the conservation and sustainable use of biological diversity, taking also into account risks to human health' (Article 17 of the Cartagena Protocol). This is also consistent with the interpretation of the general rule of international law reflected in several international instruments without an explicit reference to such threshold of damage.[9]

The obligation to prevent unintentional transboundary movements of LMOs is a due diligence obligation. The objective of the obligation is the prevention of transboundary damage. States are required to exercise due diligence with the aim of achieving the objective, but a failure to achieve the objective will not automatically result in non-compliance with the obligation. Compliance with a due diligence obligation requires States to adopt, implement, supervise, and enforce policies and measures to achieve the objective,[10] in this case policies and measures to prevent the release of an LMO that leads or may lead to an unintentional transboundary movement. Such policies and measures can only be designed on the basis of an assessment of the risk of the release of an LMO. This presupposes the introduction of mandatory risk assessment procedures. The objective of such risk assessment is to identify and evaluate the potential adverse effects of the LMO in the 'likely potential receiving environment' (cf. paragraph 1 of Annex III of the Cartagena Protocol). Since the level of risk is related to the nature of the organism, the nature of the genetic modification, the intended use of the genetically modified organism and the likely potential receiving environment, risk assessments are to be carried out on a case-by-case basis (cf. paragraph 6 of

---

8   Legality of the Threat or Use of Nuclear Weapons, Advisory Opinion of 8 July 1996, ICJ Reports 1996, para. 29; see also Article 3 of Convention on Biological Diversity; Principle 2 of Rio Declaration on Environment and Development, adopted on 16 June 1992, UN Doc. A/CONF.151/26/Rev.1 (Vol. I) (1992), pp. 3–8; and Principle 21 of Stockholm Declaration on the Human Environment, 16 June 1972, UN Doc. A/CONF.48/14/Rev.1 (1972), pp. 3–5.

9   On the interpretation of Principle 2 of Rio Declaration on Environment and Development (1992) and Principle 21 of Stockholm Declaration on the Human Environment (1972), see René Lefeber, see note 6, pp. 86–89.

10   Case Concerning Pulp Mills on the River Uruguay (Argentina v. Uruguay), Judgment of 20 April 2010, *ICJ Reports 2010*, para. 197; Seabed Disputes Chamber of the International Tribunal for the Law of the Sea, Responsibilities and Obligations of States Sponsoring Persons and Entities with respect to Activities in the Area, Advisory Opinion of 1 February 2011, *ITLOS Reports 2011*, paras 110–120 and 218.

Annex III). Depending on the risks identified and the level of such risks, policies and measures must be established and maintained to regulate, manage and control the risks (see also Article 16 of the Cartagena Protocol). If the risk materialises (i.e. a release of an LMO occurs that leads or may lead to an unintentional transboundary movement), such policies and measures must also provide for actions to address such an event, including the notification of affected States or potentially affected States and the provision of information to these States (see also Article 17). If a State exercises the required degree of due diligence and significant transboundary damage nevertheless occurs, the obligation has not been breached.

Only the breach of a general or specific rule of international law through an act attributable to a State entails the responsibility of that State for an internationally wrongful act, including for damage that is caused by that act. Such a breach is governed by the rules of general international law with respect to the responsibility of States for internationally wrongful acts.[11] These rules permit the development of special rules on the responsibility for a specific internationally wrongful act, but this would require an agreement among negotiating States to deviate from the rules of general international law. Such an agreement could not be reached in the negotiations on the Supplementary Protocol.[12] It was agreed that this Protocol shall not affect the rights and obligations of States under the rules of general international law on state responsibility (Article 11 of the Supplementary Protocol).

IV The responsibility of States for the injurious consequences of activities under their jurisdiction or control

1 Introduction

In the absence of an internationally wrongful act or any other special rules of international law, damage can only be redressed by recourse to domestic law. In cases involving multiple jurisdictions, such recourse may be frustrated by procedural difficulties, such as the absence of a competent or appropriate forum, or the denial of access to assets to satisfy claims on the basis of a foreign judgment, or substantive difficulties, such as the burden of proof. Such difficulties can only be overcome by international cooperation, which is warranted on the basis of the application of the 'polluter-pays' principle at the international level (see Section II). States should not

---

11   Articles on the Responsibility of States for Internationally Wrongful Acts, *Yearbook of the International Law Commission 2001*, Vol. II, Part Two, p. 20, taken note by UN Doc. A/RES/56/83 (2001), Annex.

12   For a compilation of submissions by negotiating Parties on State responsibility, see Chapter I.A of Annex II, Report of the Open-Ended *Ad Hoc* Working Group of Legal and Technical Experts on Liability and Redress in the Context of the Cartagena Protocol on Biosafety on the Work of its Third Meeting, UNEP/CBD/BS/WG-L&R/3/3 (15 March 2007); see also Gurdial Singh Nijar, Sarah Lawson-Stopps and Gan Pei Fern, *Liability and Redress under the Cartagena Protocol on Biosafety: A Record of the Negotiations for Developing International Rule, Vol. 1* (Centre of Excellence for Biodiversity Law, 2008), Chapter 2.

walk away from (or should not be able to, in any event) the responsibility that comes with permitting activities under their jurisdiction or control that create a significant risk of causing domestic and transboundary damage.

Hence, in order to fill the gap that would otherwise be left, additional obligations should be imposed on States for permitting such activities to be carried on within their jurisdiction or control. In the case of unintentional transboundary movements, the source State should be the subject of such additional obligations; in the case of intentional transboundary movements, both the exporting State and/or the importing State could be appropriate subjects of such additional obligations. Since the advent of new technologies, in particular after the Second World War, the international community has developed three approaches to imposing these additional obligations on States and implement the 'polluter-pays' principle at the international level: (a) the obligation of States to pay compensation; (b) the obligation of States to ensure prompt, adequate and effective compensation (via a civil liability approach); and (c) the obligation of States to ensure prompt, adequate and effective response measures (via a regulatory liability approach).

2 The obligation of States to pay compensation

The most straightforward approach to addressing the injurious consequences of activities that create a significant risk of causing significant transboundary damage would be to require States to prevent the causation of such injurious consequences in absolute terms. This approach would render the causation of significant damage unlawful when the risk materialises and might give rise to claims for termination of the activity. In the aftermath of the occurrence of significant transboundary damage, it should always be assessed whether adjustments of the activity can be made to minimise the risk of future occurrences. However, States are not required under inter-national law to terminate an activity under its jurisdiction or control if the activity only creates a risk of causing significant damage irrespective whether the risk has materialised or not. International law requires States to exercise due diligence with the aim of preventing significant transboundary damage, but does not require them to prevent significant transboundary damage in absolute terms. This does not necessarily exclude imposing an obligation on that State to pay compensation for the damage caused without labelling the activity or its injurious consequences as unlawful. Pursuant to this approach, the injurious consequences are allocated to the State under whose jurisdiction or control an activity is carried on. This State may recover the costs from private actors within its jurisdiction or control that carry on the activity.

Such an obligation to pay compensation has been imposed on States for damage caused on the surface of the Earth by activities in outer space.[13] When this

---

13 Article 7, Treaty on Principles Governing the Activities of States in the Exploration and Use of Outer Space, including the Moon and Other Celestial Bodies, adopted on 23 January 1967 (in force), *United Nations Treaty Series*, Vol 610, p. 205; Convention on International Liability for Damage Caused by Space Objects, adopted on 29 March 1972 (in force), *United Nations Treaty Series*, Vol. 961, p. 187.

obligation was introduced in outer space treaties, in the late 1960s and early 1970s, outer space activities were predominantly carried on or procured by governments. However, these treaties are also applicable to damage caused by commercial outer space activities, which have spread in recent years. There is no other treaty in force that imposes an obligation on States to pay compensation for the full amount of damage caused. The only other field where an obligation has been introduced for States to pay compensation relates to the peaceful use of nuclear energy. Nuclear liability conventions impose a primary obligation to pay compensation on the operator of the nuclear installation for damage caused by nuclear material in the installation or in transport.[14] Only if payments by the operator up to the amount set by the conventions are insufficient to compensate the damage is the installation State required to provide supplementary compensation.[15]

In the absence of consistent State practice and a common *opinio juris*, no customary obligation can be said to have emerged imposing an obligation on States to pay compensation for significant transboundary damage caused by activities carried on under their jurisdiction or control.[16] States are also not willing to accept such an obligation, as illustrated by the proposals to that end in the negotiations on damage resulting from transboundary movements of LMOs, which gathered little support and provoked strong repudiations.[17]

States have also been reluctant to accept a procedural approach to the payment of compensation for significant transboundary damage caused by activities under their jurisdiction or control. Pursuant to this approach, States would be required to negotiate a compensation arrangement with potentially affected States or affected States.[18] Such an arrangement would ideally be negotiated before the activity creating a significant risk of causing significant transboundary damage is permitted, but it could also be negotiated after the materialisation of the risk. An obligation to negotiate a compensation arrangement has been introduced for damage caused by the non-navigational uses of international watercourses.[19] This obligation, which is part of a treaty that is not yet in force, is to date the only multilateral example of this procedural approach.

---

14   Paris Convention on Third Party Liability in the Field of Nuclear Energy, adopted on 29 July 1960 as amended (in force), *United Nations Treaty Series*, Vol. 956, p. 251; Vienna Convention on Civil Liability for Nuclear Damage, adopted on 21 May 1963 as amended (in force), *United Nations Treaty Series*, Vol. 1063, p. 265.

15   Brussels Convention Supplementary to the Paris Convention on Third Party Liability in the Field of Nuclear Energy, adopted on 31 January 1963 as amended (in force), *United Nations Treaty Series*, Vol. 1041, p. 358; Protocol to Amend the Vienna Convention on Civil Liability for Nuclear Damage, adopted on 12 September 1997 (in force), *United Nations Treaty Series*, Vol. 2241, p. 270.

16   Lefeber, see note 6, Chapter 5.

17   For a compilation of submissions by negotiating Parties on State liability, see Chapters I.B, IV.2 (a) and V.A of Annex II, Report of the Open-Ended *Ad Hoc* Working Group of Legal and Technical Experts on Liability and Redress in the Context of the Cartagena Protocol on Biosafety on the Work of its Third Meeting, UNEP/CBD/BS/WG-L&R/3/3 (15 March 2007); see also Nijar *et al.*, see note 12, Chapter 6 (a).

18   Lefeber, see note 6, Chapter 6.

19   Article 7 (2), Convention on the Law of the Non-Navigational Uses of International Watercourses, adopted on 21 May 1997 (not in force), UN Doc. A/Res/51/229 (8 July 1997), Annex.

3 The obligation of States to ensure prompt, adequate and effective compensation

Claims for damages caused by activities may be brought before domestic courts under domestic civil liability regimes and, in the case of transboundary damage, domestic conflict-of-laws rules. The law generally provides for the injurious consequences of damage to lie where it falls, unless the occurrence of damage is imputable, in the sense of wrongful conduct, to the source of the damage. Accordingly, domestic civil liability regimes are based on proof of fault of the defendant by the claimant, unless a special civil liability regime has been created that introduces strict liability or reverses the burden of proof. When a risk materialises in spite of the implementation of measures to regulate, manage and control such risks, it will be difficult for victims to prove wrongful conduct, and the introduction of strict liability or the reversal of the burden of proof is therefore warranted for risk-prone activities. Strict liability regimes have, therefore, been introduced in domestic legal systems for a variety of activities that create a real or perceived significant risk of damage. In cases involving multiple jurisdictions, differences between domestic laws may still leave victims without compensation and/or impede economic development. With the dual aim of protecting victims and facilitating activities across borders, international agreements have been developed that harmonise substantive and procedural civil liability rules, in particular by imposing strict liability for specific risk-prone activities and addressing occurrences of damage involving multiple jurisdictions.[20] These international agreements oblige States to introduce uniform and effective civil law remedies to address domestic and/or transboundary damage caused by such activities.[21]

This approach has found recognition in principles, developed by the International Law Commission (ILC), on the allocation of loss in the case of

---

20 Paris Convention on Third Party Liability in the Field of Nuclear Energy, see note 14; 1963 Vienna Convention on Civil Liability for Nuclear Damage, see note 14; International Convention on Civil Liability for Oil Pollution Damage, adopted on 29 November 1969 as amended (in force), *United Nations Treaty Series*, Vol. 973, p. 3; International Convention on Liability and Compensation for Damage in Connection with the Carriage of Hazardous and Noxious Substances by Sea (HNS), adopted on 3 May 1996 (not in force), IMO/LEG/CONF.10/8/2 (9 May 1996); International Convention on Civil Liability for Bunker Oil Pollution Damage, adopted on 23 March 2001 (in force), IMO/LEG/CONF.12/19 (27 March 2001); Basel Protocol on Liability and Compensation for Damage Resulting from Transboundary Movements of Hazardous Wastes and Their Disposal, adopted by Decision V/29 on 10 December 1999 (not in force), UNEP/ CHW.5/29 (10 December 1999) Annex III [Basel Liability Protocol]; Protocol on Civil Liability and Compensation for Damage Caused by the Transboundary Effects of Industrial Accidents on Transboundary Waters to the 1992 Convention on the Protection and Use of Transboundary Watercourses and International Lakes and to the 1992 Convention on the Transboundary Effects of Industrial Accidents, adopted on 21 May 2003 (not in force), Doc. ECE/MP.WAT/11- ECE/CP.TEIA/9 [Kiev Protocol on Civil Liability].

21 Lefeber, see note 6, Chapter 7.

transboundary harm arising out of hazardous activities.[22] 'Hazardous activities' are defined as those that have a high probability of causing significant trans-boundary damage or a low probability of causing disastrous transboundary damage.[23] These Principles will not apply to the development and use of LMOs. The release of LMOs into the environment, such as genetically modified crops for agricultural production, is not likely to fall within the scope of this definition, as no government may be expected to approve such release if the risk assessment reveals either a high probability of causing significant transboundary damage or a low probability of causing disastrous transboundary damage. The concerns with respect to the release of these LMOs relate to risks not identified in a risk assessment and the correctness of the evaluation of the risk. Yet, the development of other LMOs will meet the requirements of the definition: the development of the genetically modified avian influenza virus in a maximum-security laboratory creates, without doubt, a low probability of causing disastrous transboundary damage. The Principles would, in any event, only apply to unintentional trans-boundary movements of LMOs, because the transboundary damage must have been caused by activities through their 'physical consequences'.[24] This means that the physical link must connect the activity with its transboundary effects. Damage resulting from intentional transboundary movements is thus not covered by these Principles.

One of the objectives of the ILC's Principles is to ensure prompt and adequate compensation to natural or legal persons that are victims of transboundary damage (Principle 3 (a)). In its commentary, the ILC adds that the Principles serve other objectives as well, including preserving and promoting the viability of economic activities that are important to the welfare of States and peoples.[25] Pursuant to the Principles, States 'should' take necessary measures to ensure that prompt and adequate compensation is available to victims (Principle 4.1). Some substantive and procedural standards have been formulated by the ILC to elaborate on what these measures should be. Substantively, primary liability should rest with private persons and not with States; should not require proof of fault; should be covered by financial security; and, in appropriate cases, should be supplemented by industry-wide funds at the national level (Principles 4.2–4.4). If such measures are insufficient to provide adequate compensation, States should ensure the alloca-tion of additional financial resources (Principle 4.5). Procedurally, prompt, adequate and effective remedies must be made available to domestic judicial and administrative bodies to adjudicate claims arising out of transboundary damage

---

22   Principles on the allocation of loss in the case of transboundary harm arising out of hazardous activities, *Report of the International Law Commission 2006*, UN Doc. A/61/10 (2006), p. 101, taken note by UN Doc. A/RES/61/36 (2006), Annex [Allocation of Loss Principles].

23   Paragraph 2 of commentary to Principle 1, Allocation of Loss Principles, ibid., p. 106.

24   Paragraph 4 of commentary to Principle 1, ibid. See also commentary on Article 1 of the Draft Articles on Prevention of Transboundary Harm from Hazardous Activities, *Yearbook of the International Law Commission 2001*, Vol. II, Part Two, p. 151, paras 16–17.

25   Paragraph 10 of commentary to Principle 3, Allocation of Loss Principles, see note 22.

caused by hazardous activities (Principle 6.1). Since the Principles only address transboundary damage, the victims of transboundary damage should additionally have access to remedies that are no less prompt, adequate and effective than those available to victims that suffer damage within the State in which the damage-causing hazardous activity is carried on (Principle 6.2).

Although the ILC's approach to provide for prompt, adequate and effective compensation through effective civil law remedies finds support in international agreements that harmonise substantive and procedural liability rules, only a few of these agreements have entered into force, notably those governing the use of nuclear energy and the transportation of oil.[26] Numerous other international special civil liability regimes are no longer expected to ever enter into force, such as those in fields of water-related industrial activities and the transboundary movement of hazardous wastes and their disposal.[27] Although differences were overcome during long and intense negotiation processes preceding their adoption, negotiating States either accepted the agreement without the intention of becoming a Party or encountered legal and/or policy difficulties when considering implementation of these agreements in domestic law.

This poor record of international special civil liability regimes was an important reason that no consensus could be achieved on the development of such a regime for damage resulting from transboundary movements of LMOs. Although elaborate text proposals on civil liability were submitted and discussed,[28] the negotiations on civil liability resulted in a process solution (Article 12 (2) of the Supplementary Protocol). Although this solution falls short of imposing an obligation on Parties to ensure prompt, adequate and effective compensation for damage caused by transboundary movements of LMOs, it requires a State to pay serious attention to the regulatory framework for such compensation when it considers becoming a Party to the Supplementary Protocol. At that time, a State will have to determine whether: (a) existing civil law remedies provide 'adequate rules and procedures' for personal and material damage; or (b) additional civil law remedies are required to redress such damage. Although the scope of this provision is limited to personal and material damage that is associated with 'adverse effects on the conservation and sustainable use of biological diversity, taking also into account risks to human health' (Article 2 (2) (b) of the Supplementary Protocol), it may be expected that the parliamentary approval processes in many States will involve a comprehensive assessment and discussion of domestic law related to personal injury, property damage and economic loss (traditional damage) caused by LMOs.[29]

26   See note 20.
27   Ibid.
28   For a compilation of submissions by negotiating Parties on civil liability, see Chapter IV.2 (b) of Annex II, Report of the Open-Ended *Ad Hoc* Working Group of Legal and Technical Experts on Liability and Redress in the Context of the Cartagena Protocol on Biosafety on the Work of its Third Meeting, UNEP/CBD/BS/WG-L&R/3/3 (15 March 2007); see also Nijar *et al.*, see note 12, Chapter 5 (b).
29   On civil liability in the Supplementary Protocol, see further Chapters 7 and 8 of this book, by Gurdial Singh Nijar, and Elmo Thomas and Mahlet Teshome Kebede, respectively.

4 The obligation of States to ensure prompt, adequate and effective response measures

Obliging States to ensure prompt, adequate and effective compensation may be suited for addressing damage to private goods (traditional damage), but is less so for addressing damage to public goods, notably the environment. Although scientifically sound models could be designed to determine the monetary equivalent for irreversible environmental loss (e.g. by determining the discounted value of future ecosystem services), the award of compensation is not likely to produce an optimal solution to redress such loss. First, the valuation of irreversible environmental loss in monetary terms is surrounded by uncertainty inherent in any model that seeks to incorporate future uses of a specific environmental component; there is currently no such internationally agreed model available. Second, the rigorous application of such models is likely to result in awards that are beyond the financial capability of the liable person. Third, the value of an environmental component cannot always be reflected in a price, because components like it are indispensable for people to survive (e.g. the availability of water resources). Fourth, the award of compensation necessitates the identification of a beneficiary and raises the question of guidance for the allocation of financial resources to environmental or other purposes. Yet, it can be done and has been done, as may be illustrated by the awards of the United Nations Compensation Commission addressing environmental claims.[30]

The award of compensation only emerges as a remedy when prevention of a loss-causing event has failed and, under such circumstances, it should only be resorted to when restoration of the *status quo ante* is not possible. In the event of environmental loss, or threat of loss, the environment benefits most from the avoidance of loss or further loss, or from the restoration of the loss. If the loss is irreversible, the *status quo ante* can be approached through restoration by equivalent. This can be achieved through the replacement of the lost components by other components for the same use or a similar type of use at the same location or an alternative location. In international law, the primacy of restoration over compensation to address the injurious consequences of an internationally wrongful act is well established.[31] The internationally agreed objective to protect and preserve the environment also favours alternatives for the award of compensation for environmental loss. Such an alternative has emerged and was referred to in the negotiations on the Supplementary Protocol as an administrative approach to liability – it is also known as regulatory liability. This approach requires the implementation of response measures in the event of environmental loss or threat of loss in order to avoid loss or further loss, or to restore the loss. The primary

---

30   On the work of the United Nations Compensation Commission, see Cymie R. Payne and Peter H. Sand eds, *Gulf War Reparations and the UN Compensation Commission: Environmental Liability* (Oxford University Press, 2011).

31   Article 35 and its commentary, Articles on Responsibility of States for Internationally Wrongful Acts, see note 11, p. 96, para. 3.

responsibility for the implementation of such response measures should rest with the polluter. If the polluter fails to implement response measures or if the urgency of the situation requires the immediate implementation of such measures, a third party should be entitled, or even obliged, to implement response measures. Such a third person could be the State under whose jurisdiction or control the loss occurs; any State if the loss occurs in an area beyond the limits of national jurisdiction; a private actor that is geographically in the best position to implement response measures; or a private actor that has an interest in the protection and preservation of the environment. Finally, the recovery of the costs of response measures from the polluter by such a third person should be facilitated.

This alternative approach has also found recognition in the ILC's Principles on the allocation of loss in the case of transboundary harm arising out of hazardous activities. The protection and preservation of the environment in the event of transboundary damage is one of the objectives of these Principles (Principle 3 (b)). The Principles require the State under whose jurisdiction or control a hazardous activity is carried on to ensure that appropriate response measures are taken upon the occurrence of an incident involving that activity which results in or is likely to result in transboundary damage (Principle 5 (b)); and the States affected or likely to be affected by the transboundary damage are required to take all feasible measures to mitigate and, if possible, eliminate the effects of such damage (Principle 5 (d)).[32]

The ILC's approach to ensure prompt, adequate and effective response measures is supported by developments in international law, including the conclusion of international agreements. At first, such regulatory measures were incorporated in special civil liability regimes as incidental provisions.[33] These provisions are generic and do not provide detailed arrangements for the implementation of response measures. They typically oblige persons in operational control to adopt measures to mitigate damage or a threat of damage. It was only in 2005 that the first international agreement focused primarily on response measures was concluded, namely Annex VI to the Protocol on Environmental Protection to the Antarctic Treaty on Liability Arising from Environmental Emergencies. It had appeared in the negotiations on this agreement that, on the one hand, the protection and the preservation of the environment was the primary objective of the negotiations and, on the other, no agreement could be reached on the conclusion of a comprehensive special civil liability regime.[34] After many years of unsuccessful negotiations, the

---

32   Paragraphs 3–8, 10 of commentary to Principle 5 (b), Allocation of Loss Principles, see note 22.

33   Article 6, 1999 Basel Liability Protocol, see note 20; Article 6, 2003 Kiev Protocol on Civil Liability, see note 20; see also International Oil Pollution Compensation Fund 1992, *Claims Manual*, December 2008 edn. Available at www.iopcfunds.org/uploads/tx_iopcpublications/2008_claims_manual_e.pdf (accessed 1 August 2013).

34   This paradigm shift in the focus of the negotiations is rooted in the personal report that the chairman of the negotiations on liability issued during the twenty-third Antarctic Treaty Consultative Meeting (ATCM); see Personal Report of the Chairman of the Liability Discussion in WG1, ATCVM XIII, Working Paper 041 (1999).

negotiators moved away, for the time being, from the development of a special civil liability regime that would also address traditional damage and, instead, focused on addressing environmental loss through the introduction of regulatory liability. The scope of this agreement is modest. It only provides for response measures in the event of an environmental emergency to avoid loss or further loss; in particular, it does not provide for restoration measures.

Thus, the regulatory approach to liability is reflected in incidental provisions in a number of international agreements and only in one international agreement in a prominent way; this latter agreement is not in force, is regionally confined, only involves a limited number of States, and only introduces measures to avoid loss or further loss resulting from environmental emergencies. Hence, it cannot be said that a customary obligation of States has yet emerged to ensure the implementation of prompt, adequate and effective response measures in case of environmental loss or threat of such loss. Of course, this does not prevent the introduction of this obligation in new international instruments. The launch of the negotiations on damage resulting from the transboundary movement of LMOs coincided with the adoption of Annex VI and a directive on environmental liability by the European Union that introduces regulatory liability.[35] Proposals tabled in the negotiations that captured this alternative approach to liability for damage to the environment logically ensued from the adoption of these instruments.[36] It appeared subsequently that this approach was the only option for the adoption of a legally binding instrument. Eventually, the negotiating States agreed to 'work towards' a legally binding instrument on regulatory liability that would include an article on civil liability.[37] This work resulted in the adoption of the Supplementary Protocol.

The Supplementary Protocol provides for regulatory liability. It requires States to ensure that response measures are taken in the event of damage or a sufficient likelihood of damage caused by activities falling within its scope (Article 5). The definition of 'response measures' is broad and covers: (a) measures to prevent further adverse effects or, in the case of a sufficient likelihood of damage, to avoid any adverse effects; and (b) measures to return to baseline conditions or an equivalent alternative (Article 2 (2) (d)). The definition of 'damage' is limited to adverse effects on the conservation and sustainable use of biological diversity that is

---

35 Directive 2004/35/CE of the European Parliament and of the Council of 21 April 2004 on environmental liability with regard to the prevention and remedying of environmental damage, *Official Journal of the European Communities* 2004, L 143/56. The evolution of this directive is also marked by a paradigm shift in the focus of the negotiations from a special civil liability regime to a regulatory liability regime; see Commission of the European Communities, White Paper on Environmental Liability, COM (2000) 66.

36 For a compilation of submissions by the negotiating Parties on the administrative approach, see Chapter IV.2 (c) of Annex II, Report of the Open-Ended *Ad Hoc* Working Group of Legal and Technical Experts on Liability and Redress in the Context of the Cartagena Protocol on Biosafety on the Work of its Third Meeting, UNEP/CBD/BS/WG-L&R/3/3 (15 March 2007); see also Nijar *et al.*, see note 12, Chapter 5 (a).

37 See Decision BS-IV/12 (2010), Liability and redress under the Cartagena Protocol on Biosafety, UNEP/CBD/BS/COP-MOP/4/18 (25 June 2008), p. 84.

measurable or otherwise observable and are considered significant on the basis of a list of factors, including the long-term or permanent change; the extent of the qualitative or quantitative changes; the reduction of the ability to provide goods and services; and the extent of any adverse effects on human health (Article 2 (b)). The response measures consist of obligations of the person in control of the LMO (operator) and the competent authority. The responsible operator must be required to: (a) immediately inform the competent authority; (b) evaluate the damage; and (c) take appropriate response measures in the event of damage or a sufficient likelihood that damage will result if timely response measures are not taken (Articles 5 (1) and 5 (3)). The competent authority is required to: (a) identify the operator; (b) evaluate the damage; and (c) determine which response measures should be taken by the operator (Article 5 (2)). The competent authority may also implement appropriate response measures and recover the costs from the operator (Articles 5 (4) and 5 (5)). The decisions of the competent authority are subject to procedural safeguards, including administrative or judicial review (Article 5 (6)).[38] The Supplementary Protocol does not, however, provide for cross-border enforcement of such decisions.

It appears from the Supplementary Protocol that a large number of other issues were identified and considered relevant in the context of a regulatory liability regime. The Supplementary Protocol does not provide for harmonisation in respect of these issues, but leaves discretion to the Parties whether and how to address them in domestic law. These issues include the identification of the operator (Article 2 (2) (c)); the right of the operator to invoke exemptions (Article 6); time limitation of liability (Article 7); financial limitation of liability (Article 8); and the establishment and maintenance of financial security by the operator (Article 10). There was no agreement to harmonise these issues and the only agreement that could be reached was to forego harmonisation. The identification of these issues in the Supplementary Protocol and leaving discretion to Parties to address them in domestic law were nevertheless essential. Leaving these issues out of the Supplementary Protocol could be interpreted as a rejection of a Party's right to address the issue in domestic law. It may also reflect the novelty and complexity of the new approach to address liability for damage to the environment and, as in the case of the Supplementary Protocol, damage to biological diversity.[39]

V The responsibility of the private sector for the injurious consequences of their activities

In an international community dominated by States with exclusive territorial sovereignty, the exercise of jurisdiction with respect to natural and legal persons (or their assets) in another State is impeded by legal and practical difficulties.

---

38 On administrative approach to liability in the Supplementary Protocol, see further Chapter 5 of this book, by Alejandro Lago Candeira.

39 On this issue, see further Chapter 10 of this book, by Worku Damena Yifru and Kathryn Garforth.

In the event of civil liability, judgments of domestic courts and tribunals are not automatically recognised and enforced in other States in the absence of an international agreement. In the event of regulatory liability, administrative decisions related to response measures can only be recognised and enforced in other States on the basis of an international agreement. Since States are reluctant to assume liability for damage caused by activities carried on by private actors under their jurisdiction or control (Sections III and IV.2) or to harmonise domestic liability regimes in whole or part (Sections IV.3 and IV.4), effective legal remedies to address damage resulting from transboundary movements may not be available. To demonstrate corporate social responsibility and to facilitate international transboundary movements, the private sector should consider resorting to self-regulation to address such claims.

In the negotiations concerning liability and redress in the context of the Cartagena Protocol, the private sector did not only actively participate in the inter-governmental negotiations, but also developed a proposal for self-regulation. This proposal eventually evolved into a contractual mechanism for response in the event of damage to biological diversity caused by the release of an LMO (Compact).[40] The membership consists of six companies with large market shares in the agricultural biotechnology market, but is open to other entities that meet the conditions of membership. This private sector initiative was 'noted' in the decision by which the Supplementary Protocol was adopted.[41]

A member is contractually bound to respond under the terms of the Compact if the release of an LMO into the environment by that member causes damage to biological diversity irrespective of the place of release and the place of damage. States are third-party beneficiaries of the Compact with the right to bring claims under a claims process that provides for recourse to binding arbitration under the auspices of the Permanent Court of Arbitration (PCA). States may seek the implementation of remediation measures and/or monetary compensation in speci-fied situations. A member may avail itself of a number of exemptions, of limitation of liability in time, and of limitation of liability in amount. Each member is required to demonstrate their financial capacity to meet their financial obligations under the Compact, including by proof of self-insurance.[42]

The Compact is not intended to be an alternative to domestic regulatory liability regimes. Although the Compact precludes the multiple recovery of damage and the simultaneous pursuit of claims under the Compact and domestic law, it provides States with an option that is complementary to the Supplementary Protocol and domestic law implementing the Supplementary Protocol or otherwise

---

40   The Compact, as amended on 18 September 2012. Available at www.biodiversitycompact.org (accessed 1 August 2013).

41   10th preambular paragraph, Decision BS-V/11 (2010): International rules and procedures in the field of liability and redress for damage resulting from transboundary movements of living modified organisms, reproduced in Appendix 2 of this book.

42   On the Compact, see further Chapter 14 of this book, by J. Thomas Carrato, John Barkett and Phil Goldberg.

providing for regulatory liability. This may be the only option for States if the damage cannot be recovered on the basis of domestic law, including in cases where a Compact member does not have sufficient assets in that State. Furthermore, the Supplementary Protocol and the Compact were both finalised in 2010, but only the Compact is currently and universally operational.

The provisions of the Compact address in much more detail than the Supplementary Protocol the issues that will need to be implemented in domestic law to make it operational. In some respects, the Compact is more restrictive than the Supplementary Protocol (it does not address threats of damage) and in other respects it may be more restrictive than domestic law (it provides for exemptions, limitation in amount, limitation in time and rules on the standard of proof). However, in other respects, it is more progressive than the Supplementary Protocol (it provides for monetary compensation, compulsory financial security and action to develop commercial insurance).

It thus appears that the Compact fills a regulatory gap that States have not been able to fill, but it should be borne in mind that the rules were set by the private sector. An opportunity was provided to States and other stakeholders, including civil society, to comment on draft texts in regional dialogues, and these comments resulted in significant improvements of the original text.[43] Yet, there were red lines that could not be crossed, notably on the standard of proof, defences, time limits and financial limits. Be that as it may, the Compact is a unique demonstration of corporate social responsibility that may become an innovative model for addressing damage to the environment.

VI Conclusion

The Parties to the Cartagena Protocol demonstrated their responsibility for the protection and preservation of the environment by adopting the Supplementary Protocol. The Supplementary Protocol is the first global and comprehensive agreement providing for regulatory liability and a definition of damage to biological diversity. It is global as States from all United Nations regions participated in its development. It is comprehensive as response measures include avoidance as well as restoration of damage, and must be implemented to address damage arising from environmental emergencies as well as damage with a slow onset.

Although States have the right to provide for regulatory liability without an international agreement, the Supplementary Protocol requires its Parties to implement it in domestic law. By voluntarily assuming a binding obligation to provide for prompt, adequate and effective response measures in the event of damage caused by the transboundary movement of LMOs, States expressly accept the responsibility that comes with their consent to the import of them. By adhering

---

43 Dialogues were held in Asia (Singapore in January 2009 and the Philippines in January 2010), America (Costa Rica in June 2009), Europe (Belgium in November 2009), and Africa (Kenya in August 2010).

to and implementing the Supplementary Protocol, States give effect, at the inter-national and national level, to the principle that the polluter must pay for the injurious consequences of activities under their jurisdiction or control that create a significant risk of significant damage. The Supplementary Protocol contributes to filling the gap in international law with respect to addressing damage involving multiple jurisdictions.

The Supplementary Protocol only partially fills the gap, though. It only covers damage to biological diversity and fails to cover traditional damage, as intended by the States pushing for a liability regime at the time of adoption of the Cartagena Protocol. Although this limited approach finds justification in the objectives of the Convention of Biological Diversity and the Cartagena Protocol, there is no legal impediment to address traditional damage in a liability instrument in the context of these Conventions. But a regulatory liability regime is not suited to address traditional damage: this type of damage needs to be addressed through a civil liability regime.

Furthermore, the Supplementary Protocol places the responsibility for the implementation of response measures on the importing State. This was also not the intention of the States pushing for a liability regime at the time of adoption of the Cartagena Protocol. These States aimed at channelling liability to the developers of LMOs and, hence, at requiring exporting States imposing liability on the developers for damage caused by their products. The importing State may be in a better position to assess the impact of an LMO on the receiving environment, but its knowledge of the risks of the technology is likely to be limited and depends on its capacity to review risk assessments. The State of import may require a foreign developer to implement response measures under its domestic law, but the Supplementary Protocol does not provide for the transboundary recognition and enforcement of decisions related to response measures. Since the Compact allows for recourse against foreign developers, it adds value to the Supplementary Protocol.

Whether the regulatory liability approach to address damage to the environment will be successful depends on the entry into force of and the adherence to the Supplementary Protocol, as well as the future applications of this approach. The functional scope of the Supplementary Protocol is limited as it only addresses damage to biological diversity resulting from transboundary movements of LMOs. Regulatory liability is suited for application to other activities and/or types of damage. It could, for example, be introduced for: (a) damage to biological diversity caused by other activities, such as the transboundary movement of invasive alien species, under the Convention on Biological Diversity;[44] (b) damage to the environment under other multilateral environmental agreements; or (c) other types

---

44   It may be noted that Article 14 (2) of CBD calls for the examination, on the basis of studies to be carried out, of the issue of liability and redress, including restoration and compensation, for damage to biological diversity, except where such liability is a purely internal matter; for the latest develop-ment, see Decision IX/23 (2008): Report of the Conference of the Parties to the Convention on Biological Diversity on the Work of Its Ninth Meeting, UNEP/CBD/9/29 (2008), p. 190.

of damage, such as public health costs resulting from unexpected negative effects of the introduction of medicines.

The adoption of the Supplementary Protocol originates in regional and domestic precedents. It may therefore not have been a paradigm shift in addressing liability for damage to the environment, but it is certainly part of a 'paradigm evolution' of international liability law. In times when harmonisation of domestic civil liability regimes is not, or is no longer, an acceptable option for many States to address liability for damage involving multiple jurisdictions, developing and agreeing on an alternative approach to address the common concern of preventing and restoring damage to the environment is a paradigm shift. Yet, it remains to be seen whether the regulatory liability approach will survive and evolve further to become a sustainable approach to address liability and redress for damage to the environment.

5 Administrative approach to liability

Its origin, negotiation and outcome

Alejandro Lago Candeira

I Introduction

The European Union (EU) introduced the administrative approach with regard to liability and redress in the context of the Cartagena Protocol on Biosafety (Cartagena Protocol). This is based on the system that the EU adopted internally through Directive 2004/35 on environmental liability with regard to the prevention and remedying of environmental damage.[1] The adoption of the Directive coincided with the commencement of the negotiating process under Article 27 of the Cartagena Protocol. Its negotiating positions were heavily conditioned by this internal EU legislation and the outcome of the negotiation was influenced by that legislation as well, culminating in the adoption of the Nagoya-Kuala Lumpur Supplementary Protocol on Liability and Redress to the Cartagena Protocol (Supplementary Protocol); the influence on its administrative approach to liability was especially felt in the core of this legally binding instrument. At first sight, one could interpret this outcome as the direct effect of transposing to the Supplementary Protocol internal legislation of the EU and its 27 Member States, undoubtedly a large block of countries involved in the negotiation. However, a deeper analysis will demonstrate that it was the result of a limited transposition of the EU legislation to the international sphere and was actually the side effect of some decisions taken by other regional groups during the negotiation. This chapter will introduce the core elements of the administrative approach to environmental liability under EU legislation and track the circumstances in which this approach was converted into the main element of the liability regime for living modified organisms (LMOs) in the negotiations under Article 27 of the Cartagena Protocol. In this context, it is important to note that this is one of the main circumstances directly linked to the negotiation of the Cartagena Protocol itself, particularly for the EU. Thus, it is necessary to first describe correctly the framework of the negotiation process under Article 27 of the Cartagena Protocol in order to elaborate on international rules and procedures in the field of liability and redress for damage resulting from LMOs.

---

1 Directive 2004/35/CE of the European Parliament and of the Council of 21 April 2004 on environmental liability with regard to the prevention and remedying of environmental damage, *Official Journal of the European Union 2004*, L 143/56.

1 Relevance of the Cartagena Protocol for the EU

The EU followed a cautious approach in the negotiation of the Cartagena Protocol, based on the existence of its own internal rules that regulate the safety of bio-technology in the entire EU.[2] Given these as a premise, and not knowing very well what would be at stake in the negotiation of the biosafety protocol, the EU assumed that the best possible position was to promote a two-staged approach. The idea was to negotiate and adopt guidelines that could be rapidly implemented by all the Parties to the Convention on Biological Diversity (CBD). This initial step of adopting guidelines could be complemented, if necessary, with the adoption by the Conference of the Parties to the CBD of further or stronger (legally binding) measures after the assessment of the experience gained at the national and inter-national levels. This approach had the advantage of a rapid implementation of the measures, avoiding the rather long negotiation process anticipated for a legally binding instrument and the cumbersome ratification procedures needed after its adoption in each Party. The second advantage of this approach was that the measures would be more widely applied as implementation by all the Parties to the Convention, and not only those that had ratified them (as it would be in the case of a legally binding instrument), would be recommended. In this two-staged approach, there was an expectation that more experience would be gained from the voluntary implementation of the measures.

The interests of the EU in the biosafety protocol negotiation changed quite dramatically as the visibility of this negotiation and the stakes involved in it started to rise. From an initial cautious response to the demands of developing countries, the EU moved to an active role in the negotiation with important political stakes.[3] The evolution of the internal position and approach of the EU was mainly due to the important pressure that civil society and NGOs played internally on this topic, so that, as Bail pointed out, it was 'necessary to be seen as actively advocating global action for biosafety in biotechnology . . . to reassure a public opinion extremely worried about food safety . . . and increasingly sceptical towards biotechnology'.[4]

It is evident that there are very different approaches and perceptions regarding food safety, in particular the regulation of genetically modified organisms (GMOs). In the USA, for instance, as Lucia Roda Ghisleri summarised, regulations 'consider genetically modified foods as novel foods but not a separate entity with respect to other foods', focusing on the altered characteristics introduced by the genetic modification and the intended use of the new crop. Indeed, the principle that they followed for their risk assessment is based on the substantial equivalence of those

2   At that time the relevant legislations were: Directive 90/219 of 23 April 1990 on the contained use of genetically modified microorganisms, and Directive 90/220 of 23 April 1990 on the deliberate release into the environment of genetically modified organisms (and subsequent revisions).

3   Christoph Bail, Jean Paul Decaestecker and Matthias Jorgensen, 'European Union', in Christoph Bail, Robert Falkner and Helen Marquard eds, *The Cartagena Protocol on Biosafety: Reconciling Trade in Biotechnology with Environment and Development?* (Earthscan, 2002), p. 167.

4   Ibid.

products.[5] This review process is in the hands of the Food and Drug Administration (FDA), a federal agency with a long history in the US since its establishment in 1930. In comparison, a different approach taken by the EU is noticeable, where due to previous European food crisis of a different nature, the public perception of the risk related to the regulation of food and feed is quite sensitive. The European consumers have had a low level of trust in the public authorities in this field;[6] thus, the requirements and procedures for food/feed regulations are much more complex and are based on the precautionary principle.[7] The recognition of the precautionary principle in the Cartagena Protocol was in itself an important outcome for the EU as this principle is not only contained in the EU regulations on GMOs, but is also reflected in the basic principle of the EU environmental policy, recognised in the Treaty establishing the European Communities (TEC).

Due to the huge differences in regulation at both the international and regional levels, at a certain point in the biosafety negotiations, the EU realised that the protocol could become central to the definition of the relationship between multilateral environmental agreements and WTO rules. It was clear at the time of the negotiation that the EU approach to the regulation and the approval of GMOs for the EU market would, sooner or later, be challenged before the WTO. Indeed, in 2003, the United States, Canada and Argentina took that step, requesting the establishment of a panel within the Dispute Settlement Body of the WTO against the European Community position, in which they claimed that the application between 1999 and August 2003 of a *de facto* moratorium on the approval of agricultural products obtained by use of modern biotechnology restricted the import of GM crops from those countries (also known as *EC-biotech products*).[8] Although the relationship between the environmental treaties and the WTO has never been previously recognised or established by the WTO panels, some considered that the mere existence of the Cartagena Protocol would limit the claim against the EU in the WTO panel report in this case.[9] The EU tried to use the Cartagena Protocol to justify some of its most controversial internal measures. As the Protocol entered into force after the adoption of those measures, the EU used the Cartagena Protocol as a crystallisation of international customary law. However, the panel ignored not only this argument, but also the relationship between the Cartagena Protocol and all of the authorisation processes under the

---

5   Lucia Roda Ghisleri *et al.*, 'Risk Analysis and GM Foods: Scientific Risk Assessment', *European Food and Feed Law Review*, Vol. 4 (2009), p. 247.

6   It is expected, however, that this may change with the work of the European Food Safety Authority established in 2002.

7   For a deeper analysis and comparison of the different international and national systems on the regulation of risk and in particular on the regulation of GMOs, see Roda Ghisleri *et al.*, see note 5, pp. 235–250.

8   EC- Measures Affecting the Approval and Marketing of Biotech Products, Constitution of the Panel Established at the Requests of the United States, Canada and Argentina, WT/291/24, WT/292/18, WT/293/18 (5 March 2004).

9   See EC- Measures Affecting the Approval and Marketing of Biotech Products, Reports of the Panel, WT/DS291/R, WT/DS292/R, WT/DS293/R (29 September 2006).

WTO. This could be justified in this case because the Cartagena Protocol entered into force in September 2003.[10]

The third element that could have exerted some pressure on the EU and other developed Parties was the fact that the CBD was not at that time completely consolidated and, therefore, posed a hypothetical risk that a failure in the negotiation of the biosafety protocol could have a negative impact on the development of the Convention. Some Parties were even implying that a failure could have led to the collapse of the Convention as a whole.[11]

All of these considerations, forced by an internal increase in interest driven by certain NGOs in some EU Member States, stimulated a more active participation by the EU in efforts towards formation of a legally binding instrument: the Cartagena Protocol on Biosafety.

2 Open issues under the Cartagena Protocol: liability and redress

One of the most remarkable characteristics of multilateral environmental agreements is that most of them have some kind of open clauses. This is the international approach to addressing issues that need a decision but are not ready for a full agreement. In some cases, these clauses are the way to address scientific uncertainties; in others, they hide the absence of total agreement. In all cases, they are perceived as a way to keep matters under open discussion. The Cartagena Protocol is not an exception in this regard, and its main enabling clause relates to the issue of liability and redress.

There are many peculiar features connected with the inclusion of this clause in the Protocol that were relevant in its subsequent process of negotiation. Article 27 was an important part of the final agreement that led to the adoption of the Cartagena Protocol. At a certain point in the discussion, some badges with 'No Liability, No Protocol' clauses made clear the importance of this issue for some countries, in particular for developing countries that were concerned about their limited capacity for risk assessment and risk management. However, it is also true that it was not among the open issues that were closed in the final deal because it had been closed previously during the 6th Meeting of the Biosafety Working Group in Cartagena de Indias (Colombia) in 1999.

It is peculiar how the issue of liability and redress, even though it was not the final element to be closed, was crucial to the adoption of the Cartagena Protocol. This was peculiar because most of the liability regimes, at least those established at the international level, involved some cases of damage that had actually occurred

---

10   Alejandro Lago Candeira *et al.*, 'GMOs and Resolution of Conflicts under the WTO', *European Food and Feed Law Review*, Vol. 4 (2009), pp. 282–294.

11   This argument or idea had been also used by developing countries in the negotiation of the Nagoya Protocol on access to genetic resources and fair and equitable sharing of the benefits derived from their utilisation (ABS), although in this case it was a convincing argument as the ABS is the third objective of the CBD.

before the start of negotiations. These also cover hazardous activities, usually ultra-hazardous ones. In the case of LMOs, there has not been any known case of damage caused by their transboundary movement – 'there was no LMO equivalent of the Torrey Canyon disaster or Chernobyl'.[12] Thus, views of the negotiation of the Cartagena Protocol on this issue were extremely polarised, with those that wanted to include a full-fledged liability and redress regime into the Protocol standing opposed to those who denied the need of such a regime. Indeed, some delegates also argued that the introduction of a specific liability and redress regime related to biosafety could be interpreted as an unjustified discrimination to be used as a trade barrier. In this way, the heated debate over the issue of financial security continued until the very end of the negotiation on the Supplementary Protocol.[13] The only difference from the 1999 negotiations was that at the time of the Supplementary Protocol, the confrontation was between Southern countries only, rather than being a North-South conflict as in 1999.

After lengthy discussions, it was clear that there would not be an acceptable biosafety protocol for the African group without a provision on liability and redress. Consequently, a middle ground solution, namely the insertion of an enabling clause, started to emerge as a possible compromise. The final agreement acknowledged that this issue would not be resolved during the Cartagena Protocol negotiations and that more time was needed.

Open issues in an international environmental instrument and ways to handle them are key to the conclusion of negotiations. Liability and redress was a key issue in obtaining the final compromise leading to adoption of the Cartagena Protocol. The EU, as one of the major supporters of this agreement, was politically bound by it. The political support that the EU gave to the Cartagena Protocol was reaffirmed by the fact that eight of its 15 EU Member States, plus the EU as a group, were Parties to the Protocol when it entered into force on 11 September 2003, and by the fact that 18 of its 25 Member States,[14] again plus the EU as a group, were Parties to the Protocol by the time its first COP-MOP was held in February 2004 in Kuala Lumpur, Malaysia.[15] At this Kuala-Lumpur meeting, the negotiating process under Article 27 officially began (Decision BS I/8).

II The EU context: the Directive 2004/35 on environmental liability

The EU was bound and very much attached to the Cartagena Protocol, but it was also bound by its internal legislation on environmental liability. The adoption of

12   Kate Cook, 'Liability: "No Liability, No Protocol"', in C. Bail, R. Falkner and H. Marquard, see note 3, pp. 372–373.
13   See Chapter 9 of this book, by Rodrigo C. A. Lima.
14   The reference here to the EU of the twenty-five member States is anticipating the official date of the enlargement of the EU to twenty-five member States (1 May 2004) in order to highlight the political commitment to this instrument.
15   The high relevance at the political level of the Cartagena Protocol for the EU could also be demonstrated by the fact that, at the end of 2004, twenty-six of the twenty-seven member States of the EU (plus the EU as a group) were Parties to the Protocol.

the Directive 2004/35 on environmental liability (EU-ELD) in 2004 was preceded by a long and difficult discussion at the EU level. The first document where the Commission presented this issue for public discussion was the 1993 Green Paper on remedying environmental damage,[16] in which the European Commission suggested 'individual and collective compensation mechanisms under a civil law system'.[17] This preliminary proposal by the Commission certainly could have opened the debate on the issues of environmental liability for the first time at the European level, but unfortunately the proposal found direct opposition from the industry, which led to its progressive abandonment by the Commission. Fortunately, this development attracted the attention of the European Parliament, which adopted in April 1994 a resolution calling on the Commission to submit a proposal for a directive on civil liability in respect of environmental damage. The issue of environmental liability was raised by the Parliament on several occasions, stressing in particular the need to have liability provisions in existing community legislation in the field of biotechnology.

It took the Commission seven years to present a new proposal, the White Paper on Environmental Liability (2000),[18] which introduced a new line clearly differentiating between damage to biodiversity and the contamination, on one hand, and traditional damage, on the other. Under this proposal, traditional damage would remain under the competence of Member States, although some basic provisions would be established at the EU level in order to ensure coherence.

The regulation of liability relating to GMOs, as previously mentioned, was one of the main reasons for the proposal on environmental liability. The second paragraph of the foreword of the White Paper on Environmental Liability (2000) already made reference to the specific need to address liability relating to GMOs, echoing the serious public concern that GMOs may affect the health of European citizens or may have negative effects on the environment. Some Member States linked their assessment of the proposal to the question of liability for environmental damage connected to the deliberate release and sale of GMOs, leading to a strong connection between the general proposal and the specific issue of environmental liability caused by GMOs.

The core idea of the White Paper was to introduce an administrative law system for damage to biodiversity and contaminated land. In this regard, the Commission proposal was clearly US oriented. In the US, environmental clean-up, at federal level, is in the hands of the Environmental Protection Agency. 'The Commission thought that the administrative law approach in the USA was reasonable; it only

---

16   Communication from the Commission to the Council, the Parliament and the Economic and Social Committee: Green Paper on Remedying Environmental Damage, COM (93) 47 final (14 May 1993). Available at http://ec.europa.eu/green-papers/pdf/environmental_damage_gp_com_93_47.pdf (accessed 1 August 2013).

17   Gerd Winter, Jan H. Jans, Richard Macrory and Ludwig Krämer, 'Weighing up the EC Environmental Liability Directive', *Journal of Environmental Law*, Vol. 20, Issue 2 (2008), p. 164.

18   White Paper on Environmental Liability presented by the Commission, COM (2000) 66 final (9 February 2000). Available at http://ec.europa.eu/environment/legal/liability/pdf/el_full.pdf (accessed 1 August 2013).

tried to avoid the very high litigation costs in the USA'.[19] The concept of the administrative approach, therefore, was not original to the EC, but was very much influenced by the system already put in place 20 years earlier in the US.[20] The proposal of the administrative approach did not meet much opposition by the EU Member States, as they were very reluctant to make concessions on anything related to traditional damage, an area with important differences between the current common law and civil law approaches of different EU Member States. They were not prepared to change them at a national level.

These strong lines of the debate forced the Commission to abandon any proposal on the approximation of laws related to traditional damage, leaving only the so-called 'administrative approach' on the final proposal, now covered under Directive 2004/35 on environmental liability with regard to the prevention and remedying of environmental damage.[21]

The administrative approach is based on the designation of a competent public authority in charge of the system. Competent public authorities play a fundamental role, ensuring that environmental damage is prevented and repaired. Their normal duties under an administrative approach are to establish which polluter has caused the damage (and, under EU-ELD, the imminent threat of damage), to assess the significance of the damage, and to determine which remedial measures should be taken. The main obligation is nevertheless borne not by the public authority, but by the polluter, that is the liability is channelled to the operator. The operator has the obligation to take response measures in cases where environmental damage has occurred or where there is an imminent threat that such may occur. This is one of the main merits of the administrative approach, its preventive character, because there is no need to wait – indeed, there is an obligation not to wait for damage to occur. The operator, even the competent authority, is able to take measures where there is an imminent threat of damage. With this approach, the competent authority becomes an active participant that can directly take measures where the operator has failed to do so and, if necessary, later look for the reimbursement of the cost of those measures from the operator.

The second merit of the administrative approach as compared to most of the civil liability regimes is that the public authority is a key feature in avoiding or redressing so-called 'orphan damage' to the environment. Civil systems are rooted on property rights. Thus, in most cases with environmental damage, there would be many environmental assets that might not be covered, or only covered in a very limited way, by the civil liability regimes.

Another important merit of the administrative approach is that it channels liability to the operator (strict liability), and this reinforces the preventive character

---

19   Winter *et al.*, see note 17, p. 165.

20   Oil Pollution Act 1990 and its natural resource damage assessment regulations (NRDA). See Edwards H. P. Brans, 'Liability for Damage to Public Natural Resources under the 2004 EC Environmental Liability Directive Standing and Assessment of Damages', *Environmental Law Review*, Vol. 7 (2005), p. 90.

21   Directive 2004/35/CE, see note 1.

of the system, giving an element of predictability to the market. This is because the operator knows in advance the likelihood of causing damage, and thus it can prepare for its potential consequences through internal procedures (e.g. insurance or financial guarantees). Finally, the administrative approach does not substitute the classic civil liability regimes, but does have a clear complementary character. This is also a positive value, as in other fields the existence of different liability systems entails their operation as alternatives and not as a complement.

The fact that the process is left to the discretion of the competent public authority may be considered a demerit with the potential to become an advantage. This could lead to some arbitrary interpretation or uneven implementation. However, in the case of the EU Directive on Environmental Liability, this issue has been solved through the 'request for action' and the 'review procedures', respectively established under Articles 12 and 13. The request for action consists of the right of certain affected or interested natural or legal persons to submit to the competent authority any observations relating to instances of environmental damage or imminent threat of damage. This request for action must be accompanied by relevant information, and the competent authority, if the information is plausible, must take action, informing the affected or interested person of the steps taken. The review procedures consist of the right of the affected or interested person to have access to a court or similar procedures for review of the decisions taken by the competent authority.

III The negotiation: the famous 'two-staged approach' of the EU

The adoption of the Directive, just after the initiation of the negotiation process in the context of Article 27 of the Cartagena Protocol, entirely conditioned the approach of the EU to this negotiation. First of all, the internal EU process was far from complete with the adoption of the directive, as directives need to be transposed by the Member States into their national systems. In order to do that, each directive establishes a deadline for its implementation, which was 30 April 2007 in the case of the EU-ELD. The degree of complexity involved in the implementation of the Directive at the national level was made apparent by the fact that the Commission instituted infringement procedures against eight Member States for the late transposition into national law of the Directive, although only six of them ended in court procedures before the European Court of Justice. According to the European Commission, transposition of the Directive was completed by July 2010,[22] four months before the final adoption of the Supplementary Protocol.

Another important background element to confirm the EU position in this negotiation was the negative experience under other environmental liability regimes based on civil liability, in particular by their lack of effectiveness. The

---

22 Information retrieved from http://ec.europa.eu/environment/legal/liability/index.htm (accessed 1 August 2013).

several instruments on environmental liability and redress had been negotiated and adopted, but most of them were (and still are) awaiting their entry into force.[23]

The main question addressed by the EU when preparing for this negotiation was how to design and implement an effective liability and redress regime for LMOs that accounted for such limitations and conditions. The natural answer was to propose a regime to be developed in two stages: first, through development of guidelines that could be easily adopted by the COP-MOP and quickly implemented by all the Parties to the Cartagena Protocol, then decide on whether further steps were needed, such as a legally binding instrument on the subject, after proper experience with the implementation of those guidelines was gained.

The first step would mean that all Parties to the Cartagena Protocol would have to implement the guidelines, avoiding one of the major problems that other environmental liability regimes face, namely the difficult internal ratifications processes at the national level that impede the minimum number of ratifications needed to allow entry into force of those instruments. The second step would be in practice a review process of the guidelines subject to a certain period of time and to the appropriate decision of the COP-MOP on further measures. This so-called 'two-staged approach' was indeed very similar to the approach that the EU had followed in the negotiation of the Cartagena Protocol. It was thought to be the optimum procedure through which to address the EU internal situation on the subject and to give an opportunity at the international level for effectiveness in the field of environmental liability, where such a trait is normally the exception rather than the rule.

The main disadvantage of this approach is that it assumes from the beginning that most of the measures are going to be taken at the national level. This assumption clashed with the views of those who defend truly international liability and redress rules and who wanted the development and negotiation of such a regime in order to compensate for their lack of capacity to perform appropriate risk assessments at a national level. These proponents were thinking about the classic liability regimes for oil pollution or other hazardous activities rather than of a new regime that focuses on standardising measures implemented at the national level. Another important shortcoming of this approach is that the first stage may not address adequately the issue of enforcement of national liability rules across jurisdictions based on a COP decision.

IV The assumption of a legally binding instrument on liability and redress

The proposal of the EU of having a 'two-staged approach' was vehemently opposed by those countries that during the negotiation of the Cartagena Protocol had defended the need to have a legally binding regime on liability and redress.

23   See Chapter 1 of this book, by Akiho Shibata.

In their view, the EU proposal in particular seemed to question or reopen the agreement obtained in Article 27 of the Cartagena Protocol to elaborate the 'international rules and procedures in the field of liability and redress'. Unfortunately, this view connected the liability issue with the old sensitivities arising from the negotiation of the Cartagena Protocol, and it was difficult or even impossible to look into the substance of the issue. The negotiation of those rules over all those years showed that the appropriate implementation of the rules of the Cartagena Protocol could reduce the relevance of liability and redress rules. However, other Parties were still very much attached to the political compromise reached at the time of adoption of the Cartagena Protocol and were not prepared to have anything less than a legally binding instrument, no matter the content.

This lack of readiness to even consider the two-staged approach proposed by the EU, which was indeed a lack of readiness to consider the position and situation of the EU in the negotiation, was a determining factor in the future direction and the result of the overall negotiation. The EU, as a major actor of both the CBD and the Cartagena Protocol, could not afford to be left outside of the results of this negotiation, and if the only possible outcome was a legally binding regime, the degree of flexibility for the EU was going to be strictly reduced to the limits of its internal legislation. The only room for manoeuvre for the EU in this context, while supporting both its negotiating partners who successfully adopted the final compromise under the Cartagena Protocol and a legally binding instrument on liability and redress arising in connection with LMOs, was to have something at the international level that would not collide with the EU system.

The EU offered varying external signals of these closely linked factors, although some of these signals might have been difficult to detect or interpret from outside the EU. The major signal to the outside world, apart from the repeated insistence on the two-staged approach, lay in its representation, namely the composition of EU negotiators. It is obvious that not many can follow or understand (often even within the EU) how the EU is organised and represented in international negotiations. If that is a common feature in international negotiations, it is even more complex in a negotiation involving issues of 'shared competences' such as the environmental ones. The normal practice, at least until the Lisbon Treaty entered into force (December 2009), was that the Presidency of the Council coordinated the European position and conducted the negotiation on behalf of the EU and its Member States, with the support of interested colleagues from other Member States and from the European Commission. However, there was also an established rule that 'the granting of competence to the Community in internal legislation meant that such competence also extended to related external policy'.[24] Thus, if there is EU legislation in a particular field, this will have a direct effect on the exercise of the external competence of the EU and its Member States. The

---

24   John Vogler, 'The European Contribution to Global Environmental Governance', *International Affairs*, Vol. 81, No. 4 (July 2005), p. 839.

normal way to articulate this is through a concession by the Council to negotiating mandates to the European Commission. In this case, there was clearly European legislation on the topic (Directive 2004/35), and therefore a mandate was given to the European Commission to negotiate on behalf of the EU. However, the EU legislation did not cover all types of liability, as explained above. It covered only the so-called administrative type, meaning in this case that the Presidency was entitled to negotiate issues related to civil liability but not covered by the EU-ELD. This forced the EU to have permanently two negotiators at the negotiating table (Commission and Presidency), with clear separate areas of intervention.

The European Commission obtained its first mandate in June 2007 based on the two-staged approach. During the 5th meeting of the Open-Ended *Ad Hoc* Working Group on Liability and Redress (*Ad Hoc* WG) held in Cartagena de Indias, Colombia, in March 2008, the Co-Chairs presented their 'Core Elements Paper', based on four key elements: (1) the adoption of a legally binding instrument on the administrative approach; (2) the adoption of guidelines on civil liability; (3) the establishment of supplementary mechanisms of compensation; and (4) measures on capacity building.[25]

The original EU position, based on a two-staged approach contained in the negotiating mandate to the Commission, was amended before the COP-MOP4 (Bonn, May 2008) in order to provide the negotiators with flexibility if the 'Core Elements Paper' presented by the Co-Chairs was accepted by the other Parties. It would have been a bit strange if the EU could not accept a legally binding system based on the proposal it drew from its own system. The basis of the new mandate was that the EU could accept a legally binding instrument on liability and redress under Article 27 as far as it contained the administrative approach and it was compatible with the existing EU system established through the EU-ELD.

After long discussions during the Bonn meeting, as the failure to meet the four year deadline established in Article 27 was imminent, the Decision adopted by the COP-MOP4 (Decision BS-IV/12) at least contained the elements of a political agreement to keep the negotiation aimed 'towards a legally binding instrument on the administrative approach (with one provision on civil liability), and towards a non-legally binding instrument on civil liability' for two more years until the COP-MOP5 in Nagoya, Japan. This negotiation was entrusted to a setting much more reduced in size, namely the so-called Group of the Friends of the Co-Chairs (GFCC), which was composed of a limited number of participants from various regions and specifically named interested Parties.

The expectation in Decision BS-IV/12 was for one meeting of GFCC in 2009 and, if deemed necessary by the Co-Chairs in order to conclude the negotiations, a second meeting in 2010. In reality, though, the positions of Parties were not that close to one another, especially in their details, and the two meetings initially anticipated were extended to four in the end, concluding only on the starting day of the COP-MOP5 in Nagoya.

---

25   See Appendix 4 of this book for the 'Core Elements Paper'.

V The outcome: does the Supplementary Protocol really introduce the administrative approach in other Parties apart from the EU and its Member States?

Once the EU amended its negotiating mandate and was able to work towards a legally binding instrument on the administrative approach, its new priorities on this last stage of the negotiation (2009–2010) were to avoid any conflict between the new system and the EU-ELD, to keep the EU system without having to introduce changes,[26] and to have a liability regime that was as meaningful as possible and based on the administrative approach. In connection to the latter, the EU struggled in the negotiations when compelled to object to the adoption of a proposal under the provision on civil liability that could have functioned as an escape clause to avoid application of the administrative approach. Although the political agreement reached at COP-MOP4 was intended to work towards a legally binding instrument on the administrative approach and a non-legally binding instrument on civil liability, it became evident that some negotiating partners still had a very different regime in mind.[27] That issue arose each time the provision on civil liability within the legally binding instrument was discussed. It was also evident that different Parties were looking for enough flexibility in the provisions of the new instrument to interpret the system in a way that they could keep applying their national systems, some of which were more oriented towards civil law than administrative.

The final outcome is a mixture, of course, of all the different situations and contexts that interacted during the negotiation, but in this case the EU position clearly drove the outcome. The first important remark after the statement of objective presents the definition of damage. One of the most difficult elements of the negotiations of liability and redress regimes is the definition of 'damage to the environment' because these regimes hardly ever provide a definition of the 'environment' as a subject of legal protection. The Supplementary Protocol has a proper definition of damage and a proper definition of response measures, key for meaningful implementation of this system.

However, does the Nagoya-Kuala Lumpur Supplementary Protocol really introduce the administrative approach to liability at the international level? The core elements of the administrative approach are present in the Supplementary Protocol, in particular the adoption of response measures by the operator and the designation of the competent authority and its leading role in the process with the establishment of its different duties are there. It is also true that other key features are difficult to find in the adopted outcome, such as the use of response measures not only for damage, but under the 'imminent threat' of damage. In the Supplementary Protocol, there is only a diffuse reference to the imminent threat of damage

---

26 See Chapter 12 of this book, by Edward H. P. Brans and Dorith H. Dongelmans on the implementation of the Supplementary Protocol in the EU.
27 See Chapters 7 and 8 of this book, by Gurdial Singh Nijar, and Elmo Thomas and Mahlet Teshome Kebede, respectively, on a civil liability provision within the Supplementary Protocol.

through the phrase 'sufficient likelihood that damage will result if timely response measures are not taken' (Article 5 (3)). It is also true that the search by some Parties for flexibility at the national level has left some provisions in the Supplementary Protocol that could be interpreted to maintain business as usual if a (national) assessment of the national measures on civil liability affirmed that the scope of the response measures was already covered by those existing rules on civil liability. The most significant of these open provisions that could lead to the non-implementation of the brand new administrative approach is Article 5 (7).

Another important element of the final battle of the negotiation was the possible requirement of financial securities. The adopted article on financial securities[28] evidently demonstrates the discrepancies not only with a very soft language describing the freedom of the Parties to establish such at a national level, but also by making strange references to preambular paragraphs and odd requests to the Secretariat to undertake a study on different elements of the financial guarantees at the first COP-MOP after the entering into force of the Supplementary Protocol.

Both of these elements, namely the imminent threat and financial securities, were clearly identified by the LMO producer countries as a tool for potential disguised restrictions on trade. The final outcome reflects this interest so that the system will not promote the creation of extra burden on the marketing of LMOs at the international level.

VI Conclusion

The EU played an important role in the negotiation of the rules and procedures on liability and redress under Article 27 of the Cartagena Protocol; its role and positions clearly determined the outcome of the Nagoya-Kuala Lumpur Supplementary Protocol. Its role was conditioned by both external and internal forces. Externally, the compromise reached for the adoption of the Cartagena Protocol affected the EU role. Internally, the EU role was influenced by the adoption in 2004 of its internal rules on environmental liability (EU-ELD) that covered environmental damage caused by, among other activities, GMOs. However, it was not the intention of the EU to export its new rules on environmental liability to the international community; to the contrary, the EU was afraid of doing so due to its lack of experience in implementation. That the outcome of the administrative approach was the main element of the Supplementary Protocol resulted from the assumption of some Parties to the Cartagena Protocol, and not of the EU, that the only possible result of the negotiations under Article 27 was a legally binding instrument.

Nevertheless, the administrative approach is clearly recognised in the Supplementary Protocol through the establishment of the operator's obligation to take response measures in cases of environmental damage, and the central role of the competent public authorities in the process and their duties are well defined. The Supplementary Protocol is extremely open in many of its provisions under the clear assumption that the real measures are left to be taken at the national level. Under that perspective, only time will allow us to assess the real impact of this new and, in a sense, revolutionary instrument.

28   See Chapter 9 of this book, by Rodrigo C. A. Lima.

6 A scientific perspective on the Supplementary Protocol

Reynaldo Ariel Alvarez-Morales

I Introduction

The objective of the Nagoya-Kuala Lumpur Supplementary Protocol on Liability and Redress to the Cartagena Protocol on Biosafety (Supplementary Protocol), according to its Article 1, is 'to contribute to the conservation and sustainable use of biological diversity, taking also into account risks to human health, by providing international rules and procedures in the field of liability and redress relating to living modified organisms'. It is, therefore, a legal instrument that sets the minimum international standards on liability and redress for damage to the environment resulting from the use of living modified organisms (LMOs). Although conceived as a legal document, the nature of its subject matter is highly technical and scientific, and in some instances this fact guided the course of the decisions that were taken during the negotiations. However, the lack of a thorough and common under-standing on some of these technical issues also contributed, in some cases, to a lack of agreement, such as in the case of whether the term 'products thereof' was to be included in the document or not.

   This chapter explores the scientific justifications for some of the controversial provisions in the Supplementary Protocol, namely the definition of 'operator' in Article 2 (2) (c) and the ultimate deletion of 'products thereof' from the scope of the Supplementary Protocol (Article 3).

II The definition of 'operator'

One of the issues discussed was the very nature of LMOs, as some Parties regarded LMOs as 'intrinsically dangerous', whereas for other Parties LMOs could not be placed in the same category as radioactive material or chemical wastes. In this regard, it is worth noting that although Parties recognised the need for an LMO-specific liability regime, in part because of the potential to generate very different LMOs through modern biotechnology and in part because of the potential damage they may cause, it is also recognised that for such damage to occur, a series of biologically driven complex events have to take place that are also case specific. These biological events may be described in a simple form as follows:

(a) The LMOs must interact with the environment, either by themselves or as a result of the spread of the transgene to sexually compatible species, which would then become LMOs themselves and would be in a position to exert the damage.

(b) The LMOs must multiply and persist as a population, sorting intricate environmental interactions governed in most cases by complex factors that are part of natural selection pressures, such as changing weather patterns and biotic and abiotic interactions.

(c) The LMOs or their descendants, once established, must then exert a negative effect on the environment such as displacing native organisms or reducing the population of non-target organisms. This is what is known as the 'pathway to harm'.

This complex process will most likely take place over a relatively long period of time and will be dependent upon: (a) the trait conferred by the transgene; (b) the biology and genetics of the recipient organism; and (c) the receiving environment. These are the three elements that define a case in the 'case-by-case' approach used by the risk assessment analysis under the Cartagena Protocol on Biosafety (Cartagena Protocol). When the events mentioned above are revisited in the context of some of the other issues included in the Supplementary Protocol, such as the definition of the liable entity, which is identified as the 'operator', it becomes evident that an initial effort to define *a priori* who the operator was would not have worked.

Under the Supplementary Protocol, it is clear that to find liability, three elements need to be clearly established: (1) damage to the conservation and sustainable use of biological diversity, taking also into account risks to human health; (2) a causal link, that is establishment in fact and at law that the harm is directly attributed to the LMO or its use; and (3) existence of a person who can be identified as responsible. Only then does the issue of redress for the harm established arise.

However, identifying the 'operator' may not be simple. One must assume that when an importing Party has agreed to receive an LMO for the first time, they would do so in accord with the advance informed agreement (AIA) procedure or with their national biosafety legislation, as well as the provisions in the Cartagena Protocol,[1] and therefore a decision by the importing Party to receive the LMO in question would have been based on the results of a risk assessment performed as described in Article 15[2] of the Cartagena Protocol and following the case-by-case approach. If the three elements of the case-by-case approach described above in

1   Article 7 (Application of the Advance Informed Agreement Procedure), Cartagena Protocol. The specific legal regime of AIA is established in Articles 8 to 10 and 12 of the Cartagena Protocol.
2   Article 15 (Risk Assessment), Cartagena Protocol: '1. Risk assessments undertaken pursuant to this Protocol shall be carried out in a scientifically sound manner, in accordance with Annex III and taking into account recognized risk assessment techniques. Such risk assessments shall be based, at a minimum, on information provided in accordance with Article 8 and other available scientific evidence in order to identify and evaluate the possible adverse effects of living modified organisms on the conservation and sustainable use of biological diversity, taking also into account risks to human health.'

(a) through (c) are maintained when the LMO is released into the environment, the results of the risk assessment may very well prove to be accurate and no harm would occur. In other words, if the characteristics of the LMO are maintained, if the LMO is used for its intended purpose, if this use occurs in the intended receiving environment, and if the applicable risk management measures[3] are effectively implemented, no conceivable damage resulting in the legal liability of some person could occur. However, if unpredicted effects or an unidentified harm occurs, which was not possible to identify with the knowledge available to the risk assessors at the time of the evaluation, and if this results in damage to biodiversity or its sustainable use, the liable entity may turn out to be either the developer or the producer.

However, in other cases, the identity of the operator may not be easily determined. One can imagine a scenario in which an LMO, after it is imported following the AIA procedure, is released outside the intended environment and damage occurs after all the necessary events that comprise the 'pathway to harm' take place. When the damage is identified, a causal link must be established between the damage and the LMO, even though this may not be easy to achieve. Most likely, a considerable period of time will have passed since its importation, and either the LMO or its genetically modified progeny, which may be a wild relative, has had time to spread beyond the environment where the intended release occurred. In this scenario, how or why was the LMO released into an unintended environment? The reasons may be many and may include, among other possibilities: an accidental release; an intentional release without knowledge of the nature of the organism; an intentional release with knowledge of the nature of the organism but without the knowledge of the legal conditions required for its release; or an illicit release and use of the LMO. Deciding who would be liable in these cases may prove difficult as there may be many 'intermediaries' and many circumstances that would require thorough evaluation.

Therefore, an agreement was reached under which the operator was defined as:

> any person in direct or indirect control of the LMO which could, as appropriate and as determined by domestic law, include, *inter alia*, the permit holder, person who placed the LMO on the market, developer, producer, notifier, exporter, importer, carrier or supplier.
>
> (Article 2 (2) (c))

III 'Products thereof'

Another controversial issue already mentioned was whether or not 'products thereof' should have been included in the scope of the Supplementary Protocol.

---

3 Article 16 (Risk management), Cartagena Protocol: '1. The Parties shall, taking into account Article 8 (g) of the Convention, establish and maintain appropriate mechanisms, measures and strategies to regulate, manage and control risks identified in the risk assessment provisions of this Protocol associated with the use, handling and transboundary movement of living modified organisms.'

The Cartagena Protocol[4] refers to living modified organisms that may have adverse effects on the conservation and sustainable use of biological diversity. However, a reference to 'products thereof' is made in Article 20, Annex I, and Annex III of the Cartagena Protocol. The definition of 'products thereof' used in the Cartagena Protocol is: 'processed materials that are of living modified organism origin, containing detectable novel combinations of replicable genetic material obtained through the use of modern biotechnology'.

On the one hand, some argued that because they were mentioned in relation to risk assessment, the risks identified through the risk assessment process may materialise and hinder conservation and sustainable use of biological diversity, taking also into account risks to human health, therefore falling within the objective of the Supplementary Protocol. However, when assessing possible risks to the environment, the information required by the risk assessors relates directly to the LMO and not to the products derived from these, because it is understood that what interacts with the environment is the LMO itself and not its non-living products.

Nevertheless, the mention of 'detectable novel combinations of replicable genetic material' in the definition of 'products thereof' was a contentious issue. What does replicable mean in this context? Most dictionaries will only provide a definition such as 'capable of replication', which is still ambiguous as it does not necessarily imply 'self-replication'. The genetic material (DNA in most cases) cannot replicate itself without some minimal elements such as the enzyme that synthesises new DNA (DNA-Polymerase), the building blocks (dATP, dGTP, dCTP, dCTP) of DNA, and ATP as an energy supply; this all occurs only in an environment with the proper pH, ionic strength, and temperature. All of these elements and conditions can be found within living cells or can be provided in a cell-free environment in a laboratory.

The term 'replicable' may be understood to mean that the genetic material can be replicated outside a living cell, such as in a laboratory and with expert human assistance. If DNA is obtained from a product derived from an LMO and replicated in a laboratory, does this have any meaning within the scope of the Supplementary Protocol? Most certainly not, as it is not the DNA itself that interacts with the environment, and therefore the replicated DNA would have to be introduced into an organism and this, in turn, released into the environment. This constitutes a completely different case.

However, there is also an argument that free DNA can find its way into an organism and this in turn can interact with the environment through a phenomenon called Horizontal Gene Transfer (HGT). For instance, DNA is ubiquitous in soil as it is released during the decay of plant material, animals and microorganisms, and this DNA may be taken up and incorporated into the

---

4   Article 4 (Scope), Cartagena Protocol: 'This Protocol shall apply to the transboundary movement, transit, handling and use of all living modified organisms that may have adverse effects on the conservation and sustainable use of biological diversity, taking also into account risks to human health.'

genome of some bacteria through a process known as 'genetic transformation' or 'natural transformation'.[5] Most of the time, the acquired DNA is lost as in most cases it may not be stably integrated or it cannot be of use to the bacterium if it includes regulatory signals of plant, animal or fungal origin, as these cannot be properly interpreted by the bacterial regulatory system. In most cases, DNA from other soil microorganisms is the material used by soil bacteria, and this is an important mechanism by which bacteria acquire resistance to antibiotics and toxic metals or the ability to use certain chemical compounds.

HGT involving plants, animals or microorganisms has been accepted as a mechanism of evolution,[6] and very specific interactions such as those between soil protozoan and bacteria or between plants and bacteria[7] have been described. Nevertheless, this is far from sound evidence that DNA exchanged through HGT is a common and significant process in animals and plants that could impact the environment; the process could be very different if genetically modified bacteria are the organisms to be released into the environment.

To settle the differences between those that wanted the mention of 'products thereof' in the text and those that wanted it removed, it was agreed that although the reference to 'products thereof' would be removed from the operative text of the Supplementary Protocol, a reference to this issue would be recorded in the report of the fifth meeting of the Parties to the Cartagena Protocol. The agreed text reads as follows:

> It emerged during the negotiations of the Supplementary Protocol that Parties to the Protocol hold different understandings of the application of Article 27 of the Protocol to processed materials that are of living modified organism-origin. One such understanding is that Parties may apply the Supplementary Protocol to damage caused by such processed materials, provided that a causal link is established between the damage and the living modified organism in question.[8]

IV Conclusion

In the implementation of the Supplementary Protocol, science is going to play a major role. Identifying damage, determining its significance, quantifying the damage, and proposing and implementing mitigation or restoration measures will not be simple tasks. Therefore, the principal roles of scientists should be to

---

5   OECD, Guidance document on horizontal gene transfer between bacteria, ENV/JM/MONO (2010), p. 22, para. 40.

6   Charles G. Kurland, Björn Canbäck, and Otto G. Berg, 'Horizontal gene transfer: A critical view', *Proceedings of National Academy of Sciences of the USA*, Vol. 100 (2003), pp. 9658–9662.

7   Aaron O. Richardson and Jeffrey D. Palmer, 'Horizontal gene transfer in plants', *Journal of Experimental Botany*, Vol. 58 (2007), pp. 1–9.

8   Report of the Fifth Meeting of the Conference of the Parties to the Convention on Biological Diversity Serving as the Meeting of the Parties to the Cartagena Protocol on Biosafety, UNEP/CBD/BS/COP-MOP/5/17 (2010), para. 133, reproduced in Appendix 3 of this book.

propose the implementation of effective management/control measures, to monitor the performance of LMOs in the environment, and to examine the results of these actions and implement risk management strategies accordingly, including mitigation responses when necessary. In this way, science will rightly accompany and support compliance with the objective of the Cartagena Protocol and its Supplementary Protocol.

7 Civil liability in the Supplementary Protocol

Gurdial Singh Nijar

I What is civil liability?

Civil liability is the attachment of responsibility for any damage through the civil process (as distinct from the criminal process). Hence, it is not the State but the person suffering the damage who initiates this process by bringing an action against the person causing the damage. The remedy sought is either monetary compensation or injunctive relief intended to prevent or remove the source of the damage. Generally, all national legal systems provide a person the right of recourse against the responsible party. To recover, a causal link must be established between the damage and the source of the damage, in this case the living modified organism (LMO); the nature of the damage must be foreseeable as arising from the activity; and the person to whom the damage may be caused must also be foreseeable. The broad notion is grounded on the principle of *ubi jus ibi remedium* – where there is a grievance, there must be a remedy.

The approach for establishing international rules and procedures for such damage recovery at the national level in respect of LMOs moved from one country to another is to establish ground rules recognisable across jurisdictions as to the kind of damage recoverable; these rules include how, when, where and against whom civil action may be initiated and pursued. The rules are thus rendered intelligible to all parties affected – the plaintiff pursuing the action, as well as the defendant against whom the action is initiated.

Civil liability may also be contrasted against the administrative approach. Civil liability is established through the judicial system of a country, where liability may be contested. Under the administrative approach, the administrative authorities decide what should be done. There is no adjudication by the courts.

II Civil liability under the Supplementary Protocol

The civil liability regime under the Nagoya-Kuala Lumpur Supplementary Protocol on Liability and Redress (Supplementary Protocol) includes just one article on civil liability, namely Article 12. It reads as follows:

1   Parties shall provide, in their domestic law, for rules and procedures that address damage. To implement this obligation, Parties shall provide for

response measures in accordance with this Supplementary Protocol and may, as appropriate:

(a) Apply their existing domestic law, including, where applicable, general rules and procedures on civil liability;
(b) Apply or develop civil liability rules and procedures specifically for this purpose; or
(c) Apply or develop a combination of both.

2   Parties shall, with the aim of providing adequate rules and procedures in their domestic law on civil liability for material or personal damage associated with the damage as defined in Article 2, paragraph 2 (b):

(a) Continue to apply their existing general law on civil liability;
(b) Develop and apply or continue to apply civil liability law specifically for that purpose; or
(c) Develop and apply or continue to apply a combination of both.

3   When developing civil liability law as referred to in subparagraphs (b) or (c) of paragraphs 1 or 2 above, Parties shall, as appropriate, address, *inter alia*, the following elements:

(a) Damage;
(b) Standard of liability, including strict or fault-based liability;
(c) Channelling of liability, where appropriate;
(d) Right to bring claims.

1 Addressing damage by response measures

Article 12 obliges Parties to the Supplementary Protocol to include provisions for rules and procedures that address damage in their domestic law. 'Damage' is defined in Article 2 (2) (b), and what is 'significant' is to be determined on the basis of a non-exhaustive indicative list of factors set out in Article 2 (3).[1] To implement this obligation, Parties must provide for response measures. These measures are defined in Article 2 (d) as 'reasonable actions to (i) Prevent, minimize, contain, mitigate, or otherwise avoid damage, as appropriate; (ii) Restore biological diversity through actions to be undertaken in the following order of preference: (a) Restoration of biological diversity to the condition that existed before the damage occurred, or its nearest equivalent; and where the competent authority determines this is not possible; (b) Restoration by, *inter alia*, replacing the loss of biological diversity with other components of biological diversity for the same, or for another type of use either at the same or, as appropriate, at an alternative location'.

Parties can implement the obligation to provide such in their domestic law by exercising one of three options, namely: (a) by applying their existing domestic law, including general rules and procedures on civil liability, in other words a law that

1   For those provisions, see Appendix 1 of this book.

does not deal specifically with damage caused by LMOs; (b) by applying extant civil liability rules and procedures that deal specifically with such damage, that is a law that deals specifically with damage caused by LMOs, or, if there is no such specific law, then to develop such a law; or (c) by applying or developing a combination of both, that is the general and the specific rules and procedures.

2 Addressing material or personal damage

Article 12 (2) deals with civil liability and the traditional categories of damage, namely material or personal damage. This damage must be associated with 'an adverse effect on the conservation and sustainable use of biological diversity, taking also into account risks to human health'. It is not easy to envision what this damage may be.

In contrast with the unqualified obligation to provide a domestic law dealing with response measures in accordance with the Supplementary Protocol, Parties must 'aim to provide' adequate rules and procedures in their domestic law on civil liability for such damage. 'Aim' means to strive for or to try to attain the objective or purpose. Although the obligation is not absolute, the article nonetheless requires Parties to make *bona fide* and concrete efforts to provide adequate rules and procedures for the damage envisaged. Parties must perform their obligations in good faith, as made explicit by the Vienna Convention on the Law of Treaties (*pacta sunt servanda*).

Again to implement the obligation, the Article prescribes three possible methods. For Parties, these are: (a) continuing to apply their existing general law on civil liability; (b) developing and applying or continue to apply civil liability law specifically for that purpose; or (c) developing and applying or continuing to apply a combination of both.

A law developed to deal specifically with damage referred to in either of the situations above must address, *inter alia*, the following elements: (a) damage; (b) the standard of liability, including strict or fault-based liability; (c) channelling of liability, where appropriate; and (d) the right to bring claims. First, these elements are standard in any regime dealing with damage arising from the commission of a tort. Second, there is no substantive content for each of these elements.

3 What the civil liability provision does not deal with

The Supplementary Protocol is spectacularly deficient in providing for an effective civil liability regime. It leaves it to the Parties to implement their existing laws or develop new laws to take response measures; they must also 'aim' to provide for remedies in respect of material or personal damage that is 'associated with adverse effects on the conservation and sustainable use of biodiversity'. It is hard to ascertain what such 'associated' damage may be. Nor were countries insisting on this narrowly circumscribed definition during the course of the negotiations able to concretely identify what such damage may be. Second, the elements prescribed for inclusion in a national law are unexceptional staple fare in any law that deals with damage for torts. There is no substantive content for any of the elements either – they are vacuous.

Over the several years of negotiations, many Parties that had initiated the need for a full-fledged civil liability regime had provided text on the minimum elements for such a regime. This included elaborate text on such elements as standard of liability, channelling of liability, interim relief, exemptions or mitigation, recourse against a third party by the person who is liable on the basis of strict liability, joint and several liability, apportionment of liability, limitation of liability, and coverage.[2]

III Prospective international regimes

A reasonably meaningful international civil liability regime could have taken any one of three possible forms.[3]

1 Transnational process regime

A transnational process regime would be process orientated. It would not establish substantive standards to be applied by national courts, but merely strengthen local remedies available by eliminating or minimising difficulties relating to such common elements as subject matter, jurisdiction over natural persons, the most convenient forum for preferred claims, the applicable law to decide questions in dispute, and enforcement of judgments.

Consider this example: An individual or legal person from Party A (referred to hereafter as a 'national') suffers damage as a result of the transboundary movement of LMOs. The damage is caused by the national of Party B. The Supplementary Protocol could enable the claimant (A's national) to sue in the courts of B on the same basis as B's nationals, that is as if A were also a national of B. A, as a State, would also be allowed access to B's courts for any damage it suffers. Provision could also be made to facilitate inspections, exchange of information and consultations between States. Such an approach has been adopted in the Convention on the Protection of the Environment between Denmark, Norway and Sweden (the 1974 Nordic Convention).[4] An international fund could be established to take care of the plaintiff who lacks or has limited resources to pursue his or her claim.

Even in such an approach, there are drawbacks. The main drawback is that the provisions of the Supplementary Protocol will be left to national courts to adjudicate. Claims may succeed in one court and not another. Then again, certain

2   Gurdial Singh Nijar, Sarah Lawson-Stopps and Gan Pei Fern, *Liability and Redress under the Cartagena Protocol on Biosafety: A Record of the Negotiations for Developing International Rules, Vol I* (Centre of Excellence for Biodiversity Law, 2008), p. 183.

3   Gurdial Singh Nijar, *Developing a Liability and Redress Regime under the Cartagena Protocol on Biosafety* (Institute for Agriculture and Trade Policy, 2000), pp. 50–52.

4   Convention on the protection of environment, adopted on 19 February 1974 and entered into force on 10 May 1976, *United Nations Treaty Series*, Vol. 1092, p. 279.

claims may be accepted in some jurisdictions and not in others. Claims for life and property damage are common to most, if not all, jurisdictions. However, jurisdictions differ in allowing claims for depletion of the environment or economic loss flowing from such damage. The quantum awarded may also vary greatly. Both the procedural and substantive rules for proving a case may also vary with different jurisdictions. This lack of uniformity could give rise to unfairness in an international system of dealing with exposure to common damage.

There are solutions to these problems. One is to allow country B's courts to apply A's more favourable laws. Alternatively, country A's courts could hear the claim applying A's own laws. A third option could give the claimant a chance to pursue remedies in the court the claimant feels will give the most favourable result.

Then finally, there is the problem of ensuring compliance by the State with its obligations.

2 Negotiated international private law regime

A negotiated international private law regime approach would be an improvement to the transnational process regime. It would establish a binding agreement specifying a body of liability law enforceable in domestic courts against private individuals. In other words, a Party to any such instrument would be compelled to enact national liability laws incorporating the elements specified in the international agreement it has signed. The specific content of each important element would also be specified.

Most multilateral environmental liability agreements of the past decade have adopted this approach. In addition to covering jurisdiction over foreign persons and entities and the enforcement of judgments, such a regime will set out clear internationally recognised liability standards. These would include standards on standing to sue, nature of liability, burden of proof, damages that could be claimed, and limits on recovery. Further provisions could deal with matters of ensuring recovery of compensation awarded, such as compulsory insurance and/or an international fund.

Once accepted, the civil liability instrument would become part of national law through self-execution, that is automatically without any other national implementing legislative or executive process, or it may become national law through implementing legislation. Such a law would largely do away with the lack of uniformity inherent to a transnational process regime.

Two examples of a negotiated international private law regime are the approach of the Convention on Civil Liability for Oil Pollution Damage, which deals with liability for pollution damage from oil spills[5] and the Basel Protocol on Liability and Compensation resulting from the Transboundary Movement of Hazardous

5 International Convention on Civil Liability for Oil Pollution Damage as amended, adopted on 29 November 1969, *United Nations Treaty Series*, Vol. 973, p. 3.

Wastes and their Disposal.[6] Several conventions in the field of nuclear energy[7] also adopt this approach.

Myriad complex issues must be dealt with, such as who is to be liable, the standard of liability, any financial limitations, types of damage recoverable, satisfaction of judgment, setting up of funds or other schemes (such as insurance) for that purpose, and liability of governments to pay for shortfalls. The acceptance of such a liability regime would require Parties to incorporate the agreed provisions in a national law. Then a person who suffers damage could seek relief from a domestic court of the appropriate Party. The choice of the court will be established by the instrument. This court will have to decide the claim by applying the rules on liability and compensation set out in the instrument.

An international fund regime would likely follow the successful conclusion of a negotiated private international law regime on liability and would likely be obligatory. There would be a fund authority with specific functions such as providing funds to satisfy a judgment where, for any reason, the funds are not otherwise forthcoming or are inadequate. Funds could also be made available to pursue litigation, to provide financial aid for emergency clean-up for the damage, and to indemnify a person upon successful conclusion of the litigation. An example of such a fund is established under the 1971 Fund Convention for Oil Pollution Damages.[8]

3 International arbitral regime

In the preceding regimes, governments take the role of facilitator for private parties as they pursue their claims. The government's role is to negotiate and create an

6   Basel Protocol on Liability and Compensation for Damage Resulting from Transboundary Movements of hazardous wastes and their disposal, adopted by Decision V/29 on 10 December 1999, UNEP/CHW.5/29 (10 December 1999), Annex III.

7   The 'Paris Convention' regime was developed by the OECD and so is not global in scope. It comprises: Convention on Third Party Liability in the Field of Nuclear Energy (adopted on 29 July 1960, *United Nations Treaty Series*, Vol. 956, p. 251), and the Convention Supplementary to the 1960 Convention (adopted on 31 January 1963, *United Nations Treaty Series*, Vol. 1041, p. 358). The 'Vienna Convention' regime is global in scope, and comprises: Convention on Civil Liability for Nuclear Damage (adopted on 21 May 1963 as amended, *United Nations Treaty Series*, Vol. 1063, p. 265), and Optional Protocol concerning to the Compulsory Settlement of Disputes (adopted on 21 May 1963, *United Nations Treaty Series*, Vol. 2086, p. 94). These two regimes – the Paris and the Vienna – are tied together in the Joint Protocol Relating to the Application of the Vienna and the Paris Conventions, adopted on 21 September 1988, *United Nations Treaty Series*, Vol. 1672, p. 293. In addition, see Convention Relating to Civil Liability in the Field of Maritime Carriage of Nuclear Material (adopted on 17 December 1971, *United Nations Treaty Series*, Vol. 974, p. 255), and Convention on Liability of the Operators of Nuclear Ships (adopted on 24 May 1962, *American Journal of International Law*, Vol. 57, p. 268, but has not entered into force as it is not yet ratified by any State). See IAEA, *Civil Liability for Nuclear Damage: Advantages and Disadvantages of joining the International Nuclear Liability Regime*. Available at http://ola.iaea.org/ola/treaties/multi.html (accessed 1 August 2013).

8   International Convention on the Establishment of an International Fund for Compensation for Oil Pollution Damage as amended, adopted on 18 December 1971, *United Nations Treaty Series*, Vol. 1110, p. 57.

international instrument for this purpose. The State's role does not extend to participation in actual litigation, unless States are claiming reparation for damage to their interest as a State.

In an international arbitral regime, governments would act as claimants and defendants through an intergovernmental dispute resolution mechanism. The 1972 Space Objects Liability Convention[9] is an example of this type of regime. There, the State is held liable for activities that could have been undertaken by individuals or entities. The claims process also proceeds as between two States. In such an arbitral liability instrument, a State whose environment or nationals suffer the harmful effects of an LMO, for instance, could bring a claim against the State where the LMO originated, the State with jurisdiction over the entities in operational control of the LMO at the time of the release, or the State where the LMO was released. The instrument would then establish a claims procedure. It could make the International Court of Justice the final adjudicator, or provide recourse to a form of international arbitration through special tribunals such as the Permanent Court of Arbitration and its Optional Rules for Arbitration of Disputes Relating to Natural Resources and the Environment. A third option would be to establish a panel of experts to undertake the arbitral function.

The applicable law would have to be specified, as well as the substantive liability rules, as has been done for the Space Objects Liability Convention.

IV The approach of the Supplementary Protocol

As the earlier analysis demonstrated, the Supplementary Protocol neither adopts nor incorporates any of these liability approaches. The Supplementary Protocol essentially requires (in the case of response measures) or exhorts Parties to strive towards (in the case of traditional civil liability damage) only that which they can do in any event in the exercise of their sovereign right. It does little more than reiterate the right of Parties to apply their existing law or to develop a specific law to deal with damage caused by the transboundary movement of LMOs. An opportunity was missed to add value to the corpus of international law regarding liability that has a cross-border dimension.

Developing countries, organised as the Like-Minded Group, demanded from the early days of the negotiations that an effective civil liability regime be made pivotal to the establishment of a biosafety protocol. Yet, after six long years of arduous negotiations based on the mandate established by COP-MOP1 in 2004 at Kuala Lumpur, what emerged was a single and rather vacuous article on civil liability in a binding treaty designed to deal with liability and redress. The next part of this chapter deals with how this came about.

---

9 Convention on International Liability for Damage Caused by Space Objects, adopted on 29 March 1972, *United Nations Treaty Series*, Vol. 961, p. 187.

V Article 27 of the Cartagena Protocol

1 The arguments for and against the inclusion

When the negotiations for a biosafety protocol first started, delegates from primarily developing countries insisted that a regime dealing with the transboundary movement of LMOs had to incorporate provisions on liability and redress to deal with incidents of damage caused by such LMOs. In their minds, this was the 'crux of the biosafety issue' and many among them resorted to wearing badges with the slogan 'No Liability, No Protocol'. However, there was no consensus on the need to address such an issue in the negotiations.[10] There was a clear North-South divide over the need for inclusion of civil liability in the protocol. Those who saw themselves as recipients of foreign LMOs argued that including such provisions would instil confidence in the technology and help avert criticism from their populace when they allowed or encouraged such imports. Imports of LMOs would then be viewed as a responsible act of the government on a precautionary basis, and in the (unlikely, as industry asserted) event of damage, liability provisions would help them cope with the fallout from any incident. This was stressed as being particularly important as developing countries lacked the capacity to conduct a proper risk assessment and management. They also argued that a liability regime that channelled liability would make the polluter pay for any damage. The exhortation in the Convention on Biological Diversity (CBD) that conservation of bio-diversity was the common concern of mankind suggested, they argued, the need for international action to confront any adverse effects posed by LMOs – especially since these living forms could well cause irreparable damage. They pointed to the existence of several international treaties dealing with liability for oil and potentially hazardous waste. Hence, they argued that mere reliance on existing State responsibility was inadequate to deal with compensation for damage resulting from the transboundary introduction of LMOs into their country.

Exporting countries resisted the inclusion of a liability regime because such was said to encourage the perception that this nascent technology could be hazardous. They did not know the kind of situations envisioned and the extent of their exposure to liability. They pointed to State responsibility in international law as providing an adequate remedy. They deprecated any comparisons with other treaties dealing with proven hazardous material.

The discussions were indeed largely mired by the fact that the impact of LMOs was unclear and unknown. This prompted developing countries to insist on the inclusion of the precautionary principle as a critical component and as the overarching basis for regulatory action. It would allow governments to take peremptory action in the face of scientific uncertainty about the danger posed by the LMO.

The resistance by developed countries, backed by the biotech industry, to avoid any civil liability provisions increased the resolve of developing countries to insist

10   See Kate Cook, 'Liability: "No Liability, No Protocol"', in Christoph Bail, Robert Falkner and Helen Marquard eds, *The Cartagena Protocol on Biosafety: Reconciling Trade in Biotechnology with Environment and Development?* (Earthscan, 2002), pp. 371–384.

on the inclusion of such provisions. They simply could not understand why industry was fighting so strenuously to exclude civil liability from the Protocol in the face of its sustained argument that LMOs caused no harm. Some industry representatives suggested setting up a voluntary fund in lieu of obligatory civil liability provisions. This suggestion quickly faded out, but was revived much later at a critical stage of the negotiations. Developed countries also pointed to the protracted negotiations for liability instruments in other fields to emphasise that the inclusion of civil liability would inordinately delay the conclusion of a protocol. Liability under the Basel Convention on hazardous waste had taken six years to adopt in 1999 and it took 10 years for the International Convention on Liability and Compensation for Damage in Connection with the Carriage of Hazardous and Noxious Substances by Sea to be adopted in 1996.

However, central to the debate was the key question of whether there should be a protocol on the international regulation of the transboundary movement of LMOs absent provisions on liability and redress for any ensuing damage.

2 The negotiating positions

Three proposals were advanced during the negotiations: first, the inclusion of substantive provisions; second, the inclusion of an enabling clause that would require a civil liability regime to be negotiated later; and third, the omission of any provision on civil liability. Within each of these categories, there were variations as well. The exact positions of countries advancing each of these proposals differed widely. For example, among those advocating substantive provisions, the African Group presented a comprehensive and detailed text for a biosafety protocol, replete with an extensive article on liability and compensation. Finally, it became clear as other issues took centre stage that time was running out to develop substantive rules on civil liability. Hence, Parties resigned themselves to a proposal by Norway to include an enabling clause committing Parties to develop rules on liability and redress within a prescribed time frame. This was the genesis of Article 27 in the Cartagena Protocol on Biosafety (Cartagena Protocol) that was finally concluded and adopted on 29 January 2000.[11]

VI The negotiations on Supplementary Protocol

1 The process

At the first Conference of the Parties serving as the Meeting of the Parties to the Cartagena Protocol (COP-MOP1) at Kuala Lumpur in 2004, the process and a timetable for the process were negotiated and established. The resulting Decision

---

11 Article 27, Cartagena Protocol: 'The Conference of the Parties serving as the Meeting of the Parties, shall at its first meeting, adopt a process with respect to the appropriate elaboration of international rules and procedures in the field of liability and redress for damage resulting from transboundary movements of living modified organisms . . . and shall endeavor to complete this process within four years.'

BS-I/8 created an Open-Ended *Ad Hoc* Working Group of Legal and Technical Experts on Liability and Redress (*Ad Hoc* WG). Five meetings of the *Ad Hoc* WG were scheduled and the process was slated to be completed in May 2008, to coincide with COP-MOP4 in Bonn, Germany. However, no instrument was even near completion by this date. COP-MOP4 then directed negotiations to continue under a contact group, consisting essentially of the Group of the Friends of the Co-Chairs (GFCC), under which the negotiations had been proceeding thus far since the group was established at *Ad Hoc* WG 5 in Cartagena in 2008. As this informal grouping had yielded modest results (reducing the unwieldy text to a less bulky one), continuing this format was agreed to at the enlarged GFCC meeting immediately preceding COP-MOP4. This format consisted of a number of representatives from various regional groups: six from Asia Pacific (including Bangladesh, China, India, Malaysia, Palau and the Philippines); two from the EU; two from Central and Eastern Europe; six from the African Group; six from the Latin American and Caribbean Group (GRULAC); and the nations of New Zealand, Norway, Switzerland and Japan. Two meetings were stipulated by COP-MOP4 Decision BS-IV/12, but there was no outcome of these meetings in Mexico (February 2009) and Malaysia (February 2010). Two more meetings were held, the first in Kuala Lumpur (June 2010) and the second in Nagoya (October 2010, preceding COP-MOP5), again with no outcome. Then, during COP-MOP5, a final spurt of extended meetings over six days bore fruit. The text was concluded by the working group (essentially organised as the GFCC) and the Nagoya-Kuala Lumpur Supplementary Protocol on Liability and Redress resulted. It was formally adopted by COP-MOP5 on 15 October 2010 by Decision BS-V/11. This was right in the midst of the rather difficult negotiations over the Access and Benefit Sharing (ABS) Protocol under the CBD, which was then proceeding in another part of the meeting hall, causing the negotiators involved in both processes to almost miss that final hour.

2 The content of the negotiations

The mandate established at COP-MOP1 in Kuala Lumpur in 2004 required that the process unaddressed by the Cartagena Protocol continue until completion within the prescribed time frame. Hence, the mandate directed that the *Ad Hoc* WG elaborate on liability and redress rules arising out of the transboundary movement of LMOs. The mandate also provided for one Technical Expert Group (TEG) meeting before the commencement of negotiations at the five scheduled *Ad Hoc* WG meetings, and this proved crucial in preparing the groundwork for them. The TEG meeting laid out the potential considerations relevant to a comprehensive set of rules and procedures for liability and redress. It listed topics on which more information was needed and identified a list of options and issues for elements of an international regime. It is important to note that all these elements relate to formation of a civil liability instrument, making it abundantly apparent that this was the nature of the regime contemplated by all the Parties. The elements included damage (definition, threshold, nature, scope, and valuation of), causation, standard of liability, channelling, financial security, settling of claims, limitations (as to time and amount), and the standing to bring claims. These were appended as an Annex to the Report of the TEG and became the reference and organisational guide for further work at the *Ad Hoc* WG meetings that were to follow.

From then on, beginning with the first meeting of the *Ad Hoc* WG, the negotiations were characterised by a 'one-step-forward-two-steps-back' approach as Parties pushing for binding rules provided concrete text on the elements, while others reverted to the discussion on the 'need for' a binding instrument. At the second meeting, for example, the United States and New Zealand (members of JUSCANZ) proposed the elaboration of criteria to assess the effectiveness of (and thus the need for) a regime. This was included as an annex to the report.[12] The Co-Chairs' push for Parties to provide concrete text for these elements was often thwarted by the insistence of some Parties for more information as a precondition to providing such text. This continued until the third meeting of the *Ad Hoc* WG, with some Parties providing text on various elements, others dragging their feet in providing such text, and the Co-Chairs valiantly synthesising the presentations into a single document. At this third meeting, the Co-Chairs presented a streamlined document with unattributed text under the following general headings: (I) Possible approaches to liability and redress; (II) Scope; (III) Damage; (IV) Primary compensation scheme; (V) Supplementary compensation scheme; (VI) Settlement of claims; (VII) Complementary capacity-building measures; and (VIII) Choice of instrument.[13]

The primary compensation scheme consisted of two approaches to liability and redress: the administrative approach and the civil liability approach. The administrative approach held that issues of liability and redress would be addressed through the administrative authorities. There would be no recourse to the courts, as contrasted to civil liability. The administrative approach was an entrenched feature of European environmental law, but it was largely unheard of elsewhere as a component of civil liability. However, as its main features were identified, it received the support of all Parties at the fourth meeting of the *Ad Hoc* WG. These features included empowering a competent national authority to require an operator to address cases of damage; if it failed to do so, the authority could step in and recover the costs incurred from the operator. There was also authority to prevent damage. The liability was strict – liability attached upon proof of damage and not culpability. Significantly, this approach existed in addition to a claim for civil liability, that is a claim for damage could be implemented through the judicial

12 Report of the Open-Ended *Ad Hoc* Working Group of Legal and Technical Experts on Liability and Redress in the Context of the Cartagena Protocol on Biosafety on the Work of its Second Meeting, UNEP/CBD/BS/COP-MOP/3/10 (2006), Annex I (Indicative list of criteria for the assessment of the effectiveness of any rules and procedures referred to in Article 27 of the Protocol).

13 Report of the Open-Ended *Ad Hoc* Working Group of Legal and Technical Experts on Liability and Redress in the Context of the Cartagena Protocol on Biosafety on the Work of its Third Meeting, UNEP/CBD/BS/WG-L&R/3/3 (2007), Annex II (Synthesis of proposed operational texts on approaches and options identified pertaining to liability and redress in the context of Article 27 of the Biosafety Protocol).

process. From this meeting forward, Parties proceeded to and were required to provide text on the basis of this structure.

However, the negotiations were in danger of stalling as no significant progress was discernible. Every proposal by the group advancing the cause of civil liability was met by an almost opposite and equal proposal that negated theirs. The Co-Chairs then presented at the fifth meeting of the *Ad Hoc* WG a Core Elements Paper,[14] which consisted of four 'pieces': the administrative approach, civil liability, supplementary compensation scheme and capacity building. Elements were proposed for each of these, and as a package, the Co-Chairs then proposed the following: a binding administrative approach, a non-binding civil liability approach, and a voluntary fund agreed to by industry combined with a collective approach to be funded by the Parties and others and to be administered by the Parties. Developing countries reacted against the Core Elements Paper document as a package, but realisation soon dawned that this document was the best basis for rescuing the negotiations from failure. Nonetheless, developing countries were resolute that the civil liability approach must be binding. Up to this point, although some developed countries (and a handful of developing countries) hinted at their preparedness to consider a binding instrument, they nonetheless repeatedly asserted that this issue could only be resolved at the final stage of the negotiations when other contentious issues were resolved. The matter came to a head at the fourth meeting of COP-MOP in Bonn in May 2008. Developing countries banded together as the Like-Minded Friends, a group consisting of 83 developing countries, and insisted on a threshold commitment by countries for a binding provision on civil liability. They made it clear that without this concession, they were disengaging from the negotiations. This prompted the Co-Chairs to pose the following two questions: (1) Is there an objection to work towards a legally binding instrument on an administrative approach?; and (2) Is there an objection to work towards including in such a legally binding instrument one article on civil liability? This matter was resolved when finally, after several tense bilateral meetings that threatened to scuttle the negotiations, all Parties that were hitherto intransigent acknowledged their willingness to work on both points.

The negotiations with regard to the single binding civil liability clause then began in earnest. Some developed countries were concerned that their judicial system did not countenance rules on liability and redress for such LMO-related damage. Implicit in the arguments of others was the concern that acceding to the establishment of civil liability provisions would suggest the inherent danger of LMOs and biotechnological products. Ultimately, the weak provisions discussed earlier were agreed to. To recap, Parties were obliged to ensure that they were working towards providing adequate rules and procedures in their domestic law on civil liability for material or personal damage associated with the damage (as defined in Article 2, paragraph 2 (b)). They agreed to: (a) continue to apply their existing general law on civil liability; (b) develop and apply or continue to apply

14   See Appendix 4 of this book.

civil liability law specifically for that purpose; or (c) develop and apply or continue to apply a combination of both. Further, when developing their laws, they were obliged to include the following elements: (a) damage; (b) standard of liability, including strict or fault-based liability; (c) channelling of liability, where appropriate; and (d) right to bring claims.

VII The way forward

The unity of developing countries forged at the outset of the negotiations dissipated at the closing stages. A possible beneficent reason for this was that in the course of the six-year negotiations, some of these countries began embracing modern biotechnology in their national development plans, or hoped to do so; thus, they recoiled from their initial insistence on a strong civil liability regime in response to their national biotechnology sector. The change of position became evident at the GFCC meeting at Putrajaya, Malaysia, in 2010. This, it is submitted, was the singular cause for the adoption of the rather weak provisions on civil liability.

The position is not hopeless. First, there is now in place an international binding provision that deals with civil liability. Parties are obliged to review their domestic laws to assess whether or not they have in place adequate rules and procedures on civil liability, bearing in mind the need to address the elements set out in Article 12. They then have to act accordingly as required by Article 12 with the aim of ensuring that they have an adequate domestic law in place to deal with liability and redress for the damage caused by LMOs. Hence, the Supplementary Protocol has entrenched civil liability as a national law requirement of Parties. The statement in the introduction to the official text of the Supplementary Protocol that it adopts only the administrative approach and eschews any reference to civil liability is, with respect, woefully inaccurate. Second, Article 13 requires COP-MOP to review the effectiveness of Article 12. This must take place every five years after the entry into force of the Supplementary Protocol. Parties are required to provide information requiring such a review. This implies that COP-MOP is obliged to assess whether Parties have made efforts to assess and put in place the necessary 'adequate' laws on civil liability. These efforts must be reported to COP-MOP. Article 33 of the Cartagena Protocol,[15] which applies by virtue of Article 16 (3)[16] of the Supplementary Protocol, obliges Parties to report to the COP-MOP the measures they have taken to implement their obligations under the Supplementary Protocol.

---

15 Article 33, Cartagena Protocol: 'Each Party shall monitor the implementation of its obligations under this Protocol, and shall, at intervals to be determined by the Conference of the Parties serving as the meetring of the Parties to this Protocol, report to the Conference of the Parties serving as the meeting of the Parties to this Protocol on measures that it has taken to implement the Protocol.'
16 Article 16 (3), Supplementary Protocol: 'Except as otherwise provided in this Supplementary Protocol, the provisions of the Convention and the Protocol shall apply, *mutatis mutandis*, to this Supplementary Protocol.'

VIII Conclusion

The Supplementary Protocol does not include substantive provisions on civil liability for the defined damage by LMOs. It nonetheless imposes an obligation for Parties to enact adequate domestic laws to provide for such damage. This provides flexibility to Parties to develop laws that are compatible and workable within their national legal systems. This is as far as the negotiations could have realistically and pragmatically gone, given the diametrically opposing views of the protagonists in the negotiations. It is possible that with experience and in the ripeness of time, the process established by the Supplementary Protocol to assess the effectiveness of national regimes could well lead to the establishment of a mature regime incorporating substantive international rules on liability and redress for damage caused by LMOs.

8 One legally binding provision on civil liability

Why it was so important from the African negotiators' perspective

Elmo Thomas and Mahlet Teshome Kebede

I Introduction

During the negotiations of the 'international rules and procedures in the field of liability and redress for damage resulting from transboundary movements of living modified organisms', the text and options on the table went through many changes. What started out as negotiation over rules and procedures developed into different options, namely an administrative approach, a civil liability regime and a set of guidelines. The first two options could be legally binding or non-legally binding, expanding the options to five. From the beginning, the African Group was in favour of a legally binding civil liability regime. As the negotiations progressed, the choice narrowed to one between an administrative approach and a civil liability regime, with the majority supporting a legally binding regime for either. In Bonn, at the fourth Conference of the Parties serving as the Meeting of the Parties (COP-MOP) to the Cartagena Protocol on Biosafety (Cartagena Protocol) in 2008, the majority of the developing countries supporting a legally binding civil liability regime made a huge compromise and agreed to work towards a legally binding instrument focusing on an administrative approach, but also including a legally binding provision on civil liability.

The question is – why was it so important for the African Group to have at least one legally binding provision on civil liability in the new treaty that would later be adopted as the Nagoya Kuala-Lumpur Supplementary Protocol on Liability and Redress (Supplementary Protocol) in 2010? This chapter addresses this question in the following manner: first, it will explain why the administrative approach to liability was deemed to be insufficient for many of the African countries; second, it will describe the existence of gaps in the legislation of many African countries when addressing environmental damage through a civil liability regime; and third, it highlights the need for a legally binding international civil liability regime from the African perspective. In addition, in the case of environmental issues, it has been argued that a further development of traditional liability regimes is called for, since they are insufficient to address all dimensions of the broad ranging issues at hand including environment liability and redress for human induced global warming.[1] This argument holds very true for the complexities of possible damage to the environment resulting from living modified organisms (LMOs), in which case not much ground has been covered in terms of addressing liability. This very reality imposes an extra challenge for African countries in terms of dealing with the nature and scope of damage and the applicable liability standards at the national level. This has had a bearing on their tendency to address the issue of liability at an international level.

II The administrative approach: why it would not suffice

An administrative approach to environmental liability was introduced by the European Union by its Environmental Liability Directive 2004/35/EC.[2] Africa has had little experience in the application of an administrative approach to liability at a regional or international level. A common understanding of this approach is that through it, the burden of executing remedial measures is shifted to the competent national authority. The competent national authority must respond to damage, effectively ensuring that there is redress for damage. This also signifies that the competent national authority will have to establish the causal link between the damage and the LMO in question, as well as to determine the type of redress and the monetary value of such redress. The onerous task of pursuing the responsible operator in the process of ensuring redress also adds additional challenges, such as tracking the range of operators among whom to apportion joint and several liabilities. This additional responsibility being imposed upon the competent national authorities was a significant stumbling block for many developing countries including African countries.

In addition, during the development of national biosafety frameworks that implement the Cartagena Protocol, there was no legally binding international liability and redress regime for damage resulting from LMOs, as such a regime was still being negotiated. Thus, the implementation of the Supplementary Protocol would impact the operation of all competent national authorities for all African countries. It may also be recalled that many countries in Africa are still in the process of developing their national biosafety frameworks. While some African countries have just finalised their legislation for the regulation of LMOs, in most cases this legislation is still not operational. This means that, to date, there are still some African countries that do not have a functional competent national authority

---

1   Philippe Cullet, 'Liability and Redress for Human-Induced Global Warming: Towards an International Regime', *Standfortd Journal of International Law*, Vol. 43 A (*Symposium: Climate Change Liability and Allocation of Risk*) (2007), p. 99.

2   Directive 2004/35/CE of the European Parliament and of the Council of 21 April 2004 on environmental liability with regard to the prevention and remedying of environmental damage, *Official Journal of the European Union 2004*, L 143/56. See also Chapter 5 of this book, by Alejandro Lago Candeira.

with regards to the implementation of biosafety measures as prescribed under the Cartagena Protocol. In even the few instances among the African countries where a functional competent national authority is already in place or newly established, the obligations under the Supplementary Protocol would still be cumbersome for most of them. The tasks of newly established national competent authorities are already daunting even without the additional responsibility added by the legally binding regime of an administrative approach.

Therefore, the African Group was in favour of a legally binding civil liability regime that would make use of its existing judicial system as opposed to an administrative regime that would add to the workload of competent national authorities, which in some countries might not have been established yet. What is more, as in the case of many developing regions, for Africa, a continent grappling with governance issues, the absence of a binding civil liability provision was thought not to be conducive for the continent. It was considered that leaving all critical decisions on liability and redress in the hands of competent national authorities outside of a court system paved the way for governance challenges, including corruption.

III Civil liability in African legislation: the gaps in addressing environmental damage

As mentioned above, most legal systems of African countries have not addressed damage caused by LMOs in their existing civil liability regimes. Hence, what had been anticipated at the negotiation was a set of binding international rules and procedures, critical for the African countries to ensure that liability and compensation arising from LMOs could be established and enforced at the domestic level.

The main remedy under domestic civil laws common to countries in Africa is compensation by way of awarding damages. The objective of these laws is to compensate persons for injury or loss caused to them and, as far as possible, to put them in a position as if the damage had not occurred. The system therefore seeks to assess the value of the loss in financial terms. In the traditional civil liability regimes, recoverable losses are generally limited to personal injury, damage to property, and pure economic loss in certain cases. Accordingly, most systems do not consider pure ecological damage within the recoverable damage, and hence damage to biological diversity would not be covered either. The compensation in such circumstances is limited to consequential loss to persons and property, but does not include ecological damage *per se*.

Under the civil law principles, most systems do not impose an obligation to use the damages received to restore the environment. A number of civil liability systems impose an obligation to mitigate any damage that may involve clean-up. In addition, in a number of countries the administrative authorities may order the plaintiff to carry out clean-up operations effectively requiring use of civil damages for restoration. On the other hand, most systems operate some form of administrative system for environmental protection, and it is through these systems rather than civil law remedies that most action to protect and restore the environment is supposed to take place. The licensing and monitoring systems provide the administrative authorities with necessary information, but they usually do not have considerable powers to restore the damage and reclaim the costs.

Consequently, because of the gap that exists due to the absence of civil liability regimes relating to LMOs, it is rather common that national cases regarding damage to biological diversity and the ensuing liability and redress claims resulting from LMOs have not been brought or otherwise widely reported in most African jurisdictions. This fact alone makes it critical for African countries to have in place an elaborate civil liability structure for environmental damage caused by LMOs.

In this context, to illustrate this point, it might be interesting to explain briefly the Ethiopian legal system that deals with liability for environmental crimes. The Ethiopian Revised Criminal Code of 2004 stipulates that criminal law applies to any person, a national or foreigner, who has committed an offence under the national jurisdiction of Ethiopia[3] and establishes criminal liability also for 'juridical persons'. The term 'juridical persons' under the Criminal Code includes corporations with governmental, non-governmental, public or private structures, as well as any legally recognised institutions or associations set up for commercial, industrial, political, religious or any other purposes. However, certain institutions that are not legally recognised by Ethiopian law, such as newly emerging industries, may escape criminal responsibility because they fall outside the description of 'juridical persons'.[4] Further, under the Ethiopian law, the environmental enforcement strategy involves a three-pronged approach based on regulatory, civil and criminal enforcement. Severe punishments are stipulated for environmental crimes for certain defined activities, but the sanctions stipulated in the Revised Criminal Code hardly encompass all aspects of what are conventionally considered 'environmental crimes' and 'crimes against the wild life', such as illegal animal trafficking, deforestation, illegal hunting, etc. Suffice it to say that damage resulting from modern biotechnology (genetic engineering) including LMOs is not covered. Finally, as demonstrated by the provisions governing environmental impact assessments, the structural arrangements and institutional hierarchy among the relevant administrative bodies seem to be inconsistent and contradictory in the legal regime pertinent to environmental crimes in Ethiopia.[5] This is but one instance of the need for an international regime to harmonise the existing inconsistency and gaps present in most legal regimes in Africa in the administration of civil and criminal cases of environmental liability.

3   Article 11, Ethiopian Revised Criminal Code, 2004. Available at www.refworld.org/docid/ 49216b572.html (accessed 1 August 2013).
4   Rose Mwebaza, Philip N. Mwanika and Wondowossen S. Wondemagegnehu, *Situation Report: Environmental Crimes in Ethiopia* (1 July 2009). Available at www.issafrica.org/publications/ publication-archives/conference-reports/ (accessed 1 August 2013).
5   Ibid.

IV Binding civil liability systems at the international level: why are they so important?

The negotiations for the Supplementary Protocol were concluded with the adoption of just one legally binding provision referring to civil liability. Article 12 deals with how the Supplementary Protocol is implemented in relation to civil liability, albeit in a rather feeble manner. What is provided there is simply an obligation for Parties to assess the situation at home regarding damage resulting from LMOs and to provide rules and procedures to deal with liability in their domestic laws. Where domestic laws already address damage from LMOs, the response measures are handled applying those existing laws. As per Article 12, the necessary civil liability laws should also be in place, but the Party obviously will only consider its own existing legal arrangements. The legal problems arising from environmental loss, including insurance, have been resolved in diverse ways in different countries. The laws covering damage to the environment in most countries are heterogeneous and to some extent even ambiguous.[6] This implies that if and when a civil claim is brought before a court, one must follow the rules and procedures that are outlined by that court. The courts of different countries may have different rules. It will be difficult, then, for a foreign national or a foreign stakeholder claimant to make a claim in a court of another jurisdiction in which the rules are unfamiliar. This difficulty may indeed be settled if the fundamental rules and procedures are harmonised across jurisdictions through an international instrument.

Because of the increasing integration between countries and people and in view of the ever greater risks of transboundary environmental damage, the national legislation and systems of liability should be as uniform as possible. This works to the advantage of the person suffering damage. Variations in legislation, however, compromise the protection that should be afforded to the victims. A uniform liability system is also an advantage for liability insurers and enhances their potential for providing better policies.[7] Thus, the problems brought about by environmental damage cannot be resolved only from the national perspective. With the advances made in industry and the resulting potential transboundary damage caused by LMOs, the issue of effective compensation for victims has assumed an international character.[8] This underlines the need for international cooperation, ideally in the form of a binding international treaty on civil liability for environmental damage resulting from LMOs or, at the least, a provision in a treaty ensuring this objective. The African Group insisted that such measures are needed because of the limited possibilities offered by their national laws for adequate and effective compensation in the case of damage resulting from LMOs. The African Group acknowledges that the public law does indeed play an important role in the prevention of environmental damage. However, the rules on civil liability enter

6   Peter Wetterstein, 'Current Trends in International Civil Liability for Environmental Damage', *Annual Survey of International & Comparative Law*, Vol. 1, No. 1 (1994), p. 183.

7   Ibid.

8   Ibid., p. 184.

into the picture when administrative regulations have proved ineffective in preventing such damage. To a large extent, this is the case in the national laws of most African and other developing countries. Hence, where an adequate civil liability system recognised in the international arena in the form of a binding provision is available, the claimant has an opportunity to obtain compensation through due process of law.

Feeble as it may be, the Supplementary Protocol does stimulate the Parties to consider and develop adequate civil liability rules in the absence of such rules dealing with the damage to biodiversity resulting from LMOs, taking also into account crucial key elements such as the scope of damage (damage to biodiversity/ personal damage, etc.), standards of liability, channelling of liability, and access to justice issues (Articles 12 (2) and (3)). In the absence of any other legal provision dealing with civil liability for damage resulting from LMOs, Article 12 of the Supplementary Protocol would surely be taken by the African countries as a beacon of hope to address the complexities of civil claims and liabilities arising from LMOs, the nature of which has increasingly become international rather than domestic.

V Conclusion

While there might have seemed to be a relatively straight forward choice between a legally binding instrument on an administrative approach to liability or a civil liability regime, the challenge for the African continent was much more intricate. Achieving the effectiveness of both the administrative regulations and the civil liability system has been identified as the major challenge. For the African continent, the necessary solution was thought to be a legally binding regime.

In a legally binding international instrument on an administrative approach to liability, the execution of measures to redress the damage would shift to the competent national authority of the affected State. Such competent national authorities in Africa may have been newly established with little experience or, in some cases, non-existent. Such an approach, therefore, is not a preferred choice for Africa. On the other hand, a legally binding international instrument on civil liability system would allow the development of harmonised rules and procedures across jurisdictions. It would also address the gaps existent in many African civil liability laws that fail to address damage resulting from LMOs. Therefore, the answer to the question of why one legally binding provision on civil liability was so important is actually the same as that to the question of why there was a call for a legally binding civil liability regime in the agenda of negotiation (Article 27 of the Cartagena Protocol) in the first place.

9 Trade and the Supplementary Protocol

How to achieve mutual supportiveness

Rodrigo C. A. Lima[1]

I Introduction

In October 2010, the city of Nagoya, Japan, hosted the 5th Meeting of the Parties (COP-MOP5) to the Cartagena Protocol on Biosafety (Cartagena Protocol) under the Convention on Biological Diversity (CBD). The main objective of the Cartagena Protocol is to ensure an adequate level of protection in handling, transport and use of living modified organisms (LMOs) that may have adverse effects on the conservation and sustainable use of biological diversity, taking also into account risks to human health and specifically focusing on transboundary movements.

Since the Cartagena Protocol entered into force in September 2003, the Parties have been discussing and negotiating decisions related to identification, liability and redress, risk assessment, capacity building related to biotechnology, and recently socioeconomic considerations. The main objective for the COP-MOP5 meeting was the adoption of a supplementary protocol on liability and redress that would allow Parties to implement response measures in the event of damage to biodiversity caused by LMOs, considering also the possible adverse effects to human health that may arise from environmental damage that has already occurred to the environment.

The negotiations over the liability and redress mechanism, as stated in Article 27 of the Cartagena Protocol, started in 2004 with the establishment of the Open-Ended *Ad Hoc* Working Group of Legal and Technical Experts on Liability and Redress (*Ad Hoc* WG), and this long process came to a successful end when the COP-MOP5 adopted the Nagoya-Kuala Lumpur Supplementary Protocol on Liability and Redress (Supplementary Protocol) in 2010.

The Parties were mandated to adopt a liability and redress mechanism at the COP-MOP4 in 2008. However, the lack of agreement about three controversial issues motivated the establishment of a Group of Friends of the Co-Chairs (GFCC) in order to continue the negotiation. The three controversial issues were: (a) the discussion of whether to include 'products thereof' in addition to the LMOs themselves in the scope of the instrument; (b) the controversies relating to financial

1   The author would like to acknowledge the excellent research assistance of Paula Moura.

security or insurance to allow compensation for damages caused by LMOs; and (c) the debate about the need for a legally binding civil liability regime.

This chapter analyses one of these controversial issues, namely Article 10 of the Supplementary Protocol, which allows Parties to voluntarily adopt financial security aiming to compensate individuals or Parties for damage to biodiversity caused by LMOs. This provision is examined in light of the World Trade Organization (WTO) agreements. The objective is to verify whether a measure requiring a financial security by a Party to the Supplementary Protocol would be in line with the WTO rules and principles. In this context, it is worth noting that despite the fact that the Cartagena Protocol is a multilateral environmental treaty, its implications for trade are very clear when it comes to the regulation of trans-boundary movements of LMOs. The Cartagena Protocol does not aim at affecting trade relations, but since it imposes obligations on States and operators dealing with LMOs, it may do so worldwide.

The second section below will focus on analysing Article 10 of the Supplementary Protocol and the objectives of the Cartagena Protocol, aiming to understand the scope of and justification for adopting financial security provisions. The third section will be dedicated to the analysis of the WTO principles and agreements that may touch upon the financial security measure, namely the national treatment principle, Article XX (b) of the General Agreement on Tariffs and Trade (GATT), the Agreement on Technical Barriers to Trade (TBT) and the Agreement on the Application of Sanitary and Phytosanitary Measures (SPS). The fourth section will address the possible implications of Article 10 for the Parties to the Supplementary Protocol and the fifth section will focus on the relationship between the Cartagena Protocol and the WTO. Lastly, the conclusions will be presented.

II The liability and redress negotiations and the financial security debate

Article 27 of the Cartagena Protocol contained a mandate to create a liability and redress mechanism to allow compensation in the event of damage arising from LMOs subject to transboundary movement. In combination with Article 15 on risk assessment and Article 18 dealing with the identification of LMOs, the issue of liability and redress represented the biggest challenge of the Cartagena Protocol, since its central objective aims:

> to contribute to ensuring an adequate level of protection in the field of the safe transfer, handling and use of living modified organisms resulting from modern biotechnology that may have adverse effects on the conservation and sustainable use of biological diversity, taking also into account risks to human health, and specifically focusing on transboundary movements.
>
> (Article 1)

The negotiation of a liability and redress mechanism began at MOP1, held in Malaysia in 2004, when an *Ad Hoc* WG was created with the objectives of collecting information regarding liability for damage caused by LMOs, analysing potential or real issues related to damage scenarios and applying international rules regarding liability to them, and collecting data for defining the nature of damage, among others.[2] Since the Parties failed to adopt a decision at COP-MOP4 in Bonn, Germany, in 2008, the negotiations continued in the context of a new group, the GFCC. In this manner, the Parties agreed to boost the negotiations, which were deemed very complex. Between 2009 and 2010, the GFCC held four meetings to discuss the text on liability and redress.

The demand for an article on financial security to cover possible damage was a sensitive issue since the beginning of the negotiation under Article 27 of the Cartagena Protocol. Malaysia, India, Norway, Palau and the African countries favoured some kind of financial guarantee (mandatory, voluntary or related to the regulation of each country).[3] Since the idea of a fund within the framework of the liability and redress decision was abandoned, the financial security provision became the target for many Parties. It is safe to say that financial security became the most complex issue within the final negotiation, alongside the issue of 'products thereof'. During the fourth meeting of the GFCC, which took place just before the COP-MOP5 in Nagoya, the discussion about providing insurance or financial security became a potential deal-breaker for the negotiation. Instead of establishing a decision imposing on all countries the duty to adopt measures of this nature, a compromise was reached that left the decision whether or not to adopt financial security measures to each Party's discretion, as long as they are in compliance with obligations under international law.

It is important to highlight that such a compromise was probably the most difficult point at the pre-COP-MOP5 meeting, which led to the establishment of a small contact group composed by Brazil, Paraguay and South Africa, on the one hand, and Malaysia, Bolivia and Namibia, on the other. Only after informal and closed negotiations that went late into the night and through the weekend preceding the start of COP-MOP5, the paragraph below was approved:

Article 10. Financial Security

1   Parties retain the right to provide, in their domestic law, for financial security.

2   Parties shall exercise the right referred to in Paragraph 1 above in a manner consistent with their rights and obligations under international law, taking into account the final three preambular paragraphs of the Protocol.

---

2   Decision BS-I/8 (2004), Establishment of an Open-Ended *Ad Hoc* Working Group of Legal and Technical experts on liability and redress in the context of the Protocol, UNEP/CBD/BS/COP-MOP/1/15 (2004).

3   For a history of negotiations on financial guarantees, Gurdial Singh Nijar, Sarah Lawson-Stopps, and Gan Pei Fern, *Liability and Redress under the Cartagena Protocol on Liability: A Record of the Negotiations for Developing International Rule, Vol. 1* (Centre of Excellence for Biodiversity Law, 2008), pp. 283–293.

3   The first meeting of the Conference of the Parties serving as the meeting of the Parties to the Protocol after the entry into force of the Supplementary Protocol shall request the Secretariat to undertake a comprehensive study which shall address, *inter alia*:

(a)   The modalities of financial security mechanisms;
(b)   An assessment of the environmental, economic and social impacts of such mechanisms, in particular on developing countries; and
(c)   An identification of the appropriate entities to provide financial security.

Under Article 3 (5), the Supplementary Protocol applies in cases of damage occurring in areas within the limits of national jurisdiction of the Parties. By contrast, Article 3 (7) stipulates that domestic laws adopted to implement the Supplementary Protocol shall apply to damage resulting from transboundary movements of LMOs by a non-Party. In this sense, when a non-Party to the Supplementary Protocol is to export LMOs to a Party, the non-Party exporter may have to comply with the requirements imposed by the importing Party – otherwise the exporter may decide not to sell the LMOs.

This illustrates a close relationship between the Supplementary Protocol and trade, and indicates the possibility of measures taken under the Supplementary Protocol being considered barriers to trade. Under Article 10 (1) reproduced above, a State that ratifies the Supplementary Protocol would be allowed to request financial security (e.g. from exporters, importers, technology developers, transporters and other operators)[4] to cover possible damage to biodiversity caused by LMOs. The Parties may request such a measure at their discretion. However, Article 10 (2) stipulates that any measure of this nature must follow the three final preambular paragraphs of the Cartagena Protocol, namely:

Recognizing that trade and environment agreements should be mutually supportive with a view to achieving sustainable development,

Emphasizing that this Protocol shall not be interpreted as implying a change in the rights and obligations of a Party under any existing international agreements,

Understanding that the above recital is not intended to subordinate this Protocol to other international agreements.

The language of these preambular paragraphs aims to balance a hypothetical financial security measure adopted by a Party with the rules of international law,

---

4   It is noteworthy that the negotiation text stipulated that the financial guarantee would be required of the operators, but in the end this issue of who is the 'operator' was left pending (Article 2 (2) (c), Supplementary Protocol). It should be noted that a guarantee would naturally be required from somebody in the importing State or even in the exporting State, which requires returning to the concept of operator in Article 2 (2) (c).

especially those of the WTO. Although this balance of mutual supportiveness may be achievable, it is important to analyse how a measure would be applied in concrete cases.

It is worth noting that because the Parties will be able to define 'operators' in their domestic regulations, it is possible to imagine that in the legislation of one Party, some operators will need to adopt financial security measures, while in another Party different operators will have to bear the obligation of financial security measures. This may lead to a complex scenario that may result in the creation of barriers to trade. The same logic applies for measures adopted by a Party that require guarantees from a non-Party, as stipulated in Article 3 (7) of the Supplementary Protocol. The central question that must be addressed is to what extent these guarantees are necessary to avoid damage to biodiversity.

III Damage to biodiversity, financial security and the WTO

In stipulating that it is possible for a Party to adopt financial security measures to respond to or compensate for damage to biodiversity caused by LMOs, Article 10 (1) gives rise to a wide range of cases that can interfere in the trade of many products. It is therefore essential to consider the implications of adoption of financial security measures for the trade of LMOs and products containing LMOs or for those that have the ability to transfer or replicate that genetic material.[5] The adoption of financial security measures will be analysed in relation to the national treatment principle, Article XX (b) of the GATT, the TBT Agreement and the SPS Agreement.

1 The national treatment principle

The national treatment principle, stipulated in Article III of the GATT, seeks to prevent discrimination between similar products. According to the first section of Article III:

> The products of the territory of any contracting party imported into the territory of any other contracting party shall be accorded treatment no less favourable than that accorded to like products of national origin in respect of all laws, regulations and requirements affecting their internal sale, offering for sale, purchase, transportation, distribution or use.

---

5   It is important to emphasise that the Cartagena Protocol and its decisions, including the Supplementary Protocol on Liability and Redress, exclusively address LMOs, that is living organisms originated from modern biotechnology that are able to transfer or replicate their genetic material, under Articles 3 (g) and 3 (h) of the Cartagena Protocol. Despite the intense pressure to include products thereof from LMOs, these were left out, because they cannot necessarily transfer or replicate their genetic material, which would not be within the scope of the Cartagena Protocol. See further chapter 6 of this book, by Reynaldo Ariel Alvarez-Morales.

This principle exerts direct influence on a State's domestic policies, with the objective of avoiding the adoption of measures that apply only to similar imported products, which may lead to the imposition of restrictions on products from other countries. Since the Supplementary Protocol addresses the transboundary movement of LMOs that will later be used, handled and transported in the importing State, it is natural to imagine that financial security would be required under Article 2 (2) (c) of the Supplementary Protocol from the exporter, importer, technology developer or any other person who may be appointed as an operator.

The compliance with the national treatment principle would require the importing country to have the same policies for its operators, irrespective of the transboundary movement of that LMO. However, since the occurrence of transboundary movements is a key condition required by the Cartagena Protocol and its Supplementary Protocol, the Parties might not have intended to apply these financial security provisions to 'locally produced' LMOs. Thus, it is important to examine whether the financial security obligation would be compliant with the national treatment principle.

The example below (Figure 9.1) illustrates how a financial security measure would probably violate the national treatment principle.

2 Article XX (b) of the GATT

Article XX of the GATT addresses general exceptions that allow the adoption of restrictive measures to trade when necessary to protect a legitimate objective, as long as these do not constitute means of arbitrary or unjustifiable discrimination between States where the same conditions prevail. These measures shall not

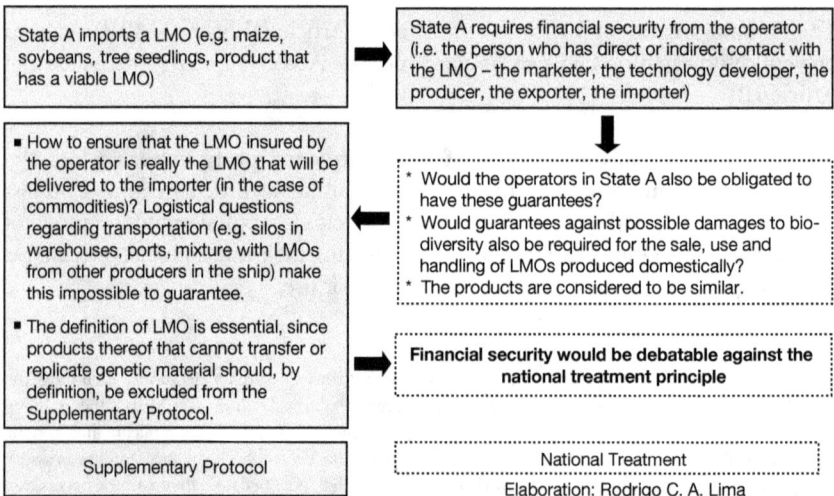

State A imports a LMO (e.g. maize, soybeans, tree seedlings, product that has a viable LMO)

State A requires financial security from the operator (i.e. the person who has direct or indirect contact with the LMO – the marketer, the technology developer, the producer, the exporter, the importer)

- How to ensure that the LMO insured by the operator is really the LMO that will be delivered to the importer (in the case of commodities)? Logistical questions regarding transportation (e.g. silos in warehouses, ports, mixture with LMOs from other producers in the ship) make this impossible to guarantee.

- The definition of LMO is essential, since products thereof that cannot transfer or replicate genetic material should, by definition, be excluded from the Supplementary Protocol.

* Would the operators in State A also be obligated to have these guarantees?
* Would guarantees against possible damages to biodiversity also be required for the sale, use and handling of LMOs produced domestically?
* The products are considered to be similar.

Financial security would be debatable against the national treatment principle

Supplementary Protocol

National Treatment

Elaboration: Rodrigo C. A. Lima

Figure 9.1 Financial security and the National Treatment Principle

be disguised barriers to trade either. Thus, the measures aimed at protecting human, animal and plant life, or health may be adopted by members of the WTO without contradicting its rules (paragraph b). The measures aimed at conservation of non-renewable natural resources may also be adopted as long as they are adopted in conjunction with restrictions to domestic production and consumption (paragraph g).

The WTO's jurisprudence related to Article XX is extensive because prior to the approval of the TBT Agreement and the SPS Agreement, Members sought to justify certain restrictions on trade based on this article. The *USA-Gasoline* (WT/DS2 and WT/DS4), the *EC-Asbestos* (WT/DS135), and the *USA-Shrimp* (WT/DS58) Panels were important in this context, consolidating some essential requirements to justify a measure based on Article XX.

It is up to the Member that applies the measure to prove that its aim is to protect human, animal and plant life, or health and that such action is necessary to achieve the intended objectives. In this regard, the financial security or insurance applied with the objective of protecting biodiversity and allowing redress in the event of damage should: (a) seek to protect biological diversity against possible damage caused by LMOs; and (b) be justifiable as a necessary measure to avoid the damage. The WTO Appellate Body emphasised the need for strict interpretations of the exceptions in Article XX as it stated:

> To permit one Member to abuse or misuse its right to invoke an exception would be effectively to allow that Member to degrade its own treaty obligations as well as to devalue the treaty rights of other Members. If the abuse or misuse is sufficiently grave or extensive, the Member, in effect, reduces its treaty obligation to a merely facultative one and dissolves its juridical character, and, in so doing, negates altogether the treaty rights of other Members. The chapeau was installed at the head of the list of 'General Exceptions' in Article XX to prevent such far-reaching consequences.[6]

It is worth noting that in this context, the concept of damage adopted in the Supplementary Protocol 'means an adverse effect on the conservation and sustainable use of biological diversity, taking also into account risks to human health, that is measurable or otherwise observable taking into account, wherever available, scientifically-established baselines recognised by a competent authority that takes into account any other human induced variation and natural variation; and is significant as set out in paragraph 3 below' (Article 2 (2) (b) of the Supplementary Protocol).

The analysis regarding point (a) above could be considered valid, since the measure itself (i.e. financial security) is adopted with the objective of avoiding damage to biodiversity as defined and allowing redress for it. However, the measure's adaptation to the objective that it seeks to achieve seems restrictive,

6   US-Measures for Import Prohibition of Certain Shrimp and Shrimp Products, Report of Appellate Body, WT/DS58/AB/R (12 October 1998), para. 156.

requiring Parties to weigh the necessity of insurance and guarantees as a way to guarantee the appropriate protection to biodiversity. Therefore, some questions should be answered, such as:

(a) In the context of the Cartagena Protocol, do LMOs usually cause damage to biodiversity? Are there examples of such damage? Can they be considered dangerous products?
(b) Are LMOs subject to transboundary movements approved by States? Did they pass a risk assessment process? Are these products considered safe for human consumption and are they approved for intentional release into the environment?
(c) To avoid any damage to biodiversity caused by an LMO and to allow redress in case such damage occurs, is it necessary to require insurance or financial security? Are there other measures that could be implemented to achieve the same level of protection to biodiversity?
(d) Is financial security or insurance applied to any LMO necessary to guarantee biodiversity protection? Is the measure specific, focusing on LMOs that demand guarantees of this nature because they have actually caused damage or because there is scientific evidence to endorse this possibility?

In order to adapt to Article XX (b) of the GATT, it is vital to answer these questions. Otherwise, a measure could be challenged under that Article. The analysis of a case based on Article XX (b) can be considered in combination with the TBT Agreement and/or the SPS Agreement, since these agreements are more specific when it comes to environmental protection. However, the violation of the SPS Agreement, for example, does not depend on the characterisation of the same measure as an infringement of Article XX. It is worth noting, however, that in cases based on the TBT or SPS, States could also plead infringement of Article XX, which would be completely possible in the financial security case.

3 Agreement on technical barriers to trade (TBT)

The TBT agreement regulates the application of technical barriers to trade or, more specifically, the rules and technical regulations that seek to achieve the legitimate objectives established under Article 2 (2) of the Agreement (i.e. national security requirements; the prevention of deceptive practices; protection of human health or safety, animal or plant life or health, or the environment).

A technical regulation can be a combination of requirements related to the characteristics of the products and the process or method of production, or it can be the requirements related to symbols, packaging and labelling, among other mandatory requirements of a technical order required by States. On the other hand, compliance with a standard required by a recognised institution, such as the International Standardization Organization (ISO), and a standard related to the processing stage of the product or to a product characteristic are not mandatory.

According to Article 2 (2) of the TBT Agreement, States shall ensure that these measures are not prepared, adopted or applied in a way that creates unnecessary barriers to international trade. For this purpose, the measures shall not be more restrictive than necessary to achieve the objective, including, for example, protection of the environment or national security. In the *EC-Sardine* case, the Panel stated that:

> Article 2.2 and this preambular text affirm that it is up to the Members to decide which policy objectives they wish to pursue and the levels at which they wish to pursue them. At the same time, these provisions impose some limits on the regulatory autonomy of Members that decide to adopt technical regulations: Members cannot create obstacles to trade which are unnecessary or which, in their application, amount to arbitrary or unjustifiable discrimination or a disguised restriction on international trade.[7]

Therefore, States shall ensure that imported products receive no less favourable treatment than that conceded to similar products produced domestically. This obligation reflects the national treatment principle and is very important for the analysis of the insurance and financial security proposition. The objective of requiring financial security is to allow liability in a case of damage to biodiversity caused by the transboundary movements of LMOs, and to assure its redress.

It is necessary to analyse the measure (financial security) and weigh it against the objective it seeks to protect (the environment). As Tatiana Prazeres emphasises:

> technical regulations should not restrict international trade beyond the exact limit necessary to guarantee a legitimate objective, considering the risks that the non-observation of these objectives could cause. Many times, the discussion of protectionist measures through technical barriers to trade resides in the content of the 'legitimate objectives' – a concept that is too vague to guarantee the adequate theoretical use of technical barriers.[8]

Conceptually, financial security required by a Party to the Supplementary Protocol with the objective of allowing liability and redress in the event of damage to biodiversity caused by an LMO can be understood as a technical regulation that seeks to protect the environment and, therefore, can be included in the context of the TBT Agreement.

Having overcome this conceptual matter, it is important to consider if there is sufficient scientific evidence to justify the financial security requirement and also if the measure is reasonable and necessary to achieve the intended objective. Figure 9.2 (overleaf) aims to analyse a hypothetical case of financial security compared to the TBT obligations.

---

7   EC–Trade Description of Sardines, Report of the Panel, WT/DS231/R (29 May 2002), para. VII.8.
8   Tatiana Prazeres, *Comércio Internacional e Protecionismo, as barreiras técnicas na OMC* (Aduaneiras, 2003), pp. 91–92.

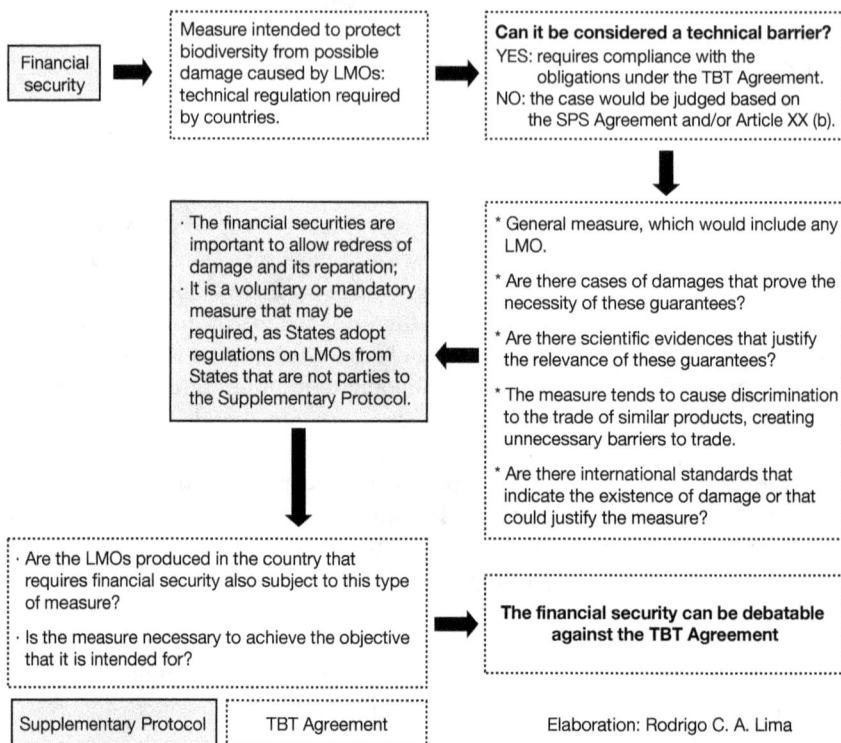

Figure 9.2 Financial security and the TBT Agreement

4 Agreement on the application of sanitary and phytosanitary measures (SPS)

Another WTO agreement that is relevant in the financial security analysis relates to the application of sanitary and phytosanitary measures to trade. Despite the independence of the TBT Agreement from the SPS Agreement, it is necessary to analyse both agreements since the possibility of adopting financial security could be questioned in either case. In practice, the applicability would depend on a concrete case (Panel), and the Dispute Settlement Body of the WTO would determine the nature of the measure: technical, sanitary or phytosanitary.

According to Annex A of the SPS Agreement, sanitary and phytosanitary measures are those applied to protect human, animal, or plant life or health from risks arising from the entry of pests, diseases, disease-carrying organisms or disease-causing organisms. Also, these can include measures that seek to protect human, animal, or plant life or health from risks arising from additives, contaminants, toxins, disease-causing organisms in foods, beverages or feedstuff, or measures to prevent or limit other damage from the entry, establishment or spread of pests. For example, when a State restricts the imports of fresh bovine meat in order to prevent the entrance of the foot and mouth virus, it applies a sanitary measure.

When it requires wood to be treated in order to prevent the presence of diseases or pests or when it requires the treatment of fruits with certain substances to avoid the entrance or dissemination of a pest, it applies a phytosanitary measure. These measures include all relevant laws, decrees, regulations, requirements and procedures; processes and production methods; testing, inspection, certification and approval procedures; quarantine treatments; sampling procedures and methods of risk assessment; and packaging and labelling requirements directly related to food safety.

There are two requirements in order for a measure to be considered sanitary or phytosanitary: (a) the intention to protect human, animal, or plant life or health; and (b) the intention to combat food hazards (*food-borne risks*) or risks related to pests and diseases (*pest- or disease-related risks*) and organisms that cause diseases. In other words, food safety and the protection of human, animal, and plant life or health are legitimate objectives that the SPS Agreement seeks to protect. Article 2 (2) establishes that States shall ensure that sanitary and phytosanitary measures be applied only to the extent necessary to achieve these objectives.

They shall also be based on scientific principles and not maintained without sufficient evidence. Furthermore, the State that applies a measure shall ensure that it does not cause arbitrary or unjustifiable discrimination between States where the same conditions prevail. In other words, States that have similar sanitary conditions, such as the presence of a disease, and adopt similar measures for fruit treatment, shall not adopt more restrictive measures without scientific support.

To justify these measures, States should have scientific evidence, which entails carrying out a risk assessment. Article 5 (1) of the SPS Agreement stipulates that 'Members shall ensure that their sanitary or phytosanitary measures are based on an assessment, as appropriate to the circumstances, of the risks to human, animal or plant life or health, taking into account risk assessment techniques developed by the relevant international organizations'. This means that States shall also 'take into account the available scientific evidence; relevant processes and production methods; relevant inspection, testing and sampling methods; prevalence of specific diseases and pests; existence of pest- or disease-free areas; relevant ecological and environmental conditions; and quarantines or other treatments' (Article 5 (2)).

The SPS establishes the adoption of international standards developed by relevant organisations, known as the 'Three Sister' organisations: World Organisation for Animal Health (OIE), the International Plant Protection Convention (IPPC) and the *Codex Alimentarius* Commission. When a State applies a measure based on a standard of one of these organisations, it is presumed to be in accordance with the SPS rules.

However, when a country adopts an appropriate level of protection, usually more restrictive than the international standard, or when there is no relevant standard, the measure or its necessity to the intended protection must be justified. According to the texts of and precedents under the SPS Agreements, it has become evident that the following steps are the necessary conditions to apply a sanitary or phytosanitary measure that may cause restrictions to trade:

(a)   The State needs to have scientific evidence that justifies the necessity of the measure to avoid, for example, the entrance of an organism, including an LMO, that can cause a disease or damage to health or the environment.
(b)   The measure should not lead to a creation of disguised restrictions to trade.
(c)   The measure can be based on international standards of the sister organisations of the SPS.
(d)   To support the measure, the State must carry out a risk assessment; otherwise it may be questioned regarding the level of protection it adopts.

The exception stipulated under Article 5 (7) of the SPS Agreement for provisional measures in cases where scientific evidences are insufficient is, in practice, a reflection of the precautionary approach or principle under international environmental law. Principle 15 of the UN Declaration on Environment and Development states that 'when there are threats of serious or irreversible damage, lack of full scientific certainty shall not be used as a reason for postponing cost-effective measures to prevent environmental degradation'.

Although the precautionary principle was not recognised as a principle of international law, the panels in the *EC-Hormones* and *Japan-Apples* cases analysed the application of the precautionary approach under Article 5 (7) and stated that the need to search for scientific evidence in order to apply a measure is the focus of the SPS Agreement. The exception may be applied as long as the following four essential requirements are fulfilled:

(a)   Scientific evidence is insufficient.
(b)   The State should consider the available information on the subject, including that arising from relevant international organisations, as well as that applied by other States.
(c)   The State should seek to obtain additional information necessary for more objective risk assessment.
(d)   The measure applied should be reviewed in a reasonable period of time.

This author stated elsewhere, in the context of LMOs, that:

It is this confrontation between substantial obligations (Articles 2.2 and 5.1 of the SPS) and the exception of Article 5.7 incorporating a precautionary approach that requires attention. This is because a case involving LMOs touches on the central point of the SPS, which is the necessity of the link between measures and science. From this observation, the discussion on the fallibility of science is reignited, which requires re-thinking the notion of sufficient evidence under Article 2.2 of the SPS regarding the foundations for the risk verification with the possibility of adopting precautionary sanitary and phytosanitary measures in line with its Article 5.7. Moreover, the duty to prove that a particular LMO is harmful to health or the environment is a matter that will inevitably raise new questions about the burden of proof in the WTO. This is because, although it seems clear that it is the Member applying the measure that has the duty to prove the harmfulness, it provides for a right to protect itself before a risk that is largely unknown actually materialises, as long as there is some scientific base for such a risk.[9]

Knowing the main obligations of the SPS Agreement, it is necessary to consider the possibility of adopting financial security in order to answer two questions: (a) Can the measure (financial security) be defined as a sanitary or phytosanitary measure and, therefore, should it follow the rules of the SPS Agreement?; and (b) Does the measure respect the SPS Agreement?

A measure can be considered as sanitary or phytosanitary if an LMO can bring disease and damage to plant life or health and, therefore, threaten biodiversity. In this sense, the measure could be judged based on the SPS Agreement and would have to respect the requirements of scientific evidence, risk assessment, and possible international standards and even the lack of scientific data. It is worth noting in this context that because Article 10 of the Supplementary Protocol does not define what financial security is, one must assume that such a measure would possibly be comprehensive and involve any LMO subject to transboundary movement that, alone, would be contrary to the SPS rules.

The risk assessment, which in practice allows assessment of whether a product is safe or not and is required for the approval of LMOs, is necessarily undertaken on a case-by-case basis. The existence of scientific evidence or the lack thereof should be related to a specific LMO and cannot be indiscriminately extended to all LMOs. Moreover, it is worth noting that there are no international standards to justify the requirement of financial guarantees to prevent possible damage from LMOs. This means that the measure would be applied to achieve an *appropriate level of protection* (according to Articles 3 (3) and 5 (3) of the SPS Agreement) desired by the State requiring the measure, which would necessarily depend on scientific justification, and this does not seem to be the case.

It is important to remember that the State's right to apply a measure more restrictive than an international standard when it wishes to protect human, animal, and plant life or health is one of the central elements of the SPS Agreement. The Appellate Body in the *EC-Hormones* case changed the understanding of the Panel and recognised the autonomous right of a State to stipulate levels of protection higher than those achieved by international standards.[10]

It is also important to mention in this context that Article 3 (3) of the SPS Agreement, which allows the introduction or maintenance of higher level of protection, is part of the core of the SPS as it refers to the risk assessment under Article 5,

9   Rodrigo C. A. Lima, *Medidas sanitárias e fitossanitárias na OMC: neoprotecionismo ou defesa de objetivos legítimos* (Aduaneiras, 2005), pp. 265–266.
10   EC-Measures Concerning Meat and Meat Products (Hormones), Report of Appellate Body, WT/DS26/AB/R, WT/DS48/AB/R (16 January 1997).

which necessarily includes the notion of scientific justification under Article 2 (2) and its exception of the precautionary principle/approach under Article 5 (7) of the SPS.[11] The problem with Article 10 of the Supplementary Protocol is that the level of protection will usually be applied in a broad way, that is to LMOs generally rather than specific LMOs, and it is necessary to have scientific evidence for that.

The requirement of financial security may be justified as necessary based on the precautionary approach, stipulated in the preamble and Article 1 of the Cartagena Protocol. However, the first argument that invalidates the use of the precautionary principle/approach in this case is the fact that financial security or insurance is required for any LMO. This would create a rule for any LMO when in fact the measure must be specific due to the lack of scientific evidence relating to any particular LMO and due to the possibility that this organism could actually cause damage to biodiversity.

The second argument is that in theory, the financial security measures would continuously be applied to LMOs until the Supplementary Protocol is amended to change this decision or until the Party ceased to require it. Even in a view of environmental NGOs,[12] this continuous application of precautionary measures by way of a financial security may violate the WTO. In fact, the vision of the precautionary approach in the Protocol and the SPS Agreement would certainly trigger a lot of discussion, as Balakrishna Pisupati argued:

> The application of the precautionary approach under the Protocol and the SPS is different. Under Article 10 (6) of the Protocol, lack of scientific certainty shall not prevent a Party from taking a decision, as appropriate, with regard to the import of the LMO in order to avoid the adverse effect of the LMO on conservation and sustainable use of biodiversity, taking into account risks to human health. Because the Protocol does not give a limit to the application of the precautionary approach, its application is very flexible based on the different purposes. However, the SPS clearly indicates that the level of sanitary or phytosanitary protection shall be appropriate (Article 3.3). The measures are not more trade-restrictive than required to achieve their appropriate level of sanitary or phytosanitary protection, taking into account technical and economic feasibility (Article 5.4). To sum up, the significance of the precautionary provisions in the Protocol is that they fill in some of the gaps in the SPS.[13]

In the *Japan-Apples* case, Japan argued that the phytosanitary measures it required to allow the import of apples from the United States could be sustained on the basis of Article 5.7 of the SPS. However, Japan did not prove that the scientific evidence available invalidated the information gathered by the experts

11   Lima, see note 9, pp. 171–172.
12   Third World Network, 'The Cartagena Biosafety Protocol and the WTO Agreements'. Available at www.twnside.org.sg/title/mop1c.htm (accessed 1 August 2013).
13   Balakhrisna Pisupati, 'Biotechnology, Cartagena Protocol and the WTO Rules', *Asian Biotechnology and Development Review*, Vol. 7, No. 2 (2005), p. 86.

group created to analyse the case scientifically, nor did it prove that it undertook a new risk analysis in order to have a deeper understanding of the case before applying the measure beginning in 1994. In this context, the Panel considered that the application of such measures was not within a reasonable period of time, since the Panel began in 2002.[14] Along these lines, Marsha A. Echols argues that all possible information and evidence must be considered:

> Since the Agreement uses the word 'insufficient', there should be some 'available scientific information' to justify even a temporary measure, such as a scientific study or report that supports or forms the basis for action. The analysis could be sufficient even if it is inconclusive or the majority scientific view has not crystallized.[15]

Figure 9.3 (below) summarises the financial security or insurance requirements before the SPS Agreement rules.

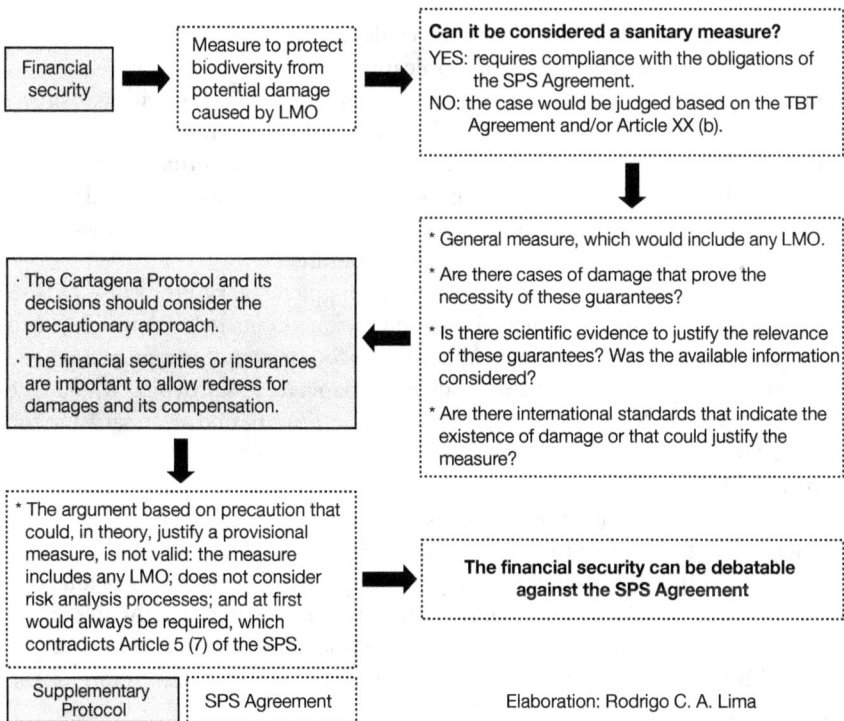

Figure 9.3 Financial security and the SPS Agreement

14   Lima, see note 9, pp. 233–234.
15   Marsha A. Echols, *Food Safety and the WTO: The Interplay of Culture, Science and Technology* (Kluwer, 2001), p. 112.

IV Implications for Parties on adopting financial security

The first concern when considering the requirement of financial security in the context of the Supplementary Protocol is that in theory, any transboundary movement of LMOs may entail such financial guarantee. This means that any operator would have to adopt a financial guarantee in order to sell, buy, handle, use and even transport an LMO. According to Article 2 (2) (c) of the Supplementary Protocol, this operator could be any person that has direct or indirect control over the LMO, which could include a person who placed the LMO on the market, a developer, an importer or an exporter.

Even small biotechnology development companies, importers, exporters and traders, among others, would be required to adopt insurance or other financial security to cover possible damage caused by LMOs, even without any case of damage to biodiversity to justify such requirements. It is important to remember that the authorised LMOs that go through risk assessment processes cannot be considered inherently dangerous products.

Considering that there is no scientific evidence that justifies these guarantees, and that the Cartagena Protocol's precautionary approach itself requires a minimum information base regarding possible damage, calling for a risk assessment that allows for reaching a more scientifically based decision, it is reasonable to question if financial security, even if voluntary, would be in accordance with WTO rules. Small, medium and large biotechnology companies would be affected in their trade and even in the development of biotechnology itself by the unnecessary increase in costs by the adoption of financial guarantees.

It is worth considering that Article 7 of the Supplementary Protocol stipulates that Parties can establish in their domestic law time limits for actions related to response measures. Since the financial security is for the costs that may be incurred in taking the response measures to biodiversity damage, this provision would give a substantial margin of discretion regarding the time period necessary for the required financial security to cover such damage. This time period may well differ depending on each Party's domestic regulation. This possibility makes the requirement of financial security more complex and difficult to implement.

Increase in the prices of food, raw materials, renewable energy and products made from LMOs would be an inevitable consequence of the adoption of financial security, which would be enormously damaging for many States. At this stage, it is relevant to remember that the debate over whether to include products made from LMOs (or the products thereof) was intense until the final hours of the negotiation on the Supplementary Protocol.

If any product made from or produced with the use of LMOs, such as dairy products, wine, beer, medicines or other products, is eligible for a financial security measure even absent the ability to transfer or replicate the modified genetic material, the door stands open to a wide range of barriers to trade not necessarily related to the objective of the Supplementary Protocol and the Cartagena Protocol.

Although, as of today, there are no such guarantees actually required by domestic laws on any LMO, Article 10 (3) of the Supplementary Protocol stipulates that at the first meeting of the Parties of the Supplementary Protocol, the Secretariat should undertake a comprehensive study on, *inter alia*, the modalities of financial security mechanisms, the impact of these mechanisms especially for developing countries and the identification of appropriate entities that can offer these financial security measures. This study should include the possibility of financial securities becoming barriers to trade and their economic and social impacts, particularly on developing countries. In such a study, it is essential to consider the extent to which these guarantees are necessary to avoid or cover potential damage to biodiversity caused by an LMO.

V Cartagena or WTO: is there a balance?

The relationship between the environment and trade is always complex and clearly present in the Cartagena Protocol and the WTO. When a State seeks to regulate the transboundary movement of LMOs to avoid possible damage caused to its biodiversity and to allow compensation for such, the State does so because the LMOs for food or processing, for scientific research, and/or for seeds are being traded. It appears that, on the one hand, the objective of the Cartagena Protocol is to regulate the transboundary movement of LMOs to avoid damage to the conservation of and sustainable use of biodiversity, and, on the other hand, the WTO rules are designed to allow the adoption of trade restrictions as long as there is scientific evidence to justify the need for such measures; these can thus be considered mutually supportive.

In fact, the Cartagena Protocol stipulates in its preamble that trade and environmental agreements should be mutually supportive with a view to promoting sustainable development.[16] Meanwhile, Article 16 (4) of the Supplementary Protocol stipulates that its rules should not affect the rights and obligations of the Parties under international law, which reinforces the idea of a harmonious relationship between the Supplementary Protocol and other treaties, including the WTO agreements.

Despite this apparently harmonious relationship, it is clear that the provisions adopted under the Supplementary Protocol may impact trade, as is obviously the case for financial security measures. In the *EC-Biotech* cases, involving measures

---

16   P. G. Gayathri and Reshma R. Kurup, 'Reconciling the Bio Safety Protocol and the WTO Regime: Problems, Perspectives and Possibilities', *American Journal of Economics and Business Administration*, Vol. 1, No. 3 (2009), p. 239 states: 'The insertion of these statements in the Preamble has only made the conflict between the Protocol and WTO Agreements appear more circular and ambiguous. It has merely restated that in the case of conflict, trade agreements and the Protocol are to be counterpoised with equal primacy. But, more importantly, looking at it from a different perspective, the three statements also emphasize that the two regimes are not to be viewed as conflicting, but as a mutual "check-and-balance mechanism" towards achieving sustainable growth. Such a shift of perception would be instrumental in bringing about a much required paradigm shift in this area'.

affecting the approval and marketing of biotech products,[17] the United States, Argentina and Canada questioned the barriers applied to biotech products and the unjustified delays in the approval of these products. The European Union argued that the measures in question could not be analysed based only on the SPS Agreement and should be considered under the Cartagena Protocol, the CBD and the precautionary principle. The Panel did not enter into the merits of these issues because the Unites States and others are not Parties to the Cartagena Protocol. This fact allowed the Panel to forgo the concrete analysis of the relationship between the Cartagena Protocol and the WTO Agreements.[18]

The issue of financial security reignites the possible conflict between the Cartagena Protocol regime, including its Supplementary Protocol, and the WTO. If any Party decides to require financial security for imported LMOs in accordance with Article 10 of the Supplementary Protocol, we may expect cases to arise before the Dispute Settlement Body of the WTO.

VI Conclusions

The main question to be answered by Parties to the Supplementary Protocol that require financial security in accordance with Article 10 relates to the necessity of adopting such measures to allow redress for possible damage to biodiversity caused by LMOs. As to this question, on the one hand, there are no cases of actual damage caused by LMOs to demonstrate the relevance of these guarantees. On the other hand, it is not clear how these guarantees would be applied by different Parties to the Supplementary Protocol. This would create an uncertain environment that would lead to the adoption of trade barriers.

The WTO rules are quite clear in requiring scientific evidence to justify protective measures for the environment and human health. Minimum evidence is required even in the case of the precautionary measures, in that these measures should consider the available evidence, be reviewed after a reasonable period of time, and should take on more risk assessment to effectively prove their necessity. It is possible that the financial security measures taken under Article 10 of the Supplementary Protocol may contradict the national treatment principle, Article XX (b) of the GATT, the TBT Agreement, and the SPS Agreement.

It is very plausible that a measure such as this could come to be questioned at the WTO and generate barriers to trade, which would create an uncertain environment in the trade of any product derived from biotechnology. In this context, it is extremely important to remember that only LMOs that can transfer or replicate their genetic material are in the scope of the Cartagena Protocol and its Supplementary Protocol. A broad measure applicable to any LMO or, even

---

17   EC- Measures Affecting the Approval and Marketing of Biotech Products, Reports of the Panel, WT/DS291/R, WT/DS292/R, WT/DS293/R (29 September 2006).

18   Elaini C. G. Silva, Rodrigo C. A. Lima and William Filgueiras, 'Comércio Internacional e Biotecnologia: o caso EC-Biotech', in *O Brasil e o Contencioso na OMC, Tomo I, Série GVLaw* (Saraiva, 2009), p. 510.

worse, to a product thereof, can create a complex and debatable scenario. Commodities such as soybeans, corn and other grains would be strongly affected not only by the costs of these guarantees, but also by barriers to trade. However, any product containing a viable LMO, such as bacteria, enzymes or yeast (e.g. dairy products and drinks, among others) could also be affected, creating even greater barriers.

Despite the fact that the Protocol's inherent focus is protection of biodiversity and that the WTO rules focus on free trade, it is essential to consider whether financial security may contradict even with the basic principle of the WTO that allows the application of measures restricting trade in order to protect the environment, that is the demonstration of the need of such measures in light of the objective that it is intended to protect. A broad measure that would cover all products derived from biotechnology and would burden many products in their trade cannot be justified as necessary to protect biodiversity and will be unacceptable, even from a solely environmental perspective. In this context, it is worth noting the possible relevant role of the International Plant Protection Convention[19] and its Secretariat in the consideration of appropriateness of financial security because it can provide scientific information related to risk assessment and monitoring of pests and diseases that affect plants. More specifically, it may also be able to provide data on possible damage caused to biodiversity by LMOs, considering the role of the organisation and of the States that are Parties to it.

It is clear that the adoption of financial security will depend on the Supplementary Protocol entering into force and on its Parties' willingness to actually implement it. Before such measures are actually applied, the Secretariat is expected to carry out the reviews stipulated under Article 10 (3) of the Supplementary Protocol in order to analyse which measures could be legitimately applied and especially what their impacts would be, particularly for developing countries. These analyses based on scientific and technical standards are essential to allow the adoption of more scientifically based financial security measures within the scope of the Supplementary Protocol that are in compliance with the WTO and other trade-related international rules.

---

19 International Plant Protection Convention, adopted on 6 December 1951, *United Nations Treaty Series*, Vol. 150, p. 67.

10 The Supplementary Protocol

A treaty subject to domestic law?

Worku Damena Yifru and Kathryn Garforth

I Introduction

The Nagoya-Kuala Lumpur Supplementary Protocol on Liability and Redress (Supplementary Protocol) has 21 articles. Seven of these articles do not concern the subject matter covered by the Supplementary Protocol. They are governance- or process-related provisions[1] that are commonly included in any multilateral agreement. There are three additional articles referring to exemptions, time limits and financial limits.[2] They address elements that are typical of liability instruments. However, these articles are merely permissive; they do not impose any hard obligations on Parties. They are essentially recommendations for how Parties may wish to address these issues in their domestic law. Therefore, this treaty contains about nine articles that address matters related to the subject of liability and redress for damage caused by living modified organisms (LMOs). Even of these articles, only the one on response measures (Article 5) has a direct bearing on liability. Article 5 appears to be the heart of the Supplementary Protocol. Yet, its implementation is subject to domestic law, a flexibility that leaves room for stringent or soft policy and legislative approaches towards damage resulting from LMOs.

In this manner, the Supplementary Protocol establishes minimum and minimal international norms and subjects these to domestic law. It remains silent on a number of key aspects of liability and redress, creating no international rules on these issues and leaving them to be addressed at the national level. Finally, the Supplementary Protocol indicates that it is not intended to affect the rights and obligations of Parties under international law; thus, it is a treaty that is both part of international law and isolated from it. In this chapter, we explore the tensions within the Supplementary Protocol and in its connections to the rest of the international legal canon, and we inquire whether and to what extent the Supplementary Protocol provides rules that have any significance at all.

---

1 These seven articles (Articles 14–15 and 17–21) cover issues related to: the governing body, secretariat, signature, entry into force, reservations, withdrawal, and authentic texts of the Supplementary Protocol.
2 Articles 6 to 8, Supplementary Protocol.

II International law, international environmental law and liability for environmental damage

Paragraph 1 of Article 38 of the Statute of the International Court of Justice recognises three sources of international law: treaties, custom and general principles of law recognised by civilised nations. Treaties are written instruments in which the Parties agree to be bound by the negotiated terms. A treaty is based on the consent of the Parties to it; in other words, the treaty will only be binding on those who agree to be so bound. Not only are treaties binding, however, but they must also be implemented in good faith. The Latin maxim *pacta sunt servanda* ('agreements must be kept') is arguably one of the oldest and most fundamental principles of international law.[3]

One of the newer branches of international law is international environmental law. Its origins stretch into the mid-nineteenth century, but its modern period is widely seen as beginning with the United Nations Conference on the Human Environment (Stockholm Conference) held in Stockholm in 1972. Three main products emerged from the Stockholm Conference: a resolution on institutional and financial arrangements (which led to the establishment of the United Nations Environment Programme); the Declaration of the United Nations Conference on the Human Environment (Stockholm Declaration) containing 26 principles; and an Action Plan.

In the four decades since the Stockholm Conference, governments and international organisations have taken unprecedented steps towards the protection of the environment. They have agreed to a large number of substantive and procedural rules and put in place a wide range of institutional arrangements. However, despite this development and expansion of international environmental law, environmental concerns and rules are still a long way from becoming an integral part of economic development policies and activities.[4] Trade and economic cooperation rules are overwhelmingly more powerful than environmental rules.

Perhaps nowhere is this clearer than in attempts to regulate liability for damage to the environment. This is also a relatively new area where the rules are evolving and need further development.[5] Principle 22 of the Stockholm Declaration highlights this point:

> States shall cooperate to develop further the international law regarding liability and compensation for the victims of pollution and other environmental damage caused by activities within the jurisdiction or control of such States to areas beyond their jurisdiction.

---

3   John H. Currie, Craig Forcese, and Valerie Oosterveld, *International Law: Doctrine, Theory and Practice* (Irwin Law, 2007), p. 74.

4   Philippe Sands, *Principles of International Environmental Law*, 2nd edn (Cambridge University Press, 2003), p. 53.

5   Ibid., p. 869

Twenty years later in 1992, the United Nations Conference on Environment and Development, which was convened in Rio, included the following in its declaration:

> States shall develop national law regarding liability and compensation for the victims of pollution and other environmental damage. States shall also cooperate in an expeditious and more determined manner to develop further international law regarding liability and compensation for adverse effects of environmental damage caused by activities within their jurisdiction or control to areas beyond their jurisdiction.
>
> (Principle 13 of the Rio Declaration)

The Convention on Biological Diversity (CBD) also includes a provision indicating the importance of addressing liability and redress. The Convention requires the Conference of the Parties to examine the issue of liability and redress for damage to biological diversity, 'except where such liability is a purely internal matter'.[6] While the Parties to the Convention have undertaken some work on this issue,[7] the provision is an open-ended commitment with no indication of any time frame when such examination should end or for what purpose it should be undertaken. This lack of a strong commitment is presumably due to the reluctance of States to tie their hands any further.

In the 20 years between the Rio and Stockholm Declarations, States moved to add emphasis to the need for the development of national laws regarding liability and compensation in addition to the development of international law in this area. In the time since 1972, States have also managed to negotiate and adopt a number of international and regional liability instruments, but many of these have not entered into force.[8] Thus, it seems that while, in principle, States agree to the need for the development of international liability rules for environmental damage, in practice, they are unwilling to establish international liability rules that they fear might impose excessive costs. In the context of the Cartagena Protocol on Biosafety

---

6   Article 14 (2), CBD.

7   Most recently, at the eighth meeting of the Conference of the Parties (COP), the Parties requested the Executive Secretary to prepare a synthesis report on technical information relating to damage to biological diversity and approaches to valuation and restoration of damage to biological diversity, as well as information on national/domestic measures and experiences (Decision VIII/29, para. 3). A document was prepared (UNEP/CBD/COP/9/20/Add.1) which was considered and welcomed by the Parties at their ninth meeting (Decision IX/23). In the multi-year programme of work adopted by COP-10 held in 2010, the Parties agreed that liability and redress could be addressed at COP-12 (Decision X/9, para. (b) (vii)).

8   Recent Developments in International Law Relating to Liability and Redress, Including the Status of International Environment-Related Third Party Liability Instruments: Note by the Executive Secretary, UNEP/CBD/BS/GF-L&R/3/INF/1 (12 May 2010). It should be noted that a number of international liability conventions in the fields of oil pollution and nuclear activity have been negotiated and entered into force. A number of these have evolved over the years to include environmental damage within their scope.

(Cartagena Protocol), this means a number of States have been reluctant to accept rules on liability for damage caused by LMOs, as they believe this will stifle the growth of their biotechnology sector. How, then, did the international community agree to adopt the Supplementary Protocol?

In practice, there are two distinct areas of liability under international law: (a) State liability, which is the liability of States and other international persons under the operation of rules of public international law; and (b) civil liability, which refers to the liability of individual legal or natural persons under the rules of national law adopted pursuant to international treaty obligations establishing harmonised minimum standards.[9] The Supplementary Protocol is said to have adopted a third approach to liability, namely an administrative approach. Some believe that this administrative approach is the most appropriate for establishing liability rules for environmental damage or damage to biodiversity. Does it create binding international rules, though?

There are those, of course, who argue that international law is not law.[10] Instead, what we call 'international law' is, according to these critics, simply politics or States acting in their own self-interest.[11] To those who critique international law as voluntary or at least unenforceable, this seems particularly to be the case with international environmental law.[12] Perhaps one of the biggest challenges for international environmental law is addressing liability for damage to the environment in a significant and legally meaningful way.

III The Supplementary Protocol

1 Context of the negotiations

Views were polarised during the negotiations of the Cartagena Protocol on the need for binding international rules and procedures on liability and redress for damage resulting from transboundary movements of LMOs. Some States were strongly against the idea of having any liability and redress rules. For others (all of them developing countries), liability rules were so important that at one stage, they expressed their intent to make the conclusion of the Cartagena Protocol

---

9 Sands, see note 4, p. 869.
10 For a good catalogue of key works contemplating the nature of international law, see Joshua Kleinfeld, 'Skeptical Internationalism: A Study of Whether International Law is Law', *Fordham Law Review*, Vol. 78 (2010), pp. 2451–2530.
11 See generally Jack L. Goldsmith and Eric A. Posner, *The Limits of International Law* (Oxford University Press, 2005).
12 See Alexandre Kiss and Dinah Shelton, *International Environmental Law*, 3rd edn (Transnational Publishers, 2004), p. 203 suggesting that '[p]rinciples are widely used in international environmental law, perhaps more than in any other field of international law'. See also Daniel M. Bodansky, 'Customary (and Not So Customary) International Environmental Law', *Global Legal Studies Journal*, Vol. 3 (1995), p. 116 characterising international environmental norms as a 'myth system' 'since these norms represent the collective ideals of the international community, which at present have the quality of fictions or half-truths'.

conditional on having 'liability' addressed in the Protocol. Some delegates expressed their strong views by wearing badges that read 'No Liability, No Protocol' during the final stages of the negotiations.

As we know, the outcome of these differing views was Article 27 of the Cartagena Protocol. This enabling provision required the first meeting of the Parties to the Protocol to adopt a process for the elaboration of international rules and procedures in the field of liability and redress for damage resulting from transboundary movements of LMOs. This process was indeed adopted by the Parties at their first meeting in 2004. Negotiation of what finally became the Supplementary Protocol commenced in earnest in 2005.

While five years had passed since the adoption of the Cartagena Protocol, it immediately became clear that little had changed in the range of views on liability and redress. States' divergent positions aligned with their different national interests. States with advanced or emerging bio-economies[13] were worried about the impact that any liability rules might have on their exports and on exporters of modern biotechnology products. States with little or no production of LMOs who considered themselves as primarily importers or consumers of the products of this technology felt they needed some kind of protection or guarantee for redressing any injury or losses they may suffer. Positions ranging from a call for State liability of LMO-exporting countries, including on behalf of exporters under their jurisdiction, to no liability rules at all continued to be advanced as they had during the negotiation of the Cartagena Protocol itself.

What had changed between 2000 and 2005 was the unity and enthusiasm of a number of developing countries for some form of liability rules. During the final phases of the negotiation of the Cartagena Protocol, the so-called Like-Minded Group negotiating bloc was formed by all developing countries and China (in other words, the Group of 77 plus China), with the exception of Argentina, Chile and Uruguay. These latter three were the only developing countries to join Australia, Canada and the US to form the Miami Group. The Like-Minded Group, or at least most of its members, strongly supported inclusion of a liability provision in the Cartagena Protocol in one form or another.

By the time negotiations on liability and redress began in 2005, the solidarity of the Like-Minded Group had fragmented. Some of the countries that had been in favour of a strong biosafety protocol in the 1990s were now either completely opposed to or at least lukewarm about any liability and redress rules for damage resulting from LMOs. The shift occurred as biotechnology industries began to emerge in some developing countries, leading these countries to seek protection of their national interests. In fact, some of these countries with emerging biotechnology industries appeared more cautious on certain issues, such as financial security, than did their developed country counterparts.

---

13   'Bio-economy' as defined by the Organization for Economic Cooperation and Development (OECD) refers to economic activities relating to the invention, development, production and use of biological products and processes. OECD, 'The Bioeconomy to 2030: designing a policy agenda' (2009). Available at www.oecd.org/futures/bioeconomy/2030 (accessed 1 August 2013).

The Supplementary Protocol should, therefore, be seen in the context of the tensions and divergence of views that evolved over the course of the past 15 years (i.e. since 1996, when negotiations on a biosafety protocol started formally). At one stage of the process in 2008, the working document that formed the basis of the negotiations was more than 60 pages long and packed with over 150 so-called 'operational texts' proposed by governments and representatives of non-governmental organisations for consideration.[14] When the Supplementary Protocol was adopted in October 2010, it was a very lean, seven-page document consisting of 21 articles in all.

The content of the Supplementary Protocol needed some interesting twists to arrive at consensus. Almost all the substantive provisions of the Supplementary Protocol are subject to domestic law. The only way out for States on all sides of the argument, it seems, was to accept an approach addressing only a few issues in a small number of provisions and qualifying these provisions by making them 'subject to domestic law'.

The practice of making rules of international agreements subject to domestic law is not unique to the Supplementary Protocol. In fact, it is a very common feature of environmental treaties. What is perhaps different in the case of the Supplementary Protocol is the fact that the practice has been used so sweepingly. As we shall see, it is very difficult to pinpoint any substantive rule in the Supplementary Protocol that creates an international obligation to be implemented unequivocally. In addition, issues that are not considered by the Supplementary Protocol are also left to be addressed by the domestic law of Parties. We also explore the relationship – or lack of relationship – between the Supplementary Protocol and international law in general.

2 Core provisions

Normally, a treaty harmonises practices or rules of national laws or creates new rules of international law. Does the Supplementary Protocol do any of these things?

(1) Definitions

The Supplementary Protocol defines 'damage' as an adverse effect on the conservation and sustainable use of biological diversity and provides some criteria that may be used to determine the occurrence of an adverse effect or damage.[15] It should also be noted that the definitions from the CBD apply to the Supplementary Protocol.[16] Thus, 'biological diversity' means the variability among living

---

14 See Revised Working Draft of Proposed Operational Texts on Approaches and Options Identified Pertaining to Liability and Redress in the Context of Article 27 of Biosafety Protocol, Note by the Co-Chairs, UNEP/CBD/BS/WG-L&R/5/2/Rev.1 (2008). This number includes only operational texts placed under any first option in cases where there were two or more options.
15 Article 2 (2) (b), Supplementary Protocol.
16 Article 2 (1), Supplementary Protocol.

organisms from all sources including, *inter alia*, terrestrial, marine and other aquatic ecosystems, and the ecological complexes of which they are part; this includes diversity within species, between species and of ecosystems.[17]

The Supplementary Protocol is perhaps the first attempt by any global environmental agreement to define damage to biodiversity. Given the broad nature of this definition and the intricacies arising from the meaning of 'biodiversity' itself, it is difficult to determine whether this definition signifies any harmonised understanding of the concept of 'damage to biological diversity' or 'damage to the conservation and sustainable use of biological diversity', and thus the influence it may have on domestic legislation. In other words, it may be possible for the domestic law of a future Party to continue using any existing definition of 'damage' or to adopt a definition different from the one in the Supplementary Protocol yet still be seen as acting within the Supplementary Protocol. For example, in the Environmental Liability Directive[18] of the European Union (EU-ELD), 'environmental damage' means: (a) damage to protected species and natural habitats; (b) water damage; and (c) land damage.[19] The term 'protected species and natural habitats' is further defined and is largely restricted to specific lists of species and habitats in other Directives.[20] From the perspective of the EU-ELD, 'damage to protected species and natural habitats' seems to be the equivalent of damage to biological diversity. For the purpose of the Supplementary Protocol, however, 'damage to biological diversity' is much broader and is not limited to protected species and natural habitats. Whether the EU will be amenable to introducing any changes to the definition in its EU-ELD now that it has decided to become a Party to the Supplementary Protocol is yet to be seen.[21]

Part of the definition of damage is a requirement for damage to be significant.[22] The Supplementary Protocol includes a list of factors that may be used to determine whether damage meets the threshold of a significant adverse effect.[23] In addition to this, however, the Supplementary Protocol also provides that 'Parties may use criteria set out in their domestic law to address damage that occurs within the limits of their national jurisdiction'.[24] The language here is puzzling as the word 'address' would seem to link this provision to Article 5 on response measures, but it is unclear how 'criteria' could be used to address damage. The intention seems to have been to refer to criteria for assessing or evaluating damage. This would link the provision

17   Article 2, CBD.
18   Directive 2004/35/CE of the European Parliament and of the Council of 21 April 2004 on environmental liability with regard to the prevention and remedying of environmental damage, *Official Journal of the European Union 2004*, L 143/56.
19   Article 2 (1), EU-ELD, ibid.
20   Article 2 (3), EU-ELD, ibid.
21   The European Union deposited its instrument of approval of the Supplementary Protocol on 21 March 2013.
22   Article 2 (2) (b) (ii), Supplementary Protocol.
23   Article 2 (3), Supplementary Protocol.
24   Article 3 (6), Supplementary Protocol.

to the definition of 'significant' and add another layer of conditionality to the indicative list of factors by subjecting them to criteria in domestic law.

The Supplementary Protocol also includes a definition of the term 'operator' as 'any person in direct or indirect control of the living modified organism'[25] in question. It goes on to indicate that the operator 'could, as appropriate and as determined by domestic law include, *inter alia*, the permit holder, person who placed the living modified organism on the market, developer, producer, notifier, importer, carrier or supplier'. While the definition does delineate the basic elements to identify who the operator might be, the determination of the person or the category of the person still needs to be made by domestic law.

(2) Scope

The Supplementary Protocol applies to damage resulting from LMOs that find their origin in a transboundary movement.[26] Obviously, the reference to 'transboundary movement' does not necessarily lend itself to the concept of 'transboundary damage' or 'transboundary harm',[27] which is the typical concern of international instruments on liability for damage.[28] The term 'transboundary movement' was required in order to justify the Supplementary Protocol as an international instrument dealing with some international problems (which, by definition, involves at least two different national jurisdictions), and also to fit the Supplementary Protocol within the scope of the Cartagena Protocol.[29] As such, transboundary damage resulting from LMOs identified by the Supplementary Protocol[30] does not

---

25 Article 2 (2) (c), Supplementary Protocol.

26 Article 3 (1), Supplementary Protocol.

27 'Transboundary harm' means harm caused in the territory of or in other places under the jurisdiction or control of a State other than the State of origin, whether or not the States concerned share a common border, Article 2 (c) of Prevention of Transboundary Harm from Hazardous Activities, *Yearbook of the International Law Commission 2001*, Vol. II, Part Two, pp. 146–148, taken note by UN Doc. A/RES/62/68 (2007).

28 See, for example, Article 3 of the 2003 Protocol on Civil Liability and Compensation for Damage caused by the Transboundary Effects of Industrial Accidents on Transboundary Waters, adopted on 21 May 2003 (not in force), Doc. ECE/MP.WAT/11-ECE/CP.TEIA/9. While not explicitly mentioned, a number of other international liability instruments would also appear to include transboundary damage within their scope. For example, the International Convention on Civil Liability for Oil Pollution Damage (adopted on 29 November 1969 and amended by 1992 Protocol, *United Nations Treaty Series*, Vol. 973, p. 3) applies to pollution damage caused in specific geographic areas of a Contracting State (see Article II for a precise definition) but there is no requirement for the incident causing the pollution damage to have also occurred in those areas. The Convention on Third Party Liability in the Field of Nuclear Energy (adopted on 29 July 1960 as amended, *United Nations Treaty Series*, Vol. 956, p. 251) and the Vienna Convention on Civil Liability for Nuclear Damage (adopted on 21 May 1963 as amended, *United Nations Treaty Series*, Vol. 1063, p. 265), follow a similar approach.

29 Article 4, Cartagena Protocol.

30 Article 3 (1) to (3), Supplementary Protocol.

appear to be covered by the Supplementary Protocol and largely remains to be dealt with at the domestic level.[31]

Furthermore, if the operator is a national of the State where the damage occurs, whether the LMO that caused the damage has its origin in a transboundary movement does not really matter. It should be relatively straightforward for the competent authority to require a domestic operator to take response measures or for the competent authority to attempt to recover the costs of the evaluation of the damage and the implementation of response measures from the operator when the competent authority implements the response measures due to the failure of the operator to do so.[32] The difficulty comes when the operator is located in a foreign jurisdiction. In this situation, compelling the operator to take response measures or endeavouring to recover costs from such an operator could be much more challenging. The Supplementary Protocol offers little or no assistance in this regard. It is silent on issues of jurisdiction, applicable law, and recognition and enforcement of judgments.[33] With no rules set at the international level, this issue is subject to domestic law, in this case two sets of domestic law: the domestic law of the State where the damage occurs and that of the State of the operator.

A question might then arise whether the notion of 'transboundary movement' as the origin of the LMO is a superficial demarcation between the national and international domains involved. The Supplementary Protocol probably goes beyond liability that is 'purely an internal matter', yet the provision on scope seems consistent with the whole architecture of the treaty, which confers more space and weight to domestic law than to international scenarios and corresponding international rules.

(3) Response measures

Article 5 provides for response measures. It appears to be at the heart of the Supplementary Protocol as it is the article that most directly provides international rules and procedures to redress damage. The definition of 'response measures'

---

31   A possible exception is unintentional transboundary movements of LMOs. Damage from an unintentional transboundary movement may also constitute transboundary damage. In this case, there is some recourse to international law particularly Article 17 of the Cartagena Protocol, which includes notification and consultation obligations in case of an unintentional transboundary movement or possible unintentional transboundary movement that is likely to have significant adverse effects on the conservation and sustainable use of biodiversity. This is also supported by Article 14 of the CBD and Principles 18 and 19 of the Rio Declaration.

32   Article 5 (1), (4) and (5), Supplementary Protocol.

33   Proposed text on the recognition and enforcement of judgements was part of the working document for the negotiations as late as the second meeting of the Group of the Friends of the Co-Chairs (held in February 2010). See Liability and Redress Draft Texts for Further Negotiations, UNEP/CBD/BS/GF-L&R/2/2 (2009). But it was deleted over the course of that meeting. See Report of The Group of the Friends of the Co-chairs on Liability and Redress in the Context of the Cartagena Protocol on Biosafety on the Work of its Second Meeting, UNEP/CBD/BS/GF-L&R/2/3 (2010). The text appeared in the section on civil liability and was not directly linked to response measures.

elaborates the specific actions that need to be taken in the event of damage.[34] In doing so, the definition might have set a minimum standard for Parties to the Supplementary Protocol to adopt and adhere to. However, response measures under Article 5 are very much subject to domestic law.

Article 5 refers to 'domestic law' six times, including two instances where obligations are to be implemented 'in accordance with domestic law'. Most critically, paragraph 8 of the Article specifies that response measures must be implemented in accordance with domestic law. What does this mean? Is it domestic law, and not Article 5, that ultimately provides for or determines the content of response measures and the manner of their implementation? What is the implication of subjecting the provision on response measures to domestic law? One could say that it is only the details of implementation that are left for elaboration by domestic law, not the principal obligation to respond to damage or likelihood of damage. However, others could argue that Parties are free either to adopt or set aside the requirements of the Supplementary Protocol related to response measures to the extent implementation at the domestic level justifies such action. The obligatory requirement to implement response measures 'in accordance with domestic law' may be used as an opening for the adoption of stringent or soft rules and approaches at the national level for addressing damage resulting from LMOs. Whatever the answer to these questions might be, one characterisation may be agreed upon. Given its strong reliance on domestic law, Article 5 may be more of an obligation of result than an obligation of conduct, despite the fact that it contains paragraphs that require Parties and their competent authorities to act in certain ways. Even this result may be called into question, however, as we shall see in the discussion on implementation and relation to civil liability below.

Also in Article 5, in the event of damage, Parties must require the appropriate operator to: (a) immediately inform the competent authority; (b) evaluate the damage; and (c) take appropriate response measures (Article 5 (1)). Interestingly, such actions may be subject to any requirements of the competent authority. It is hard to imagine how and why the Supplementary Protocol needs to go as far as giving recognition to 'any requirements' of an administrative entity at the domestic level. It is interesting to note how the Supplementary Protocol did not stop even at making itself subject to domestic law; it went further to a lower level of domestic governance and subjected the provision on response measures to domestic administrative requirements. Arguably, such requirements would be defined or recognised by the domestic law and not by the Supplementary Protocol. The intention here seems to be that the requirements applying to Parties as specified in the Supplementary Protocol may be complemented by further requirements that may be set by the authority having the legal as well as technical competence over the type of event or damage in question. However, adding layers of requirements emanating from local authorities could again be part of the general

---

34   Article 2 (2) (d), Supplementary Protocol. Apparently, the term 'response measures' was preferred to 'redress' for some reason.

scheme of the Supplementary Protocol to leave issues to be dealt with at the national level by domestic laws and institutions.

(4) Implementation and relation to civil liability

The content and placement of a rule on civil liability were highly contentious during the negotiations. The provision that was finally agreed to (Article 12) makes the provisions in the Supplementary Protocol further subject to domestic law.

Article 12 begins by largely recapping requirements contained in some of the preceding parts of the Supplementary Protocol. Thus, Parties are required to provide in their domestic law for rules and procedures that address damage and to do so by providing for response measures in accordance with the Supplementary Protocol (Article 12 (1), the chapeau). As we have already seen, however, 'providing for response measures in accordance with the Supplementary Protocol' is to be implemented in accordance with domestic law.

Article 12 goes a step further, though, and adds another layer of the application of domestic law. It states that Parties may provide for response measures by applying their existing domestic law.[35] Not only does the Supplementary Protocol state that response measures are to be implemented in accordance with domestic law, but it also protects existing domestic law by in effect determining that such existing domestic law is already providing for these response measures.

This takes us beyond the argument regarding Article 5 and response measures. While Article 5 may be an opening to take a soft approach at the national level to addressing damage resulting from LMOs, Article 12 suggests that no approach – no requirements for response measures – may be sufficient so long as this is existing domestic law. Article 12 may nullify whatever minimal international rules have been set by Article 5. It begs the question of why it was necessary to negotiate such an international instrument at all.

Article 12 also addresses civil liability. If and when a Party wishes to provide for civil liability for material or personal damage (i.e. traditional damage), it appears mandatory to continue to apply existing general law on civil liability, to develop and apply or continue to apply civil liability law specifically tailored for the purpose, or to develop and apply or continue to apply a combination of both (Article 12 (2)). One important caveat to note, however, is that the material or personal damage referred to is associated with damage as defined in the Supplementary Protocol, namely damage to the conservation and sustainable use of biological diversity. Although the paragraph is formulated in a manner that makes its implementation mandatory, the availability of the options, in particular the option to use existing general civil liability law, may provide legitimate grounds for a Party to ignore traditional damage associated with damage to biodiversity if that Party so wishes. Furthermore, the Supplementary Protocol is silent on the issue of civil liability for traditional damage not connected to damage to biodiversity, leaving it for individual States to decide if and how they wish to proceed in their domestic law.

35   Paragraph 1 (a) of Article 12, Supplementary Protocol.

(5) Relationship with the Convention and the Protocol

In addition to subjecting the obligations in the Supplementary Protocol to domestic law and leaving key aspects of liability and redress to be addressed only at the national level, the Supplementary Protocol also has a difficult relationship with the rest of international law. Article 16 lays down rules that govern the relationship of the Supplementary Protocol with its 'ancestors', the CBD and the Cartagena Protocol, as well as with other areas of international law. According to these paragraphs, the Supplementary Protocol shall '(n)either modify nor amend the Protocol' (Article 16 (1)).

What does it mean for a treaty to supplement another treaty?[36] Does it mean expanding the other pre-existing treaty? Does it mean adding some rules that do not affect the pre-existing treaty, in this case the Cartagena Protocol? Has the Supplementary Protocol not extended the Cartagena Protocol? What is really the ultimate legal or practical implications of the phrase 'neither modify nor amend the Protocol'? Presumably, this phrase cannot mean that nothing has happened following the implementation of Article 27 of the Protocol. Article 27 contemplated the elaboration of international rules and procedures on liability and redress, and the Supplementary Protocol is the realisation of this provision. From that perspective, therefore, something must have changed and that change must have something to do with the Cartagena Protocol too.

In any case, the Supplementary Protocol is an independent treaty. It needs to be signed and ratified, or acceded to, as appropriate. A treaty does not bind States that are not privy to it.[37] No Party to the Cartagena Protocol may be bound by the Supplementary Protocol after its entry into force before such Party expresses its consent by depositing its instrument of ratification, acceptance, approval or accession.

Article 16 (4) states that the Supplementary Protocol shall 'not affect the rights and obligations of a Party under international law'. This paragraph of the Supplementary Protocol is very sweeping and unusual in that it cuts off the Supplementary Protocol from the rest of international law. As indicated earlier, international law is comprised of treaties, custom and general principles of law, so the reference to 'international law' in this provision denotes a very broad concept.

Some international instruments include a provision stipulating the nature of their relationship with other treaties. For example, Article 22 of the CBD specifies the relationship of the Convention with other international conventions. It states that the provisions of the Convention shall not affect the rights and obligations of a Contracting Party deriving from any existing international agreements, except where the exercise of those rights and obligations would cause a serious damage or threat to biological diversity.[38] Clearly, the determination of relationship is limited to existing international agreements.

---

36   See Chapter 2 of this book, by Akiho Shibata, on the origin of Article 16.
37   Article 34 of the Vienna Convention on the Law of Treaties, adopted on 22 May 1969, *United Nations Treaties Series*, Vol.1155, p. 331.
38   Paragraph 1 of Article 22, CBD.

The Cartagena Protocol does not include a provision on relationship in the operative text of the treaty. After intense negotiations, it was finally agreed that some guiding statements would be included in the preamble of the Protocol, as reflected in the last three paragraphs. These recognise that trade and environment agreements should be mutually supportive, emphasise that the Protocol is not to be interpreted as implying a change in the rights and obligations of a Party under any existing international agreements, and state an understanding that the Protocol is not to be subordinated to other international agreements. Again, the emphasis is on international agreements rather than international law as a whole.

The International Law Commission's (ILC) draft articles on 'Prevention of transboundary harm from hazardous activities' (draft articles) include an article on relationship to other rules of international law. Article 18 of the draft articles states: 'The present articles are without prejudice to any obligation incurred by States under relevant treaties or rules of customary international law'.[39] It is interesting to note that the ILC article refers to 'any obligation', unlike paragraph 4 of Article 16 of the Supplementary Protocol, which mentions 'rights and obligations'. Furthermore, the ILC article uses the language of 'under relevant treaties or rules of customary international law', and not 'under international law' as in paragraph 4 of Article 16.

The references in Article 22 of the CBD to 'any *existing* international agreements' and in Article 18 of the ILC draft articles to 'any obligation *incurred* by States under relevant treaties'[40] suggest that the relationship between that text and other treaties or rules of customary international law is backwards-looking, applying only to treaties or rules already in existence. In contrast, paragraph 4 of Article 16 is open-ended in its reference to 'rights and obligations', on the one hand, and 'international law', on the other. That means the Supplementary Protocol is both retrospective and prospective; it is not supposed to affect the rights and obligations of a Party under international law – past, present or future.

A treaty once made is supposed to create new rules of international law that are *ipso facto* binding on the Parties. According to paragraph 4 of Article 16 of the Supplementary Protocol, the rights and obligations of its Parties under international law shall not be affected by the adoption and later implementation of the Supplementary Protocol. The entry into force of any treaty, though, will always have some effect on the rights of States that are Parties to that treaty under international law. The logic of paragraph 4 of Article 16 is a paradox – on the one hand, as a new treaty, the Supplementary Protocol is part of international law; on the other hand, it has been severed from international law and is to have no effect on the rest of the international legal canon. Apart from being a logical impossibility, the provision begs the question as to the point of a treaty that is to have no effect on the rights and obligations of its Parties under international law.

A further challenge is how to reconcile Article 16 with paragraph 2 of Article 10.[41] The latter article addresses financial security and was one of the final

39   Article 18, Prevention of Transboundary Harm from Hazardous Activities, see note 27.
40   Emphasis added.
41   See Chapter 7 of this book, by Rodrigo C. A. Lima.

issues to be resolved during the negotiations. Article 10 also contains what is, in effect, a relationship clause. The article recognises that Parties retain the right to provide, in their domestic law, for financial security (Article 10 (1)). It then requires Parties to exercise this right 'in a manner consistent with their rights and obligations under international law, taking into account the final three preambular paragraphs of the [Cartagena] Protocol' (Article 10 (2)). If the Supplementary Protocol is not to affect the rights and obligations of a Party under international law, is it possible to simultaneously require an existing right to be exercised in a manner consistent with a Party's rights and obligations under international law? It seems as though the negotiators were trying to have their cake and eat it too: they cut off the Supplementary Protocol from the rest of international law, yet attempted to subject the right to provide for financial security to other aspects of international law.

3 Other considerations

There are provisions in the Supplementary Protocol dealing with causation (Article 4), exemptions (Article 6), time limits (Article 7), financial limits (Article 8) and right of recourse (Article 9). Each of these provisions touches upon very important issues relevant to liability and redress as well as issues commonly considered in civil liability regimes. For this reason, though, they do not seem to fit well with the administrative approach adopted by the Supplementary Protocol. While these provisions are well suited to the adversarial nature of civil liability, they are less consistent with the tone of the Supplementary Protocol, which appears to seek a more cooperative approach to ensuring that biodiversity is restored following damage.

Including provisions on exemptions, time limits, financial limits and right of recourse in the Supplementary Protocol reminds Parties of the need to provide legal or procedural protection to the operator from any capriciousness on the part of the State. Is this reminder necessary in the context of an administrative approach to liability and redress? The provisions are not necessarily related to the other substantive rules in the Supplementary Protocol. They have little or no direct correlation with Article 5. They are recommendations for consideration when developing domestic law provisions. While they provide indications of what Parties may do, they lack the force of mandatory legal obligations. They would have more meaning and relevance if placed in guidelines or any other soft law format, such as those developed under the United Nations Environment Programme[42] or in the work conducted under the International Law Commission.[43]

---

42 Guidelines for the development of domestic legislation on liability, response action and compensation for damage caused by activities dangerous to the environment, annex to Decision SS.XI/5 B, Proceedings of the Governing Council/Global Ministerial Environment Forum at its eleventh special session, UNEP/GCSS.XI/11 (3 March 2010).

43 Principles on the allocation of loss in the case of transboundary harm arising out of hazardous activities, *Report of the International Law Commission 2006*, UN Doc. A/61/10, p. 101, taken note by UN Doc. A/RES/61/36 (2006), Annex, and the draft articles on the Prevention of Transboundary Harm from Hazardous Activities, see note 27.

IV Conclusion

The international community has called for the development of international law regarding liability and compensation for environmental damage. Achieving international consensus in this area is an enormous challenge, however. Indeed, reaching international consensus on liability and redress in general – whether tied to environmental damage or not – has been an extremely difficult task. After several decades of work on liability and redress for transboundary harm, the International Law Commission has moved away from the notion of liability and redress *per se* and towards the principle of prevention of transboundary harm and allocation of loss, presumably with a view to making better progress. States are extremely reluctant to accept liability rules that could impose new costs on themselves or their citizens.

The negotiations on liability and redress under the Cartagena Protocol and the final outcome in the form of the Supplementary Protocol support this perspective. The reluctance of a number of States to commit themselves to legally binding international rules on liability and redress seems to be why, as the review in this chapter shows, the Supplementary Protocol leaves its core obligations to elaboration by domestic law or to implementation 'in accordance' with domestic law.

Even the concept of liability and redress serves merely as a facade of the new treaty without playing much of a role in the content. Apart from its title, the Supplementary Protocol makes reference to 'liability' in Article 1 (objective) and Articles 5 and 12 in connection with civil liability only. The term 'redress' appears in the title of the Supplementary Protocol without having any real role in forming the substantive rules at the core of the treaty. It has not been mentioned in the body of the Supplementary Protocol, except in Article 1 (objective) and paragraph 3 (a) of Article 2, though indirectly. In contrast, there are 18 references to 'domestic law' spread over nine of the Supplementary Protocol's 21 articles.

The Supplementary Protocol may contain more optional rules than mandatory ones. Where every substantive provision of a treaty is subject to domestic law, the famous principle of international law that 'agreements must be kept' may be less relevant. There is too much flexibility, which makes monitoring of compliance with the terms of the agreement difficult and, in fact, pointless. This situation could, perhaps, be attributed to the nature of rules based on an administrative approach – the unavoidable consequence of dealing with liability and redress for damage to biological diversity and choosing an administrative approach as the basis to do so. Those who were advocating for a comprehensive liability regime now have the treaty, but not necessarily the rules they were looking for.

However, the Supplementary Protocol still represents an international framework for national policy and legislative action. It is a minimum agreement. As a minimum, it embodies international consensus with respect to things that were sources of deep division before, including that: (a) LMOs could cause damage to biological diversity; (b) legal and administrative measures are required to address such damage; and (c) operators that have control over the organisms should be answerable for any damage. In this regard, the Supplementary Protocol may provide the impetus to countries, in particular to those developing countries, to elaborate their domestic law in this area, heretofore addressed by few legal systems. The Supplementary Protocol provides guidance and benchmarks for how domestic law should respond to damage to biodiversity caused by LMOs, and in the process, it makes clear that the importing country will bear much of the burden in ensuring that any such damage is appropriately redressed. Those countries concerned about the possible impacts of LMOs may find the support they need in the Supplementary Protocol to take action in their domestic law.

The Supplementary Protocol can be described as less ambitious but more realistic. By providing such flexible rules, it might win the support of a sufficient number of States to allow it to enter into force, unlike many previous liability instruments. Its purpose looks to encourage and enable, rather than require, States to address, in their domestic law, damage to the conservation and sustainable use of biological diversity that may be caused by LMOs. Whether negotiating a 'treaty subject to domestic law' is an effective means of addressing damage to the environment or biodiversity remains to be seen.

Part III
The implementation

11 Challenges and opportunities in the implementation of the Supplementary Protocol

Re-interpretation and re-imagination

Dire Tladi

I Statement of the issues

The Nagoya-Kuala Lumpur Supplementary Protocol on Liability and Redress (Supplementary Protocol) is the product of long and difficult negotiations, beginning in 2005 and culminating in its adoption in 2010 in Nagoya. With the adoption of the Supplementary Protocol, the challenges of implementation must be confronted.

Like most other international law instruments, the Supplementary Protocol is a product of compromises that straddle the fault lines between the positions of various interests groups. Moreover, while these fault lines manifest themselves primarily in the course of the negotiations, they also have a tendency to re-emerge when it comes to the implementation of the instrument. These fault lines re-emerge in the form of re-interpretation and re-imagination that may take place subsequent to the conclusion of the agreement – in other words, fights that were lost may be reopened in the form of conflicting interpretations of provisions of the agreement. The re-emergence of the fault lines is to be expected given the problem of auto-interpretation in international law, that is the fact that the absence of a compulsory judicial method to settle disputes allows individual States the privilege of determining for themselves what the content of the law is. Thus, there is a possibility, even a likelihood, that in the process of the implementation of the Supplementary Protocol, hard-fought compromises may be reopened in the form of differing interpretations. However, the nature of the Supplementary Protocol as applicable to international transport may also have an impact on the extent to which re-interpretation and re-imagination could affect implementation.

The purpose of this short chapter is to consider the implementation challenges that may arise due to the re-interpretation and re-imagination of the provisions of the Supplementary Protocol by States that become party to it. The re-interpretation and re-imagination can take place at various times, including when implementing legislation is adopted or even during exchanges between Parties at the Conference of the Parties serving as a Meeting of the Parties (COP-MOP) to the Cartagena Protocol on Biosafety (Cartagena Protocol) or at other international forums. I begin by giving a general description of the forums in which Parties (and possibly non-Parties) could re-interpret the provisions of the Supplementary Protocol. I then proceed to consider specific challenges faced in implementing the Supplementary Protocol that could open up opportunities for re-interpretation and re-imagination. The provisions in the Supplementary Protocol relating to financial security and civil liability raise peculiar issues of implementation and offer additional opportunities for re-interpretation and re-imagination. I therefore offer more specific comments thereon.

II Opportunities for re-interpretation and re-imagination: the forums

'Re-interpretation and re-imagination', for the purposes of this chapter, refers to the tools, including subsequent practice, that States (or, for that matter, other actors) may use to mould their rights and obligations under a treaty in a manner that is more favourable for them.[1] 'Re-interpretation', in turn, refers to the use of language in the agreement as the primary tool for moulding the meaning of an instrument in this way, while 're-imagination' refers to reliance on discussions occurring during the negotiations of the instrument whether based on reports of the meetings, articles or the 'unwritten *travaux préparatoire*' to achieve the same ends.[2] Although re-interpretation may be comparably more faithful to the terms of the instrument, both 're-interpretation' and 're-imagination' represent acceptable tools of interpretation.[3] The extent to which either tool produces the 'objectively' correct interpretation would, however, depend on their consistency with terms of the treaty, in the given context and in the light of the treaty's object and purpose.[4] At their extreme, re-interpretation and re-imagination could lead to revisionism, which would be an 'interpretation' that is not faithful to the terms of the treaty, in the given context and in the light of the object and purpose of the treaty.

In the context of the Supplementary Protocol, the opportunities for re-interpretation and re-imagination present themselves in two different ways. In the first instance, because of the nature of international environmental regulation, domestic implementation is required. Second, even apart from the domestic implementation, States have the opportunity to re-interpret and re-imagine provisions of international environmental agreements at international forums, including but not limited to the Conferences of the Parties (COP) established under such agreements.

---

1   On what constitutes subsequent practice for the purposes of treaty interpretation, see International Law Commission, Provisional Summary Record for the 3172nd Meeting: Subsequent Agreement and Subsequent Practice in Relation to the Interpretation of Treaties, UN.Doc A/CN.4/SR.3172 (25 June 2013).

2   While Courts and academics refer to the *travaux préparatoire*, diplomats negotiating treaties sometimes find it sufficient to rely on memory, whether their own or the memory of another.

3   See Articles 31 and 32, Vienna Convention on the Law of Treaties, adopted on 23 May 1969, *United Nations Treaties Series*, Vol. 1155, p. 331.

4   This is the language used in Article 31 (1) of the Vienna Convention on the Law of Treaties, which reflects the general rule of interpretation.

The first point about re-interpretation and re-imagination in the domestic implementation arises from the nature of modern international environmental agreements. It has to be understood that modern international environmental law, and the agreements that form such a significant part of this body of law, is significantly different from classical international law, which has been concerned with purely inter-State relations or questions of government conduct.[5] Environmental harm is, by and large, caused by the conduct of non-State actors.[6] There are, of course, incidents of State-caused environmental harm such as the environmental harm that could result from nuclear testing, but these are exceptions rather than the rule.[7]

Because environmental harm is caused principally by the conduct of non-State actors, to be effective, international regulation of the environment has to have, as its primary objective, the goal of affecting the conduct of non-State actors. However, States remain the primary addressees and any international regulation remains addressed to States and would require States 'to regulate or otherwise influence the behaviour of the relevant non-State actors'.[8] Truly, the Cartagena Protocol itself is directed at the State, requiring the State of export to 'notify, or require the exporter to' notify the competent authority prior to the transboundary movement of living modified organisms (LMOs).[9] Nonetheless, it is clear that the role of the State is mainly to 'require the exporter' to undertake notification.[10] Moreover, the overall objective of the Cartagena Protocol regulation is to affect the conduct of non-State actors in the 'transfer, handling and use of living modified organisms'.[11]

This structure of international environmental agreements is equally apparent in other international agreements. To illustrate, while the Kyoto Protocol to the UN Framework Convention on Climate Change (Kyoto Protocol) provides that States shall 'elaborate policies' on, *inter alia*, 'energy efficiency in relevant sectors', 'sustainable forms of agriculture' and the 'development and increased use of renewable energy', the Kyoto Protocol does not call upon States to use energy efficiently, to engage in sustainable forms of agriculture or to develop the use of renewable energy.[12] The State is merely called upon to facilitate these various objectives. Thus, as a rule, the obligation of States is, to varying degrees, to regulate

5   Daniel Bodansky, Jutta Brunnée and Ellen Hey, 'International Environmental Law: Mapping the Field', in Daniel Bodansky, Jutta Brunnée and Ellen Hey eds, *The Oxford Handbook of International Environmental Law* (Oxford University Press, 2007), p. 6.

6   See also Dire Tladi, 'Corporates and the Flexible Mechanisms in the Climate Change Regime: The Privatisation of Sustainable Development?' *South African Yearbook of International Law*, Vol. 32 (2007), p. 396.

7   See, e.g., *Legality of the Threat or Use of Nuclear Weapons*, Advisory Opinion of 8 July 1996, *ICJ Reports* 1996, para. 29, where the Court recognised that 'the use of nuclear weapons could constitute a catastrophe for the environment'.

8   See Thilo Marauhn, 'The Changing Role of the State', in Bodansky *et al.*, see note 5, p. 739. See also Bodanksy *et al.*, see note 5, p. 7.

9   Article 8 (1), Cartagena Protocol.

10   Ibid.

11   Article 1, Cartagena Protocol.

12   Article 2, Kyoto Protocol to the UN Framework Convention on Climate Change, adopted on 11 December 1997, *United Nations Treaties Series*, vol. 2303, p. 148. See Tladi, see note 6, p. 399.

the conduct of those under their jurisdiction. To borrow the words of Bodanksy, Brunnée and Hey, the international agreement regulates 'one-step removed' from those whose conduct is regulated (the non-State actor).[13] The State thus acts as the intermediary in the regulation of the conduct of the non-State actor and has to translate the framework agreed to internationally into domestic regulation of the conduct of non-State actors.[14]

In this process of transforming the internationally agreed rules to the domestic plane the possibility of re-interpretation and re-imagination may present itself. Thus, when implementing legislation or other directives necessary to give effect to the international environmental agreement, specific provisions not reflecting the prefer-ence of the State may be redrafted in a manner that is closer to the preference of the State concerned. The more vague or ambiguous the particular provision under consideration, the greater the possibility for re-interpretation and re-imagination.

Another opportunity for re-interpretation and re-imagination will present itself in other international forums where States have the opportunity to state their views on the contents of their rights and obligation under a treaty. The most typical forum where this is likely to happen is the COP established under the particular instru-ment – in the case of the Supplementary Protocol, this will be COP-MOP.[15] As an illustration, the Cartagena Protocol provides for the COP-MOP to consider 'the need for and modalities for developing standards with regards to' handling, packaging and transport practices, *inter alia*.[16] Given the complex negotiations over the documentation required, it should not come as a surprise when delegations seek to re-interpret some aspects of Article 18.[17] Even without an explicit mandate from the international agreement, a conference of the parties can decide to take up a specific matter. The consideration of socio-economic considerations in decision-making (a hotly contested issue in the negotiations of the Cartagena Protocol) is recognised by the Cartagena Protocol.[18] The Cartagena Protocol does not man-date the further consideration of socio-economic elements, yet 'socio-economic considerations' has become an important sub-topic under the discussion on capacity-building activities – often, there is debate over its meaning as one or more delegations offer differing interpretations.[19]

13 Bodanksy *et al.*, see note 5, p. 7.
14 Marauhn, see note 8, p. 734.
15 See Article 14, Supplementary Protocol.
16 Article 18 (3), Cartagena Protocol.
17 See for discussions on the documentation negotiations, Johan Bodegard, 'Documentation', in Christoph Bail, Robert Falkner and Helen Marquand, *The Cartagena Protocol on Biosafety: Reconciling Trade in Biotechnology with Environment and Development?* (Royal Institute of International Affairs, 2002), p. 338. In the course of COP-MOP discussions under the agenda item 'handling, transport, packaging and identification' there is often robust negotiations on the meaning of the Article. See Report of the Fifth Meeting of the Conference of the Parties serving as Meeting of the Parties to the Cartagena Protocol on Biosafety, UNEP/CBF/BS/COP-MOP/5/17(2010), paras 110–121.
18 Article 26, Cartagena Protocol.
19 See paragraphs 21–31, Decision BS-V/3 (2010), Status of Capacity-Building Activities, UNEP/CBD/BS/COP-MOP/5/17 (2010), in which the Conference of the Parties makes decisions on capacity building initiatives relative to taking into account socio-economic considerations. A major difference of opinion existed over precisely how socio-economic considerations were to be taken into account.

The Supplementary Protocol specifically makes provision for regular review of the effectiveness of the Supplementary Protocol. More specifically, the Supplementary Protocol in Article 13 provides that the first review 'shall include the review of the effectiveness of Articles 10 and 12'. Without a doubt, this provision will provide an opportunity for delegations to re-interpret Articles 10 and 12 and to re-imagine compromises embodied in the two provisions, both of which are discussed below.

There are many other opportunities for re-interpretation and re-imagination. However, the World Trade Organization dispute settlement framework deserves a special mention as a possible forum for the re-interpretation and re-imagination of the Supplementary Protocol for two reasons. First, trade and environment permeates just about every fault line in the negotiations leading to the adoption of both the Cartagena Protocol and the Supplementary Protocol. Whether the issue was the definition of damage, the adoption of strict or fault-based liability, the substantive scope of the Protocol, or even the nature of the instrument, the trade and environment dimension always lurked ominously in the background. The second reason for the special significance of the WTO dispute settlement mechanisms in this discussion is that the WTO provides the only realistic possibility for a definitive interpretation – whether the interpretation arrived at is 'objectively' correct or not is, of course, a totally different question and may itself be a result of re-interpretation and re-imagination. The point is that the WTO dispute settlement mechanisms present States with yet another approach to re-interpretation and re-imagination of the provisions of an adopted instrument.[20]

These are the forums in which Parties will have an opportunity to re-interpret and re-imagine the provisions of the Supplementary Protocol. I turn now to consider the provisions in the text of the Supplementary Protocol that provide an opportunity for re-interpretation and re-imagination of the Cartagena Protocol.

III The potential for re-interpretation and re-imagination in the implementation of the Supplementary Protocol

The first step towards the implementation of the Supplementary Protocol will be its entry into force. The Supplementary Protocol was opened for signature on 7 March 2011 and will enter into force after the deposit of 40 instruments of ratification or accession. Only once the Supplementary Protocol enters force will

---

20 The cases in which the WTO dealt with the trade and environment issue are too many to list here in their entirety, but the most famous include US-Measures Standards for Reformulated Gasoline, Report of Appellate Body, WT/DS2/AB/R (29 April 1996); US-Measures for Import Prohibition of Certain Shrimp and Shrimp Products, Report of Appellate Body, WT/DS58/AB/R (12 October 1998); and EC-Measures Concerning Meat and Meat Products (Hormones), Report of Appellate Body, WT/DS26/AB/R, WT/DS48/AB/R (16 January 1997).

the question of implementation come into play. The implementation will take place through the adoption of relevant implementing legislation. In the course of implementing the Supplementary Protocol, States will have an opportunity to re-interpret and re-imagine its contents.

In implementing the Supplementary Protocol, the first point that has to be borne in mind is that the Supplementary Protocol, by its own terms, does not 'modify nor amend the Protocol' and, furthermore, does not 'affect the rights and obligations of the Parties of [the] Supplementary Protocol under the Convention and the Protocol'.[21] Thus, while Parties will engage in re-interpretation and re-imagination and will generally have a significant degree of leeway on how to implement the Supplementary Protocol, this discretion will necessarily be circumscribed by the provisions of the Convention on Biological Diversity (CBD) and the Cartagena Protocol. As an initial (and very general) example, the Supplementary Protocol could not be used to prohibit trade in LMOs in a manner inconsistent with the Cartagena Protocol.

While this circumscription is helpful to guide implementation, to the extent that there is auto-interpretation of the provisions of the Cartagena Protocol and the CBD, the scope of discretion to re-interpret and re-imagine remains wide. The difficulty of avoiding diverse interpretations can be illustrated by consideration of the term 'damage' in the Supplementary Protocol. In the course of the negotiations, one camp sought a broad definition of damage and another camp sought a narrow definition of damage.[22] Those that argued for a narrow definition advanced the view that damage can only relate to biodiversity. For others, damage covered harm to health and even economic loss. What is important to note is that this was not a new debate, but was simply the negotiations of the Cartagena Protocol replaying themselves (i.e. battles that could not be won in the negotiations of the Cartagena Protocol were being fought in the negotiations of the Supplementary Protocol) – in a sense, there was re-interpretation and re-imagination of the Cartagena Protocol in the negotiations of the Supplementary Protocol. All positions were purportedly based on the objectives and scope of the Protocol. What is interesting to note is that the Supplementary Protocol adopts an ambiguity similar to that adopted in the Cartagena Protocol. Thus, under the Supplementary Protocol, damage means:

> adverse affect on the conservation and sustainable use of biological diversity, taking also into account risks to human health.[23]

This text begs the question whether harm to human health is covered under the definition of damage. A purely literal reading may suggest that it is not, but

---

21 See Article 16 (1) and (2), Supplementary Protocol.
22 See generally on the positions of different delegations, Dire Tladi, 'Civil Liability in the Context of the Cartagena Protocol: To be or not to be (binding)', *International Environmental Agreements: Politics, Law and Economics*, Vol. 10 (2010), p. 15.
23 Article 2 (2) (b), Supplementary Protocol.

this would certainly be contested by those who argued strenuously for a wide definition of damage. The text of Article 1, under the title 'Objective', could contribute to a purposive interpretation of the definition, but is equally ambiguous and thus unhelpful. Under Article 1, the objective of the Supplementary Protocol is to 'contribute to the conservation and sustainable use of biological diversity, *taking also into account risks to human health*'. Moreover, the nature of the responsibilities under the Supplementary Protocol (i.e. the fact that the Supplementary Protocol essentially puts in place an administrative approach) does not necessarily preclude an expansive definition since whatever administrative empowerments are permitted can easily be applied for the prevention of harm to human health.[24] What has to be emphasised is that this ambiguity, while not hoped for by the drafters, is not there by accident. The ambiguity is, in fact, not new, but is rather a remnant of the ambiguity of the Cartagena Protocol itself in the context of the scope of the Cartagena Protocol. In the context of implementation (within the limits of this short chapter), the ambiguity in the definition illustrates a wide margin of discretion in the implementation of the Supplementary Protocol, which in turn increases the potential for re-interpretation and re-imagination.

Another illustration of the opportunity for re-interpretation and re-imagination in the process of implementation is the definition of 'operator' in Article 2 (2) (c) of the Supplementary Protocol. As with the definition of 'damage', there was significant contestation in the negotiations over the definition of the term 'operator', with some seeking to cast a wide net and others seeking to limit the definition to the person 'in control' at the time of the damage-causing incident. The Supplementary Protocol incorporates both views, defining 'operator' as:

> any person in direct or indirect control of living modified organisms which could, as appropriate and as determined by domestic law, include, *inter alia*, the permit holder, person who placed the living modified organism on the market, developer, producer, notifier, exporter, importer, carrier or supplier.

While the text combines both approaches, the question arises whether any of the persons specifically identified (e.g. exporter or permit holder) would be liable even if they were not in direct or indirect control of the LMO at the time of the damage-causing incident. Presumably, States seeking a narrow application would require some sort of control before imposing any of the response measures on a specific operator, while those States that had sought to cast a wide net over many possible operators would create the potential for any of the mentioned operators to be held responsible for the response measures irrespective of the element of control at the time of damage. The inclusion of the phrase 'as appropriate and as determined by domestic law' simply adds to the ambiguity: 'as appropriate' suggests a level of objectivity, while 'as determined by domestic law' suggests more

---

24 This anticipatory point is made because in the course of the negotiations, those who opposed a broad definition of damage sometimes argued that a broad definition was not consistent with an administrative approach.

discretion given to the implementer. Moreover, the Supplementary Protocol provides that the competent authority has the discretion to '[i]dentify the operator that has caused the damage'.[25] This ambiguity further adds the possibility for re-interpretation and re-imagination in the implementation of the Supplementary Protocol. Again, this is not to say that there is no objectively correct interpretation, only that the less precise the language, the greater the margin for States to implement the rule in a manner consistent with legal and policy objectives, while purporting to be faithful to the text of the instrument.

A wide margin of discretion in the implementation of the Supplementary Protocol does not, however, result only from the possibility of re-interpretation and re-imagination. Some provisions in the Supplementary Protocol, by design, leave a wide margin of discretion to the implementing State. Throughout the Supplementary Protocol, the details of implementation, and subsequently policy choices, are left to national authorities. The Supplementary Protocol, for example, does not set out response measures that are to be implemented in the event of damage, but rather leaves it to national authorities to determine.[26] Similarly, while the Supplementary Protocol requires a causal link to be established between the damage and the LMO (Article 4), how this is done is left completely up to domestic law. In the course of the negotiations, there was a divergence of views as to who should bear the onus of showing the causal link: the person asserting that damage has occurred (or could occur), or the person alleged to have caused the damage. In the text as currently drafted, the national authority in each country will have the discretion of determining the burden. Granted, the significance of the 'causation' element has diminished somewhat because the Supplementary Protocol now primarily provides for an administrative regime, but some causal link between the purported damage and the LMO will need to exist in order for the Supplementary Protocol to apply.

Discretion is also given to the implementers through provision of 'rights' to the National Implementer. For example, Article 5 (5) of the Supplementary Protocol provides that the competent authority 'has the right to recover' from the responsible operator the costs of any expenses incurred in relation to the response measures. Similarly, the Supplementary Protocol grants to Parties the discretion to decide whether to grant exemptions for acts of God or acts of war or civil unrest.[27] Thus, again, States that had sought as broad a form of responsibility/liability as possible could decide not to grant any exemptions. Additionally, the Supplementary Protocol provides absolute discretion to domestic lawmakers in respect to financial limits and time limits relating to claims for response measure-related costs.

The opportunity for re-interpretation and re-imagination brought on by deliberate ambiguity arises most sharply in the context of the extent to which free trade rules can be trumped by the Supplementary Protocol or *vice-versa*. Again,

---

25   Article 5 (2) (a), Supplementary Protocol.
26   Articles 5 (2) and 5 (4), Supplementary Protocol.
27   Article 6 (1), Supplementary Protocol.

this is a legacy of the inability to agree during the negotiations of the Cartagena Protocol on whether the provisions of the Cartagena Protocol would be subject to trade agreements or *vice-versa*.[28] In the course of the negotiations, the camp seeking a broad instrument argued for inclusion of an obligation to provide financial security for the transport of LMOs to ensure that any costs related to the required response measures could be recovered. The camp arguing for a narrow instrument (indeed, in some cases, no instrument) opposed inclusion of any requirement for financial security on the basis, *inter alia*, that such requirement could negatively impact free trade and would thus fall foul of the free trade rules. As a compromise, the Supplementary Protocol provides that Parties 'retain the right to provide, in their domestic law, for financial security'.[29] For those opposed to the requirement of financial security, the text provides comfort in that the right to require financial security does not derive from the Supplementary Protocol. It is, according to the text, a right that is based on domestic law. To the extent that any requirement for financial security falls afoul of free trade rules, so the argument goes, the Supplementary Protocol could not be offered as a justification for such a violation as the right is based not on the Supplementary Protocol, but on domestic law. For those who had argued for the right to require financial security, the text provides dual benefit. First, regardless of the source, just by its inclusion in the Supplementary Protocol, the right to require financial security is cloaked in international legitimacy and therefore could provide some defence against a trade-related attack, notably that it is a right under domestic law. Second, the Supplementary Protocol, by using the phrase 'retain', may suggest that the right already exists under international law – assuming there is an acceptance that the 'in their domestic law' qualifies not the source of the right, but the place where the right is to be exercised.

To buttress the ambiguity, Article 10 (2) provides that the right to impose financial security requirements should be exercised 'in a manner consistent with [the Parties'] rights and obligations under international law, taking into account the final three preambular paragraphs of the Protocol'. Needless to say, the final three preambular paragraphs of the Cartagena Protocol are prime illustrations of ambiguity in treaty making.[30] One author has described these preambular paragraphs as making a travesty of international law.[31]

---

28   For a discussion of the without prejudice clause in the Cartagena Protocol see generally Margarida Afonso, 'The Relationship with Other Agreements: An EU Perspective', in C. Bail *et al.*, see note 17, p. 423; Sabrin Safin, 'The Relationship with Other Agreements: Much Ado About Nothing', ibid., p. 438. See also Dire Tladi, *Sustainable Development in International Law: An Analysis of Key Environment-Economic Instruments* (Pretoria University Law Press, 2007), p. 199.

29   Article 10 (1), Supplementary Protocol.

30   The first of the three provides for a mutually supportive relationship between trade and environmental agreements. The second provides that the Cartagena Protocol is not to be interpreted as implying a change in the rights and obligations of Parties. The third provides that the second should not be read as subordinating the Protocol to any other agreements.

31   Lakshman Guruswamy, 'Sustainable Agriculture: Do GMOs Imperil Biosafety?' *Indiana Journal of Global Legal Studies*, Vol. 9 (2002), p. 491.

In a less obvious way, the trade-related opportunity for re-interpretation and re-imagination is presented in the provision on civil liability. In essence, the Supplementary Protocol provides that States shall provide for domestic law rules relating to civil liability.[32] This can be done through existing civil liability rules, civil liability rules developed specifically for transboundary movement of LMOs or a combination of the two.[33] Again, the text can provide comfort for both sides of the aisle. For those who feared that civil liability rules (and particularly stringent civil liability rules) may have a negative impact on free trade, any rules on civil liability would not be derived from the Supplementary Protocol and would thus have no international status in the context of any trade/environment dispute. For those who had sought rules on civil liability, Article 12 provides international legitimacy to any civil liability rules that such a State may come up with.[34] More-over, Article 12 could conceivably be interpreted as empowering the implementing State to include a significantly broad definition of damage, to institute a strict standard of liability, and to cast a wide net for possible operators. In a strange twist, Article 12 could, in its implementation, be re-interpreted and re-imagined to achieve what could not have been achieved if States had attempted to adopt specific rules on civil liability.

Together, the discretion explicitly provided for under the Supplementary Protocol and the ambiguity that allows national implementers the license of re-interpretation, revisionism and re-imagination allow domestic law a wide policy margin in determining how to implement the Supplementary Protocol. Nonetheless, the wide margin of discretion available to the domestic implementer is tempered by the transboundary character of the Supplementary Protocol. While a country of import (where the damage is most likely to occur) is free, within certain constraints, to apply the Supplementary Protocol as it has re-interpreted or re-imagined such, enforcement in the country of export or third country may prove difficult if such re-interpretation or re-imagination is not acceptable to the latter. As an illustration, an Implementing Authority in the country of import may struggle to reclaim the costs for response measures if, under the laws of the country where the responsible operator is present, the amount is seen to be excessive or the civil liability laws implemented under Article 12 are seen to be unreasonable. The point here is not to suggest anything about the complex rules of enforcement of foreign judgments, but only to illustrate that while the domestic authorities will have significant discretion, that discretion is not absolute, as enforcement may need to take place in different jurisdictions.

IV Conclusions

The adoption of the Nagoya-Kuala Lumpur Supplementary Protocol is an exceptional feat matched only by the skilful ambiguity employed by its drafters.

---

32   Article 12 (1), Supplementary Protocol.
33   Article 12 (1) and (2), Supplementary Protocol.
34   See Tladi, see note 22.

This skilful deployment of ambiguity represents, at once, an important example of deference to domestic law and national policy, on the one hand, and, on the other, a challenge to implementation. Through the skilful use of ambiguity, different domestic systems with different resource levels, different priorities attaching to environmental concerns, different policies towards biotechnology, and different policy concerns are free to make their own policy choices in implementing the Supplementary Protocol, whether as a result of explicit deference to domestic law or as a result of the ambiguity allowing re-interpretation and re-imagination. The challenge, however, is to ensure that the implementation of the Supplementary Protocol is respected in exporting and third countries and, equally importantly, in related international systems.

12 The Supplementary Protocol and the EU Environmental Liability Directive

Similarities and differences

Edward H. P. Brans and Dorith H. Dongelmans

I Introduction

On 15 October 2010, the Nagoya-Kuala Lumpur Supplementary Protocol on Liability and Redress to the Cartagena Protocol on Biosafety (Supplementary Protocol) was adopted, an important event as it is one, if not the only, international treaty that deals with liability for environmental damage caused by living modified organisms (LMOs). The adoption of the Supplementary Protocol is, however, not only a significant event because of the subject it deals with, but also because of the approach that has been taken by the negotiating Parties with regard to liability. Unlike the majority of international environmental liability treaties, including the International Oil Pollution Conventions,[1] which have served as a model for many environmental liability treaties,[2] such as the 1999 Basel Liability Protocol,[3] the 1996 HNS Convention,[4] and the 2001 Bunker Oil Pollution Convention,[5] the

1   1969 International Convention on Civil Liability for Oil Pollution Damage (CLC) as amended, adopted on 29 November 1969, *United Nations Treaty Series*, Vol. 973, p. 3; Protocol of 1992 to amend the International Convention on Civil Liability for Oil Pollution, adopted on 27 November 1992, *United Nations Treaty Series*, Vol. 1956, p. 255; 1971 International Convention on the Establishment of an International Fund for Compensation for Oil Pollution Damage (FUND), as amended, adopted on 18 December 1971, *United Nations Treaty Series*, Vol. 1110, p. 57; Protocol of 1992 to amend the 1971 International Convention on the Establishment of an International Fund for Compensation of Oil Pollution Damage, adopted on 27 November 1992, *United Nations Treaty Series*, Vol. 1953, p. 330.
2   See Edward H. P. Brans, *Liability for Damage to Public Natural Resources: Standing, Damage and Damage Assessment* (Kluwer Law International, 2001), pp. 311–318.
3   Basel Protocol on Liability and Compensation for Damage Resulting from Transboundary Movements of Hazardous Wastes and their Disposal, adopted by Decision V/29 on 10 December 1999 (not in force), UNEP/CHW.5/29 (10 December 1999), Annex III.
4   International Convention on Liability and Compensation for Damage in Connection with the Carriage of Hazardous and Noxious Substances by Sea (HNS), adopted on 3 May 1996 (not in force), IMO/LEG/CONF.10/8/2 (9 May 1996).
5   International Convention on Civil Liability for Bunker Oil Pollution Damage, adopted on 23 March 2001, entered into force on 21 November 2008, IMO/LEG/CONF.12/19 (27 March 2001).

Supplementary Protocol adopts an 'administrative approach' to liability rather than the civil liability approach taken by those international treaties.

Interestingly, one finds this so-called administrative or public law approach in the 2004 EU Environmental Liability Directive (EU-ELD)[6] as well.[7] This EU Directive establishes a liability framework based on the polluter-pays principle and is focussed on the prevention and remediation of damage to protected natural resources and habitats caused by occupational activities, including the deliberate release into the environment, transport, and marketing of genetically modified organisms.[8]

In this chapter, we compare both liability regimes and discuss whether this common administrative approach to liability will make it likely that it is implemented in EU law once the EU has ratified the Supplementary Protocol by a simple modification of the EU-ELD, if necessary. As will be shown, there are substantial differences between these regimes, especially where it concerns the scope of the level of detail of the provisions and requirements that have been introduced in them. The latter is especially the case where it concerns the measure of damages and the determination of the measures that need to be taken to remediate environmental damage. Implementing the Supplementary Protocol into EU law might be possible, but given the differences between both regimes, it is less simple than one might expect.

In the following section, we discuss the Supplementary Protocol and its history. We thereby focus on the objective and scope of the Supplementary Protocol, the nature of the regime, the type of environmental damage that is recoverable, and the measure of damages. We then introduce the EU-ELD and discuss its key provisions, as well as the novel and controversial elements of this regime. We will thereby also refer to relevant case law and the limited experience there is in EU Member States with the application of the EU-ELD. Finally, in Section IV, we address whether it is possible to implement the Supplementary Protocol into EU law through a simple modification of the EU-ELD or more drastic changes to the Directive are necessary to make this possible. We end our contribution with a conclusion.

---

6   Directive 2004/35/CE of the European Parliament and of the Council of 21 April 2004 on environmental liability with regard to the prevention and remedying of environmental damage, *Official Journal of the European Union 2004*, L 143/56 (EU-ELD).

7   Gerd Winter, Jan H. Jans, Richard Macrory and Ludwig Krämer, 'Weighing up the EC Environmental Liability Directive', *Journal of Environmental Law*, Vol. 20, Issue 2 (2008), p. 164.

8   See Annex III of the EU-ELD, wherein there is reference to Council Directive 90/219/EEC of 23 April 1990 on the contained use of genetically modified microorganisms, *Official Journal of the European Communities 1990*, L 117/1, as amended; and Directive 2001/18/EC of the European Parliament and of the Council of 12 March 2001 on the deliberate release into the environment, transport and placing on the market of genetically modified organisms, *Official Journal of the European Communities* 2001, L 106/1, as last amended by Directive 2008/27/EC of 11 March 2008, *Official Journal of the European Union 2008*, L 81/45.

II The Supplementary Protocol

The Supplementary Protocol is intended to overcome the gap between the economic motivation of biotech companies to introduce LMOs in international trade and the concerns of the State Parties and others for the consequences thereof to biodiversity, whereby it is to be noted that prior to the adoption of the Supplementary Protocol, there was no specific international regime available providing rules for holding such companies accountable for biodiversity damage caused by the intentional or accidental introduction of LMOs into the environment and to compel these companies to take appropriate response measures.[9] The underlying purpose of the Supplementary Protocol is thus to contribute to the conservation and sustainable use of biological diversity by providing the State Parties and the EU with rules and procedures in the field of liability and redress relating to LMOs.[10]

1 Scope of the regime

Given this objective of the Supplementary Protocol to provide international rules and procedures related to LMO liability and redress, the Supplementary Protocol covers an array of LMOs, including those that are: (a) intended for direct use as food or feed, or for processing; (b) destined for contained use; or (c) intended for intentional introduction into the environment (Article 3 (1)).[11]

The Supplementary Protocol only applies to damage resulting from LMOs within the meaning of Article 3 of the Protocol if they find their origin in a transboundary movement.[12] Where it concerns intentional transboundary movements of LMOs, the Supplementary Protocol only covers damage resulting from *any authorised use* of such LMOs.[13] This seems to be a significant restriction of the scope of the Supplementary Protocol. However, given the text of Article 3 (3), the scope of the regime is less limited than one might expect. According to this provision, the Supplementary Protocol also applies to damage resulting from illegal and unintentional transboundary movements.[14] Although an illegal or unintentional transboundary movement is seemingly to be distinguished from an unauthorised use of LMOs following an intentional transboundary movement, Article 3 (3) of the Protocol provides an important extension of the scope of the regime and probably makes

---

9   Anastasia Telesetsky, 'The 2010 Nagoya-Kuala Lumpur Supplementary Protocol: A New Treaty Assigning Transboundary Liability and Redress for Biodiversity Damage caused by Genetically Modified Organisms', *ASIL Insight*, Vol. 14, Issue 41 (10 January 2011), p. 2.

10   Article 1, Supplementary Protocol.

11   Article 3 (1) (a), (b) and (c), Supplementary Protocol.

12   Article 3 (2), Supplementary Protocol. If one takes this definition of LMOs, it might be the case that not all LMOs are covered. However, we use the term LMOs in this chapter without taking into account this possible limited coverage.

13   Article 3 (2), Supplementary Protocol.

14   With regard to the meaning of the terms unintentional and illegal transboundary movements, Article 3 (2) of the Supplementary Protocol refers to Articles 17 and 25 of the Cartagena Protocol, respectively.

up part of the gap between authorised and unauthorised uses of LMOs following an intentional transboundary movement of LMOs.

Given the above, the Supplementary Protocol does not apply to domestic damage caused by LMOs when the damage does not originate from transboundary movement. The underlying reason is that the Parties to the Supplementary Protocol have, with some exceptions, sovereignty over their natural resources and the natural habitats located within their borders.[15] Parties to the Supplementary Protocol thus must fall back on domestic law to address damage that is not the result of a transboundary movement of LMOs and that occurs within the limits of their national jurisdiction.[16] This will also be the case if the biodiversity damage results from a transboundary movement of LMOs from non-Parties.[17]

2 Damage

The Supplementary Protocol applies to damage resulting from LMOs. Damage is defined in the Supplementary Protocol as 'an adverse effect on the conservation and sustainable use of biological diversity, taking also into account risks to human health'. Biodiversity is defined in the Supplementary Protocol in the same manner as in the Convention on Biological Diversity (CBD): 'the variability among living organisms from all sources including, *inter alia*, terrestrial, marine and other aquatic ecosystems and the ecological complexes of which they are part'.[18] Note that biodiversity is more than just the number of species in a certain area. There are four levels at which biodiversity is assessed: genetic diversity within species, the variability among species, functional diversity (which refers to the variety of biological functions of ecosystems), and ecosystem diversity (which refers to the variety of communities of organisms with particular habitats).[19] Damage to

---

15   Without going into detail here, we note that the 1971 Ramser Convention on wetlands of international importance especially as waterfowl habitat (adopted on 2 February 1971, *United Nations Treaty Series*, Vol. 996, p. 245), and the 1979 Convention on the conservation of European wildlife and natural habitats (Bern Convention) (adopted on 19 September 1979, *United Nations Treaty Series*, Vol. 1284, p. 209), and other international (regional) instruments may limit the freedom of Parties to the Supplementary Protocol to exhaust their natural resources and use or exploit their habitats.

16   See Article 3 (6) of the Supplementary Protocol, which seems to affirm this. However, it might also be that Article 3 (6) is intended to address differences between the national liability regimes of the Parties to the Protocol and that of the Supplementary Protocol and allow these Parties to use criteria, thresholds, etc. set out in their domestic law to establish liability for any damage that falls within the scope of this Supplementary Protocol where such damage occurs within the limits of their national jurisdiction (see Section IV below).

17   Article 3 (7), Supplementary Protocol provides that the domestic law implementing this Supplementary Protocol shall also apply to LMOs from non-Parties.

18   Article 2, CBD.

19   John L. Harper, David L. Hawksworth, 'Preface', in David L. Hawksworth ed., *Biodiversity: Measurement and Estimation* (Chapman & Hall, 1996), pp. 7–10. For comparable definitions of the term 'biodiversity', see California Biodiversity Council, 'Scientific definition of biodiversity'. Available at http://biodiversity.ca.gov/Biodiversity/biodiv_def2.html (accessed 1 August 2013).

biodiversity is thus more than damage to protected natural habitats and natural resources, as it is the starting point of the EU Environmental Liability Directive (see further Section III below).

Not all damage to biodiversity is covered by the Supplementary Protocol. Only damage that is of such a nature and extent that it has an adverse effect on the conservation and sustainable use of biological diversity, taking also into account risks to human health, and is '(i) measurable or otherwise observable taking into account, if available, scientifically-established baselines recognized by a competent authority that takes into account any other human induced variation and natural variation, and (ii) is significant'.[20] Whether or not an adverse effect on the conservation and sustainable use of biological diversity is significant is to be determined on the basis of a non-exhaustive list of factors listed in Article 2 (3) of the Protocol. Factors that can be taken into account are the nature and extent of the change to biodiversity caused and the duration thereof. Is it a long-term or permanent change that is caused?[21] Or is it a short-term and non-permanent change that will recover through natural recovery within a reasonable period of time? Other factors concern the reduction of the ability (of components) of biological diversity to provide goods and services to, we presume, other natural resources and/or humans, and the extent of any adverse effects of, we assume, the LMOs in question on human health.

Although the latter suggests that the Supplementary Protocol also covers personal injury and other traditional forms of damage, such as economic loss suffered as a consequence of personal injury, such types of damage are not covered by the Supplementary Protocol. It is left to the State Parties and the EU to deal with such types of loss.[22] The focus of the Supplementary Protocol is on damage to biological diversity resulting from LMOs that find their origin in a transboundary movement.

As will be noted below, according to the Supplementary Protocol, a person in direct or indirect control of an LMO can be forced to take response measures in the event damage has occurred. Being able to determine the consequences of a deliberate or accidental release into the environment of an LMO for biodiversity is thus essential for the application of the regime. It is now striking that given the text of Article 2 (2) (b) (i) of the Supplementary Protocol, the Parties to the Supplementary Protocol are more or less free to establish the method for determining whether an instance of damage to biodiversity is such that the threshold criteria of the Supplementary Protocol are met. It is clear from the text of the Supplementary Protocol that there is a preference for measuring the extent of the damage caused by using baseline data and data on natural and other variations. However, a Party to the Supplementary Protocol may also decide to consider observations sufficient to trigger administrative liability. It is obvious that the result

20   Article 2 (2), Supplementary Protocol.
21   According to the Supplementary Protocol, the latter is to be understood as a change that will not be redressed through natural recovery within a reasonable period of time.
22   Article 12 (2), Supplementary Protocol.

of this freedom of choice is that the new regime will not be implemented in the national law of the various parties in a uniform manner.

There are other elements of the Supplementary Protocol that will result in considerable differences between States where it concerns the application of the regime. Take, for instance, the non-exhaustive list of factors that has been introduced to determine the significance of the damage caused. As a result, where one Party to the Supplementary Protocol will determine certain consequences of the introduction of an LMO into the environment sufficient to regard the person in direct or indirect control of the LMO to be liable, other Parties to the Supplementary Protocol will not. Thus, it is unlikely that the Supplementary Protocol will result in a uniform worldwide regime on liability and redress for biodiversity damage caused by LMOs.

It should be noted that the same has happened with the Environmental Liability Directive. EU Member States were given many choices with regard to the implementation of some of the key provisions of this Directive. As a result, there is a broad divergence between EU Members States on the implementation of these provisions and thereby the application of the Directive in the EU.[23] Although the lack of uniformity is not necessarily a problem, the result is that where a responsible party can be held liable in one EU Member State for natural resource damage, in another EU Member State this will not be the case, even where it concerns the very same type of damage. The differences between the EU Member States with regard to the implementation of the EU-ELD are the most striking in cases with cross-border effects or where a certain incident has an effect on a nature protection area that is located in one EU Member State, but is of importance to a neighbouring Member State.

3 Person liable, defences and the extent of the liability

Under the Supplementary Protocol, liability is channelled to the operator. 'Operator' is defined in the Supplementary Protocol as 'any person in direct or indirect control of the living modified organism'. This could include, depending on domestic law, the permit holder, the person who placed the living modified organism on the market, and/or the developer, producer, modifier, exporter, importer, carrier or supplier of the LMOs concerned.[24] Taking the definition of

---

23   See Report of the European Commission to the Council, the European Parliament, the European Economic and Social Committee and the Committee of the Regions under Article 14 (2) of Directive 2004/35/CE on the environmental liability with regard to the prevention and remedying of environmental damage, COM (2010) 581 final, pp. 3–4. Paul Horswill, 'The biodiversity provisions of the Environmental Liability Directive – benefits, challenges and implications of inconsistent transposition', *Environmental Liability*, Vol. 17, No. 2 (2009), pp. 57–61. Tanja Munchmeyer, Valerie Fogleman, Leonardo Mazza and Shailendra Mudgal, Implementation Effectiveness of the Environmental Liability Directive (ELD) and related Financial Security Issues (2009), pp. 26–31. Available at http://ec.europa.eu/environment/legal/liability/pdf/ELD%20Study%20November%202009.pdf (accessed 1 August 2013).

24   Article 2 (2) (c), Supplementary Protocol.

'operator' in the Supplementary Protocol, it is clear that liability is not channelled to a single (legal) person. An advantage thereof is that depending on how the Supplementary Protocol is being implemented in domestic law,[25] a larger group of potential and possibly solvent addressees is available in the event of damage to force to take response measures than if liability would have been channelled to one specific legal entity or person.[26] Thus, in the event of damage, there might be more than one addressee of an administrative order available to not only immediately inform the competent authority of the damage that occurred or is occurring and to evaluate such damage, but also to take the appropriate response measures (see further Subsection 5 below).[27]

The Supplementary Protocol does not provide specific defences to the operator, such as the state-of-the-art defence or the permit defence. However, apart from classic exemptions such as 'act of God' and 'act of war', the Supplementary Protocol gives the Parties the option to provide in their domestic law other exemptions or mitigations they consider appropriate.[28] The latter makes it possible for the Parties to the Supplementary Protocol to introduce key defences, such as the state-of-the-art defence and/or the permit defence.

It is obvious that the foregoing could lead to situations whereby an operator can escape liability in one country because of the possibility to invoke an exemption, while in another country, where domestic law does not provide for that exemption for the operator, this would not be the case. A uniform implementation of the Supplementary Protocol in the various State Parties is unlikely, as is a uniform application of the regime. As will be shown, this is to some extent the same for the EU-ELD.

According to Article 4 of the Supplementary Protocol, not every operator may be given an order to take response measures. Parties to the Supplementary Protocol may only do so after they have established a causal link between the damage and the LMOs in question. The Supplementary Protocol does not stipulate how this is to be done. It only stipulates that the causal link is to be established in accordance with domestic law. The same approach has been taken in the EU-ELD. It is left to the EU Member States to decide how to establish a causal link between the damage that has occurred and the activities of individual operators.[29]

---

25   Note that Article 12 (3) of the Supplementary Protocol gives its Parties the option to include rules in their domestic civil liability laws on channelling of liability and thus to limit the group of potential liable persons to one or more specific persons and/or legal entities.

26   See Article 5 (1), Supplementary Protocol.

27   It is not explained what is meant by the term 'appropriate operator' in Article 5 (1) of the Supplementary Protocol, but we presume it is the Parties to the Supplementary Protocol that have to determine on the basis of their national laws who can be considered to take the appropriate response measures.

28   Article 6 (1) and (2), Supplementary Protocol.

29   See Article 4 (5) of the EU-ELD and ERG and Others v Ministero dello Sviluppo Economico and Others, Case C-378/08, Judgement of the European Court of Justice (Grand Chamber) of 9 March 2010, *European Court Reports 2010 I-1919*, paras 55–57.

The Supplementary Protocol does not provide a liability limit.[30] This does not, however, mean that the operator's liability is unlimited. First of all, the Supplementary Protocol gives Parties the option to introduce in their domestic laws financial limits for the recovery of costs and expenses related to response measures. Second, it provides that an operator can only be required to take response measures that are considered 'reasonable actions' (Article 2 (2) (d)). Although Article 2 (2) (d) of the Supplementary Protocol does not refer to the costs of such measures, considering the elements listed in subparagraph (d) to determine the type of response measures to be taken, it seems that an operator cannot be forced to take response measures that are disproportionately costly. No further guidance is provided in the Supplementary Protocol as to how to determine at what level response measures become disproportionately costly. However, taking the wording of Article 2 of the Supplementary Protocol into consideration, it seems safe to presume that the economic value of the impacted natural resources is not decisive.[31]

4 Response measures

Damage to biological diversity is only recoverable if a certain threshold is met. As stated above, this will be the case if the 'adverse affect on the conservation and sustainable use of biological diversity, taking also into account risks to human health' is measurable or otherwise observable and is of such a nature that it is significant.

In order to determine whether this is the case, one must compare the condition of the natural resources affected after the incident has occurred using, if available, scientifically established baselines.[32] The Supplementary Protocol does not include a definition of 'baseline'. However, given the text of Article 2 (2) (b), it means the condition the biological diversity would have been in if the incident that caused the damage had not taken place, taking into account seasonal influences and human-induced and natural variations. This definition is comparable with the one included in the EU-ELD.[33]

It should be noted that a baseline condition can only be determined if data are available regarding the status of the affected biodiversity just before the incident occurred, although under certain conditions a reference date may also be used.[34] The Supplementary Protocol does not include an obligation to collect such data,

---

30 See Article 8, Supplementary Protocol.
31 In the United States, this issue caused much debate. See Edward H. P. Brans, see note 2, p. 112 *et seq.* See also Michael Faure and Liu Jing, 'New Models for the Compensation of Natural Resources Damage', *Kentucky Journal for Equine, Agriculture, and Natural Resources Law*, Vol. 4, No. 2 (2012), pp. 269–270.
32 Article 2 (2) (b) (i), Supplementary Protocol.
33 Article 2 (14), EU-ELD.
34 See Resource Equivalency Methods for Assessing Environmental Damage in the EU (REMEDE), Toolkit for Performing Resource Equivalency Analysis to Assess and Scale Environmental Damage in the European Union, p. 80. Available at www.envliability.eu/docs/D13MainToolkit_ and_Annexes/REMEDE_D13_Toolkit_310708.pdf (accessed 1 August 2013).

which is understandable considering the scope of the Supplementary Protocol as it does not limit itself to certain natural resources. In that respect, the EU-ELD has a more limited scope. The scope of the EU regime is in principle limited to natural habitats and species protected under the Habitats Directive and Wild Birds Directive, water protected under the Water Framework Directive, and soil.[35] EU Member States are required under these Directives to collect data on the conservation status of natural resources and on the quality of these waters. Provided EU Member States fulfil their obligations under these Directives, data are available to determine baseline conditions of the habitats, species and waters protected under these EU Directives, but not on biodiversity as such, since the focus of these EU Directives is primarily on the protection and conservation of certain natural habitats, species and waters (see further Section III below).

As noted earlier, not every change to biodiversity that results from the release of LMOs is recoverable under the Supplementary Protocol. Only adverse affects to biodiversity that can be considered significant are deemed to be 'damage' within the meaning of the Supplementary Protocol. Once it is likely that damage of that extent occurred or is imminent, the Supplementary Protocol dictates that its Parties require the appropriate operator or operators to immediately inform the competent authority, to evaluate the damage, and to take appropriate response measures. 'Response measures' are defined as reasonable actions to:

(a) prevent, minimise, contain, mitigate or otherwise avoid damage, as appropriate; and
(b) restore biological diversity through actions to be undertaken in the following order of preference:

   • restoration of biological diversity to the condition that existed before the damage occurred, or its nearest equivalent; and where the competent authority determines this is not possible,
   • restoration by, *inter alia*, replacing the loss of biological diversity with other components of biological diversity for the same, or for another type of use, either at the same or, as appropriate, at an alternative location.

Unlike the EU Environmental Liability Directive, the Supplementary Protocol does not require that interim losses are compensated. 'Interim losses' can be described as the loss or impairment of biological diversity during the restoration period. Under the Supplementary Protocol, therefore, an operator can thus not be forced to take measures to compensate for the loss or impairment of biological diversity during the period of (natural) recovery.

Considering the above, the extent of the responsible party's liability is determined on the basis of: (a) the measures taken to prevent, minimise, contain, mitigate or otherwise avoid damage; (b) the cost of evaluating the damage; and (c) the restoration measures taken to remediate the adverse affect on the conservation

35   Article 2 (1) (a), (b) and (c), EU-ELD.

and sustainable use of biological diversity to baseline condition. In principle, the nature and extent of these measures and of the costs of evaluating the damage determine the extent of the financial burden the responsible party is faced with once an incident occurs, which is covered by the Supplementary Protocol.

Since no financial liability limits have been introduced in the Supplementary Protocol and forcing the appropriate operator or operators by administrative order to take restoration measures may have serious financial consequences, competent authorities are required under the Supplementary Protocol to reason their decisions with regard to the response measures they require to be taken. In order to stimulate well-reasoned decisions, the Supplementary Protocol stipulates that competent authorities are required to evaluate the damage caused, to explore (we assume) available restoration options, and to determine the response measures that are to be taken by the operator.[36] In addition, the addressee of an administrative order to take restoration measures is also to be given the opportunity of administrative or judicial review.[37]

5 Ordering the taking of response measures: an administrative approach

As stated above, most international treaties that include rules on liability for environmental damage are civil liability regimes. They use the general principles of tort law as a starting point. The Supplementary Protocol is, to our knowledge, the first international treaty that uses an administrative public law approach to hold certain (legal) persons accountable for environmental damage caused or that is likely to be caused.[38] The administrative approach is laid down in Article 5 of the Supplementary Protocol. According to this provision, in the event of damage resulting from LMOs, Parties to the Supplementary Protocol shall require the appropriate operator or operators to take appropriate response measures, if necessary, by order of the competent authority.[39]

Under the civil liability approach, in most cases, it is the competent authority who takes the appropriate response measures. As a consequence, in the first instance, the competent authority bears the costs and often cost recovery procedures are necessary to be compensated for the costs made. Before a competent authority institutes such a legal action against the appropriate operator(s), the competent authority needs to verify whether there is a sufficient legal basis to initiate legal proceedings, as a claimant under civil law is obliged to substantiate his claim.

Compared to the civil liability approach, this new approach has the advantage of shifting the primary responsibility for appropriate response measures to

---

36   Article 5 (2) and (6), Supplementary Protocol.
37   Article 5 (6), Supplementary Protocol.
38   One of the reasons for the negotiating Parties to choose an administrative approach was that many international civil liability regimes have not been successful. See Chapter 4 of this book, by René Lefeber.
39   Article 5 (1) and (6), Supplementary Protocol.

the operator. He can be ordered, if needed, to take these measures, and if the operator obeys the order and takes the appropriate response measures, it is the operator who bears the costs. A cost recovery action by the public authorities in that case is not necessary, as the operator has funded the response measures. Another advantage of the administrative approach is that the operator can be forced to take the appropriate response measures soon after the incident that caused the damage or is likely to cause the damage. This probably occurs sooner than if the civil liability approach was followed.

However, it should be taken into account that Article 5 (6) of the Supplementary Protocol requires the public authorities to reason their decisions to require an operator to take the appropriate response measures. It is for that reason necessary to determine whether there is a sufficient legal basis for ordering these measures, which will take time. How thorough such an examination should be is not stipulated in the Supplementary Protocol, although the public authorities are required to evaluate the damage, to identify the operator that caused the damage, to determine whether this operator can be considered the 'appropriate operator' under the Supplementary Protocol, and to determine whether the damage results from LMOs within the meaning of the Supplementary Protocol. All of this is important as one should keep in mind that in the case that an operator who acts in conformity with a legal order and incurs the costs is of the opinion that the competent authority has wrongly taken the position that there is a legally enforceable obligation for that operator to take appropriate measures, the operator will file a civil law claim against the competent authority based on its allegedly unlawful act. Where the national law of a State Party provides for administrative remedies against the order, the operator will exploit the administrative remedies in order to obtain compensation for the costs incurred.

From this perspective, there is not that much of a difference between a civil liability regime and a liability regime that is based on an administrative approach. Eventually, almost the same legal issues are to be addressed under both approaches: has damage been caused by the incident or is it likely to occur, and if so, is it of such an extent that it can be considered significant; who caused the damage; and what response measures can reasonably be required? Thus, in our opinion, the 'administrative approach' does not imply that difficult legal discussions can be prevented. It might be that under the 'administrative approach', these discussions are postponed in time, and nothing more. These difficulties would arise even under the administrative approach, especially if the operator who is the addressee of a legal order refuses to take the response measures required or starts legal proceedings after he or she has taken such measures. In both cases, the legality of the administrative order is subject to a legal debate. The subjects that are to be addressed in that sort of administrative proceedings do not differ much from those that are to be dealt with in civil liability cases aimed at the recovery of costs incurred.

The EU-ELD also takes an administrative approach and is, in that respect, comparable with the Supplementary Protocol. An important difference with the

Supplementary Protocol is, however, that some of the provisions of the EU-ELD are so-called self-executing provisions, which means that no legal order of a public authority is necessary to make these provisions operational.[40] Such provisions have legal effect without aid of an administrative order. Examples of such provisions are Articles 5 (1) and 6 (1) (b) of the EU-ELD, which require the operator to take preventive measures where environmental damage has not yet occurred but is likely to occur, or to take remedial measures where environmental damage has occurred.

Like the EU-ELD, the Supplementary Protocol allows the public authorities to take response measures where the operator fails to do so and to recover the costs of such measures. Both the EU-ELD and the Supplementary Protocol allow the national legislature to determine the situation in which the operator may be excused from these costs.[41] The Supplementary Protocol leaves it to the national legislature to determine when this will be the case. The stricter EU-ELD determines in what type of cases a Member State may decide not to recover the costs of preventive or remediation measures.[42]

6 Financial security

Like the EU-ELD, the Supplementary Protocol addresses the issue of financial security (Article 10),[43] a highly important issue since the availability of financial security determines, to a large extent, the success of a legal regime.[44] However, like the EU-ELD, no decisions have been taken with regard to this issue yet. No provision is included in the Supplementary Protocol that forces its Parties to introduce some sort of financial security. The Supplementary Protocol only determines that research will be started as to the available options and modalities after the entry into force of the Supplementary Protocol. Despite the importance of the subject, nothing has been decided yet. The approach is strikingly similar to that of the EU-ELD, according to which the EU Member States must encourage the development of financial security instruments and markets. However, the Directive goes no further. Considering the recent study on the EU-ELD and its effectiveness, this might change, but it will take time, and as yet, the outcome is uncertain.[45]

---

40 See Valerie Fogleman, 'Enforcing the Environmental Liability Directive: Duties, Powers and Self-Executing Provisions', *Environmental Liability*, Vol. 14, No. 2 (2006), p. 127 *et seq.*

41 Article 8 (4), EU-ELD and Article 5 (4), Supplementary Protocol.

42 Article 8 (4), EU-ELD.

43 See Chapter 9 of this book, by Rodrigo C. A. Lima.

44 See Michael G. Faure and David Grimeaud, *Financial Assurance Issues of Environmental Liability* (2000), p. 230. Available at http://ec.europa.eu/environment/legal/liability/pdf/insurance_gen_finalrep.pdf (accessed 1 August 2013).

45 See Report from the Commission, see note 23. Currently, the European Commission is investigating the feasibility of creating a fund to cover environmental liability and losses caused by industrial accidents. See http://eldfund.biois.com/home (accessed 1 August 2013).

III The European Union Directive on Environmental Liability (2004/35/CE)

In this section, we will discuss the EU-ELD in more detail. The focus here is the nature of the regime, the types of damage covered and the measure of damages.

1 The scope of the EU-ELD[46]

The EU-ELD establishes a liability framework based on the polluter-pays principle and is focused on the prevention and remediation of damage to protected natural recourses and habitats caused by occupational activities. The EU-ELD imposes on the operator of an occupational activity either a strict or fault-based liability for environmental damage caused, depending on the type of activity involved. Operators who undertake an activity that is covered by the EU legislation listed in Annex III of the Directive can be held strictly liable for damage to EU-protected species and natural habitats, contamination of land (soil pollution), and damage to waters covered by the Water Framework Directive,[47] provided the damage is above a certain threshold. The EU legislation listed in Annex III includes Directive 96/61/EC concerning Integrated Pollution Prevention and Control (IPPC Directive) and legislation on the transportation of dangerous substances, on waste management operations, and on the deliberate release into the environment, transport of, and marketing of genetically modified organisms.

Operators that undertake an activity not covered by the Directives listed in Annex III may only be held liable if they are at fault and only if damage has been caused or is likely to be caused to flora and fauna protected under the EU Wild Bird Directive and the Habitats Directive.

The scope of the EU-ELD as it concerns protected species and habitats is, in principle, limited to the species and natural habitats protected by the Wild Birds and Habitats Directives. However, Member States have the option to bring other species and natural habitats under the scope of the EU-ELD.[48] The EU-ELD also covers damage to waters, however only insofar as these waters are covered by the Water Framework Directive. The Directive also covers soil pollution damage. However, this type of damage is only recoverable if it 'creates a significant risk of human health being adversely affected' (Article 2 (1) (c)) and if it is caused by an activity listed as potentially dangerous. If the latter is not the case, the operator will escape liability (at least under EU law). Under the EU-ELD, risks to human health are only taken into account where it concerns soil pollution damage, not where damage to protected natural resources and habitats and damage to waters

---

46   For further details on the EU-ELD, see Lucas Bergkamp and Barbara Goldsmith eds, *The EU Environmental Liability Directive: A Commentary* (Oxford University Press, 2013).

47   Directive 2000/60/EC of the European Parliament and of the Council of 23 October 2000 establishing a framework for Community action in the field of water policy, *Official Journal of the European Communities*, L 327/1.

48   Article 2 (3) (c), EU-ELD. This is only possible if such natural resources are protected by national protection and conservation laws.

are concerned. The EU-ELD does not cover 'traditional damage' (personal injury, damage to goods and property, and pure economic loss). These categories of damage are excluded from the scope of the Directive because the losses are already recoverable under the liability laws of the Member States.

In the preamble of the Habitats Directive, there is a reference to 'biodiversity'.[49] However, in the EU-ELD itself, the term 'biodiversity' cannot be found. One of the reasons that the Directive does not refer to 'biodiversity' is the confusion resulting from its use. In earlier versions of the Directive, the term was used but its interpretation differed from more authoritative and generally accepted interpretations, such as the one provided by the CBD. The focus of the EU-ELD is basically on natural resources that are protected under EU nature conservation Directives. The legal status of these natural resources – owned or not owned – is irrelevant. The natural resources covered are considered to be of public interest and are in need of protection, for instance, by the designation of special protection areas (the Natura 2000 network). Although the EU-ELD likely helps prevent the loss of biodiversity, its focus and scope is more limited compared to the Supplementary Protocol. The EU-ELD does not cover biodiversity as defined under the CBD, as biodiversity is more than just damage to protected natural habitats and species.

Biodiversity as defined in the CBD is not covered by the EU-ELD. However, it is to be noted that this does not mean that loss of biodiversity cannot be considered when planning and implementing restoration measures to remediate impacted natural resources and natural resource services to baseline conditions.

2 Damage: threshold approach to natural resource damage

The EU-ELD only applies to damage to the natural resources covered if the damage is of such a nature and extent that the damage can be considered significant. According to Article 2 (1) of the Directive, this is the case for habitats and species covered if the damage is such that it has 'significant adverse effects on reaching or maintaining the favourable conservation status' of these natural resources. In order to determine whether a particular incident has such an effect, it is noted in the EU-ELD that a comparison of the post-incident condition of the natural resources with the baseline condition of these natural resources is needed. In Annex I of the Directive, guidance is provided on how to determine whether a certain event caused significant adverse changes to the impacted natural resources. Note that the threshold criteria are based on the Habitats Directive.[50]

---

49   See Preamble, Council Directive 92/43/EEC of 21 May 1992 on the conservation of natural habitats and of wild fauna and flora, *Official Journal of the European Communities*, L 206/7.

50   For the case law of the European Court of Justice regarding the interpretation of the relevant clauses of the Habitats Directive, see Landelijke Vereniging tot Behoud van de Waddenzee and Nederlandse Vereniging tot Bescherming van Vogels v Staatssecretaris van Landbouw, Natuurbeheer en Visserij, Case C-127/02, Judgement of the Court (Grand Chamber) of 7 September 2004, *European Court Reports 2004 I-07405*, especially the conclusion of the Advocate General J. Kokott.

A comparable approach is taken with regard to damage to the waters covered by the EU-ELD.[51]

3 Person liable, defences and the extent of the liability

Under the EU-ELD, liability is channelled to the operator of an occupational activity. The 'operator' is any natural or legal person who operates or controls the occupational activity, or where this is provided for in national legislation, to whom decisive economic power over the technical functioning of such an activity has been delegated, including the holder of a permit or authorisation for such an activity or the person registering or notifying such an activity.[52]

The EU-ELD cannot be applied in cases where environmental damage has been caused by pollution of a diffuse character, unless it is possible for the public authorities to establish a causal link between the damage and the activities of individual operators.[53] As the Directive does not specify how such a link is to be established, Member States have broad discretion here.[54] With regard to the extent of the discretion, the Court of Justice of the European Union (ECJ) held in a judgement of 9 March 2010 that legislation of a Member State may provide the competent authority the power to impose measures for remedying environmental damage, presuming a causal link between the pollution found and the activities of the operator or operators concerned. However, according to the ECJ, the competent authority must have plausible evidence capable of justifying its presumption.[55]

An operator may escape liability if he or she proves that the damage was caused by a third party (provided appropriate safety measures were in place), or if he or she proves that the damage resulted from compliance with an order or instruction from a public authority.[56] The EU-ELD also allows Member States to introduce the so-called permit-defence[57] and/or state-of-the-art defence.[58]

The EU-ELD does not provide for a liability limit. This does not, however, mean that liability is unlimited. Under the Directive, damages are preferably assessed on the basis of the actual costs of remediation. The Directive contains a set of

---

51 Article 2 (18), EU-ELD.
52 Article 2 (6), EU-ELD.
53 Article 4 (5), EU-ELD.
54 See Case C-378/08, see note 29, paras 55–57.
55 Ibid.
56 See Article 8 (3), EU-ELD.
57 See Article 8 (4) (a), EU-ELD. The permit defence entails that the operator can escape liability if the operator is able to demonstrate that he or she was not at fault or negligent, and that the environmental damage caused resulted from an emission or event expressly authorised by the regulatory authority.
58 See Article 8 (4) (b), EU-ELD. The state-of-the-art defence entails that the operator can escape liability if the operator is able to demonstrate that he or she was not at fault or negligent, and that the environmental damage caused resulted from an emission or event not considered likely to cause environmental damage according to the state of scientific and technical knowledge at the time the emission was released or the activity took place.

guidelines on selecting the most appropriate measures to remedy the environmental damage caused.[59] These guidelines have been introduced in order to, among other things, prevent liable operators from being confronted with disproportionate costly restoration measures or a disproportionate claim. The Directive does not contain a specific standard for determining at what point the costs of a certain restoration option becomes disproportionate.

4 Measure of damages and the objective of remediation measures

The EU-ELD emphasises restoration and chooses restoration costs as the primary and preferred method to assess damages.[60] However, because it takes time to restore the damaged natural resources to baseline condition, the operator will also be held liable for the loss or impairment of natural resources and their services during the restoration period (interim losses).[61] According to Annex II of the Directive, the restoration of damage to waters and protected species and natural habitats is to be achieved by way of so-called primary, complementary and compensatory remediation measures. 'Primary remediation' is defined in Annex II as 'any remedial measure which returns the damaged natural resources and/or impaired services to, or towards, baseline condition'. Thus, the focus of these measures is to directly restore the natural resources and services that have been impacted to the baseline condition.[62] The complementary remediation is defined in Annex II as 'any remedial measure taken in relation to natural resources and/ or services to compensate for the fact that primary remediation does not result in fully restoring the damaged natural resources and/or services'. The purpose of this type of remediation measures is to provide a similar level of natural resources and/or services at an alternative site similar to what would have been provided if the damaged site would not have been impacted.

Because neither of these remediation measures compensate for the loss of ecological and/or human services during the restoration period, compensatory remediation measures are needed to compensate for the interim loss of natural resources and their services pending recovery. This compensation consists of additional improvements to protected natural habitats and species or waters either

---

59   See Annex II of EU-ELD. For further details on these guidelines and a toolkit regarding the application thereof, see www.envliability.eu/ (accessed 1 August 2013). See further Joshua Lipton, Ece Ozdemiroglu and David J. Chapman eds, *Equivalency Methods for Environmental Liability in the EU: Assessing Damage and Compensation under the Environmental Liability Directive* (Springer, forthcoming); and Lucas Bergkamp and Barbara Goldsmith eds, *The Environmental Liability Directive: A Commentary* (Oxford University Press, 2013).

60   See Article 7 (1), EU-ELD.

61   See Article 2 (11), (13) and Annex II, para. 1 (c) and (d), EU-ELD. In addition to restoration costs (and interim losses), the responsible party can be held liable for the costs of assessing damages as well as the administrative, legal and enforcement costs, the costs of data collection and monitoring, and oversight costs. See Articles 8 (2) and 2 (16), EU-ELD.

62   See in this respect Annex II, paras 1.1.1 and 1.2.1, EU-ELD.

at the damaged site or at an alternative site. In order to determine the scale of the complementary and compensatory remediation measures, specific methods are proposed in Annex II, such as the use of resource-to-resource or service-to-service approaches (i.e. Habitat Equivalency Analysis).[63]

The objective of these remediation measures is thus not only to bring back the damaged natural resources to baseline condition, but also to restore the impaired natural resource services to baseline condition. 'Natural resource services' (sometimes merely 'services') is defined in the Directive as 'the functions performed by a natural resource for the benefit of another natural resource or the public'. When developing reasonable remediation options under the Directive, the loss of natural resource services contributing to human welfare must be taken into account as well.[64]

According to Annex II of the EU-ELD, a reasonable range of remediation options, each consisting of a primary, and, if necessary, a complementary and compensatory component, must be developed.[65] The various remediation options are to be evaluated and the most appropriate ones are selected on the basis of a set of criteria.[66] The process of identifying, evaluating and selecting restoration options is important for determining the extent of the polluter's liability. According to Article 7 (1) of the Directive, it is up to the potentially liable person to identify, in accordance with its Annex II, potential remediation measures and to submit these to the competent authority for approval. The competent authority must decide which remediation option, each including primary, compensatory, and, if necessary, complementary remediation measures, is to be implemented.[67]

5 Ordering the taking of response measures: an administrative approach

The EU-ELD contains provisions that create a duty for competent authorities to act, that authorise competent authorities to act, and that impose a duty on operators to act. An example of the latter can be found in Article 5 (1). According to this provision, the operator who caused an imminent threat of environmental damage occurring has to notify the competent authority of such an event and has to prevent the damage from occurring or to remediate the environmental damage caused.[68] For this chapter, Articles 6 through 8, along with 11, of the Directive are the most relevant. These provisions boil down to the following: according to Article 6 (1), which

---

63   See note 59 for reference.
64   See Article 2 (15) and Annex II, paras 1 (b)–(d), EU-ELD.
65   Annex II, para. 1.3.2, EU-ELD.
66   Annex II, paras 1.3.1–1.3.3, EU-ELD. These criteria include: the costs of implementing the various options; the extent to which each option avoids collateral damage and benefits each damaged natural resource and/or service; the likelihood of success of each option; the length of time it will take under these options to restore the damaged resources and services to baseline condition; and the extent to which each option achieves the restoration of the site, or geographical linkage to the damaged site if measures are taken elsewhere.
67   See Article 7 (2), EU-ELD.
68   See Articles 5 to 7, and 11, EU-ELD.

is a self-executing provision,[69] the operator him or herself takes the necessary remedial measures without waiting for an administrative order. The operator has to identify, in accordance with Annex II of the Directive, the potential remedial measures and submit them to the competent authority for approval. It is up to the competent authority to decide which remedial measure is to be implemented.

The competent authority may also require by administrative order the operator to take the necessary measures or may take the remedial measures itself, as a means of last resort. If the competent authority takes the remedial measures, the competent authority 'shall recover . . . the costs it has incurred in relation to the . . . remediation actions taken under the Directive'.[70] However, under certain conditions, the competent authority may decide not to recover the (full) costs of these measures. For example, this is the case if the expenditure required to recover the costs is likely to exceed the recovered sum, or if the Member State concerned introduced the permit-compliance defence, the operator demonstrates that he or she was not at fault or negligent and that the environmental damage was caused by an emission or event expressly authorised by, and fully in accordance with, a permit.

IV Implementation of the Supplementary Protocol into EU law

1 The position of the EU with regard to the Supplementary Protocol

The European Union ratified the Cartagena Protocol on 27 August 2002. Following the ratification, the EU took part in the negotiations to establish a liability regime relating to damage to biodiversity caused by LMOs. One of the goals of the European Union during the negotiations was to make sure that the result was consistent with relevant Union legislation and consistent with the basic principles of EU Member States' law on liability and redress. In addition, a regime that could be implemented in EU law without introducing or amending substantive rules on (civil) liability was desired.[71] Because the final compromise that was reached in the second half of 2010 was within the limits set by the European Commission, the EU supported the Supplementary Protocol.[72] The Council of the EU welcomed the adoption of the Supplementary Protocol.[73] In March 2011, the Commission proposed signing by the Council of the Supplementary Protocol,[74] and on 11 May

---

69 See Fogleman, see note 40, p. 127 *et seq.*
70 See Article 8 (2), EU-ELD.
71 See Proposal for a COUNCIL DECISION on signing the Nagoya-Kuala Lumpur Supplementary Protocol on Liability and Redress to the Cartagena Protocol on Biosafety, COM (2011) 130 final (21 March 2011), para. 6.
72 See ibid., para. 7.
73 Council Conclusions on Convention on Biological Diversity: outcome of and follow-up to the Nagoya Conference (11–29 October 2010), 20 December 2010, para. 2.
74 Proposal for a COUNCIL DECISION on signing the Nagoya-Kuala Lumpur Supplementary Protocol, see note 71.

2011, the EU signed the Supplementary Protocol. Finally, the EU deposited its instrument of approval of the Supplementary Protocol on 21 March 2013.

How is this new liability regime going to be implemented in EU law? Since most of the liability provisions of the Supplementary Protocol are covered by the EU-ELD, it is most likely that this will be done by changing the Directive. In this section, we will discuss whether any substantive changes to the Directive are needed if the Supplementary Protocol is implemented in EU law by bringing this new regime under the scope of the EU-ELD.

2 Are substantive changes to the ELD necessary?

Obviously, there is an overlap between the Supplementary Protocol and the EU-ELD. Both regimes cover damage to natural resources, apply an administrative approach, and are focused on the actual remediation of the environmental damage done and not on awarding monetary compensation for it. The Supplementary Protocol offers the important advantage of being to some extent a flexible regime as it leaves it to the Parties to decide how to deal with some key legal issues. Examples of this are the determination of the threshold, the establishment of a causal link between the damage and the LMO, legal defences, and exemptions. That the regime will not be implemented in a uniform manner worldwide poses a disadvantage, but conversely, it is an advantage that European legislators have the option to pick and choose those elements of the Supplementary Protocol that are similar or almost similar to the EU-ELD.

There are, however, also some important and more fundamental differences between the Supplementary Protocol and the EU-ELD. These differences are such that they make an easy implementation into EU law less likely. The differences concern the scope of both regimes and their measures of damages. Let us begin by discussing the first one.

The Supplementary Protocol covers biodiversity damage, the concept of biodiversity being defined in CBD. The EU-ELD, on the other hand, does not cover that type of environmental damage at all. The term 'biodiversity' is not even used in the Directive (only in its preamble and only in general terms). The scope of the EU regime is, briefly put, limited to the natural habitats and species listed in annexes to the Wild Birds Directive and the Habitats Directive, along with the nature areas designated by Member States on the basis of the Directives.[75] In addition, the EU-ELD covers waters under the Water Framework Directive and soil pollution. The latter applies only if the soil pollution is such that it causes a risk to human health or is likely to cause such a risk. The scope of the EU-ELD is thus far more limited than the scope of the Supplementary Protocol.

---

75   Note that the EU-ELD allows Member States to extend the scope of the regime to natural resources not covered by EU law to natural resources covered by national nature conservation laws.

Since the Supplementary Protocol is not flexible where it concerns this part of its scope and does not allow its Parties to make any reservations in that regard, implementation of the Supplementary Protocol into the EU-ELD will likely be complex. In that regard, we note that we do not consider it very likely that the EU-ELD will be extended to biodiversity damage. Member States find the Directive, as it is now, already complex to apply, especially its Annex that determines how to remediate damage to natural habitats and species. It is also relevant that under the Wild Birds Directive, the Habitats Directive and the Water Framework Directive, Member States collect data on the status of natural resources, but the focus thereof is not (at least not in our knowledge) on collecting data on biodiversity; rather, researchers focus 'just' on the status of various natural habitats, species and waters covered in the respective Directives.

The second difference concerns the loss of natural resource services following an incident that has an impact on the natural habitats, species and waters covered by the EU-ELD. Such a loss, which is defined in the Directive as a loss of 'the functions performed by a natural resource to other natural resources or the public', falls under the scope of the EU-ELD. In fact, it can be considered one of the elements of the regime that makes the regime different from other national and international environmental liability regimes. Only in the United States do we see a number of liability regimes that cover such a loss. It is unlikely that the Supplementary Protocol covers this type of environmental damage. In Article 2 (2) (b) of the Supplementary Protocol, there is a reference to the 'conservation and sustainable use of biodiversity', but it is unlikely that this makes a loss of natural resource services during the time of recovery to baseline one of the types of damage that are covered by the Supplementary Protocol. Even if the Supplementary Protocol could be read to include these losses, it seems to concern only the functions humans rely on and no other natural resources.

Third, the measure of damages differs, although not in relation to its financial limits. Both regimes have omitted a liability limit. The difference concerns the compensation of interim losses. Under the Supplementary Protocol, an operator cannot be forced to take (compensatory) remediation measures in order to compensate for the loss of impairment of biological diversity during the period of (natural) recovery. Using EU-ELD terminology, under the Supplementary Protocol, an operator can only be forced to take primary and complementary restoration measures. This is an important difference and concerns the very essence of the EU-ELD. The compensation of interim losses has been introduced to provide an incentive for polluters to take remediation measures soon after the incident occurred instead of waiting for natural recovery and to make a fuller application of the polluter pays principle likely. Now that the Supplementary Protocol does not provide for the recovery of interim losses and does not, so it seems, have a provision allowing Parties to extend the measure of damages under this regime, we consider this issue, along with the above mentioned biodiversity issue, to be the most difficult issues in the decision to be dealt with when preparing the implementation of the Supplementary Protocol into EU law by amending the EU-ELD.

It could be argued that Article 3 (6) of the Supplementary Protocol gives its Parties the possibility to bring interim losses under the scope of the regime. However, the meaning of this provision of the Supplementary Protocol is not entirely clear. It notes that the Parties 'may use criteria set out in their domestic law to address damage that occurs within the limits of their natural jurisdiction'. Addressing damage is, however, not necessarily the same as the 'recovery of damages for damage caused' or 'liability for damage caused'. For that reason, we question whether Article 3 (6) of the Supplementary Protocol can be used to overcome the difference in scope of both regimes and their measures of damages. If Article 3 (6) of the Supplementary Protocol could provide a solution for the difference in scope, in our opinion, this is the case with regard only to the recovery of interim losses and not for the biodiversity issue.

V Conclusion

The Supplementary Protocol and the EU Environmental Liability Directive do have a lot in common. The most striking similarities are the nature of both regimes (administrative approach) and the emphasis of both regimes on restoration instead of a monetary compensation for the damage caused. Another similarity is that both regimes are flexible with regard to some of the essentials of a liability regime, such as defences and exclusion.

There are also, however, some important differences between both regimes. As explained above, these concern the scope of both regimes and their measure of damages. In essence, it comes down to the following: the focus of the EU-ELD is more limited than that of the Supplementary Protocol as the Directive does not cover damage to biodiversity; the Directive's focus is on the natural habitats, species and water covered by the EU nature conservation Directives and on soil pollution. With regard to the measure of damages, the difference concerns the recovery of interim losses. Under the Directive, an operator may be under an obligation to take measures to compensate for such losses. However, it seems that the interim losses are not recoverable under the Supplementary Protocol, although Article 3 (6) may provide a solution for the EU legislator on this issue.

Despite the similarities as described above, the differences in scope and measure of damages will make it likely that the EU legislator will have to make some important and maybe difficult choices once it is decided that the Supplementary Protocol is to be implemented into EU law by extending the scope of the EU-ELD. Will the scope of the Directive be extended in order to cover damage to biodiversity or is this only going to be done with regard to damage caused by LMOs, or maybe not at all? What about interim losses, one of the essential elements of the Directive's measure of damages; is the EU legislature willing to let loose the recovery of this type of loss if damage is caused by LMOs? It might take a few months or maybe years to tackle these interesting issues. It will be interesting to follow the various steps the EU legislator will take to implement the Supplementary Protocol.

13 A Japanese approach to the domestic implementation of the Supplementary Protocol

Eriko Futami and Tadashi Otsuka

I Introduction

At the fifth meeting of the Conference of the Parties serving as the Meeting of the Parties (COP-MOP) to the Cartagena Protocol on Biosafety (Cartagena Protocol), which was held in Nagoya, Japan, the Nagoya-Kuala Lumpur Supplementary Protocol on Liability and Redress to the Cartagena Protocol on Biosafety (Supplementary Protocol) was adopted on 15 October 2010. This finally resolved the issue that had been left open by Article 27 of the Cartagena Protocol, which mandated an elaboration of rules on liability and redress for damage to biodiversity resulting from living modified organisms (LMOs). In other words, the Supplementary Protocol established a system of liability for 'biodiversity damage' caused by LMOs subject to transboundary movements.

It must be noted that the 'biodiversity damage' dealt with by the Supplementary Protocol is one type of damage to the environment *per se*. Japan has the important role of taking the initiative in demonstrating how to implement the Supplementary Protocol domestically, because Japan hosted the COP-MOP at which the Supplementary Protocol was adopted. This is especially so because this is the first opportunity for Japan to introduce and institute a liability system for damage to the environment *per se*, and, thus, her experience in its domestic implementation will be watched with keen interest. In Japan, the term 'environmental damage' is employed to convey two meanings.[1] In some cases, 'environmental damage' is used in its wider sense to mean all damage caused by environmental impacts. In other contexts, 'environmental damage' is used in its narrower sense to mean damage caused by environmental impacts excepting those related to personal and property interests. This narrow meaning of the term refers to damage to the environment *per se*. In this chapter, the term 'environmental damage' is used in the latter, narrower meaning of environmental damage *per se*.

---

1   Tadashi Otsuka, 'Kankyo Shufuku Sekinin, Hiyou Futan ni tuite: Kankyo Songairon eno Doutei' (Liability and Apportion of Costs for Remedying the Environment: A Step towards an Environmental Liability Theory), *Hougaku Kyoushitsu (The Law Classroom)*, No. 329 (2008), pp. 94–95.

This chapter discusses the challenges facing Japan as it seeks to domestically implement the Supplementary Protocol. First, it reviews the Japanese law that domestically implements the Cartagena Protocol, which will form the legal basis for the implementation of the Supplementary Protocol (Section II). Second, after briefly pointing out the features of the Supplementary Protocol, it examines in detail the possible means of implementing the Supplementary Protocol under the Japanese legal system and will explore the challenges facing Japan in that process (Section III).

II The Cartagena Protocol and the Japanese Cartagena Law[2]

The Cartagena Protocol was adopted in 2000. The Cartagena Protocol emanated from the mandate under Article 19 (3) of the Convention on Biological Diversity (CBD), adopted in 1992, to establish the procedures for preventing adverse effects by LMOs on the conservation and sustainable use of biological diversity. In 2003 in Japan, the Law Ensuring Biological Diversity through the Regulation of Use of Living Modified Organisms (Cartagena Law)[3] was enacted for the purpose of ratifying and domestically implementing the Cartagena Protocol. The Cartagena Law distinguishes two types of use of LMOs, Type 1 Use and Type 2 Use, the specific content of which are described below and establishes procedures and regulations for each of these types of use.

1 The purpose of the Cartagena Law

The purpose of the Cartagena Law is to ensure the precise and smooth implementation of the Cartagena Protocol, by taking measures to regulate the use of LMOs for ensuring biological diversity (Article 1). The Cartagena Law defines 'use' of an LMO as the 'use for provision (of LMO) as food, animal feed or other purposes; its cultivation and other growing; its processing; its storage; its transportation and its disposal; and other acts attendant with these' (Article 2 (3)).

---

2   Tadashi Otsuka, 'Idenshi Kumikae Seibutsu no Biosafety to Yobou teki Approach' (Biosafety of Genetically Modified Organisms and the Application of Precautionary Approach), Touru Iwama and Kenichiro Yanagi eds, *Kankyo Risk Kanri to Hou (Environmental Risk Governance and Law)* (Jigakusya Publishing Corporation, 2007), pp. 127–150.

3   Idenshi Kumikae Seibutsu to no Shiyo to no Kisei niyoru Seibutsu Tayousei no Kakuho ni kansuru Houritsu (Law Ensuring Biological Diversity through the Regulation of Use of Living Modified Organisms), Law No. 97 of 5 June 2003, as amended. The Japanese Ministry of the Environment understands that the Japanese term 'seibutsu tayousei no kakuho' (ensuring biological diversity) means the same as 'seibutsu tayousei no hozen oyobi jizoku kanouna riyou' (conservation and sustainable use of biological diversity). Kankyosho (The Ministry of the Environment), Idenshi Kumikae Seibutsu tou no Kisei niyoru Seibutsu no Tayousei no Kakuho ni Kansuru Houritsu no Kaisetsu (Commentary on the Law Ensuring Biological Diversity through the Regulation on the Use of Living Modified Organisms) (modified on 1 April 2007), p. 1. Available at www.bch.biodic. go.jp/bch_2.html (accessed 1 August 2013). Thus, the Ministry considers that an adverse effect on biological diversity is the same as that on conservation and sustainable use of biological diversity.

For the definition of biological diversity, the Law simply refers to that provided in Article 2 of the CBD (Article 2 (4) of the Japanese Cartagena Law).

The objective of the Cartagena Protocol is to contribute to ensuring an adequate level of protection in the field of uses of LMO that may have adverse effects on the conservation and sustainable use of biological diversity, *taking also into account risks to human health* (Article 1 of the Cartagena Protocol, emphasis added). However, as the protection of human health is not included as an objective of the CBD, it is the understanding of the Japanese Cartagena Law that the protection of human health is to be considered only incidentally when providing for the conservation of bio-diversity; thus, the objective of the Cartagena Law is not directly to contribute to the protection of human health.[4] Generally speaking, the risks dealt with by environmental legislation fall into two types, namely risks to human health and risks to the environment (or ecological risk). The Cartagena Law is considered to be concerned only with the latter, the ecological risk. According to the European Environment Agency, a risk can be divided into three categories: risk, uncertainty and ignorance.[5] Using that matrix, the Cartagena Law concerns itself with mainly uncertainty and ignorance regarding ecological risk.[6] As the existing environmental legislation in Japan have mainly dealt with risks to human health, the enactment of the Cartagena Law concerning itself with ecological risk has had a ground-breaking level of significance for Japan.

2 Type 1 Use

Type 1 Use can be understood simply as the open use of LMOs. More specifically, according to the Japanese Cartagena Law, Type 1 Use is the use of LMOs with no preventive measures to control dispersal into the air, water or soil outside of facilities, equipment or structures. This is the use of LMOs without containment measures. The cultivation of LMOs in semi-isolated fields or those in conventional fields, commercial distribution of LMOs, and transportation of LMOs in a lorry in bulk will be considered as Type 1 Use.[7] Currently, Type 1 Use of LMOs is far

---

4 The Ministry of the Environment, Commentary, see note 3, p. 1.
5 European Environmental Agency, Late lessons from early warning: the precautionary principle 1896–2000 (2001), pp. 170, 184, 192. Available at www.eea.europa.eu/publications/environmental_issue_report_2001_22/Issue_Report_No_22.pdf (accessed 1 August 2013).
6 Otsuka, see note 2, p. 128. Using the same matrix, the Cartagena Protocol takes into consideration the risks to human health incidentally, so it can be considered as directly covering the uncertainty and ignorance regarding risks to human health. On the other hand, the Japanese Cartagena Law, merely as a result of conserving biodiversity and indirectly covering risks to human health through the environment, may include the uncertainty and ignorance regarding risks to human health. Actually, the Japanese Cartagena Law may be considered as taking no account at all of human health. Under this construction, the scope of protection afforded by the Japanese Cartagena Law could be seen as narrower than that of the Cartagena Protocol.
7 Yutaka Tabei, 'Idenshi Kumikae Shokubutsu no Riyo niokeru Idenshi kumikae Seibutsu tou no Kisei niyoru Seibutsu no Tayousei no Kakuho ni kansuru Houritsu (Cartagena Hou) no Gaiyo to Seibutsu Tayousei Eikyo-hyouka' (Outline of Cartagena Law Biological Diversity Risk Assessment of Living Modified Organisms (LMO)), *Nihon Nouyaku Gakkai Shi (Journal of Pesticide Science)*, Vol. 35, No. 2 (2010), p. 146.

greater in the agricultural and forestry sectors (such as maize and rice) than in other sectors, including research and development or pharmaceuticals. Under the Cartagena Law, a person who wishes to make Type 1 Use of an LMO must obtain the approval from the competent minister on the management plan stipulating the names and types of LMO involved and intended content and methods of use for each type of LMO (Type 1 Use Management Plan) (Article 4 (1)). A person who wishes to obtain such approval must conduct a risk assessment and submit to the competent minister the Biological Diversity Risk Assessment Report along with an application form detailing the Type 1 Use Management Plan and other necessary data (Article 4 (2)).

The Biological Diversity Risk Assessment is the result of the assessment of the adverse effects on biological diversity that may be caused by Type 1 Use of each type of LMO. Under the Cartagena Law, the 'Adverse Effect on Biological Diversity' is defined as those adverse effects that are caused by the use of LMOs that threaten to impair biological diversity (Article 3 (i)).[8] Accordingly, the criterion for approval by the competent minister is certification that 'no adverse effect that threatens to impair the preservation of species or populations of wild fauna or flora or any other Adverse Effect on Biological Diversity could arise' (Article 4 (5)). Thus, the Cartagena Law specifies one type of Adverse Effect on Biological Diversity focusing on the LMO's adverse effects on the preservation of wild flora and fauna. The risk assessment required under the Law does not include the assessment of possible adverse effects on animals bred or plants cultivated by people, nor does it take into consideration hybridisation or other interaction with cultivated crops,[9] because they are not 'wild'.

Under the Cartagena Law, when it has come to be recognised that due to environmental changes that could not have been foreseen at the time of the approval or due to the progress of scientific knowledge, there exists a risk that an Adverse Effect on Biological Diversity could arise even when a Type 1 Use of LMO is made in accordance with the Type 1 Use Management Plan for which the approval had previously been obtained, the competent minister must change or abolish the said Type 1 Use Management Plan (Article 7 (1)), and shall consult experts in advance concerning such changes or the abolition of the Management Plan (Article 7 (2)). This is arguably an application of the precautionary principle. It takes into account

---

8   An unofficial translation by the Ministry of the Environment includes the concept of 'unacceptable risks' as stipulating: 'adverse effects that are caused by the use of living modified organisms and posing unacceptable risks that impair biological diversity'. The original Japanese text does not contain, at least explicitly, this concept of 'unacceptable risks', which seems to raise the threshold of adverse effect. The concept of 'unacceptable risks' also appears in the translation of Article 4 (5).

9   The Ministry of the Environment, Commentary, see note 3, p. 14; Nozomu Koizumi and Yuichiro Nakayama, 'Idenshi Kumikae (GM) Natane no Koboredane to Seibutsu Tayousei' (Spilled Genetically Modified (GM) Rapeseed and Biodiversity), *Bioscience & Industry*, Vol. 68, No. 5 (2010), p. 362. Additionally, municipalities are making progress in formulating ordinances and guidelines on measures to address concerns about hybridisation and mixture with cultivated non-GM crops by future commercial harvesting of LMOs in their regions. Yutaka Tabei, 'Idenshi Kumikae Sakumotsu no Kokunai Saibai nitsuite' (On the Domestic Cultivation of Genetically Modified Crops: Foreign and Domestic Trends in the Cultivation of Genetically Modified Crops and Future Responses), *Nogyo to Keizai (Agriculture and Economics)*, Vol. 73, No. 4 (2007), pp. 61–63.

the remaining uncertainties regarding the effects on biodiversity arising from LMOs. This reflects two elements of the precautionary principle. The first is the provisional nature of management, which depends on risk assessment.[10] The second is step-by-step control, by which a reassessment is conducted immediately when the situation changes even after permission has been granted.[11]

Under the Cartagena Law, three types of measures concerning Type 1 Use may be ordered by the competent minister that are designed to prevent Adverse Effect on Biological Diversity in order to ensure the precise and smooth implementation of the Cartagena Protocol (Article 3 (i)). First, the competent minister may order a person who has made or is making a Type 1 Use of an LMO without the necessary approval and/or in violation of Type 1 Use Management Plan to take steps to 'recall the LMO'[12] or to take other necessary measures (Article 10 (1)). Second, when urgent measures are necessary to prevent Adverse Effect on Biological Diversity when, as mentioned above, due to environmental changes or the progress of scientific knowledge, it has come to be recognised that there exists a risk that an Adverse Effect on Biological Diversity could arise even when a Type 1 Use of an LMO is made in accordance with Type 1 Use Management Plan, or when other exceptional circumstances have arisen, the competent minister may order a person who is making, has made, or has caused another person to make Type 1 Use of an LMO to suspend the said Type 1 Use or take other necessary measures (Article 10 (2)). These are measures required when, on the basis of the progress of scientific knowledge, it is necessary to change or abolish approved Type 1 Use Management Plan (Article 7). The phrase 'when other exceptional circumstances have arisen' is understood to refer to situations in which an Adverse Effect on Biological Diversity would arise when a person continues to use an LMO that had been identified and designated by the competent minister as clearly not causing any Adverse Effect on Biological Diversity and, thus, was allowed to use without the need for approval of Type 1 Use Management Plan (second sentence of Article 4 of the Cartagena Law).[13] Third, in the event that Type 1 Use Management Plan can no longer be observed due to the occurrence of an accident, and an Adverse Effect on Biological Diversity could arise, the Law requires a person who is making a Type 1 Use to immediately take emergency measures to prevent such effects and to notify the competent minister. If it is determined that such measures have not been taken by that person, the competent minister may order such person to take 'such preventative emergency measures' (Articles 11 (1) and (2)).[14]

10   Otsuka, see note 2, p. 134.
11   Ibid., p. 143.
12   In the original Japanese, the term 'Kaishu', in addition to the act of recalling, will also include an act of recovery, collection and retrieval.
13   The Ministry of the Environment, Commentary, see note 3, p. 18. The second sentence of Article 4 of the Japanese Cartagena Law is intended to implement Article 7 (4) of the Cartagena Protocol, which provides for a possibility of not applying the advance informed agreement procedure for an LMO identified in a decision of COP-MOP as being not likely to have adverse effects on the conservation and sustainable use of biological diversity.
14   In the original Japanese, the term 'Boushi surutameno Oukyu-u no Sochi' signifies also a provisional nature of the measure to prevent adverse effects.

3 Type 2 Use

Type 2 Use can be understood simply as a contained use of LMOs. More specifically, according to the Cartagena Law, the use of LMOs with the intention of preventing the dispersal of the LMO into the air, water or soil outside of facilities is a Type 2 Use. Thus, any use of LMOs inside facilities that are sealed off from the outside environment such as laboratories, closed-system greenhouses, and special greenhouses with screens[15] can be considered as a Type 2 Use. Since a Type 2 Use is controlled and does not allow the LMO to come into contact with the external world of biodiversity in the first place, it causes no Adverse Effect on Biological Diversity. A person who makes a Type 2 Use of an LMO must take containment measures, when the ordinance of the competent ministers stipulates such containment measures to be taken in connection with such use (Article 12). However, even when no containment measures are stipulated in the ordinance, a person who makes a Type 2 Use of an LMO must take containment measures confirmed in advance by the competent ministers (Article 13 (1)).

Similar to a Type 1 Use, the competent minister may order three types of measures concerning a Type 2 Use. First, the competent minister may order a person who has made or is making the Type 2 Use of LMOs in violation of Articles 12 and 13 above to take the containment measures or other necessary measures stipulated in the ordinance or those confirmed in advance by the competent ministers (Article 14 (1)). Second, when it has come to be recognised that due to the progress of scientific knowledge, there is an urgent need to prevent dispersal of an LMO outside of facilities, the competent minister may order a person who is making or has made a Type 2 Use to take measures to improve said containment measures or other necessary measures (Article 14 (2)). This is considered a mechanism allowing additional measures to be ordered as the scientific knowledge is enhanced. Third, when containment measures stipulated in the ordinance or confirmed in advance by the competent ministers cannot be implemented because of an accident, the Law requires a person who is making a Type 2 Use to take emergency measures to respond to the accident and notify the competent minister. The competent minister may order that person to take emergency measures to respond to such an accident if a person had not already taken them (Article 15).

As examined above, the Japanese Cartagena Law gives the competent minister a broad authority to approve the use of LMOs and to change/modify or abolish such use. The competent authority may also issue orders requiring measures be taken to address the problems arising from the uncertainties related to the use of LMOs and from accidents involving them. This basic structure is positively appreciated as being a pioneering mechanism for establishing the precautionary principle.[16]

---

15   Tabei, see note 7, p. 146.
16   Hiroki Oikawa, *Seibutsu Tayousei toiu Logic: Kankyo Hou no Shizukana Kakumei (The Logic of Biodiversity: Quiet Revolution in Japanese Environmental Law)* (Keisou Shobo, 2010), p. 76.

III Challenges for domestic implementation of the Supplementary Protocol

It is noteworthy that the Supplementary Protocol adopts the administrative approach as the basis for its liability regime. The administrative approach under the Supplementary Protocol is a mechanism by which the competent authorities (administration) require operators as defined in Article 2 (2) (c) of the Supplementary Protocol to take response measures in the event of damage (Article 5). If operators do not take response measures, the competent authorities have the right to take response measures themselves and recover the costs from operators. The required response measures are defined as reasonable actions to prevent, minimise, contain, mitigate or otherwise avoid biodiversity damage; to restore the biodiversity to its original condition that existed before the damage occurred; and, if this is not possible, to restore biodiversity by replacing the loss with other components of similar biodiversity (Article 2 (2) (d)). It is significant that the restoration of damage to biodiversity is required. The Supplementary Protocol also contains provisions covering the concept of biodiversity damage and criteria for determining damage covered by the Supplementary Protocol (Articles 2 (2) (b) and (3)), as well as its scope (Article 3). It also contains provisions on civil liability (Articles 12 and 5 (7)). One of the prominent features of the Supplementary Protocol is that these provisions, which form the general framework, allow much flexibility for domestic implementation. It is therefore likely that the Supplementary Protocol's effectiveness will depend on the domestic laws of the Parties.

It is necessary to consider how the Supplementary Protocol will be incorporated into the Japanese legal system, and especially whether there are any inconsistencies between the Supplementary Protocol and the Cartagena Law, which was enacted as a relevant domestic law to implement the Cartagena Protocol. If the Cartagena Law is inadequate as the relevant domestic law for the implementation of the Supplementary Protocol, what should be done to overcome the inadequacy? Will it involve a fundamental revision or will a new domestic law be needed?

This discussion will centre on the flexibility provisions in the Supplementary Protocol. First, how should we understand the administrative approach that constitutes the basis of the liability regime under the Supplementary Protocol,[17] and how can we ensure that the required response measures are taken? Second, how should we make the determinations about biodiversity damage as one of the types of environmental damage which has been newly introduced into Japan? Although the Supplementary Protocol has many flexibility provisions, it is said that the domestic implementation of a liability system based on an administrative approach that requires response measures will be a new challenge for many countries including Japan.[18] Therefore, this chapter focuses on the administrative approach

---

17 See Chapter 1 of this book, by Akiho Shibata.
18 Akiho Shibata, 'Saitaku Mokuzen! LMO ki-in Seibutsu Tayousei Songai nikansuru Sekinin Hosoku Giteisho no Seiritsu no Igi to Kadai' (Liability Supplementary Protocol for Biodiversity Damage caused by LMOs: Significance and Remaining Issues), *Law and Technology*, No. 49 (2010), p. 32.

that constitutes the basic framework of the Supplementary Protocol and examines the challenges for Japan in establishing appropriate provisions in its domestic law, precisely because the Supplementary Protocol has so many flexibility provisions.

1 Administrative approach

The administrative approach to liability was first introduced by the EU Environmental Liability Directive (EU-ELD).[19] Its characteristic feature is that the administrative authorities become the actors that pursue the liability of responsible persons. Additionally, responsible persons are not to pay monetary compensation, but to implement the measures (actions) to restore (improve) the damaged environment.

Is there any law in Japan that incorporates a liability regime with such an administrative approach? Is the administrative approach understood to be a new liability regime? A survey of the liability systems related to environmental remediation in existing Japanese laws in the field of the environment demonstrates the existence of legislation under which administrative authorities issue orders to take such remediation measures. It is a liability regime that can be described as a 'regulation-based polluter pays system'.[20] Among such laws, it would be useful to review those in the field of nature conservation that allow the competent authorities to order the suspension of activities, restoration measures and even alternative measures when such restoration is exceedingly difficult. It is noteworthy that under these laws, the competent authorities may order such measures not because the activity in question caused personal injury or damage to the environment *per se*, but because such activity lacked necessary permission or violated the permit conditions. Those provisions can be found in the Natural Parks Law (Article 34), the Nature Conservation Law (Articles 18 (1), 30 and 46 (2)), and the Wildlife Protection and Proper Hunting Law (Article 30 (2)). Under all of these laws, the administrative authorities impose orders to take measures on the basis of a violation of permit conditions or when the permit was not obtained.[21] They treat the suspension of activity and the order of restoration measures as an integral part of the substantive content of the order by the competent authorities requiring certain measures to be taken by the violators.

In the administrative approach regime under the Supplementary Protocol, the competent authority becomes the actor in pursuing liability of the operator in the

---

19 Directive 2004/35/CE of the European Parliament and of the Council of 21 April 2004 on Environmental Liability with regard to the Prevention and Remedying of Environmental Damage, *Official Journal of the European Union 2004*, L 143/56. See also Chapter 5 of this book, by Alejandro Lago Candeira.
20 Otsuka, see note 1, pp. 96–97.
21 Eriko Futami, 'Seibutsu Tayousei Songai no "Kaifuku" Sekinin ni kansuru Ichi Kousatsu: EU Kankyo Sekinin Shirei to OPA to Yudaku Minjisekinin Jouyaku no Hikaku wo Toushite (ni/kan)' (Liability for the Restoration of Biodiversity Damage: Comparison with EU Environmental Liability Directive, OPA, and CLC (Part 2/End)), *Waseda Hougakukaishi (Waseda Law Journal)*, Vol. 63, No. 2 (2013), pp. 302–303.

case that damage or the sufficient likelihood of damage occurs. As examined above, under the exiting Japanese legal system in the field of nature conservation, the administrative authorities may issue orders to take appropriate measures based on a violation of permit conditions, whereas the Supplementary Protocol has a system under which the competent authority requires the operator to take response measures based on the fact of its causing damage to the biodiversity. While the existing Japanese laws and the Supplementary Protocol have a different legal basis for issuing orders to take certain measures, there is arguably no great difference in the general framework by which the administrative authorities play the central role in pursuing the liability of responsible persons. Therefore, although the administrative approach to a liability regime is being introduced into Japan for the first time, it is likely that such an approach will easily be adapted to the Japanese legal system.

The administrative approach to liability in the Supplementary Protocol must then be examined in light of the current legal framework of the Japanese Cartagena Law. As examined above, under the Cartagena Law, the competent minister issues orders to take measures to a person who has made or is making use of LMOs before damage occurs. For a Type 1 Use, this is to prevent an Adverse Effect on Biological Diversity, and for a Type 2 Use, this is to prevent the dispersal of LMOs in the first place. On the other hand, in addition to prevention, the Supplementary Protocol has an aim of restoring the damaged biodiversity by pursuing liability of operators after the damage has occurred. It is conceivable that since the Cartagena Law provides an important and central role for the administrative authorities by allowing them to impose liability through the issuance of orders to take measures even before damage occurs, the Law would also allow the administrative authorities to pursue 'post-damage' liability for restoration of biodiversity damage by requiring responsible persons to take 'response measures' when damage has actually occurred. This expansion of the applicability of the Cartagena Law can be done without changing its basic structure and by just amending it to include the response measures discussed below.

2 Response measures

The Cartagena Law established two types of orders to take measures in connection with the intentional use of an LMO. First, as a response to the violation of the Type 1 Use Management Plan or the Type 2 Use ordinance/conditions, the competent minister's order is meant to indirectly prevent an Adverse Effect on Biological Diversity, as well as to deal with the violation itself (Articles 10 (1) and 14 (1)). Second, as a response to the progress of scientific knowledge, in the case of a Type 1 Use, the competent minister's order, recognising the inadequacy of the approved Management Plan, is meant directly and urgently to prevent the Adverse Effect on Biological Diversity (Article 10 (2)). In the case of a Type 2 Use, the competent minister's order, recognising the inadequacy of the containment measures in the ordinance or approval, is meant to directly and urgently prevent the dispersal of LMOs, as that LMO is not permitted to come into contact with external biodiversity in the first place (Article 14 (2)). In this second type of measure, since the Type 1 Use and Type 2 Use are in compliance with the original Management Plan and the containment measures, the orders to take measures are issued in order to pre-empt an Adverse Effect on Biological Diversity and, thus, can be considered as concrete implementation of the precautionary principle.[22]

In connection with the unintentional use of LMOs, namely in the case of accidents, the Cartagena Law establishes different rationales for Type 1 Use and Type 2 Use. In the case of Type 1 Use, when it is impossible to comply with Type 1 Use Management Plan and when an Adverse Effect on Biological Diversity could arise, the emergency measures are required to prevent such an Adverse Effect on Biological Diversity (Article 11 (1)). In the case of Type 2 Use, on the other hand, just like the second type of orders discussed above, the emergency measures are required only because the containment measures cannot be taken, even without the potential for such a situation to affect biodiversity (Article 15 (1)). Again, the LMO under Type 2 Use presupposes no contact with external biodiversity in the first place.

Therefore, the Cartagena Law addresses the situation where there is a threat of an Adverse Effect on Biological Diversity and, as such, the purpose of the orders of the competent ministers to take measures including the case of accidents is limited to preventing such effects. On the other hand, the purpose of response measures required under the Supplementary Protocol is not limited to prevention, minimisation, or avoidance of biodiversity damage (Article 2 (2) (d) (i) of the Supplementary Protocol), but also includes its restoration (Article 2 (2) (d) (ii) of the Supplementary Protocol). Presupposing the legal framework of the Cartagena Law, the question becomes whether we can interpret its scope of orders by the competent ministers to be expanded to include not only measures to prevent an Adverse Effect on Biological Diversity, but also those taken after damage to biodiversity has occurred to restore it.

In order to answer this question, it is important to refer to the different legal reasons for the various measures that are provided in the Cartagena Law, as examined above. A competent minister requiring the operators to take response measures as provided in the Supplementary Protocol when their intentional use of LMOs has caused biodiversity damage would most likely base their authority on either the first or second type of measures as examined above in connection with the intentional use of LMOs. In the event of biodiversity damage due to the unintentional introduction of LMOs under the Supplementary Protocol, it is conceivable that the competent minister could order the response measures by using its authority provided in the case of accidents (as examined above). Basing the competent minister's authority to order response measures in the case of biodiversity damage on the above provisions of the current Cartagena Law, and considering the fact that the Law distinguishes the purpose and content of measures to be ordered by the competent minister in relation to different situations and conditions, it is necessary to carefully examine whether all 'appropriate' (Article 5 (1) (c)) and 'reasonable' (Article 2 (2) (d)) response measures as envisaged by the Supplementary Protocol can indeed be implemented through the current Japanese

---

22   Oikawa, see note 16, p. 76.

Cartagena Law. The administrative approach to liability itself may be adaptable to the current Japanese legal system as examined above, but could the current Cartagena Law ensure the implementation of appropriate and reasonable response measures as provided in the Supplementary Protocol?

First, it is difficult to reach an interpretation that the types of orders to take measures envisioned under the current Cartagena Law would include restoration in response to Adverse Effects on Biological Diversity. It is inconceivable that a situation involving damage to biodiversity that necessitated restoration was taken into account at the time of the enactment of the Cartagena Law. Further, the Cartagena Law emphasises the precautionary principle, that is the prevention of a risk of Adverse Effects on Biological Diversity, and not the response to a situation where such risk materialises. In addition, in connection with the open use of LMOs (Type 1 Use), the Cartagena Law distinguishes the far-reaching measures to 'recall LMOs' from those merely to 'suspend its use' by reference to the culpability of the operator being in violation of the permit conditions. Therefore, especially when biodiversity damage has occurred without any connection to a violation of the approval or permit conditions, it is difficult to interpret the term 'suspension of use and other (similar) necessary measures' to include restoration as in the response measures.[23] Moreover, under the Supplementary Protocol (Article 2 (2) (d) (ii)), when biodiversity damage occurs, the response measures are to be taken in the following order of preference: first, restore the biodiversity to the condition that existed before the damage occurred or to its nearest equivalent; second, replace the loss of biodiversity with other components of diversity either at the same or at an alternative location. In the light of the Cartagena Law as examined above, it is the view of the authors that the Law needs to be amended to include a new explicit provision dealing with response measures. This amendment may touch upon the conceptual differences between an Adverse Effect on Biological Diversity in relation to preventative measures under the current Cartagena Law and biodiversity damage in relation to the newly introduced response measures in the implementation of the Supplementary Protocol (this issue will be discussed under Subsection 4 below in more detail). If the details of such response measures are provided explicitly in the Cartagena Law, the power of administrative authorities to implement response measures and recover the costs from operators (Articles 5 (4) and (5) of the Supplementary Protocol) would likely be exercised as administrative subrogation by administrative authorities pursuant to Articles 1 and 2 of the Law on Substitute Execution by Administration.[24]

---

23   Shibata, see note 18, p. 39, footnote 37.
24   Akiko Toi, 'Biosafety ni kansuru Cartagena Giteisho Dai Gokai Teiyakukoku Kaigou no Seika to Kadai: Sekinin to Kyusai ni kansuru Nagoya Kuala Lumpur Hosoku Giteisho no Saitaku wo Chuushin to shite' (The Achievements and Challenges of The Fifth Meeting of the Conference of the Parties serving as the Meeting of the Parties to the Cartagena Protocol on Biosafety: With a central focus on the Adoption of the Nagoya-Kuala Lumpur Supplementary Protocol on Liability and Redress to the Cartagena Protocol on Biosafety), *Jurist*, No. 1417 (2011), p. 50; Akiho Shibata, Hokudai GCOE Kenkyukai Houkoku (Presentation at Hokkaido University GCOE Study Group) (9 December 2009) (on file with the authors).

Second, the response measures required under the Supplementary Protocol include measures to prevent or minimise biodiversity damage (Article 2 (2) (d)) when such damage may occur. There is a question whether orders to take measures preventing Adverse Effects on Biological Diversity under the current Cartagena Law will adequately cover the necessary measures to be taken just before biodiversity damage occurs. Again, as for Type 1 Use, the response to this question must take into account the distinction made under the current Cartagena Law between the measures to 'recall the LMOs' when there is a violation of permit conditions and those merely to 'suspend the use of LMOs' when such a violation is not involved. It would seem difficult that the orders to take measures to prevent Adverse Effects on Biological Diversity under the current Cartagena Law will be interpreted to include all measures envisaged under the Supplementary Protocol including the measures to prevent, minimise and avoid biodiversity damage as response measures.

3 Exemption or mitigation

The Supplementary Protocol allows its Parties to provide for exemptions or mitigations in their domestic laws (Article 6 (2)). In this regard, it is necessary to examine whether and to what extent the permit defence and state-of-the-art defence may be allowed against the liability of operators to take response measures under the Japanese implementing legislation.

When imposing liability to take response measures, the Supplementary Protocol focuses on the damage caused by LMOs subject to transboundary movements rather than the activities involving such LMOs (Article 3). On the other hand, under the Cartagena Law, it is the certain activities, namely the broadly defined 'use of LMOs' either as Type 1 Use or Type 2 Use that is the subject of either an advance approval by the competent minister or stipulation by an ordinance issued by the competent ministers. The approval of Type 1 Use under the Cartagena Law can be assimilated as a permit. For Type 2 Use, the user may invoke the defence of compliance with binding administrative orders. In such a legal system under the Cartagena Law, if we allow these defences, the liability of operators for almost all activities that caused damage would be exempted or mitigated. This would be a departure from the intention of the Supplementary Protocol to address damage caused by LMOs. However, if we do not allow such defences, the operator would almost invariably be held liable to take response measures if its LMO causes damage in spite of his or her compliance with the permit or the ordinance. This might be considered as unreasonably severe to the users of LMOs. The question of permit defence should be carefully examined when implementing the Supplementary Protocol under the current Cartagena Law.

What of the state-of-the-art defence under the Cartagena Law? Under the current Cartagena Law, when (due to the progress of scientific knowledge) it has come to be recognised that there exists a risk that an Adverse Effect on Biological Diversity could arise, the competent ministers may order suspension of the Type 1 Use or take other necessary measures (Article 10 (2)). It would be problematic to allow the state-of-the-art defence to take response measures, because such defence would disregard the legislative intent of Article 10 (2) to address an adverse effect that was still unknown at the time of initial approval of the LMO. Allowing such defence would also be an obstacle in the realisation of the precautionary principle.

The present authors argued in Subsection 2 above that in order to implement the Supplementary Protocol appropriately, a new explicit provision dealing with response measures should be inserted into the Cartagena Law separately from the preventative measures that can be ordered by the competent minister under the current Law. Thus, it is necessary for us to examine whether the state-of-the-art defence against response measures should be allowed, distinguishing that from the preventative measures including those allowed under Article 10 (2) of the Cartagena Law. Although this issue needs to be considered further in detail, at this time, the following two points should be mentioned. First, we may be able to suppose a situation where damage has occurred as a result of the fact that the competent minister could not detect the Adverse Effect on Biological Diversity even though they had the latest scientific knowledge and, therefore, did not order the operator to suspend the Type 1 Use or to take other necessary measures. In such a hypothetical situation, we may be able to allow the operator to invoke the state-of-the-art defence so as to avoid imposing entire liability on the operator.

Second, under the Cartagena Law, Type 1 Use is required to obtain the approval of the competent ministers. Such approval is to be reviewed according to the progress of scientific knowledge, and, based on such review, the Use may be suspended. This review scheme makes it possible in the approval to reflect the latest scientific knowledge. This means that the permit defence by the operator incorporates the latest scientific knowledge, which is also connected to the state-of-the-art defence. As the state-of-the-art defence is pleaded on the basis of the scientific knowledge at the time when the activity is made, not when the approval is given, the state-of-the-art defence may be admitted to a limited situation when it is based on the latest scientific knowledge. The extent to which the state-of-the-art defence is admitted would be limited compared to that of the permit defence.

4 The concept of biodiversity damage

Whether the liability required under the Supplementary Protocol can be adequately implemented under the Japanese legal system depends on more than just the specific content of the response measures. Under the administrative approach to liability as envisaged by the Supplementary Protocol, it also depends on the way the administrative authorities exercise their discretionary powers to implement the liability. In other words, in order to impose the liability of operators to take response measures, especially restoration measures, the competent Japanese authorities under the Cartagena Law must evaluate and determine that there is an Adverse Effect on Biological Diversity in the situation, that is one that involves damage to biodiversity.

The basic objective of the Cartagena Law is to prevent Adverse Effects on Biological Diversity, which are defined as adverse effects that are caused by the use of an LMO that threatens to impair biological diversity.[25] For a Type 1 Use, certain criteria have been established by the guidance issued by the relevant ministries to assess such adverse effects.[26] For example, the assessment criteria for genetically modified plants include competitiveness against wild relatives, productivity of harmful substances, ability to cross-breed with wild relatives, etc. The procedures involve, for each assessment criterion, the identification of wild relatives likely to be affected, the evaluation of the concrete details of any adverse effect on the wild relatives, the evaluation of the likelihood of such adverse effects, and finally the determination whether the LMO in question threatens to impair the preservation of species or populations of wild fauna or flora. These assessment criteria and the detailed procedures for their evaluation are laid out and implemented in order to prevent Adverse Effect on Biological Diversity.[27]

By contrast, in comparison with the concept of an Adverse Effect on Biological Diversity under the Cartagena Law, the 'damage' covered by the Supplementary Protocol means 'an adverse effect on the conservation and sustainable use of biological diversity, taking also into account risks to human health, that is measurable or otherwise observable taking into account scientifically-established baselines, and significant' (Article 2 (2) (b)). Thus, it can be assumed that the concept of biodiversity damage under the Supplementary Protocol would be more limited than that of an Adverse Effect under the Cartagena Law. On the other hand, the concept of biodiversity damage under the Supplementary Protocol is broader in scope because it includes, as a factor for the determination of 'significant', the reduction of the ability of components of biological diversity to provide goods and services, in addition to the adverse effects on the components of biodiversity themselves (Article 2 (3)). Considering the facts that the Cartagena Law, in determining whether there is Adverse Effect on Biological Diversity, does not take into account the goods and services provided by biodiversity and does not have a criterion for the magnitude of the effect (significant), there seems to be an important difference between the concept of an Adverse Effect on Biological Diversity under the Cartagena Law and biodiversity damage as defined by the Supplementary Protocol.

In order to streamline the two concepts, the present authors suggest that the existing concept of Adverse Effect on Biological Diversity be abolished and, instead, the concept of biodiversity damage be introduced to the Cartagena Law.

---

25   See note 8.

26   Ministry of Finance; Ministry of Education, Culture, Sports, Science and Technology; Ministry of Health, Labour and Welfare; Ministry of Agriculture, Forestry and Fisheries; Ministry of Economy, Trade and Industry; and Ministry of Environment, The Guidance of Implementation of Assessment of Adverse Effects on Biological Diversity of Type 1 Use of Living Modified Organisms, Public Notice No. 2 of 2003.

27   Tomoki Mizutani, 'Idenshi Kumikae Seibutsu niyoru Seibutsu Tayousei eno Eikyo ni tsuite' (Adverse Effects on Biological Diversity caused by LMOs), *Kikan Kankyo Kenkyu (Environmental Research Quarterly)*, No. 132 (2004), p. 53; Yutaka Tabei, 'Idenshi Kumikae Sakumotsu no Riyou no Genjyo to Seibutsu Tayousei Eikyo Boushi no Torikumi' (Cultivation of Genetically Modified Crops and Approach to Conserve Biological Diversity), *Kikan Kankyo Kenkyu (Environmental Research Quarterly)*, No. 132 (2004), p. 34; Tabei, see note 7, p. 145.

Then, the concept of biodiversity damage will be defined as an adverse effect on biodiversity that is measurable or otherwise observable taking into account scientifically established baselines and, omitting the concept of 'significant' from its definition under the Cartagena Law, which is present in the Supplementary Protocol. By doing so, the Cartagena Law would still be addressing a situation of adverse effect with a lower threshold (the same threshold as the current Adverse Effect on Biological Diversity) by the preventative measures as authorised by the current Cartagena Law. Thus, it maintains the precautionary nature of the present Cartagena Law. The requirement of 'significance' will be added in order to ensure the more far-reaching response measures to be taken when a situation of 'damage' as defined by the Supplementary Protocol occurs. By substantively retaining the authority of the competent ministers to order the preventative measures to address Adverse Effects on Biological Diversity but adding the authority to order response measures when there is damage or a sufficient likelihood of damage, the Cartagena Law with such amendments would provide more rigorous regulations on a wider range of possible adverse effects posed by LMOs than the Supplementary Protocol itself requires. Truly, the Cartagena Law will become an implementing legislative instrument for both the Cartagena Protocol and the Nagoya-Kuala Lumpur Supplementary Protocol.

The above suggestion will mark the first ever legislation in Japan that explicitly establishes a liability regime for environmental damage *per se*.

5 Identifying operators

An operator who shall bear the liability under the Supplementary Protocol is defined as 'any person in direct or indirect control of the LMO which could, as appropriate and as determined by domestic law, include, *inter alia*, the permit holder, person who placed the LMO on the market, developer, producer, notifier, exporter, importer, carrier or supplier'. When implementing this broad definition of operator based on the current Japanese Cartagena Law, a person liable under the Law to take response measures would be within the same scope as those persons who may be ordered to take preventative measures under the current Cartagena Law. Namely, it would include a person who is making, has made or has caused another person to make use of an LMO (including, in the case of a foreign exporter, its domestic administrator) for Type 1 Use (Article 10 (2) of the Cartagena Law). In the case of a Type 2 Use, it would be a person who is making or has made use of an LMO in accordance with the ordinance, and a person who has received the confirmation for the containment measures to make use of an LMO (Article 14 (2) of the Cartagena Law).[28] As the concept of 'Use' under the Cartagena Law is

---

28   Akiho Shibata, 'Idenshi Kumikae Seibutsu-tou ni Ki-in suru Seibutsu Tayosei Songai ni kansuru Nagoya-Kuala Lumpur Hosoku Giteisho no Igi to Kadai' (Nagoya-Kuala Lumpur Supplementary Protocol on Liability and Redress for Biodiversity Damage caused by LMOs: Significance and Problems), *Bioscience and Industry*, Vol. 69, No. 3 (2011), p. 230.

defined broadly (Article 2 (3)) as explained above, almost all entities dealing with the LMO in the territory of Japan, including importers, permit holders, transporting companies carrying the LMO, researchers and growers, can be identified as an operator bearing the liability to take the required response measures. Under the Cartagena Law, the operator can be conceived broadly in response to the different situations and circumstances in which biodiversity damage can occur.

The Supplementary Protocol requires the establishment of a causal link between the damage and the LMO in question (Article 4) and does not require, at least explicitly, the establishment of a causal link with the act and/or activity of the operator causing the biodiversity damage. In other words, in determining liability, the nature of the activity of the operator may not be taken into account. Thus, as long as damage occurs that can be linked to an LMO subject to transboundary movement, any of the possible operators as defined in the Supplementary Protocol may be held liable even when the LMO in question was duly imported with the approval of the importing government after the risk assessment. The same holds true when the LMO in question was subject to an unintentional transboundary movement or even an illegal trade by a third party. Whether the operator acted in negligence will not be determinative when establishing its liability.

It has been argued that the operator liable for the damage will only be identified after having considered the nature of the biodiversity damage caused by an LMO.[29] Assuming that the current Cartagena Law would be applied to implement the concept of operator, it is probably difficult to interpret the term 'person who is making, has made, or has caused another person to make use of LMO' to include developers of LMOs. However, once biodiversity damage caused by an LMO has occurred, it is usually difficult to determine who caused it among the many entities involved in the complex chain of process from development, through production, marketing, supply and use. It may well be a case in which only the developer of the LMO can be identified. For this reason, one possible approach to legislation might be to consider including LMO developers among the possible operators as someone who would be obliged, as a last resort, to take response measures against the biodiversity damage caused by an LMO.

6 Civil liability

The Supplementary Protocol provides that in order to address the biodiversity damage, the Parties 'may, as appropriate', apply existing domestic law on civil liability or develop specifically civil liability rules and procedures for the purpose of addressing such damage (Article 12 (1)). On the other hand, 'with the aim of providing adequate rules and procedures in domestic laws on civil liability for material or personal damage associated with biodiversity damage', the Supplementary Protocol obliges its Parties to continue to apply existing general law on civil liability or to develop civil liability law specifically for the purpose of

---

29   Toi, see note 24, p. 50; Shibata, see note 18, pp. 34–35.

addressing such material or personal damage associated with biodiversity damage (Article 12 (2)).

With respect to the biodiversity damage, it would seem difficult for existing Japanese tort law to address the concept of damage to the environment *per se*. A new set of legislation will perhaps be necessary if its civil liability system is to address such damage. With respect to the 'material or personal damage associated with biodiversity damage', there will be no need of enacting a special civil law for that purpose and such damage can be addressed by the existing Japanese general tort law and possibly by civil injunctions.

IV Conclusion

Many of the provisions under the Supplementary Protocol allow their implementation in accordance with the domestic laws of the Parties. It is therefore important to closely examine how the Supplementary Protocol is implemented domestically in order to assess its actual effectiveness. This chapter examined the Japanese Cartagena Law as one possible example of such implementing legislation, focusing on the flexibility provisions introduced under the Supplementary Protocol mainly because it has taken an innovative approach to liability (the administrative approach). The present authors conclude that although there may be a need to amend the Cartagena Law to incorporate the additional authority of the competent ministers to impose restoration measures in response to biodiversity damage, the core provisions of the Supplementary Protocol based on the administrative approach can be effectively implemented by applying the basic legal framework of the current Cartagena Law. The explicit introduction of the concept of biodiversity damage into the Cartagena Law, thereby strengthening its regulatory powers to respond to a wider range of possible adverse effects posed by LMOs, would be the first ever legislation in Japan that establishes a liability regime for environmental damage *per se*.

The Supplementary Protocol contains other provisions; the way in which they will be implemented under the Japanese legal system will have significant impact not only for the operators in Japan, but also for the exporters of LMOs abroad. One such provision is Article 10 on financial security. In addition, there are technical issues that will need to be addressed if Japan will have a comprehensive legal system of effective implementation of the Supplementary Protocol, such as the concrete criteria considered when addressing damage to biodiversity, the proof of causation, and possible exemptions and mitigations. As the host country of COP-MOP5, where an epoch-making new treaty with its city name in the title was adopted, Japan needs to address these matters quickly, establish an implementing scheme under its domestic legal system, and obtain approval from the Diet (its Parliament) on the Supplementary Protocol along with the amendments to the Cartagena Law. Such efforts will assuredly become a model for its implementation that can be emulated by other countries, thereby speeding up the entry into force of the Nagoya-Kuala Lumpur Supplementary Protocol.

14 The industry's Compact and its implications for the Supplementary Protocol

J. Thomas Carrato, John Barkett and Phil Goldberg[1]

In June 2010, leading agricultural biotechnology providers BASF, Bayer CropScience, Dow Agrosciences, DuPont, Monsanto Company and Syngenta signed 'the Compact', an agreement designed to provide States with a process for binding arbitration to seek redress in the event that a living modified organism (LMO) causes damage to biological diversity. A few months later in October 2010, the Nagoya-Kuala Lumpur Supplementary Protocol on Liability and Redress for transboundary movements of LMOs was adopted. Both the Compact, a private sector remedy, and the Supplementary Protocol, developed under the auspices of the United Nations, place an emphasis on preventing damage to biological diversity and assuring timely remediation should damage occur. This chapter discusses the development of the Compact, how it works and how it can be used to complement the liability and redress remedies available to a State under the Supplementary Protocol.

I Historical context for the Compact

New technology was developed for cross-breeding of plants towards the end of the last century. Previously, crops such as corn and soy were improved by cross-breeding in the field using traditional techniques developed over centuries. These techniques, however, had well-understood limitations: results produced were variable, reaching the desired transformations took time and multiple generations of cross-bred seed had to be grown to find plants with the desired traits.

Modern techniques such as genetic modification (LMOs) and molecular breeding allow the desired traits from one plant to be 'cross-bred' into another plant at the genetic level. The resulting transformation is precise and predictable, and seed producers can accurately, efficiently and reliably address local farming

---

1 See also an article with substantially similar content, but applied in a different context in: J. Thomas Carrato, John Barkett, Darren Abrahams and Phil Goldberg, 'The "Compact" in the Context of the Biosafety Protocol (A Voluntary Contractual Supplemental Mechanism)', in David Raič and K. Guo eds, *Globalisation, the Nation-State and Private Actors: Re-thinking Public-Private Cooperation in Shaping Law and Governance* (Eleven Publishers, forthcoming 2014).

needs. For example, where drought and insects present particular problems for farmers, crops can be made drought- or insect-resistant. Other biotech crops reduce pesticide applications or minimise the need for tillage. Over the past 15 years, LMOs incorporating such desirable traits have become commercially available and have increased yield and sustainability of many types of food, feed, fibre and fuel.

During those years, LMOs never caused damage to biological diversity. They have been safely grown on more than 2 billion acres by 12 million farmers. In large part, this excellent record of safety is due to the risk assessments completed by the leading producers of LMO seeds to ensure that, when commercialised, their LMO crops will not cause damage to biological diversity. As part of these risk assessments, producers examine all relevant factors, including effects of the LMO on the environment and human and animal health. In many countries, the regulatory approval process for LMOs, which is very thorough and rigorous, can take up to six years.

Nevertheless, since LMOs have been commercialised, some in the international community have voiced concerns about what would or *could* happen. What if a risk assessment was wrong? What if there is an unintended or unwanted movement of genetic material from an LMO? What if some market entrants are not as careful as others in bringing technologies to market? What if, as a result of such events, an LMO causes damage to biological diversity? How does a State obtain redress?

1 International development of a liability and redress system for damage to biological diversity

The international community started answering these questions when it adopted the Convention on Biological Diversity (CBD) and the Cartagena Protocol on Biosafety (Cartagena Protocol) to the CBD. Together, these two treaties addressed global concern about the conservation and sustainable use of biological diversity. They enabled States to receive the information necessary for making timely, competent decisions about authorising specific LMOs for import and use in their territories, even in the absence of domestic regulation. Article 27 of the Cartagena Protocol, which addresses the topic of 'liability and redress', set in motion a process for elaborating a liability and redress mechanism in the event that an LMO damages biological diversity. Article 27 led to several years of earnest, lengthy and often contentious discussions and negotiations leading up to adoption of the Nagoya-Kuala Lumpur Supplementary Protocol on Liability and Redress (Supplementary Protocol), the details of which have been examined in Chapter 3 of this book.

2 Misinformation about biotechnology

Early in this process, company representatives recognised that there was a fear of modern agricultural biotechnology. In part, this was due to the fact that the technology was new, powerful and unfamiliar. These sentiments were also driven, to a significant extent, by persistent misinformation about the safety of LMOs.

Since the advent of biotechnology, reports have proliferated purporting mis-information or misunderstandings about the safety of LMOs. Some of these inaccurate reports may have been the result of simple mistake, but others appeared designed to influence laws governing biotechnology products. For example, in 1999, nearly 1,000 articles in newspapers and magazines around the world declared that bioengineered corn was causing the demise of the monarch butterfly.[2] The impetus for these stories was an experiment conducted by a young professor in his upstate New York laboratory, culminating in a seven-paragraph article in the journal *Science*, which the author viewed as preliminary. Anti-biotechnology activists dressed this report up and misrepresented it as evidence that the monarchs were 'felled by killer corn', calling for an immediate ban of the LMO.[3] Two years later, after several studies jointly sponsored by the biotech industry and the United States Environmental Protection Agency, the claim that the LMO caused the demise of the monarch butterfly was debunked. The stories were untrue.[4]

More recently, assertions with regard to various genetically modified seed products were made without any basis in fact or science. One group, in an effort to discredit biotechnology, falsely compared biotechnology foods to tobacco, asbestos and DDT, calling them 'inherently unsafe' and labelling them as the cause of 'widespread death and disease'.[5] Another group said that 'genetic engineering, because of its unpredictable nature, means blind experimentation with the very basis of life on Earth. This must be banned before irreparable damage occurs'.[6] Other claims falsely associated biotechnology seeds with infertility[7] or suggested that doctors 'prescribe non-GMO diets . . . [for] individuals, especially those with autism, Lyme disease, and associated conditions'.[8] As the *New Scientist* has observed, 'committed opponents seize on every opportunity to demonize' biotechnology, which 'may have even cost lives by distracting attention from other potential causes'.[9]

2   See Carol Yoon, Pollen from Genetically Altered Corn Threatens Monarch Butterfly, Study Find, *New York Times*, 20 May 1999; see also Rick Weiss, Gene-Altered Corn May Kill Monarchs, *Washington Post*, 20 May 1999.

3   For background on the development of the monarch butterfly scare, see Peter Pringle, The Butterfly Flap, *Prospect Magazine*, Issue 88, July 2003.

4   See Andrew Pollack, Data on Genetically Modified Corn Reports Say Threat to Monarch Butterflies is 'Negligible', *New York Times*, 8 September 2001.

5   See Institute for Responsible Technology, State-of-the-Science on the Health Risks of GM Foods (2008). Available at www.responsibletechnology.org/gmo-dangers/health-risks/State-of-the-Science-on-the-Health-Risks-of-GM-Foods-May-2008 (accessed 1 August 2013).

6   Physicians & Scientists for Responsible Application of Science and Technology, Our New Position on Genetic Engineering (2007). Available at http://psrast.org/bange.htm (accessed 1 August 2013).

7   See Barry Shlachter, Genetically Altered Corn at Issue, *Fort Worth Star-Telegram*, 14 November 2008, at C5.

8   See Lyme Induced Autism (LIA) Foundation, Position Paper Urging the Prescribing of Non-GMO Diets (2009). Available at www.lymeinducedautism.com/images/LIA_Foundation_GMO_Position_Paper.pdf (accessed 1 August 2013).

9   Editorial, 'Seeds of Truth over Genetic Modification', *New Scientist*, Vol. 200, 5 November 2008, p. 5.

These tactics and stories were presumably intended to scare the public, push public officials into over-regulating biotechnology, and create barriers to the technology's successful use in providing increased and healthy food, as well as environmentally sustainable feed, fibre and fuel. These effects were seen during the Article 27 negotiations. Rather than apply traditional liability concepts for advancements in product technology, some Parties sought civil liability regimes with strict (absolute) liability, mandatory collective compensation funds or prohibitive financial security requirements. The problem with these regimes is that rather than require the responsible persons to remediate actual damage, they would lead to considerable liability or other chilling burdens on non-responsible or non-culpable persons in the research, development, supply and use chains.

3 Industry engagement in the Article 27 process

The Global Industry Coalition (GIC)[10] actively participated as observers in the Article 27 discussions. Initially, the GIC's position was that no new binding international regime for liability and redress was warranted. This position was primarily based on Article 27's mandate 'to adopt a *process* for the *appropriate* elaboration of international rules and procedures' (emphasis added), although the GIC was also influenced by the initial focus of the negotiating group on onerous civil liability regimes. The GIC consistently urged rejection of such provisions, including absolute civil liability, mandatory compensation funds, shifting burdens of proof to the accused, and eliminating or severely limiting defences. In reaction, some Parties disregarded industry; others charged that industry was hindering the Article 27 process.

As the negotiations progressed, industry became more engaged in, and identified means for advancing and complementing, the Article 27 process. Leaders in agricultural biotechnology recognised that if liability decisions were improperly influenced by misunderstanding or misinformation, liability would likely be based on political grounds, instead of scientific knowledge and processes and the assessment of actual risk (assessed as hazard multiplied by exposure). They also found the *status quo*, which consisted of a variety of State laws that would create inconsistent and unpredictable results, unworkable. It became increasingly important to the GIC that legal systems for biotechnology become fair, efficient and harmonised, and that they not create unwarranted and unwise barriers to research, trade and international movement of LMOs.

In 2006, to facilitate industry involvement in the Article 27 discussions, CropLife International identified a set of principles essential to appropriate systems of liability and redress: science-based decision-making, respect for precedent, social

10 The Global Industry Coalition (GIC) for the Cartagena Protocol on Biosafety receives input and direction from trade associations representing thousands of companies from all over the world. Participants include associations representing and companies engaged in a variety of industrial sectors such as plant science, seeds, agricultural biotechnology, food production, animal agriculture, human and animal health care, and the environment.

responsibility and commercial practicality. It commissioned several independent experts to write papers on these and other aspects of liability and redress mechanisms useful for LMOs.[11] Some papers focused on existing legal structures that could address claims for damage to biological diversity, the interplay between domestic and international liability regimes, and the appropriate regulatory systems for authorising LMOs and safeguarding biological diversity.

The GIC used these materials to increase its involvement in the Article 27 negotiations, and it also studied the feasibility of an administrative approach to redressing damage to biological diversity. An administrative approach is one based on the powers and duties of public authorities (rather than individuals and courts as implemented through civil liability) that seeks to determine how, when and who should take response measures in the event of damage to biological diversity. It is typical of the administrative approach that State governments use licensing to authorise the commercialisation of LMOs in a State and to provide measures that require the license holder or permit holder to prevent and remediate any harm or for the authority itself to take such measures.

The GIC developed a concept paper for use in the discussions on the administrative approach based on an analysis of the European Union's Directive on Environmental Liability (EU-ELD).[12] After many discussions with the Parties and other observers, this approach was introduced and accepted in the negotiations. The GIC embraced this movement, supporting it within the context of the Parties' commitment to elaborating a binding international regime, and changed its position to support adoption of such a binding regime, offering compromise proposals on the provisions under negotiation.[13] Thus, by 2008, industry was positively and proactively engaged in Article 27's liability and redress process.

The Article 27 negotiations were intense and difficult, alternating between progress toward consensus on some issues and emotional impasse and fundamental philosophical differences on others. In October 2010, there was a final extraordinary session in Nagoya, Japan. At this meeting, the Parties agreed to adopt a basic framework for an administrative approach to address damage to the conservation and sustainable use of biological diversity resulting from the transboundary movement of LMOs and their subsequent release to the environment. The framework included several essential elements, but left many terms to be developed and implemented at the national level. Industry supported this compromise because it embraced an administrative approach, required science-

11   For example, Stanley H. Abramson, 'Implications of Proposed TWN and OAU Model Liability Language' (1 January 2006); and Laura van der Meer, 'Environmental Liability Regimes: Approaches and Best Practices' (1 January 2006). Available at www.croplife.org/Resources (accessed 1 August 2013).

12   Directive 2004/35/CE of the European Parliament and of the Council of 21 April 2004 on environmental liability with regard to the prevention and remedying of environmental damage (EU-ELD), *Official Journal of the European Union 2004*, L 143/56.

13   The GIC remains supportive of the express recognition of sovereign national legal systems and opposed to strict (absolute) civil liability, mandatory compensation funds, and onerous prohibitive financial security requirements.

based evidence of damage, focused the Parties on remediating any damage, and took steps to ensure that the operator responsible for causing damage would be the one who is responsible for remediation.

II Development of 'the Compact'

Concurrent with the GIC's increased involvement in the Article 27 discussions, the six major biotechnology providers came together under CropLife International's auspices to develop 'the Compact'. What exactly, then, is 'the Compact'?

The Compact is a private sector mechanism that States can use to ensure that a person or business responsible for releasing an LMO that causes damage to biological diversity remediates that damage. Unlike the Supplementary Protocol, which is a public treaty ratified by States for universal application, the Compact is a private contract signed by and obligating only its Members. States can bring claims against Members under the Compact, and those claims are resolved through binding arbitration.

Suppose a State asserts that a Compact Member's release of an LMO caused damage to biological diversity within that State's borders; that State can now choose to use the Compact to hold the Member responsible for remediating that damage. The Compact includes all of the legal standards, definitions and processes that will be used for the administration of a claim, from its filing through binding arbitration. When it is ready to file a claim, the State signs a mutual agreement for binding arbitration, completes a claim form and files the claim with the Compact's executive director. Pursuant to the Compact, independent neutrals under the auspices of the Permanent Court of Arbitration (PCA) will make all substantive determinations related to the claim. Each Member, in signing the Compact, has legally obligated itself to participate in this binding arbitration and to implement any response plan set forth by an arbitral tribunal.

1 The Compact's genesis

The idea for the Compact arose from discussions industry representatives had with their State counterparts as part of the Article 27 negotiations. The industry representatives were regularly asked, 'If your products are so safe, why won't the companies stand behind them?' There was also growing concern among some States that the absence of a liability and redress regime could compromise access to biotechnology products.

In 2006, several companies came together and concluded that one way to address these concerns would be to develop ideas for addressing damage to biological diversity on their own. Collectively, they endeavoured to: (a) offer a model system tailored to addressing damage to biological diversity; (b) express their commitment to the protection of biological diversity; (c) demonstrate their resolve to 'stand behind their products' and the safety of those products; and (d) respond to direct requests from certain Parties to contribute to the negotiation process with some form of complementary redress mechanism.

As their first order of business, the companies established core principles to guide their work. These principles were ultimately written into the Compact's preamble:

(a) Each Member is committed to rigorous stewardship, risk assessment and risk management to prevent any of its LMOs from causing damage to biological diversity.
(b) Biological diversity is a public good which States have a special responsibility to protect. Claims for damage to biological diversity should be pursued only by States.
(c) Legal due process must govern the adjudication of any claim for damage to biological diversity, and all substantive decisions must be made by an independent, neutral authority.
(d) Science-based evidence must support decisions on all aspects of a claim for damage to biological diversity, which is also required under the Rio Declaration on Environment and Development (Rio Declaration), the CBD, and the Cartagena Protocol.
(e) A party will only provide a remedy for damage to biological diversity when it is responsible for that damage and only to the extent of that party's responsibility for the damage.
(f) Companies involved in the biotechnology industry must have the financial capacity, through insurance or otherwise, to implement the appropriate remedy for any damage to biological diversity for which they are responsible and must timely provide that remedy.
(g) A company must not be held financially responsible for double or multiple recoveries for the same incident of damage to biological diversity.

During their subsequent work on a model redress regime, the companies concluded that the only approach that could work *inter se* was to write and sign a contract binding themselves such that if the release of an LMO by a signatory to that contract caused damage to biological diversity, that signatory would be required to respond appropriately. This idea of a 'binding contract' led to many complex questions, including whether such an agreement would be legal under anti-trust and anti-competition laws. Darren Abrahams and his colleagues at the Brussels, Belgium, office of Steptoe & Johnson LLP researched and analysed this issue, ultimately answering it in the affirmative. Additional questions remained. How would industry gain the acceptance for this contract by States? Would States adhere to dispute resolution rules established in a *private* contractual mechanism? Could they do so while at the same time fully respecting their own sovereignty?

2 Drafting the Compact

In 2007, representatives from BASF, Bayer CropScience, Dow Agrosciences, DuPont, Monsanto Company and Syngenta started working under the auspices of CropLife International to answer these questions and draft such a contract. The contract is now titled 'The Compact, a Contractual Mechanism for Response in the Event of Damage to Biological Diversity Caused by the Release of a Living Modified Organism'. It is widely referred to as simply 'the Compact'.

When the companies' representatives set out to draft the Compact, each of them was well aware that if the Compact could be agreed to, his or her company would be assuming a duty that it did not currently have: to provide redress for damage to biological diversity caused by the release of an LMO by that Member with very few defences and regardless of whether a State had or could obtain personal jurisdiction over the company. Its processes also would have to be accessible and trusted by States. It was not clear that the six companies would or could agree to a common framework, but they began the process so that, at the very least, they could offer the international community a set of concepts that either complemented some of the ideas already under consideration, such as the administrative approach, or were alternatives to others, such as absolute civil liability, mandatory compensation funds and potentially prohibitive financial requirements.

The first conceptual draft of the Compact was written in mid-2007 by Mr Abrahams, based in part on the EU-ELD[14] and in part on a paper by Thomas Nickson *et al.* In spring 2008, the group arrived at an acceptable framework that was consistent with the principles set out in the Rio Declaration,[15] under which a technology provider would be responsible for its own LMO with few available defences. In March 2008, the Compact's drafting group chair, J. Thomas Carrato of Monsanto Company, announced that work was underway on the Compact and described its basic concepts. Soon thereafter, the companies signed a Memorandum of Understanding to execute the Compact on completion. During COP-MOP4 in Bonn, Germany, the companies announced the Memorandum of Understanding, presented the basic concepts and approach of the Compact, and provided an early draft of the text.

Over the next two years, the Compact underwent continuous rigorous review, both internally and among the States, and numerous iterations were produced. Shook Hardy & Bacon attorneys John Barkett, an expert in international arbitration and environmental law based in Miami, Florida, and Phil Goldberg, a Washington, DC liability public policy attorney, assisted with these revisions and adapted the PCA rules for use with the Compact.

3 Assuring the Compact's value to States

The Co-Chairs of the negotiations on liability and redress, René Lefeber and Jimena Nieto Carrasco, graciously facilitated numerous open dialogues on the Compact with States and other stakeholders in the international community. The first dialogue was held in Singapore in January 2009 for representatives of Southeast Asian countries and NGOs. Subsequent dialogues were held in Costa

---

14 EU-ELD, see note 12.
15 Principle 16 of Rio Declaration on Environment and Development, adopted on 16 June 1992, UN Doc. A/CONF.151/26/Rev.1 (Vol. I) (1992), pp. 3–8.

Rica for the GRULAC countries, in Brussels for the European Union Member States and Eastern European countries, in Manila for other Asia Group countries, and in Africa for nations of that continent. In addition to representatives of State Parties and non-State Parties, interested stakeholders, including representatives from Greenpeace, the International Grain Trade Coalition, the Permanent Court of Arbitration, academics, and seed law experts also participated in these dialogues.

Feedback during these dialogues was supportive of industry self-regulation and remarkably constructive on how to improve the Compact. This process led to numerous iterations of the Compact text and extensive development and refinement of its concepts to address comments from the participants in these dialogues. In the summer of 2010, the initial six Members finalised and executed the Compact. The Compact remains a 'living document' that will be continuously improved. The Members have since approved two sets of post-enactment revisions to incorporate further feedback from States and stakeholders. There will no doubt be other revisions in the years to come.

III How does the Compact work?

1 The contract

The contract that comprises the Compact is divided into three parts: main text, Bylaws and Appendices. The main text provides the governing structure for the Compact, including requirements for membership, rules for the Compact's operation, and the standards, rights and obligations for adjudicating a claim for damage to biological diversity against a Member.

The Bylaws provide the rules and procedures the tribunal and Members will follow in carrying out their functions under the Compact. The Bylaws largely adopt the PCA arbitration rules for adjudicating a claim. The PCA Rules envision that Parties will modify the rules to pertain to the specifics of the Parties' arbitration,[16] and the Bylaws include such modifications to bring the rules up to date with modern arbitration practice and to guide the tribunal in implementing the claims and arbitration processes under the Compact.

The initial Appendices included the Mutual Agreement for Binding Arbitration that States and Members sign to initiate a claim, a Claim Form to instruct States how to submit a completed claim, a joinder agreement for non-Members to join a claim's arbitration, and non-disclosure agreements. In 2012, an Appendix on criteria related to experts to be engaged for a claim's adjudication was added. Additional Appendices, including rosters of those experts and both criteria and rosters for neutral arbiters, are still being developed.

---

16 'The Framers of existing and future agreements may need to determine the relationship between the [PCA] Rules and those agreements, and may modify them as necessary'. Permanent Court of Arbitration Optional Rules for Conciliation of Disputes Relating to Natural Resources and/or the Environment (effective 16 April 2002), Introduction.

2 Membership

As stated previously, the current Members of the Compact are BASF, Bayer CropScience, Dow Agrosciences, DuPont, Monsanto Company and Syngenta. All Members are treated equally. Each has an equal voice in the Compact's operations. Also, a Member's cost is its pro rata share of the Compact's operating costs (salaries and the supplies and costs related to running the Compact and administering claims), as well as costs associated with defending any claims against that Member and providing any required remedies.

The Members' goal, along with that of CropLife International, is to encourage open and broad membership from the biotechnology industry. Any entity, whether a private company, public research facility or government agency, can become a Member of the Compact if it satisfies the membership requirements. These requirements include: (a) a commitment to being a good steward of the technology and of biological diversity; (b) the undertaking of rigorous risk assessments; and (c) the financial capacity to provide a remedy ordered under the Compact. The Compact and Bylaws contain conditions and processes for membership that embody these principles. Should other provisions be needed to facilitate broad membership, they will be added in consultation with States and other stakeholders.

The primary benefit of joining the Compact is having one's responsibilities for damage to biological diversity clearly defined, premised on science-based evidence of causation and damage, and determined in a neutral adjudicatory process. The certainty of this process is also intended to encourage the development of commercial insurance to cover a Member's responsibilities under the Compact. The availability of such insurance, in turn, should facilitate a prospective Member's ability to demonstrate the financial capacity necessary to join the Compact and to create the financial incentive for doing so.

The importance of commercial insurance to the success of any liability and redress system was highlighted during discussions on the Supplementary Protocol. The CBD's Executive Secretary, in a note to the *Ad Hoc* Working Group in 2005, reported on the failures of several other international liability and redress conventions. Most strikingly, the Executive Secretary said a key reason that the Basel Liability Protocol had not been ratified was the '[l]ack of insurance policies . . . to cover the risks associated with the transboundary movement of hazardous waste'.[17]

Some entities may decide not to join the Compact, and the Members have taken steps to ensure that the Compact cannot and does not have any impact on non-Members. The Compact and arbitration agreement both require that all materials, decisions and processes specific to the claims process under the Compact are to be used only for determining whether a Member must provide redress under the Compact. Should an arbitral tribunal determine that damage to biological diversity was caused by a non-Member, the non-Member will have no obligations under

---

17 Note by the Executive Secretary, Status of third-party liability treaties and analysis of difficulties facing their entries into force, UNEP/CBD/BS/WG-L&R/1/INF/3 (2005), para. 10 (a).

the Compact. Further, in signing the arbitration agreement, States will be agreeing not to use determinations made in arbitration outside of the Compact. The non-Member's legal rights and responsibilities will not have changed; the non-Member will remain subject to the same laws and liability systems as if the Compact had never existed.

3 Organisational structure

The Compact creates an Executive Committee, a Technical Committee and an Advisory Committee to facilitate its operations. With regard to claims, neutrals operating under the administering authority of the PCA make all substantive decisions.

The Executive Committee governs the Compact's operations. It consists of representatives of all Members, with each Member having equal voting weight. The Executive Director is responsible for the day-to-day operations of the Compact and is the point person for receiving claims submitted by States. The Technical Committee, comprised of scientific experts from each Member, provides technical advice to the Executive Committee. It also works to establish and maintain criteria for and rosters of neutral individuals and experts who can be retained to assist in resolving claims. The Advisory Committee is chaired by the Executive Director with the goal of facilitating discussions and ensuring that the Compact is responsive to the States that use it. Its responsibilities include working with the Technical Committee on criteria and names for the experts and neutrals described above. It also will provide counsel on membership criteria, issues related to financial capacity to respond to damage and general operation of the Compact. The importance of receiving such constructive input from the international community was demonstrated throughout the many dialogues the Members had with States and other stakeholders in developing and refining the Compact.

To ensure that the Advisory Committee will offer representative viewpoints, the Compact instructs the Committee to invite the participation of up to 40 individuals along the following formula: at least two officials from each of the seven regions of the Food and Agriculture Organization (FAO); at least three Regional or International Government Organisations, such as the European Union; at least two non-governmental organisations; at least two public and private sector research firms; at least two small- and medium-sized enterprises; at least four other stakeholders (e.g. grain traders, processors, growers); and at least two Members. In the event there are more applicants than slots, the Executive Committee will ask the applicants to come up with a plan for filling the positions.

The representatives of the PCA were consulted during the Compact's formation and have provided helpful guidance, feedback and support on how the Compact Members should use the PCA in the claims adjudication process. As discussed below, the PCA will appoint a Commissioner to handle the initial review of a claim and possible claim-related fact-finding, and will facilitate the formation of a tribunal for the adjudication of that claim.

4 Claims process

Any State in the United Nations or the World Trade Organization (WTO) can initiate a claim under the Compact for damage to biological diversity in that State. It need not be a signatory to the CBD or the Cartagena Protocol. The purpose of the Compact is to complement domestic law by providing an additional mechanism for a State's recovery.

If a State pursues a claim under the Compact, the claim must be brought within three years of when the State knew or should have known of the damage to biological diversity and within 20 years of the time the LMO was authorised or released. If the State chooses not to pursue a claim under the Compact, or is outside these time frames, the State retains whatever options were available for pursuing action against a Member under applicable domestic or international law. The Compact cannot and does not have any impact on these alternative means of redress. Private citizens and non-governmental organisations can avail themselves of that applicable law or ask a State to file a claim under the Compact.

To initiate a claim under the Compact, an authorised representative of the State submits to the Executive Director a signed Mutual Agreement for Binding Arbitration, a completed Claim Form, and plausible evidence establishing damage and the concerned Member's responsibility. The State does not sign or submit any of these materials unless or until it chooses to file a claim. Just as the Compact does for Members, the Arbitration Agreement sets forth the terms and obligations for the State in arbitrating the claim: the claim will be adjudicated under the Compact's terms and conditions, the State will protect the integrity of the Compact's processes, and a Member cannot be subject to recovery under the Compact in addition to a State's administrative or civil liability system for the same incident of damage.

In an effort to facilitate the Compact's use, the Members will work with States to resolve any conflicts that might exist between the Arbitration Agreement and domestic law. The Members have a significant interest in making sure the voluntary, binding arbitration system embodied in the Compact works to the satisfaction of both States and Members.

During the first 20 days after a State submits a claim to the Executive Director, the Members named in the claim will sign the Arbitration Agreement and the Executive Director will request that the PCA appoint a commissioner. The Commissioner will work with the State to ensure that its claim is properly completed, is supported by plausible evidence, and is in compliance with the Compact's requirements. As with the EU-ELD,[18] the plausibility standard is a minimal threshold ensuring that a tribunal is convened only when there are facts supporting a reasonable inference that a claim may result in a finding against a Member. If the commissioner needs additional information to make these determinations, it may suggest fact-finding commence under the PCA's rules. A State will be given up to one year to resolve any deficiencies a commissioner finds with its claim.

---

18   EU-ELD, see note 12.

When a Commissioner determines that a claim is properly submitted, the Member will be asked to provide information responsive to the claim. The Parties may also engage in mutually agreed fact-finding. At the end of this process, the Parties will have 90 days to try to settle the claim. This period can be extended by agreement of the Parties, and the talks can be managed by a neutral conciliator separately appointed by the PCA.

If settlement is not reached, a three-person PCA tribunal will be convened to adjudicate the claim. In assessing the evidence, the tribunal will consider information from the Parties and, if desired, seek help from neutral experts. The standard of proof for each element of a claim and for all defences is 'clear and convincing evidence'. This standard is defined in the Compact to mean the degree of proof that will produce a firm belief as to the truth of the allegations, which is more than that required under the preponderance of the evidence standard, but less than that required for proof beyond a reasonable doubt. The decision to use the clear and convincing evidence standard was based on long-standing common law principles and on precedent for legal disputes of this nature.[19]

All tribunal decisions are final and cannot be appealed. If, after the tribunal has ruled, significant material information comes to light that would prove a claim, the State can file a new claim so long as the Compact's claims processes are not used to harass a Member by repeated filings that are the same or substantially similar.

The procedural requirements set forth above should not be costly to States. The general rule is that Members will pay the costs of commissioners, unless a commissioner rejects a claim and the State does not cure the claim's deficiencies within a year. For claims that proceed to conciliation or arbitration, each Party will pay an equal share of the costs of conciliation or arbitration and of the fees of the conciliator and the tribunal. To keep costs down, the Executive Committee will look into establishing a fee-chart for what commissioners, conciliators and arbitrators can charge. Each Party will also bear its own costs of preparing for and participating in the conciliation and arbitration process, which may include investigation, research, attorney, and other costs and fees.

If the State is considered a 'least developed',[20] 'small island developing',[21] or 'megadiverse'[22] country and prevails on its claim, the Member will pay the portion

19   This is the same standard of proof adopted in the famous Trail Smelter decision in which the Tribunal held that 'under the principles of international law, as well as the law of the United States, no State has the right to use or permit the use of its territory in such a manner as to cause injury by fumes in or to the territory of another or the properties or persons therein, when the case is of serious consequence and the injury is established by clear and convincing evidence'. Arbitral Tribunal, Trail smelter case (United States, Canada), Award of 11 March 1941, *Reports of International Arbitral Awards*, Vol. 3, p. 1965.
20   Least Developed Country: A State recognised by the United Nations' Office of the High Representative for the Least Developed Countries, Landlocked Developing Countries and Small Island Developing States as such. Available at www.unohrlls.org/en/ldc/25/ (accessed 1 August 2013).
21   Available at www.un.org/special-rep/ohrlls/sid/list.htm (accessed 1 August 2013).
22   One of the following 17 countries that formed in 2002 a group entitled 'Like-Minded Megadiverse Countries': Bolivia, Brazil, China, Colombia, Costa Rica, Democratic Republic of Congo, Ecuador, India, Indonesia, Kenya, Madagascar, Malaysia, Mexico, Peru, the Philippines, South Africa and Venezuela. This group collectively holds more than 70 per cent of the world's biodiversity and 45 per cent of the world's population.

of a State's costs of submitting, pursuing and arbitrating the claim correlated to that Member's percentage of responsibility for the damage. By way of illustration, if the tribunal determines that a Member is fully responsible for the damage to biological diversity in one of these States, it will assign all reasonable and properly documented costs of the arbitration to that Member. If a Member is determined to be 20 per cent responsible for the damage, the Member will pay 20 per cent of such reasonable documented costs.

5 Claim assessment

To hold a Member responsible for providing a remedy under the Compact, the tribunal must assess each element of the claim and defences asserted and conclude that there is damage to biological diversity that was caused by the release of an LMO by that Member. The amount of the Member's responsibility will then be adjusted, taking into account any of the limited affirmative defences that the Member was able to establish and the cost of appropriate response measures.

(1) Damage to biological diversity

To prove damage to biological diversity, the tribunal must conclude that there is a measureable, significant and adverse change in a species or a change in its ecosystem that result in the loss of a natural resource service essential to sustain the species. The State must first establish, through science-based analysis, a base-line of biological diversity for the affected species or natural resource service in the habitat prior to the change in biological diversity allegedly caused by the LMO. If pre-existing inventories or studies are not available, a State can develop a base-line in preparation for filing a claim. To reduce the burden of retrieving historical information on both parties, the tribunal will only consider data from the 25-year period immediately preceding the date on which the alleged damage occurred.

The change from that baseline is then measured. A State must show that this measureable change is significant and adverse. A significant and adverse change is one where: (a) a species cannot maintain itself as a viable component of its natural habitat; (b) the natural range of the species has been reduced to an unsustainable level; (c) a sufficient habitat no longer exists to maintain species population on a long-term basis; or (d) some other species in the affected ecosystem related to or dependent upon the species in question cannot maintain itself as a viable component of the ecosystem.[23] Data points for this determination may include the life histories, geographic distribution, frequencies of different genes and other biological parameters associated with the species. Some changes, such as those within historic or expected ranges of fluctuation, that are unavoidable from

---

23 As with the EU-ELD, the Compact acts as a guide to the tribunal on conditions that are not themselves considered significant and adverse.

natural causes or are the anticipated effects of a State-authorised LMO do not qualify standing alone as significant and adverse change, but may be considered along with other evidence.

This change-from-the-baseline approach is common in claims alleging environmental damage. There must be a starting point from which any alleged change can be measured. For example, the EU-ELD defines the baseline it requires as 'the condition at the time of the damage of the natural resources and services that would have existed had the environmental damage not occurred'.[24] The Directive also requires damage to have 'significant adverse effects'.[25]

(2) Causation

Once damage is established, the tribunal must determine the cause of the damage. Determining causation also is a science-based, fact-driven analysis. The Compact requires an assessment of all three traditional causation factors: (a) whether the LMO caused the damage (specifically, a showing that the LMO can cause the change to the species or ecosystem alleged and that damage actually resulted from the genetic modification to the LMO); (b) whether the Member is responsible for releasing the LMO that caused the damage; and (c) whether a superseding event or a logically unrelated or remote event altered the chain of events that otherwise might have connected the Member's release of the LMO to the damage. This causation determination reflects the Rio Declaration on Environment and Development's principle that a responsible party should repair damage to biological diversity that it causes.[26] It also directs responsibility, absent extenuating circumstances, to the Member who placed the LMO on the market, most often the technology provider, and not to others in the supply and use chain. The Compact ensures this allocation of responsibility through several provisions.

First, a Member who placed the LMO on the market in the State where it was released is considered to have 'released' the LMO. If the LMO goes through multiple States, a Member that placed the LMO on the market in the original State is also deemed to have placed the LMO on the market in the destination State and in all States through which the LMO moved. Second, there is no requirement for the State to show that a Member did anything wrong in releasing the LMO. A Member can be responsible for responding to damage to biological diversity even when it took reasonable care to prevent the damage. Third, by contrast, downstream economic actors (exporters, importers, handlers, processors, sellers, distributors, planters and users) must have done something wrong in a way that caused the damage in order to be considered the party that 'released'

---

24   Paragraph 14 of Article 2, EU-ELD, see note 12.
25   Paragraph 1 (a) of Article 2, ibid.
26   See note 15.

the LMO. Finally, if the tribunal determines that there are multiple causes of the damage, including the release of the LMO by the Member, it will assign percentages of responsibility for each cause. A Member's responsibility for providing a remedy will be commensurate with its percentage of responsibility. If a Member is 50 per cent responsible for causing the damage, it will provide or pay for half of the award. If the Member is wholly responsible, it will provide the full response. This system is the fairest way to ensure that each Member is responsible for the portion of any damage it caused.

(3) Defences

Should a State successfully establish that a Member's release of an LMO caused damage, the Member has available six limited affirmative defences. The Member has the burden of proving these defences by clear and convincing evidence. As with the causation determination above, if a defence is proven, the tribunal will assign a percentage of responsibility to the activity giving rise to the defence. The amount of the response the Member will provide will be reduced by any percentage assigned to a defence.

Three of the Member's limited defences account for factors that break the chain of causation because they are outside of the Member's control: act of God; act of war, terrorism, or civil unrest; and misuse of the LMO by someone else. The other three defences cover activities and events accepted or authorised by the State bringing the claim. These include a risk explicitly assessed and accepted as part of the State's authorisation process for the LMO, a risk posed by an activity specifically authorised or permitted by the State, and damage caused by compliance with a compulsory measure imposed by the State.

The defences most discussed during the dialogues with the States were act of God, a risk explicitly accepted or authorised by the State, and misuse. An act of God is a natural phenomenon of exceptional, inevitable and irresistible character, namely an earthquake, flood, tornado or weather event of great magnitude. Pollen flow, the transformation creating an LMO, and subsequent changes that result directly from that transformation are not acts of God. The defence for realisation of a risk specifically assessed and authorised is comparable to a 'warning defence'. It requires that the Member, in the risk assessment submitted to the State, fully and accurately warned that such damage may occur. Specifically, the Member must have identified the type, magnitude and probability of the damage so that when the State authorised the LMO, it determined that the risk of that harm was acceptable (regardless of whether the State imposed risk management measures). This defence gives Members a critical incentive to provide States with accurate and thorough risk assessments. It also relates back to an original purpose of the Compact, which was to promote environmental stewardship by having Members remove uncertainty ('what about the unknown?') through the risk assessment process.

The misuse defence can be invoked only when someone else wrongfully caused the damage. The Member must establish the following four elements: (a) another person or entity violated a law or regulation, or a prescribed condition, safety measure or standard governing the LMO; (b) violation caused the improper release of the LMO; (c) the LMO released caused the damage to biological diversity; and (d) compliance with the law, regulation, condition, safety measure or standard would have prevented the LMO's release and the damage. This defence is important because, if it was not included, a 'misuser' would know that it could violate the law and not be held accountable. Also, one should only be responsible for its own product or conduct. Incidentally, if the 'misuser' is another Member, the tribunal will require that other Member to respond to the damage caused by its misuse.

By way of illustration, suppose a Member receives an authorisation from a State to place an LMO on the market in that State. The State enacts a regulation requiring the LMO to be transported in sacks in sealed containers. The Member contracts with a company to transport the grain and communicates this requirement to the transporter in writing. In violation of this requirement, the LMO grain is transported in open-air rail cars, causing grain to be blown from the car. In the same area, farms produce the LMO in compliance with the State's conditions of use. If the LMO causes damage to biological diversity, the misuse defence applies to damage the Member can prove by clear and convincing evidence was caused by the LMO blown from the rail car. Assuming the terms and conditions of the Compact are met, the Member is responsible only for damage caused by the farms' production of the LMOs.

The Compact provides no other defences. Consequently, traditional products liability defences, such as the 'state-of-the-art' and 'reasonable alternative design' defences, do not apply.

(4) Response

If the tribunal finds that a Member is responsible, in whole or part, for damage to biological diversity, the tribunal will determine the response award. As the claimant, the State is responsible for submitting an initial response plan and, as needed, a financial valuation of the alleged damage. The responsible Member can work with the State to further develop the plan in an effort to assist the tribunal in determining the most appropriate resolution of the claim.

Restoration is the preferred response. An acceptable restoration plan will result in the species or natural resource service being restored to a suitable end point. This objective is reached when the species or ecosystem in question is restored to the condition that existed before the damage occurred, which is satisfied when: (a) population dynamics data for the species in question demonstrate that the species can maintain itself on a long-term basis as a viable component of its natural habitat; (b) the natural range of the species has been increased to a sustainable level; (c) a sufficient habitat is generated to maintain the species population on a long-term basis; and/or (d) one or more other species in the affected ecosystem related to or dependent upon the species in question can maintain itself on a long-term basis as a viable component of its natural habitat.

The means for reaching this objective must account for and seek to preserve the LMO's benefits. If the tribunal determines that those benefits cannot be preserved under the State's plan, it can tailor the restoration plan to better balance benefits and damage, develop a new restoration plan with the State to replace the species or ecosystem with another species or ecosystem or restore the damaged species in another location, combine partial restoration with an award of appropriate compensation, or replace the restoration plan entirely with the requirement that the Member compensate the State for the value of the damage. Compensation, though, is not the preferred response and is only available when restoration is impossible or restoration would cost more than the value of the damage. As with all determinations under the Compact, assessing compensation, including the value of the damage, must be done through objective processes and criteria supported by science-based evidence.[27]

There are several other factors that should be considered in determining the appropriate response, whether that be compensation or restoration. First is the nature of the ecosystem where the damage occurred. If the damage occurred in a centre of origin or protected area, for example, the economic value of the damage might be greater and the restoration more specialised than if the damage had occurred in an industrialised or degraded environment. Second is the public health impact of the damage; a response order can include measures to address imminent and substantial endangerments to public health. Public health is the physical health and well-being of a whole community, as managed by the responsible governmental agencies in a State. It does not include personal injury. As discussed above and consistent with the Supplementary Protocol, personal injury claims are not covered by the Compact and would need to be pursued under otherwise applicable domestic or international law.[28]

Finally, the award must stay within the Compact's financial limits. The Compact states these limits in the International Monetary Fund's (IMF) monetary unit, Special Drawing Rights (SDR), which can be converted into any State's currency. To encourage restoration, the restoration limits are 30 million SDR for a single incident and 150 million SDR for all incidents caused by an LMO, whereas the corresponding limits for compensation are 15 million SDR and 75 million SDR. Should awards include both restoration and compensation, the limits are 30 million SDR for a single incident, of which no more than 15 million SDR can be for compensation, and 150 million SDR for all incidents caused by an LMO, of which no more

---

27 See Secretariat of the CBD, *An Exploration of Tools and Methodologies For Valuation of Biodiversity and Biodiversity Resources and Functions* (CBD Technical Series No. 28, 2007), which contains case studies on the application of valuation methodologies described in the manuscript and which may be applicable in the Assessment Process if consistent with the terms and conditions of this Compact.

28 Similarly, '[t]raditional damage, which is common in third-party civil liability instruments, and which includes personal injury, loss of damage to property or economic interests, is not covered by the Supplementary Protocol'. Secretariat of the CBD, The Nagoya-Kuala Lumpur Supplementary Protocol on Liability and Redress to the Cartagena Protocol on Biosafety: An Introductory Note in Preparation for Signature and Ratification (2011), p. 3, para. 11. Available at http://bch.cbd.int/nkl_suppl_protocol/introductorynote.pdf (accessed 1 August 2013).

than 75 million SDR can be for compensation. These limits should be adequate for remedying damage to biological diversity and will be regularly revisited.

The financial limits serve two important purposes. From a practical perspective, they were essential in persuading Members to voluntarily sign the Compact and assent to provide States with jurisdiction, expedited adjudication and limited affirmative defences. They also should make Compact membership accessible to small companies, public research facilities and others who will need to purchase commercial liability insurance to demonstrate their ability to pay for an award. Without such financial limits, it is unlikely that a private insurance market will develop to cover response measures under the Compact.

(5) Enforcement

To provide assurance to States that a Member will provide the response required, the Compact includes austere measures for enforcing its terms, conditions and response awards. If a State or Member alleges a breach, the Party alleging the breach must provide written notice to the accused Party, who will have 10 days to respond or correct the breach. If not resolved, the tribunal's presiding arbitrator or other PCA-appointed individual will determine if there is a breach. Members are required to cooperate with this inquiry. If a Member is deemed in breach, the Member is responsible for all reasonable and documented costs associated with the enforcement proceedings, and a State can file an enforcement action in its own jurisdiction, or in the Member's domicile State among other jurisdictions.

In addition, once a Member is deemed in breach, the other Members are required to file a separate specific enforcement action against the recalcitrant Member. This option, which is unique to the Compact, may be preferable for many States because it does not tie up State resources. Also, Members have granted their advance consent to such an action in any jurisdiction or venue selected by the other Members, including where the breaching Member has assets that may be appropriated to fund the response obligation.

In the event that a Member needs to enforce the Compact against a State (for example, in order to avoid double or multiple recovery), their primary option is to enforce the Compact under the judicial system of the State that signed the arbitration agreement. Also, because the Arbitration Agreement is by its terms a commercial instrument, it can be enforced in accordance with the rules of the New York Convention.[29]

IV The Compact complements the Nagoya-Kuala Lumpur Supplementary Protocol

When taken together, the Compact and Supplementary Protocol provide States with two viable options for assuring that a responsible party will respond to any

29   See Convention on the Recognition and Enforcement of Foreign Arbitral Awards, adopted on 10 June 1958, *United Nations Treaties Series*, Vol. 330, p. 3.

damage to biological diversity caused by its release of an LMO. Both offer administrative processes with decisions made by independent neutrals or competent authorities based on scientific evidence and causation. Because States that adopt the Supplementary Protocol can still choose to file a claim under the Compact as the primary means for seeking such redress, States can take advantage of the differences between the two instruments. In fact, an important objective of the Compact's Members has been to make the Compact the preferred option for resolving claims of damage to biological diversity.

Specifically, the Members took several steps to ensure that the Compact will have value to States and that States will find its terms and processes fair, accessible and effective for adjudicating claims. As discussed above, Members held numerous intensive dialogues with States and others in the international community, during which they received constructive comments for ways to enhance the Compact. They also institutionalised a process for this feedback through the establishment of the Advisory Committee. In addition, Members took these measures in recognition that for States that do not adopt the Supplementary Protocol, the Compact may offer the *only* mechanism for addressing biological diversity-related claims.

Of greatest benefit is that the Compact covers more States and more potential situations for redress than the Supplementary Protocol. First, for the several States that have not adopted the Cartagena Protocol, the Compact is and likely will remain their only international mechanism for the remediation of damage to biological diversity caused by an LMO. Second, because it is an international treaty, the Supplementary Protocol requires transboundary movement of an LMO. The Compact does not. It is available for all LMOs, whether moved internationally or used only domestically. Third, the Compact is also broader than the EU Environmental Liability Directive, which covers only species that are protected by State law. A State can file a claim under the Compact for damage to any species or ecosystem. This 'all-LMOs' and 'any-damage' approach is important to the Compact and was enhanced by suggestions in the dialogues, including by Greenpeace's representative.

In addition, the Compact gives States a means for pursuing technology providers and other Members, even when the States do not have jurisdiction over them under applicable domestic law or when such law would not subject them to liability. Under the Supplementary Protocol, States are to pursue the appropriate 'operator' to remediate the damage. The Supplementary Protocol defines 'operator' as the person in direct or indirect control of the LMO.[30] Technology providers and other Members, though, may not qualify as such 'operators'; they may not be in control of the LMO or have facilities or assets in the State where the alleged damage occurred. As a result, the only 'operator' available within the jurisdiction of the State for an action to redress the alleged damage would be the importer, carrier, farmer or other domestic entity. By providing States the opportunity to pursue Members under the Compact, the Compact allows States to file claims

---

30   Paragraph 2 (c) of Article 2, Supplementary Protocol.

against any Member – domestic or foreign – whose release of an LMO caused the damage.

Finally, the Compact can help States satisfy the terms of the Supplementary Protocol. Most importantly, under the Supplemental Protocol, States retain the right to require a company to meet a financial security requirement. As discussed above, certain types of financial security, such as compensation funds that are mandatory regardless of whether a company's products or services ever lead to damage to biological diversity, are likely to impede access to and adoption of this proven and beneficial technology. For this reason, at the first meeting of the Conference of the Parties after the entry into force of the Supplementary Protocol, the Secretariat will be requested to undertake a comprehensive study addressing the modalities of financial security mechanisms and offering advice for appropriate entities to provide financial security.[31] The Compact is such a form of financial security. In signing the Compact, each Member has demonstrated its financial ability and has obligated itself to respond to damage to biological diversity caused by its release of an LMO. Therefore, should a State decide to require financial security, Compact membership can satisfy that requirement.

Similarly, the Compact's terms and processes can serve as a model for States in adopting the Supplementary Protocol. The strength of the Supplementary Protocol is that it sets a framework for an administrative system for redressing damage to biological diversity. However, it requires States themselves to establish more than a dozen standards and procedures needed for the system to work. Accordingly, after signing the treaty, States will have to assess and add, repeal or revise their domestic laws to establish a liability and redress system that complies with the Supplementary Protocol. The Compact, which is based on a similar platform and common concepts, can be a resource for States in completing this task. The Compact defines key terms, including damage to biological diversity and causation, fair and reasonable standards and processes for protecting biological diversity as a 'public good', legal due process both for States and those against which claims are made, determinations pursuant to science-based evidence, and independent decision-makers.

V Conclusion

The Compact's Members are committed to protecting biological diversity and standing behind the safety and performance of their LMOs in an effort to advance the world's sustainable production of food, feed, fibre and fuel. They believe that the Compact provides a model that can be adapted by other industries to protect the environment and biological diversity, and may be appropriate as a mechanism for redress in other international regimes.

To achieve their goals for the Compact, the Members actively engaged in the talks that led to the Supplementary Protocol and, at the same time, created

---

31   Paragraph 3 of Article 10, Supplementary Protocol.

the Compact to make sure States had useful liability and redress options. Its Members undertook extensive efforts to establish credibility and gain acceptance of the Compact. They realise that they have a significant stake in making sure that the Compact, which is a voluntary, binding arbitration system, works to the satisfaction of States who might bring claims under its auspices. This is the reason its Members agreed that if States use the Compact, they will provide prompt, appropriate and necessary remedial measures if found responsible for damage to biological diversity.

The Members ultimately also want States to be comfortable with agricultural biotechnology and LMOs. Rigorous risk assessments, stewardship and financial responsibility are fundamental requirements for membership in the Compact, just as they are core principles of the Supplementary Protocol. Should damage to biological diversity occur, however, Members encourage States to have workable administrative mechanisms for redress pursuant to the Supplementary Protocol and hope that States that choose to use the Compact will find it to be a timely, valuable and effective claims-adjudication system.

15 Conclusion

Beyond the Supplementary Protocol

Akiho Shibata

This book examined in depth the highlights of the Nagoya-Kuala Lumpur Supplementary Protocol on Liability and Redress to the Cartagena Protocol on Biosafety (Supplementary Protocol) from the perspective of both the negotiators and the academia. Because the Supplementary Protocol was able to shelve many of the potential difficulties and complexities particular to biotechnology and LMOs, its legal design was premised mainly on addressing biodiversity damage in an international liability regime. This book considered that this aspect of the Supplementary Protocol might have profound precedential and theoretical implications that go beyond the LMOs and biotechnology.

The preceding 14 chapters of this book identified the core issues that needed to be examined to appropriately comprehend the significance and *problématique* of the Supplementary Protocol. They include:

(a) Its incorporation, for the first time in a global liability treaty, of an administrative approach, requiring response measures, including far-reaching restoration measures, as a direct legal consequence of causing biodiversity damage. Relevant articles: Article 2 (2) (d), Article 2 (3), Article 5 and Article 12 (1).

(b) Its establishment, for the first time in a liability regime, of the concept of biodiversity damage. Relevant article: Article 2 (2) (b).[1]

(c) Its imposition of liability on 'operators' without channelling such liability to a defined actor at the international level. Relevant articles: Article 2 (2) (c) and Article 4.

(d) The necessity for, and the significance of, one civil liability provision, its review clause and the reference to Principle 13 of the Rio Declaration in its preamble. Relevant articles: Article 12, Article 13 and second preambular paragraph.

(e) Its financial security provision and its review clause. Relevant articles: Article 10 and Article 13.

---

1 This book proceeded with the assumption that the concept of damage to biological diversity (or biodiversity damage) and that of damage to conservation and sustainable use of biological diversity can be used interchangeably. See Chapter 2 of this book, by Akiho Shibata.

(f) Its relegation to Parties' domestic law of the authority to determine several elements of the liability regime in the process of implementing the Supplementary Protocol ('in accordance with domestic law'), and the source of information for the prospective Parties in such a process (EU Directive, Japanese Cartagena Law and the Compact).

(g) Its negotiation process, including its normative framework and its relation to other fields of international law, the role of precedents (United Nations International Law Commission's (ILC) Allocation of Loss Principles and EU Environmental Liability Directive), and the role of the Co-Chairs and the negotiating techniques utilised by them. Relevant articles: Article 10 (2), Article 11 and Article 16 of the Supplementary Protocol, and Article 27 of the Cartagena Protocol.

The examination of the above core issues by the contributors, often from different perspectives, has led the present author to reach certain conclusions, the implication of which may go beyond the text of the Supplementary Protocol. The author is well aware of the admonition that the success of the Supplementary Protocol, including its power to have such implications, much depends on its entering into force.[2] However, even without entering into force, the Supplementary Protocol would affect, of course, not the rights and obligations of States under international law (Article 16 (4)), but the fundamental thinking on the legal design of environmental liability regimes under international law.

I A response to 'liability occlusion'

The 'liability occlusion'[3] was very much embedded in the minds of the Parties negotiating the Supplementary Protocol.[4] The Supplementary Protocol was thought as a saviour of international environmental liability regime, after the 'sensibility' of negotiating international civil liability regimes was seriously questioned in the academia, which in turn was based on the actual experience both at the international (1999 Basel Liability Protocol and ILC discussion on 'international liability') and regional (EU environmental liability directive) levels. Undeniably, as this book amply demonstrated, the Supplementary Protocol was an *ad hoc* political compromise out of the specific political configuration of the Parties negotiating it at a particular moment of history, as well as the result of diplomatic skills of a personal nature, especially of the Co-Chairs and the leading negotiators, many of whom are the contributors of this book.[5] On top of this

---

2 See Chapter 4 of this book, by René Lefeber.

3 See Chapter 1 of this book, by Akiho Shibata.

4 See Chapters 2, 3 and 5 of this book, by those authors representing Japan (Akiho Shibata) and the EU (Alejandro Lago Candeira), and by the Co-Chairs (René Lefeber and Jimena Nieto Carrasco).

5 See Chapters 3, 7 and 10 of this book, by René Lefeber and Jimena Nieto Carrasco, Gurdial Singh Nijar, and Worku Damena Yifru and Kathryn Garforth, respectively.

unavoidable characteristic, however, the Supplementary Protocol did have a more fundamental agenda to address.

A tentative and still evolving response to the 'liability occlusion' provided in the Supplementary Protocol seems to comprise of the following thought process. First, a liability regime should clearly distinguish between addressing environmental damage *per se*, including biodiversity damage, on one hand, and the traditional damage to persons and property, and economic loss, on the other. Second, in addressing environmental damage *per se*, an administrative approach to liability would provide a more effective regime as it addresses such damage more directly by obliging the liable operator to take restoration measures. In addition, the administrative approach has a better chance of reaching an agreement among the States with vastly divergent domestic legal systems. Third, as the administrative approach to liability is novel, with a limited experience in its actual application, the details of the legal design of the liability regime based on an administrative approach were left for the time being to the domestic law of each Party.

II On administrative approach to liability, again!

The incorporation of an administrative approach to liability in the Supplementary Protocol in 2010 might not have been a 'paradigm shift',[6] or it might not be characterised as 'revolutionary'.[7] However, from the comparative examination of previous liability treaties,[8] the Supplementary Protocol surely brought a significant and explicit shift in emphasis in an international environmental liability system to ensure effective restoration measures in addressing environmental damage. The Supplementary Protocol attests to an agreement among the Parties that the most effective response to biodiversity damage is through speedy restoration measures.[9] Under the prevalent civil liability treaties, damage to the environment was addressed by letting the competent authority, or any other actor in a position to do so, voluntarily effectuate the restoration measures, and, then, as a legal requirement under the liability treaties, by obliging the responsible operator to reimburse for the costs of such measures if and when a claim is brought to a court. The administrative approach to liability, on the other hand, pre-emptively obliges the operator as a direct legal consequence of causing damage to the environment (in other words, as a liability for damage) to take restoration measures, in addition to the obligation afterwards to reimburse the costs if claimed by the competent authority that had taken such measures.[10] The obligation of the operator to take

---

6   See Chapter 4 of this book, by René Lefeber.
7   See Chapter 5 of this book, by Alejandro Lago Candeira.
8   See Chapter 2 of this book, by Akiho Shibata.
9   See Chapter 12 of this book, by Edward Brans and Dorith Dongelmans.
10   The fact that the Supplementary Protocol in its Article 5 (5) provides only for the 'right' of the competent authority to recover from the operator the costs of response measures, and not explicitly the obligation of the operator to pay such costs, clearly demonstrates its emphasis on the obligation to take response measures as the liability of the operator for causing biodiversity damage.

the response measures is effectuated and enforced primarily by the administrative organ of State in application of administrative, or public, law, rather than by the court in application of civil, or tort, law. Thus comes the denomination of 'administrative approach'.

What qualities of this new approach to liability established in the Supplementary Protocol would pull the States towards its acceptance? First, it is argued that the administrative approach to liability for environmental damage is based on a firm theoretical pedigree of 30 years of arduous discussion on 'international liability' within the ILC. It is claimed that the Supplementary Protocol is a faithful model of specific implementation of the ILC's Allocation of Loss Principles.[11] Second, it is suggested that the process of negotiation has been conducive to Parties' assuming ownership of the evolving negotiated text. Such ownership, it is argued, is even more important than achieving consensus as only true ownership will enhance the probability that the instrument will enter into force and attract broad participation.[12] Those substantive and process qualities, it is argued, would confer legitimacy to the Supplementary Protocol that pulls States towards its acceptance.

The domestic implementation of an administrative approach to liability, however, could take many avenues. The EU and its members, utilising its Environmental Liability Directive (EU-ELD), will be implementing the Supplementary Protocol faithfully by establishing the liability of the operator to take response measures. Under a self-executing provision of the EU-ELD, the operator is directly held liable to take such measures where environmental damage has occurred. In addition, under the EU-ELD, the competent authority is obliged to issue orders against operators to take such measures.[13] On the other hand, Japan, utilising its existing Cartagena Law, will be implementing the Supplementary Protocol by *authorising* the competent authority to issue an order against operators to take such measures on the basis of such operator causing biodiversity damage. Under this mode of implementation, the liability of the operator to take response measures does not arise directly from the operators causing biodiversity damage, but from the discretionary administrative order of the competent authority.[14] This mode of implementation is, arguably, within the allowable margin of discretion of the Parties as provided in Article 5 (8) of the Supplementary Protocol, which allows the Parties to determine the manner in which they implement the response measures in accordance with their domestic law, without in any way compromising the objective of the Supplementary Protocol.

The weaknesses of the administrative approach to liability have been identified. Except for the more general *problématique* of its overly open-ended nature, which will be addressed below, the difficulty and even impossibility of its transnational implementation touches upon the very heart of the limit of an administrative approach based on the territoriality principle in the application of the administrative

11   See Chapter 2 of this book, by Akiho Shibata.
12   See Chapter 3 of this book, by René Lefeber and Jimena Nieto Carrasco.
13   See Chapter 12 of this book, by Edward Brans and Dorith Dongelmans.
14   See Chapter 13 of this book, by Eriko Futami and Tadashi Otsuka.

law of States.[15] It is extremely challenging to compel the operator situated abroad to take response measures, or to endeavour to recover costs from such an operator when it does not have any assets in the territory of the State where the bio-diversity damage occurred. As the Supplementary Protocol applies to LMOs 'which find their origin in a transboundary movement', these challenges are real. The Supplementary Protocol offers little or no assistance in this regard. A few chapters of this book, however, suggested possible solutions. One such solution is 'The Compact, a Contractual Mechanism for Response in the Event of Damage to Biological Diversity Caused by the Release of a Living Modified Organism', which operates regardless of whether a State had or could obtain personal jurisdiction over the liable company.[16] The second is a creative means under the domestic law, as suggested by the Japanese Cartagena Law. Under the Law, an LMO developer that intends to export its LMO to Japan may be required to establish a 'domestic manager' in Japan, which is responsible to submit the necessary risk assessment documents and to respond to calls from the competent authority in emergencies.[17] When such a domestic manager of a foreign LMO developer can be identified as an operator under the implementing legislation, perhaps as a permit holder, a State of import where the biodiversity damage occurred may be able to enforce the liability of a foreign LMO developer to take the required response measures through that domestic manager.

III Everything 'in accordance with domestic law'?

There are 18 references to 'domestic law' within nine of the Supplementary Protocol's 21 articles. It is criticised that the Supplementary Protocol contains more optional rules than mandatory ones, and that there is too much flexibility, which makes monitoring compliance with the terms of the agreement difficult and almost pointless. Interestingly, it is argued that this situation could be attributed to the nature of rules based on an administrative approach.[18] According to another view, these flexibilities, as the result of compromises during the negotiation, straddle the fault lines between the positions of various interests groups. These fault lines, it is argued, have a tendency to re-emerge during implementation of the instrument, allowing for re-interpretation and re-imagination that may lead to serious implementation challenges, including disputes.[19]

Reflecting on the EU-ELD, where Member States were given many choices with regard to the implementation of some of its key provisions, it is argued that the lack of uniformity in the implementation of international instrument is not necessarily wrong or unusual.[20] Over-anxiety over the potential lack of uniformity

---

15   See Chapters 4 and 10 of this book, by René Lefeber, and Worku Damena Yifru and Kathryn Garforth, respectively.
16   See Chapter 14 of this book, by J. Thomas Carrato, John Barkett and Phil Goldberg.
17   See Chapter 13 of this book, by Eriko Futami and Tadashi Otsuka.
18   See Chapter 10 of this book, by Worku Damena Yifru and Kathryn Garforth.
19   See Chapter 11 of this book, by Dire Tladi.
20   See Chapter 12 of this book, by Edward Brans and Dorith Dongelmans.

in its domestic implementation should not overshadow the key achievement of the Supplementary Protocol in establishing an important shift in emphasis regarding the operationalisation of the liability for biodiversity damage. The key threshold of effectiveness of the Supplementary Protocol, according to this view, is whether its Parties establish an administrative apparatus that responds to a case of bio-diversity damage by ensuring that the operator takes effective response measures.[21] As long as this cardinal obligation is implemented, even in accordance with the domestic law of the Parties that reflects their particular legal and socio-economic conditions and circumstances, it is argued that the objective of the Supplementary Protocol can be considered as achieved, at least for the time being.

From this perspective, the most problematic re-imagination entering into the realm of revisionism is to re-interpret Articles 5 (7) and 12 (1) to mean that a Party need not establish an administrative approach to liability, but is obliged only to require the operators to take response measures as an outcome of application of civil liability law, invariably involving cumbersome and time-consuming court procedures. Article 5 (7) must be read in a way so as to allow the application of civil liability law only when, in 'defining the specific response measures to be required' from the operator, such an application is more effective in responding to the biodiversity damage than implementing an administrative approach to liability established in accordance with Articles 5 and 12 of the Supplementary Protocol. In other words, Articles 5 (7) and 12 (1) should not be read as exonerating the obligation of the Parties to establish a system of an administrative approach to liability in the case of biodiversity damage.

True, if a provision in a treaty when implemented by more than one State is bound to cause a dispute or objection, admittedly, it is flawed lawmaking. Some of the chapters suggest the provisions on financial security (Article 10) and on the exemptions (Article 6)[22] as examples of such flawed lawmaking. However, the Supplementary Protocol, as part of the legal order established by general inter-national law, does provide sufficient safety valves that would avoid, and resolve if necessary, such an outright confrontation between the Parties with different positions. Article 26 of the Vienna Convention on the Law of Treaties (VCLT) stipulates the overarching principle of good faith in the performance of a treaty,[23] whereas Articles 16 and 10 (2) of the Supplementary Protocol provide for an encouragement of mutually supportive and integrative interpretation among the relevant international law, rather than an interpretation based on isolationist unilateralism.[24] For example, a science-based approach to the implementation of

21 See Chapters 2 and 5 of this book, by Akiho Shibata, and Alejandro Lago Candeira, respectively.
22 Compare the discussion on exemptions under the Japanese law implementing the Supplementary Protocol and that under the Compact, in Chapters 13 and 14 of this book, by Eriko Futami and Tadashi Otsuka, and J. Thomas Carrato, John Barkett and Phil Goldberg, respectively.
23 Article 26 ('*Pacta sunt servanda*'), VCLT: 'Every treaty in force is binding upon the parties to it and must be performed by them in good faith'.
24 Report of the Study Group on Fragmentation of International Law: Difficulties arising from the Diversification and Expansion of International Law (full report), UN Doc. A/CN.4/L. 682 (13 April 2006).

the Supplementary Protocol in light of the WTO obligations is an excellent example of an integrative interpretation encouraged by one contributor of this book.[25] It could occur that some legislation implementing the Supplementary Protocol would be viewed by others as based on a dubious interpretation of the Supplementary Protocol. This is an abstract 'dispute' or 'objection' that can well be resolved, as it has on numerous occasions under various MEAs, by an amicable consultation process involving the Secretariat as interlocutor, through the constructive discussion among the Parties in the COP-MOP, and, if necessary, by drafting and adopting by consensus a set of guidelines on the implementation of specific articles of the Supplementary Protocol. Articles 13 and 10 (3) should be read as providing for such an opportunity of resolving, and not engendering, implementation problems if and when they actually arise.

IV Civil liability: what was the issue and where will it lead us?

No contributor in this book questioned that when Article 27 of the Cartagena Protocol was adopted in 2000, the prospective international rules and procedures in the field of liability and redress for damage resulting from transboundary movement of LMOs would be based on the prevalent model, at that time, of civil liability regimes. There is no need to repeat why and how this original thinking changed during the intervening decade of critical reflection, both in the academia and the practice of States. What, then, were the reasons that the 82-member Like-Minded Group continued to demand a legally binding provision on civil liability in the Supplementary Protocol?

A close reading of the two chapters that address this fundamental question conveys a nuanced difference in emphasis. On one hand, it is claimed that in certain parts of the world, the domestic law on liability for environmental damage has not yet well developed, and, referring to an example of environmental liability for human-induced global warming, a further development of *traditional* liability regimes is called for to address complexities involved in such areas as global warming and biodiversity damage caused by LMOs.[26] On the other hand, a treaty provision on civil liability is called for from a more technical-legal reason. Focusing on the transnational aspect of LMOs, being developed in one country, and imported and used in another country, litigation claiming for damage to the environment often involves multiple jurisdictions, and legally binding provisions in a treaty will promote level playing fields as regards to both the procedural issues, such as equal access to courts, and the substantive issues, such as the standard of

---

25   See Chapter 9 of this book, by Rodrigo C. A. Lima.
26   See Chapter 8 of this book, by Elmo Thomas and Mahlet Teshome Kebede. See a similar endeavour in the field of climate change: Richard Lord, Silke Goldberg, Lavanya Rajamani, and Jutta Brunnée eds, *Climate Change Liability: Transnational Law and Practice* (Cambridge University Press, 2012).

liability and scope of damages available.[27] This reasoning assumes that there are already domestic laws on environmental liability established in the relevant States, so that the treaty is needed to harmonise them.

It is understandable for some countries to demand an impetus in the form of a treaty to develop anew or to improve their existing domestic laws to cope with environmental damage. However, without an internally initiated policy determination as to the necessity of such domestic laws, a treaty text alone would not materialise in their establishment. The 1999 Basel Liability Protocol attests to this reality. Moreover, if there is such an internally motivated initiative, there is actually an array of more useful material to assist those States in their endeavours, such as UNEP's *Guidelines for the development of domestic legislation on liability, response action and compensation for damage caused by activities dangerous to the environment.*[28] The fact that the Like-Minded Group did not insist on having a set of guidelines on civil liability for damage caused by LMOs[29] suggests that the Group was not so much concerned with the details of a possible liability law dealing with the complexities of LMOs and biodiversity damage caused by them. As to the demand for a harmonisation of relevant domestic laws relating to biodiversity damage caused by LMOs, in light of the lack of actual cases of damage caused by LMOs and the fundamentally different views on LMOs and biotechnology, the negotiating Parties simply could not agree on the necessity for such harmonisation, beyond having the general conflict of laws and transnational litigation provisions in their civil procedure laws.

The Like-Minded Group was, at the same time, pushing for the inclusion of damage to human health in the general scope of damage under the Supplementary Protocol. The Group succeeded in retaining the phrase 'taking also into account of risks to human health' within the definition of biodiversity damage, and in having the phrase 'the extent of any adverse effect on human health' as one element of determining the significance of the damage. The Group was also adamant in referring to traditional damage to persons and property in paragraph 2 of Article 12 relating to civil liability. After an arduous negotiation, the Group succeeded in providing for an obligation, albeit a soft one, to provide a 'domestic law on civil liability for material or personal damage associated with the damage' to biodiversity. From these claims, it could be speculated that their concern was more with the adverse effect of LMOs on humans and, consequently, to have liability rules that address damage to humans, both individually and to the public

---

27   See Chapter 7 of this book, by Gurdial Singh Nijar.

28   Annex to Decision SS/XI/5B (2010), UNEP, Report of the Governing Council/Global Ministerial Environment Forum on the Work of its Eleventh Special Session (Bali, Indonesia, 24–26 February 2010), UN Doc. A/65/25 (2010), pp. 16–19.

29   Draft Guidelines on Civil Liability and Redress in the Field of Damage Resulting from Transboundary Movements of Living Modified Organisms, Report of the Group of the Friends of Co-Chairs on Liability and Redress in the Context of the Cartagena Protocol on Biosafety on the Work of its Third Meeting (15–19 June 2010), UNEP/CBD/BS/GF-L&R/3/4 (19 June 2010), pp. 16–22. See paragraph 129 of the Report of the fifth COP-MOP, Appendix 3 of this book.

health generally. In fact, one contributor of this book foresees, as a side effect of Article 12, that the parliamentary approval processes in many States may involve a comprehensive assessment and discussion of domestic law related to personal injury, property damage and economic loss caused by LMOs.[30] Furthermore, Article 13 on assessment and review implies that COP-MOP is obliged to assess whether Parties have made efforts to assess and put in place the necessary 'adequate' laws on civil liability to address material or personal damage caused by LMOs.[31] Without the guidelines, however, there is no international standard to gauge 'adequateness' of such domestic laws.[32] There is both the expectation for further development along this line of argument, on one hand,[33] and the concern for potential revisionism in such a process, going beyond the CBD-Cartagena legal framework, on the other.[34]

V Importance of capacity building and science

It became abundantly clear from the several chapters of this book that the *raison d'être* of the Supplementary Protocol providing for a liability for biodiversity damage lies at the perception and the reality, especially among the developing countries, that those countries lack the capacity to conduct, in accordance with the requirement of the Cartagena Protocol, a proper risk assessment and management of LMOs imported into their territories. In the face of such capacity gap, it is argued that having an effective liability system is a pre-requisite for instilling confidence in the technology and averting criticism from their populace when they allowed or encouraged the import of LMOs.[35] The Cartagena Protocol does recognise the importance of capacity building in risk assessment and risk management for biosafety in developing countries together with their needs for financial resources and access to, as well as transfer of, technology and know-how (Article 22, Cartagena Protocol). Financial mechanisms and resources are provided for this purpose (Article 28, Cartagena Protocol). The implementation of those articles of the Cartagena Protocol, however, still needs improvement and strengthening.[36]

It is also argued that some developing countries showed only lukewarm support for an administrative approach to liability, because, for those countries that have

---

30 See Chapter 4 of this book, by René Lefeber.
31 See Chapter 7 of this book, by Gurdial Singh Nijar.
32 See Chapter 4 of this book, by René Lefeber.
33 See Chapters 7 and 8 of this book, by Gurdial Singh Nijar, and Elmo Thomas and Mahlet Teshome Kebede, respectively.
34 See Chapter 11 of this book, by Dire Tladi.
35 See Chapter 7 of this book, by Gurdial Singh Nijar.
36 Decision BS-VI/3 (2012): Capacity-building; Decision BS-VI/4 (2012): Capacity-building: roster of experts; Decision BS-VI/5 (2012): Matters related to the financial mechanism and resources, Report of the Sixth Meeting of the Conference of the Parties to the Convention on Biological Diversity as the Meeting of the Parties to the Cartagena Protocol on Biosafety, UNEP/CBD/BS/ COP-MOP/6/18 (21 November 2012), pp. 36–68.

only newly established and still fragile administrative authorities for biosafety, the new and additional tasks envisaged in the Supplementary Protocol are daunting to accept.[37] While this reasoning does not by itself constitute an objection to, or undermine, the potential effectiveness of the international liability regime for biodiversity damage based on an administrative approach, it raises an important issue of the need for additional capacity-building measures and the means to implement them. In fact, the decision of the COP-MOP that adopted the Supplementary Protocol recalls Article 22 of the Cartagena Protocol and recognises the need for capacity-building measures to implement the Supplementary Protocol.[38] Section C of the same decision, entitled 'Complementary capacity-building measures', urges the Parties to cooperate in the development and strengthening of human resources and institutional capacities, including through facilitating private sector involvement, and invites Parties to take account of such needs in their bilateral, regional and multilateral assistance to developing country Parties that are in the process of developing their domestic implementing legislation.[39]

As called for in the same decision,[40] the new *Framework and Action Plan for Capacity-Building for the Effective Implementation of the Cartagena Protocol on Biosafety*, adopted at the sixth meeting of the COP-MOP in 2012,[41] identifies liability and redress as one of the focal areas of capacity-building measures, and sets the objective of such measures to establish institutional mechanism and process to facilitate implementation of the Supplementary Protocol. Some of the activities include the development of guidance to assist competent authorities in discharging their responsibilities under the Supplementary Protocol (item 4.3), and the organisation of training activities to strengthen the scientific and technical capacity of the competent authorities to be able to evaluate damage, establish causal links and determine appropriate response measures (item 4.4).[42]

The important role of science and scientists in the effective implementation of the Supplementary Protocol was rightly emphasised. It is said that in the implementation of the Supplementary Protocol, science is going to play a major role in the process, such as identifying damage, determining its significance, quantifying the damage, and proposing and implementing mitigation or restoration measures. The establishment of the causal link between the damage and the LMO would be predominantly science-driven. The scientists, therefore, should have a primary role in proposing the implementation of effective management and control measures,

---

37 See Chapter 8 of this book, by Elmo Thomas and Mahlet Teshome Kebede.

38 Decision BS-V/11 (2010): International rule and procedures in the field of liability and redress for damage resulting from transboundary movement of living modified organisms, Appendix 2 of this book.

39 Ibid., paras 9 and 10.

40 Ibid., para. 11.

41 Annex I: Framework and Action Plan for Capacity-Building for the Effective Implementation of the Cartagena Protocol on Biosafety, Decision BS-VI/3 (2012), see note 36, pp. 38–54.

42 Ibid., pp. 49–50.

in monitoring the performance of LMOs in the environment, and in examining the results of these actions and implementing risk management strategies accordingly, including mitigation responses when necessary. In this way, it is argued, science will rightly accompany and support compliance with the objective of the Cartagena Protocol and its Supplementary Protocol.[43]

Science is also needed, it is claimed, to ensure that the implementation of the Supplementary Protocol shall be consistent with the WTO rules, as these rules are designed to allow the adoption of trade restrictions, provided that there is scientific evidence to justify the need for such measures.[44] Without entering into the debate on the (in)famous three preambular paragraphs of the Cartagena Protocol that were reinstated by reference in Article 10 (2) of the Supplementary Protocol, no Party to the Supplementary Protocol would invoke its provisions for the purpose of deviating from, or avoiding, the obligations under other international law, including those under the WTO. Rather, it is assumed that a Party shall utilise a certain margin of discretion in implementing the Supplementary Protocol, in good faith, to better cope with a potential case of biodiversity damage that may be caused by specific LMOs that are imported by that State in its specific environmental and socio-economic circumstances. In this good faith endeavour, the science-based implementation of the Supplementary Protocol will be *sine qua non* for a mutually supportive application of all relevant international law in the field. Thus, the present author agrees with the argument that a comprehensive study that is envisaged by Article 10 (3) on financial security should encourage an analysis based on scientific and technical standards that will allow the adoption of more scientifically based financial security measures within the scope of the Supplementary Protocol.[45]

VI The debate continues

The above final analysis demonstrates that the Nagoya-Kuala Lumpur Supplementary Protocol on Liability and Redress is only the beginning of a new phase in the development of international liability regimes for environmental damage, including biodiversity damage. This new phase is characterised by the distinction between traditional damage and environmental damage *per se*, and by addressing the latter by an administrative approach to liability. Although the core elements of such an approach have been identified and concretised in the Supplementary Protocol, its substantive details, especially the specific ways in which the approach will be implemented, are left to the domestic law of the prospective Parties. Thus, it is still an 'approach', rather than an established international legal design.

The implementing legislation of the Parties and the experience in their application would provide valuable State practice to fertilise the substantive content of the administrative approach to liability. In order to have a regionally

---

43   See Chapter 6 of this book, by Reynaldo Ariel Alvarez-Morales.
44   See Chapter 9 of this book, by Rodrigo C. A. Lima.
45   Ibid.

balanced development of such State practice, the scientific and technical capacity of the competent authorities, especially in the developing world, to be able to evaluate damage, establish causal links and determine appropriate response measures, should be strengthened. Such capacity-building measures should be implemented even before the Supplementary Protocol enters into force.

How a civil liability approach to address damage, including environmental damage, caused by LMOs would evolve, both at the international and domestic levels, is not clear from the text of the Supplementary Protocol. There are both hopes and concerns for the Supplementary Protocol becoming a platform for discussion on possible liability rules for damage to human and public health caused by LMOs. Again, a potential evolution of a civil liability approach in this regard depends on the practice of States, particularly how they implement Article 12 of the Supplementary Protocol and how its review under Article 13 would be undertaken, five years after the entry into force of the Supplementary Protocol.

Thus, the debate continues as to the appropriate legal design for an international liability regime for biodiversity damage. The adoption of the Nagoya-Kuala Lumpur Supplementary Protocol in 2010 and its academic examination are important steps in such continuing debate.

Appendix 1

Nagoya-Kuala Lumpur Supplementary Protocol on Liability and Redress to the Cartagena Protocol on Biosafety, adopted on 15 October 2010, at Nagoya, Japan

The Parties to this Supplementary Protocol,

Being Parties to the Cartagena Protocol on Biosafety to the Convention on Biological Diversity, hereinafter referred to as "the Protocol",

Taking into account Principle 13 of the Rio Declaration on Environment and Development,

Reaffirming the precautionary approach contained in Principle 15 of the Rio Declaration on Environment and Development,

Recognizing the need to provide for appropriate response measures where there is damage or sufficient likelihood of damage, consistent with the Protocol,

Recalling Article 27 of the Protocol,

Have agreed as follows:

Article 1

Objective

The objective of this Supplementary Protocol is to contribute to the conservation and sustainable use of biological diversity, taking also into account risks to human health, by providing international rules and procedures in the field of liability and redress relating to living modified organisms.

Article 2

Use of terms

1   The terms used in Article 2 of the Convention on Biological Diversity, hereinafter referred to as "the Convention", and Article 3 of the Protocol shall apply to this Supplementary Protocol.

2   In addition, for the purposes of this Supplementary Protocol:

(a) "Conference of the Parties serving as the meeting of the Parties to the Protocol" means the Conference of the Parties to the Convention serving as the meeting of the Parties to the Protocol;

(b) "Damage" means an adverse effect on the conservation and sustainable use of biological diversity, taking also into account risks to human health, that:

(i) Is measurable or otherwise observable taking into account, wherever available, scientifically-established baselines recognized by a competent authority that takes into account any other human induced variation and natural variation; and

(ii) Is significant as set out in paragraph 3 below;

(c) "Operator" means any person in direct or indirect control of the living modified organism which could, as appropriate and as determined by domestic law, include, *inter alia*, the permit holder, person who placed the living modified organism on the market, developer, producer, notifier, exporter, importer, carrier or supplier;

(d) "Response measures" means reasonable actions to:

(i) Prevent, minimize, contain, mitigate, or otherwise avoid damage, as appropriate;

(ii) Restore biological diversity through actions to be undertaken in the following order of preference:

a. Restoration of biological diversity to the condition that existed before the damage occurred, or its nearest equivalent; and where the competent authority determines this is not possible;

b. Restoration by, *inter alia*, replacing the loss of biological diversity with other components of biological diversity for the same, or for another type of use either at the same or, as appropriate, at an alternative location.

3   A "significant" adverse effect is to be determined on the basis of factors, such as:

(a) The long-term or permanent change, to be understood as change that will not be redressed through natural recovery within a reasonable period of time;

(b) The extent of the qualitative or quantitative changes that adversely affect the components of biological diversity;

(c) The reduction of the ability of components of biological diversity to provide goods and services;

(d) The extent of any adverse effects on human health in the context of the Protocol.

Article 3

Scope

1   This Supplementary Protocol applies to damage resulting from living modified organisms which find their origin in a transboundary movement. The living modified organisms referred to are those:

(a)   Intended for direct use as food or feed, or for processing;
(b)   Destined for contained use;
(c)   Intended for intentional introduction into the environment.

2   With respect to intentional transboundary movements, this Supplementary Protocol applies to damage resulting from any authorized use of the living modified organisms referred to in paragraph 1 above.

3   This Supplementary Protocol also applies to damage resulting from unintentional transboundary movements as referred to in Article 17 of the Protocol as well as damage resulting from illegal transboundary movements as referred to in Article 25 of the Protocol.

4   This Supplementary Protocol applies to damage resulting from a transboundary movement of living modified organisms that started after the entry into force of this Supplementary Protocol for the Party into whose jurisdiction the transboundary movement was made.

5   This Supplementary Protocol applies to damage that occurred in areas within the limits of the national jurisdiction of Parties.

6   Parties may use criteria set out in their domestic law to address damage that occurs within the limits of their national jurisdiction.

7   Domestic law implementing this Supplementary Protocol shall also apply to damage resulting from transboundary movements of living modified organisms from non-Parties.

Article 4

Causation

A causal link shall be established between the damage and the living modified organism in question in accordance with domestic law.

Article 5

Response measures

1   Parties shall require the appropriate operator or operators, in the event of damage, subject to any requirements of the competent authority, to:

(a)   Immediately inform the competent authority;

(b) Evaluate the damage; and
(c) Take appropriate response measures.

2 The competent authority shall:

(a) Identify the operator which has caused the damage;
(b) Evaluate the damage; and
(c) Determine which response measures should be taken by the operator.

3 Where relevant information, including available scientific information or information available in the Biosafety Clearing-House, indicates that there is a sufficient likelihood that damage will result if timely response measures are not taken, the operator shall be required to take appropriate response measures so as to avoid such damage.

4 The competent authority may implement appropriate response measures, including, in particular, when the operator has failed to do so.

5 The competent authority has the right to recover from the operator the costs and expenses of, and incidental to, the evaluation of the damage and the implementation of any such appropriate response measures. Parties may provide, in their domestic law, for other situations in which the operator may not be required to bear the costs and expenses.

6 Decisions of the competent authority requiring the operator to take response measures should be reasoned. Such decisions should be notified to the operator. Domestic law shall provide for remedies, including the opportunity for administrative or judicial review of such decisions. The competent authority shall, in accordance with domestic law, also inform the operator of the available remedies. Recourse to such remedies shall not impede the competent authority from taking response measures in appropriate circumstances, unless otherwise provided by domestic law.

7 In implementing this Article and with a view to defining the specific response measures to be required or taken by the competent authority, Parties may, as appropriate, assess whether response measures are already addressed by their domestic law on civil liability.

8 Response measures shall be implemented in accordance with domestic law.

Article 6

Exemptions

1 Parties may provide, in their domestic law, for the following exemptions:

(a) Act of God or *force majeure*; and
(b) Act of war or civil unrest.

2 Parties may provide, in their domestic law, for any other exemptions or mitigations as they may deem fit.

Article 7

Time limits

Parties may provide, in their domestic law, for:

(a) Relative and/or absolute time limits including for actions related to response measures; and
(b) The commencement of the period to which a time limit applies.

Article 8

Financial limits

Parties may provide, in their domestic law, for financial limits for the recovery of costs and expenses related to response measures.

Article 9

Right of recourse

This Supplementary Protocol shall not limit or restrict any right of recourse or indemnity that an operator may have against any other person.

Article 10

Financial security

1   Parties retain the right to provide, in their domestic law, for financial security.
2   Parties shall exercise the right referred to in paragraph 1 above in a manner consistent with their rights and obligations under international law, taking into account the final three preambular paragraphs of the Protocol.
3   The first meeting of the Conference of the Parties serving as the meeting of the Parties to the Protocol after the entry into force of the Supplementary Protocol shall request the Secretariat to undertake a comprehensive study which shall address, *inter alia*:

   (a) The modalities of financial security mechanisms;
   (b) An assessment of the environmental, economic and social impacts of such mechanisms, in particular on developing countries; and
   (c) An identification of the appropriate entities to provide financial security.

Article 11

Responsibility of States for internationally wrongful acts

This Supplementary Protocol shall not affect the rights and obligations of States under the rules of general international law with respect to the responsibility of States for internationally wrongful acts.

Article 12

Implementation and relation to civil liability

1   Parties shall provide, in their domestic law, for rules and procedures that address damage. To implement this obligation, Parties shall provide for response measures in accordance with this Supplementary Protocol and may, as appropriate:

   (a)   Apply their existing domestic law, including, where applicable, general rules and procedures on civil liability;
   (b)   Apply or develop civil liability rules and procedures specifically for this purpose; or
   (c)   Apply or develop a combination of both.

2   Parties shall, with the aim of providing adequate rules and procedures in their domestic law on civil liability for material or personal damage associated with the damage as defined in Article 2, paragraph 2 (b):

   (a)   Continue to apply their existing general law on civil liability;
   (b)   Develop and apply or continue to apply civil liability law specifically for that purpose; or
   (c)   Develop and apply or continue to apply a combination of both.

3   When developing civil liability law as referred to in subparagraphs (b) or (c) of paragraphs 1 or 2 above, Parties shall, as appropriate, address, *inter alia*, the following elements:

   (a)   Damage;
   (b)   Standard of liability including strict or fault-based liability;
   (c)   Channelling of liability, where appropriate;
   (d)   Right to bring claims.

Article 13

Assessment and review

The Conference of the Parties serving as the meeting of the Parties to the Protocol shall undertake a review of the effectiveness of this Supplementary Protocol five years after its entry into force and every five years thereafter, provided information requiring such a review has been made available by Parties. The review shall be undertaken in the context of the assessment and review of the Protocol as specified in Article 35 of the Protocol, unless otherwise decided by the Parties to this Supplementary Protocol. The first review shall include a review of the effectiveness of Articles 10 and 12.

Article 14

Conference of the Parties serving as the meeting of the Parties to the Protocol

1   Subject to paragraph 2 of Article 32 of the Convention, the Conference of the Parties serving as the meeting of the Parties to the Protocol shall serve as the meeting of the Parties to this Supplementary Protocol.
2   The Conference of the Parties serving as the meeting of the Parties to the Protocol shall keep under regular review the implementation of this Supplementary Protocol and shall make, within its mandate, the decisions necessary to promote its effective implementation. It shall perform the functions assigned to it by this Supplementary Protocol and, *mutatis mutandis*, the functions assigned to it by paragraphs 4 (a) and (f) of Article 29 of the Protocol.

Article 15

Secretariat

The Secretariat established by Article 24 of the Convention shall serve as the secretariat to this Supplementary Protocol.

Article 16

Relationship with the Convention and the Protocol

1   This Supplementary Protocol shall supplement the Protocol and shall neither modify nor amend the Protocol.
2   This Supplementary Protocol shall not affect the rights and obligations of the Parties to this Supplementary Protocol under the Convention and the Protocol.
3   Except as otherwise provided in this Supplementary Protocol, the provisions of the Convention and the Protocol shall apply, *mutatis mutandis*, to this Supplementary Protocol.
4   Without prejudice to paragraph 3 above, this Supplementary Protocol shall not affect the rights and obligations of a Party under international law.

Article 17

Signature

This Supplementary Protocol shall be open for signature by Parties to the Protocol at the United Nations Headquarters in New York from 7 March 2011 to 6 March 2012.

Article 18

Entry into force

1   This Supplementary Protocol shall enter into force on the ninetieth day after the date of deposit of the fortieth instrument of ratification, acceptance, approval or accession by States or regional economic integration organizations that are Parties to the Protocol.
2   This Supplementary Protocol shall enter into force for a State or regional economic integration organization that ratifies, accepts or approves it or accedes thereto after the deposit of the fortieth instrument as referred to in paragraph 1 above, on the ninetieth day after the date on which that State or regional economic integration organization deposits its instrument of ratification, acceptance, approval, or accession, or on the date on which the Protocol enters into force for that State or regional economic integration organization, whichever shall be the later.
3   For the purposes of paragraphs 1 and 2 above, any instrument deposited by a regional economic integration organization shall not be counted as additional to those deposited by member States of such organization.

Article 19

Reservations

No reservations may be made to this Supplementary Protocol.

Article 20

Withdrawal

1   At any time after two years from the date on which this Supplementary Protocol has entered into force for a Party, that Party may withdraw from this Supplementary Protocol by giving written notification to the Depositary.
2   Any such withdrawal shall take place upon expiry of one year after the date of its receipt by the Depositary, or on such later date as may be specified in the notification of the withdrawal.

3   Any Party which withdraws from the Protocol in accordance with Article 39 of the Protocol shall be considered as also having withdrawn from this Supplementary Protocol.

Article 21

Authentic texts

The original of this Supplementary Protocol, of which the Arabic, Chinese, English, French, Russian and Spanish texts are equally authentic, shall be deposited with the Secretary-General of the United Nations.

IN WITNESS WHEREOF the undersigned, being duly authorized to that effect, have signed this Supplementary Protocol.

DONE at Nagoya on this fifteenth day of October two thousand and ten.

Appendix 2

Decision BS-V/11 (2010)

International rules and procedures in the field of liability and redress for damage resulting from transboundary movements of living modified organisms, adopted on 15 October 2010

The Conference of the Parties to the Convention on Biological Diversity serving as the meeting of the Parties to the Cartagena Protocol on Biosafety,

Recalling Article 27 of the Cartagena Protocol on Biosafety,

Recalling its decision BS-I/8 by which it established an Open-Ended *Ad Hoc* Working Group of Legal and Technical Experts on Liability and Redress in the Context of the Cartagena Protocol on Biosafety, with the terms of reference set out in the annex to the decision, to carry out the process pursuant to Article 27 of the Cartagena Protocol on Biosafety,

Noting with appreciation the work of the Open-Ended *Ad Hoc* Working Group of Legal and Technical Experts on Liability and Redress in the Context of the Cartagena Protocol on Biosafety, as contained in the reports of its five meetings,

Recalling also its decision BS-IV/12 by which it established a Group of the Friends of the Co-Chairs to further negotiate international rules and procedures in the field of liability and redress for damage resulting from transboundary movements of living modified organisms in the context of the Cartagena Protocol on Biosafety on the basis of the annex to the decision,

Noting with appreciation the work of the Group of the Friends of the Co-Chairs, as contained in the reports of its meetings,

Noting the valuable work carried out by the two Co-Chairs of the Working Group, Ms. Jimena Nieto (Colombia) and Mr. René Lefeber (Netherlands), over the past six years in steering the process in the context of Article 27 of the Cartagena Protocol on Biosafety, through both formal and informal ways,

Recalling Article 22 of the Cartagena Protocol on Biosafety, which calls upon Parties to cooperate in the development and/or strengthening of human resources and institutional capacities in biosafety,

Recognizing the need to facilitate the implementation of this decision through complementary capacity-building measures,

Noting initiatives by the private sector concerning recourse in the event of damage to biological diversity caused by living modified organisms,

(A) Nagoya-Kuala Lumpur Supplementary Protocol on Liability and Redress to the Cartagena Protocol on Biosafety

1   *Decides* to adopt the Nagoya-Kuala Lumpur Supplementary Protocol on Liability and Redress to the Cartagena Protocol on Biosafety, as contained in the annex to the present decision (hereinafter referred to as "the Supplementary Protocol");

2   *Requests* the Secretary-General of the United Nations to be the Depositary of the Supplementary Protocol and to open it for signature at the United Nations Headquarters in New York from 7 March 2011 to 6 March 2012;

3   *Encourages* Parties to the Cartagena Protocol on Biosafety to implement the Supplementary Protocol pending its entry into force;

4   *Calls upon* the Parties to the Cartagena Protocol on Biosafety to sign the Supplementary Protocol on 7 March 2011 or at the earliest opportunity thereafter and to deposit instruments of ratification, acceptance or approval or instruments of accession, as appropriate, as soon as possible;

5   *Decides* that during the budget period 2011–2012, the activities of the Nagoya-Kuala Lumpur Supplementary Protocol on Liability and Redress will be funded from the trust funds of the Cartagena Protocol on Biosafety;

6   *Notes* that the Secretariat may need additional human resources for the implementation of the Supplementary Protocol once it enters into force;

(B) Additional and supplementary compensation measures

7   *Decides* that, where the costs of response measures as provided for in the Supplementary Protocol have not been covered, such a situation may be addressed by additional and supplementary compensation measures;

8   *Decides* that the measures referred to in paragraph 7 above may include arrangements to be addressed by the Conference of the Parties serving as the meeting of the Parties;

(C) Complementary capacity-building measures

9   *Urges* the Parties to cooperate, taking into account the Action Plan for Building Capacities for the Effective Implementation of the Cartagena Protocol on Biosafety, as contained in the annex to decision BS-III/3, in the development and/or strengthening of human resources and institutional capacities relating to the implementation of the Supplementary Protocol, including through

existing global, regional, subregional and domestic institutions and organizations and, as appropriate, through facilitating private sector involvement;

10 *Invites* Parties to take the present decision into account in formulating bilateral, regional and multilateral assistance to developing country Parties that are in the process of developing their domestic law relating to the implementation of the Supplementary Protocol;

11 *Decides* to take the present decision into account, as appropriate, in the next review of the Action Plan referred to in paragraph 9 above.

Appendix 3

Paragraphs 128–139 of the
Report of the Fifth Meeting of the
Conference of the Parties to the Convention
on Biological Diversity Serving as the
Meeting of the Parties to the Cartagena
Protocol on Biosafety, adopted on
15 October 2010

Item 12. Liability and Redress (Article 27)

128 Agenda item 12 was taken up at the 1st plenary session of the meeting, on 11 October 2010. In considering the item, the meeting had before it the final report of the Group of Friends of the Co-Chairs concerning Liability and Redress in the context of the Cartagena Protocol on Biosafety (UNEP/CBD/BS/COP-MOP/5/11).

129 Ms. Jimena Nieto (Colombia), Co-Chair of the Group of Friends of the Co-Chairs, reviewed the work of the Group, which was more fully described in its report. She said that although the Group had before it consolidated draft guidelines on civil liability and redress, taking into account the Group's agreement made at its first meeting to develop a legally binding supplementary protocol based on an administrative approach, the Group had agreed that it was not necessary to further elaborate those guidelines. However, that did not affect any steps that might be taken in the future with regard to the development of binding rules on civil liability for damage resulting from living modified organisms.

130 The Group had also considered the critical negotiations that had taken place at Nagoya, as well as the common practice of naming treaties after the place of their adoption. However, the Group had also recalled that the Government of Malaysia had hosted its two previous meetings and the mandate for the negotiations on liability and redress had been adopted in Kuala Lumpur in 2004 by the first meeting of the Conference of the Parties serving as the meeting of the Parties to the Protocol. The Group had therefore agreed to name the draft supplementary protocol after the cities of Nagoya and Kuala Lumpur.

131 Mr. René Lefeber (Netherlands), Co-Chair of the Group of Friends, stated that the draft decision was subject to a review by a legal drafting group in order to ensure the legal clarity and consistency of the text of the proposed

supplementary protocol in all six official languages of the United Nations. He also informed the meeting that the negotiations had demonstrated that multilateral environmental negotiations could still produce valuable results. It had been many years since the last multilateral environmental agreement, and the adoption of a new such agreement during the International Year of Biodiversity would give new impetus to multilateral environmental negotiations. Further, the supplementary protocol provided a new approach to addressing liability for damage to biological diversity that was complementary to existing approaches including, in particular, civil liability. A definition of damage to biological diversity had also been agreed to at the international level which formed the basis for redressing such damage. He remarked that the supplementary protocol would be an important contribution to the ongoing work under the Convention on Biological Diversity.

132   Mr. Lefeber also said that the process of the negotiations had been as transparent as international negotiations could be and had enabled the effective participation of both Parties and observers. It had sparked initiatives that would unite all who had an interest in biosafety matters to effectively address any damage to biological diversity. He thanked the *Earth Negotiations Bulletin* for their daily reports and the Secretariat for its support, as well as his Co-Chair, Ms. Jimena Nieto.

133   It was noted that it had emerged during the negotiations of the Supplementary Protocol that Parties to the Protocol hold different understandings of the application of Article 27 of the Protocol to processed materials that are of living modified organism-origin. One such understanding is that Parties may apply the Supplementary Protocol to damage caused by such processed materials, provided that a causal link is established between the damage and the living modified organism in question.

134   Paraguay expressed concern regarding the reference to the last preambular paragraph of the Cartagena Protocol on Biosafety in paragraph 2 of Article 10 of the Supplementary Protocol.

135   The President thanked the Co-Chairs for their work and asked them to co-chair the legal drafting group and report back to the subsequent session of the plenary.

136   At the 2nd plenary session of the meeting, on 13 October 2010, Ms. Jimena Nieto (Colombia), Co-Chair of the legal drafting group, said that the group had made minor legal and editorial changes to the text of the draft supplementary protocol, working mainly on the English version, and a revised text would be submitted to the plenary for adoption once all language versions were ready.

137   At the 3rd plenary session of the meeting, on 15 October 2010, the Conference of the Parties serving as the meeting of the Parties to the Protocol considered draft decision UNEP/CBD/BS/COP-MOP/5/L.2, containing the proposed text of the Nagoya-Kuala Lumpur Supplementary Protocol on Liability and Redress to the Cartagena Protocol on Biosafety, and adopted it as orally amended as decision BS-V/11. The text of the decision is contained in the annex to the present report.

138   The representative of Brazil congratulated all those who had been involved in the long negotiation process on having successfully agreed on the Supplementary Protocol and thanked the Co-Chairs of the legal drafting group for their guidance, patience and commitment. The Supplementary Protocol not only added greater significance to the current International Year of Biodiversity, but also strengthened the Cartagena Protocol and the Convention on Biological Diversity. In order to address the environmental and socioeconomic concerns deriving from its unique position of being simultaneously a mega-diverse country, a producer of living modified organisms and the biggest exporter of commodities among the Parties to the Cartagena Protocol, Brazil had striven tirelessly to build a flexible and constructive approach to the negotiations of the Supplementary Protocol, which reflected the diversity of interests among Parties and took account of the concerns of Parties, civil society and the private sector. In his view, Article 10 of the Supplementary Protocol was a good example of the efforts made to accommodate divergent views. He noted that financial guarantees were not environmental guarantees and would not in themselves prevent damage to biological diversity. Implementation of the Supplementary Protocol must be consistent with that of other international agreements, particularly those on trade, in order to avoid creating costly and burdensome barriers. International agreements on trade and on the environment should be mutually supportive with a view to achieving sustainable development.

139   Statements were also made by representatives of Argentina, Peru and South Africa.

Appendix 4

Core Elements Paper

Submitted by the Co-Chairs of the *Ad Hoc* Working Group
at its fifth meeting in Cartagena, Columbia, March 2008

Piece A: Primary compensation scheme (administrative approach)

1   Supplementary Protocol to the Cartagena Protocol on Biosafety in annex I
    to COP-MOP decision (*provided that content justifies a legally binding instrument*)
2   Broad functional scope
3   Narrow geographical scope
4   Damage to the conservation and the sustainable use of biological diversity
5   Obligations incumbent on person in operational control of LMOs to inform
    competent authorities in the event of damage or imminent threat of damage,
    and to take response and restoration measures
6   Discretion of competent authorities to take such measures and recover the
    costs
7   Exemptions and mitigation: domestic discretion on the basis of an exhaustive
    list
8   Limitation in time:

   a.   relative time limit not less than [x] years
   b.   absolute time limit not less than [y] years

9   Limitation in amount: not less than [z] SDRs
10 Coverage: domestic discretion to require evidence of financial security upon
    import of LMOs, including through self-insurance
11 Causation: domestic law approach
12 Encouragement in COP-MOP decision to implement the Supplementary
    Protocol pending its entry into force

Piece B: Primary compensation scheme (civil liability)

1   Guidelines for implementation in domestic law in annex II to COP-MOP
    decision
2   Broad functional scope

3   Narrow geographical scope
4   Any type of damage resulting from the transboundary movement of LMOs to legally protected interests, including damage to the conservation and sustainable use of biological diversity not redressed through administrative approach (no double recovery)
5   Standard of liability: fault-based liability for intentional transboundary movements of LMOs, unless approval of import has been made subject to strict liability
6   Channeling of strict liability: to importer or, on a subsidiary basis, to person in operational control of LMOs
7   Exemptions and mitigation to strict liability: domestic discretion on the basis of an exhaustive list
8   Limitation of strict liability in time:

   a.   relative time limit not less than [x] years
   b.   absolute time limit not less than [y] years

9   Limitation of strict liability in amount: not less than [z] SDRs
10 Coverage of strict liability: domestic discretion to require evidence of financial security upon import of LMOs, including through self-insurance
11 Causation: domestic law approach
12 Civil procedures: enabling clause on private international law and an encouragement to recognize and enforce foreign judgments when they are based on domestic law that is compatible with Guidelines

Piece C: Supplementary compensation scheme

1   Operational provisions in main body of and/or annex III to COP-MOP decision
2   Supplementary compensation schemes for the reimbursement of costs of response and restoration measures to redress damage to the conservation and sustainable use of biological diversity

   (a) Supplementary contractual compensation mechanism by the private sector
   (b) Supplementary collective compensation mechanism of COP-MOP providing for the allocation of financial resources by COP-MOP at the request of the State in which the damage occurred, if damage has not been redressed through domestic law implementing the Supplementary Protocol or supplementary contractual compensation mechanism of the private sector

3   Access to supplementary collective compensation mechanism of COP-MOP conditional on implementation of Supplementary Protocol in domestic law
4   No residual state liability

Piece D: Complementary capacity-building measures

1   Operational provisions in main body of and/or annex IV to COP-MOP decision
2   Review of Action Plan for Building Capacities for the Effective Implementation of the Cartagena Protocol on Biosafety to address liability and redress
3   Establishment of institutional arrangement with its terms of reference in main body of and/or annex IV to COP-MOP decision
4   Functions of the institutional arrangement to include, upon request, the provision of advice to:

(a) Parties on the compatibility of draft domestic legislation with Supplementary Protocol and Guidelines
(b) COP-MOP on access to supplementary collective compensation mechanism of COP-MOP
(c) domestic public entities of State in which recognition and enforcement of a judgment is sought on the compatibility with Supplementary Protocol and Guidelines of domestic law of State where judgment was rendered

Index

Page references to Figures or Tables are in *italics*

For Product Safety Concerns and Information please contact our EU
representative GPSR@taylorandfrancis.com
Taylor & Francis Verlag GmbH, Kaufingerstraße 24, 80331 München, Germany

www.ingramcontent.com/pod-product-compliance
Lightning Source LLC
Chambersburg PA
CBHW050702280326
41926CB00088B/2430